LIFE IN
JEFFERSON
DAVIS' NAVY

LIFE IN
JEFFERSON
DAVIS' NAVY

BARBARA BROOKS TOMBLIN

Naval Institute Press

Annapolis, Maryland

Naval Institute Press
291 Wood Road
Annapolis, MD 21402

Library of Congress Cataloging-in-Publication Data

Names: Tomblin, Barbara, author.
Title: Life in Jefferson Davis' Navy / Barbara Brooks Tomblin.
Description: Annapolis, Maryland : Naval Institute Press, [2019] | Includes
    bibliographical references and index.
Identifiers: LCCN 2018054264 (print) | LCCN 2018060457 (ebook) | ISBN
    9781682471197 (ePDF) | ISBN 9781682471197 (epub) | ISBN 9781682471180 |
    ISBN 9781682471180 (hardcover : alk. paper) | ISBN 9781682471197 (ebook)
Subjects: LCSH: Confederate States of America. Navy—History. | Confederate
    States of America—History, Naval. | United States—History—Civil War,
    1861–1865—Naval operations.
Classification: LCC E596 (ebook) | LCC E596 .T665 2019 (print) | DDC
    973.7/57—dc23
LC record available at https://lccn.loc.gov/2018054264

♾ Print editions meet the requirements of ANSI/NISO z39.48-1992
(Permanence of Paper).
Printed in the United States of America.

27 26 25 24 23 22 21 20 19   9 8 7 6 5 4 3 2 1
First printing

All images are courtesy of the U.S. Naval Institute photo archive.
Maps created by Chris Robinson.

Contents

Maps

Introduction

In March 1862 twenty-one-year-old Francis W. Dawson reported to a ship of the line, formerly the *United States*, "which had escaped destruction by the Federals upon the evacuation of the navy yard."[1] Although he was an Englishman born in London in 1840, Dawson had "a sincere sympathy for the Southern people in their struggle for independence, and felt that it would be a pleasant thing to help them to secure their freedom."[2] To that end he had sought passage to the Confederacy on the steamer *Nashville*. At Southampton, England, those who were friendly to the North spoke of her as a pirate, "and her officers and crew were dubbed buccaneers," Dawson recalled. The steamer's captain, Pegram, however, explained in an article to the *Times* that he was a regularly commissioned officer of the Confederate States Navy and the *Nashville* was a vessel of war "entitled to the consideration that would be shewn to the war vessel of any other Government."[3] Nonplussed by the *Nashville's* reputation, Dawson convinced Pegram to allow him to sail with the ship as a common sailor. So he donned a sailor's outfit, "a blue woolen shirt open at the neck, a black silk handkerchief with ample flowing ends, ties loosely around the neck; blue trousers, made very tight at the knee and . . . on my head a flat cloth cap ornamented with long black ribbons" and boarded the *Nashville* for a sea adventure that ended with the steamer slipping through the Union blockade into the harbor at Beaufort, North Carolina.[4]

After obtaining an appointment as a master's mate in the Confederate States Navy and donning a new uniform of navy gray, Dawson reported to Commo. French Forrest at Norfolk, who ordered him to the receiving ship *Confederate States*. On board the *Nashville*, young Dawson had suffered seasickness, learned to go aloft to the yards, climb the shrouds, carry buckets of coal, polish brightwork, and scour the deck. He had his trunk stolen by fellow sailors and survived the tossing of the ship in a gale, but he had never slept in a hammock.[5]

Dawson's experience on board the *Nashville*, as a volunteer in a gun crew of a field artillery company, and as a prisoner of war at Fort Delaware mirrors many aspects of the experiences of officers and men of the Confederate States Navy. A number of these men were foreigners with sympathy for the Southern cause or desire for adventure and prize money.

Although the lives of Union navy sailors have been the subject of two full-length works, *Life in Mr. Lincoln's Navy* by Dennis J. Ringle and *Union Jacks: Yankee Sailors in the Civil War* by Michael J. Bennett, the history of the Civil War from the Confederate perspective remains, with a few exceptions, a "soldiers' war." Raimondo Luraghi, Tom Wells, and William Still Jr. have recently authored histories or edited compilations of articles about the Confederate States Navy. Historians Spencer Tucker and James McPherson have covered both navies in recent histories, and the work of James Coski on the James River Squadron and Maurice Melton on the Savannah Squadron have added to our knowledge of these Confederate navy squadrons. These works touch on various aspects of the Confederate States Navy, but none have fully examined the everyday lives of Confederate sailors.

In *Life in Jefferson Davis' Navy*, I draw upon letters, diaries, journals, regulations, and official reports to illustrate the life of the common sailor in the Confederate States Navy as well as the experience of Confederate naval officers. Looking back on their Civil War service, a number of officers, midshipmen, and sailors took pen to paper and wrote their memoirs or composed articles about engagements in which they took part. Their candid thoughts and observations, written at the time or soon after the war, bring vividly to life the routines of their daily lives and the challenges of wartime service on board ships, serving in gun batteries ashore, or surviving imprisonment or hospitalization.

The following chapters endeavor to bring to light how these men were recruited, trained, and disciplined; how they enjoyed liberty ashore or created their own entertainment afloat; and how they fought side by side afloat in ironclads, commerce raiders, and wooden gunboats or ashore manning gun batteries or on foot as naval infantry. Their wartime service saw many of them suffering from illness or injuries or struggling to survive in federal prisoner of war camps. A number of these sailors, having grown weary of war, chose to desert.

Chapter 1 describes how the Confederate States Navy Department recruited seamen to man a burgeoning fleet, establishing naval rendezvous in major Southern port cities, advertising in newspapers, and sending out agents to round up seamen. Their efforts to convince men to join the navy netted new recruits, but the navy faced manpower shortages during the war and came to rely on foreign seamen shipped in foreign ports or enticed by commerce raider captains to join their ships.

Once these recruits joined the navy they usually went to receiving ships and then to their shipboard assignment to be trained and learn naval traditions and routine, a process described in chapter 2. Chapter 3 explores how Confederate sailors spent their free time on board ship, took advantage of liberty ashore, and worshiped on the Sabbath.

Liberty calls ashore frequently led to problems with alcohol and sailors engaging in brawls or returning late to their ships. Others took the opportunity during port calls to desert. Chapter 4 deals with these issues of enforcing discipline and apprehending or punishing deserters. If apprehended or returned, deserters could be court-martialed and sentenced to various punishments, including being deprived of pay, employed in public works, imprisoned, or executed.

Confederate naval personnel fell victim to many illnesses, some potentially fatal, as well as injuries caused by accidents or engagements with the enemy. Cases of malaria, dysentery, smallpox, yellow fever, and scurvy proved especially serious and required competent medical care by naval surgeons on board ship or in hospitals ashore. Chapter 5 details the work of the Office of Medicine and Surgery and the medical care and treatment afforded officers and sailors alike by navy surgeons, surgeons' stewards, and hospital personnel.

Naval warfare along the coast is explored in chapter 6 with the exploits of the mosquito fleet and life on board Confederate ironclads. Warfare on the high seas on board the commerce raiders *Sumter, Florida, Alabama, Clarence,* and *Shenandoah* is recounted in chapter 7, followed by the Confederate navy's creation of the torpedo bureau and various experimental craft, which are the subject of chapter 8. Naval action on the rivers is highlighted in chapter 9, which chronicles the daring attempt by the rebel ram CSS *Arkansas* to attack the federal fleet on the Mississippi River as well as the capture of the USS *Underwriter,* one of the less-well-known Civil War naval actions. The memorable experiences of Confederate naval personnel who attempted to destroy Union blockaders with spar torpedoes or who dueled with federal ironclads on the James River are addressed as well. Fortuitously, these actions have on occasion been the subject of officers' and sailors' accounts or are mentioned in their letters home.

Hundreds of Confederate naval personnel became prisoners of war, and their struggles to survive their imprisonment are discussed in depth in chapter 10. Journals and letters written by Confederate army officers and men give an intimate account of their shared experience at prison camps such as Point Lookout, Fort Delaware and Fort Lafayette, Elmira, Johnson's Island, Camp Chase, and other federal prisons.

The final chapter of *Life in Jefferson Davis' Navy* describes the experiences of Confederate navy officers and men during the final months of the war both afloat on the James River and ashore, manning gun batteries at Fort Fisher and Drewry's Bluff or fighting the Yankees as naval infantry with Raphael Semmes' Naval Brigade at Saylor's Creek.

The total enlisted strength in the Confederate States Navy during the Civil War probably never exceeded 4,500 men, one-tenth of the number of sailors who served in the Union navy, but their legacy of courage, endurance, and ability deserves to be recognized.[6] In the following pages of *Life in Jefferson Davis' Navy,* I paint a realistic picture of the wartime service of the officers and men of the Confederate States Navy.

1

Navy Gray

Manning the Confederate States Navy

O NE OF THE MOST IMPORTANT responsibilities of the newly organized Confederate States Navy was to recruit and train enlisted men to man the navy's vessels and to find assignments for 259 former U.S. Navy officers who had resigned their commissions and "gone South" in early 1861, when the newly created Confederate Committee on Naval Affairs sent telegrams to all regular navy officers of Southern birth instructing them to resign and report to Montgomery, Alabama.[1] With a limited pool of mariners and seamen to draw from, the Confederate navy had to establish naval recruiting offices or "rendezvous" and advertise in local newspapers, eventually even offering a bounty to men willing to serve in the navy.

When the navy began converting steamers to commerce raiders, many commanding officers induced seamen on prize vessels or foreign-born sailors in Southern ports or foreign ports to man the new commerce raiders, promising them adventure and prize money.[2] The Provisional Confederate Congress at Montgomery quickly accepted those commissioned officers, warrant officers, and midshipmen who had resigned or been dismissed from the U.S. Navy. "Thus, at its very beginning, the new government found itself embarrassed with a wealth of officers, while it was poor beyond description in every other essential of navy," J. Thomas Scharf explained.[3] The naval officer corps was initially established at 4 captains, 4 commanders, 30 lieutenants, and various other nonline officers

but was expanded in April 1862 to 4 admirals, 10 captains, 31 commanders, 100 first lieutenants, 25 second lieutenants, and 20 masters in line
for promotion.[4]

Secession

At the time of secession in 1861 almost half of the 1,550 officers on the
U.S. Navy's active list hailed from Southern states. For most Southern-
born officers, this time proved an anxious one as they considered their
loyalties and weighed a decision to remain in the U.S. Navy or resign
their commissions.[5] Even prior to the secession of South Carolina, career
naval officers feared the country's sectional controversy would not be
resolved. "I cannot see any way out of our present political troubles except
secession," William Brooke wrote to his brother, John Mercer Brooke, in
December 1860. The growing tensions between North and South troubled
John Brooke, a career naval officer, who confided in mid-February 1861,
"But whilst I have great faith in the good sense of my countrymen, I can
not but apprehend disastrous consequences from the violent and aggres-
sive disposition of party heads in and out of power."[6]

When Virginia seceded on April 17, Brooke wrote, "I laid down my
pencil on the chart of French Frigate Shoals which I was drawing, went
to the Navy Department and handed in my resignation." Although raised
and schooled in the North, Brooke's decision to resign his commission
was surely influenced by the pro-Southern sentiments of his brother
William and a close friend, John McCollum, as well as his wife, who was
a devout Southerner. Navy Secretary Gideon Welles refused to accept
Brooke's resignation and directed that his name be "stricken from the rolls."[7]

Loyalty to one's home state figured in many of these officers' decisions,
leaving many facing a difficult decision when their home state seceded.
The secession of South Carolina, for example, dealt a blow to the ambi-
tions of Eugenius A. Jack, who had planned to become an engineer in the
U.S. Navy. He had obtained an apprenticeship in the department of steam
engineering at the Gosport Navy Yard and was awaiting the call for can-
didates for the naval engineering corps. When whispers of secession and
war were heard, Jack recalled, "Then I saw my dream of service under the

stars and stripes began to fade, for if war came, I must cast my lot with my state and section to which I felt that I owed my allegiance." Jack decided to continue his trade and pass on an opportunity to join the navy. Following the fall of Fort Sumter and not yet twenty-one years of age, Jack enlisted in the Old Dominion Guards, Company K, 9th Virginia Regiment. Before his company could go into winter quarters, however, Jack was detailed to duty in the navy yard at Gosport as a journeyman machinist.[8]

Midn. Charles "Savez" Read was serving in the frigate *Powhatan* at Vera Cruz, Mexico, when the state of Mississippi's ordinance of secession passed on January 9, 1861. He immediately tendered his resignation; the commodore forwarded Read's resignation to the secretary of the navy, and within weeks he unofficially learned it had been accepted. When his ship returned home to New York, he went to Montgomery, the capital of the Confederate States of America, and called on Secretary of the Navy Stephen Mallory. He was advised to return home and assured that, if war came, "the army of the South would be the place for a young man with a military education."[9] Read dutifully went home to Mississippi, but within days the war had commenced. "It was hard for me to keep from volunteering for the army, but I remembered that the South had but few sailors and would need them all on the water." Indeed, in April he received the welcome news that he had been appointed a midshipman in the Confederate States Navy.[10]

News of secession did not, however, immediately reach many of those American naval officers serving on distant stations in 1861. In Hong Kong James I. Waddell received orders to the *John Adams*, which, having ended her service, was preparing to return home. "I was pleased to receive the order, I had determined if the North made war on the South to go south and assist those people." When Waddell heard news of the Battle of Bull Run, he resolved to resign his commission, writing to the secretary of the navy, "I wish it to be understood that no doctrine of the right of secession, no wish for disunion of the States impel me, but simply because my home is the home of my people in the south, and I cannot bear arms against it or them."[11]

The new Lincoln administration and Secretary Welles had taken another line of reasoning. Welles considered officers who resigned to be deserters and ended the navy's lenient acceptance of naval officer resignations, although he did admit that many of the naval officers who left federal service might have easily turned their vessels over to the Confederacy, "but, without exception, they returned the ships entrusted to them to the Federal Government before leaving the service, thus 'retiring with clean hands.'"[12] For example, officials in Washington regarded Lt. John Newland Maffitt with suspicion for he had property in South Carolina and they viewed him as a slave owner. Maffitt relinquished command of the *Crusader* but did not resign his commission in the U.S. Navy until after the fall of Fort Sumter in April. By that time his name had been added to a list of officers subject to arrest, so he had to quickly and quietly leave Washington for Montgomery, the capital of the Confederacy.[13]

Former U.S. Navy officers and civilians as well went to Montgomery seeking appointments as surgeons or paymasters from the Confederate navy secretary, Stephen Mallory. With just a dozen small ships to man, Mallory had to assign many of the officers to duty procuring ordnance supplies, devising means of defense, and defending shore batteries and their states.

In early 1861, before an act of organization established the Confederate States Navy, a number of U.S. Navy officers who had resigned their commissions offered their services to state navies. When Georgia passed the ordinance of secession, for example, John M. Kell was in Milledgeville and immediately forwarded his resignation to the government.[14] With his resignation accepted, Kell tendered his services to Gov. Joseph E. Brown, who commissioned him to proceed to Savannah, purchase a steamer, take command of the vessel, and hold himself in readiness for harbor and coast defense as there was not a yet a Confederate navy. "The secession movement of Georgia drew her sons to her soil," Kell remembered, "and soon all were within her borders."[15] On February 13, 1861, Kell took the oath of allegiance to the Confederacy and accepted a commission in the Georgia State Navy as a commander, a promotion in rank that might have taken years to attain in the regular navy. Charles Morris joined him in the Georgia State Navy as a commander, and William Hull, a passed midshipman, was commissioned a master.[16]

In time, officers like Kell were transferred from their state navies to the Confederacy for appointment in the navy. Most entered the Confederate navy with the same rank they held in the U.S. Navy. However, as historian Scharf has noted, the loss or destruction of naval records made it impossible to follow the changes and details that took place in the Confederate Navy Department. Early in the war, assignments were made hastily, and officers were sent to duty at stations with no record of their orders.[17]

The secession of Southern states and subsequent organization of the Confederate navy caught many of the young midshipmen at the U.S. Naval Academy at Annapolis off guard. During the years before the Civil War, the number of midshipmen in the navy from Southern states had increased, and by 1842 approximately 44 percent hailed from the South. Secession and the outbreak of war in April 1861 prompted many of their fathers to submit their sons' resignations. From December 4, 1860, to November 12, 1861, 111 acting midshipmen of 267 at the U.S. Naval Academy resigned. Although in the patriotic fervor of the first months of the war some chose to enlist in the Confederate States Army, many others accepted appointments to the Confederate States Navy as midshipmen. Most of those appointed midshipmen or acting midshipmen were young men in their late teens, born in the 1840s. A few were in their early twenties.[18]

Most of these young men entered Confederate naval service with the rank of midshipman or acting midshipman, but the need for officers quickly gained some a promotion to master or to lieutenant. Daniel Trigg had received an appointment to the U.S. Naval Academy at age fifteen in 1858, but after his native state of Virginia seceded from the Union on April 20, 1861, he resigned. Sixty-six other midshipmen had already resigned, and Trigg was joined on that day by four others from Virginia. Trigg's classmates Henry Marmaduke, Ivey Foreman, H. B. Littlepage, and Charles K. King would resign as well. However, his roommate at Annapolis, Silas Wright Terry, chose to remain in the U.S. Navy.[19] So, after being a midshipman for two and a half years, Trigg packed his bags and left Annapolis, slipping through the lines to Richmond where he joined the Virginia Navy. From Richmond he was ordered to Craney Island at the mouth of the Elizabeth River to assist in building a battery. On June 11, 1861, Trigg accepted appointment in the Confederate States Navy as an acting midshipman. His first assignment in August 1861 was to the *Confederate States* anchored in the Elizabeth River at the Gosport Navy yard.[20]

The New Confederate States Navy

When the war began, the Confederate States Navy assigned former U.S. Navy midshipmen to duty on shipboard or at naval stations. They continued their studies when they could, much as midshipmen had done in the old navy before the founding of the U.S. Naval Academy in 1845. Some were fortunate to have a conscientious school teacher or surgeon on board to hold classes in navigation, seamanship, mathematics, and science.[21]

Confederate Navy Secretary Mallory, who had chaired the Naval Affairs Committee before the war, appreciated the importance of formal training and was familiar with the accomplishments of the U.S. Naval Academy. "The instruction of midshipmen is a subject of greatest importance to the Navy," he wrote to Confederate president Jefferson Davis. He argued that most midshipmen had been appointed from civil life, possessed little knowledge of the duties of an officer, and "rarely even the vocabulary of their profession."[22]

In his 1862 report, Mallory recommended that a naval school be established to properly educate junior officers, but little was done to create such a naval school for the Confederacy.[23] The naval school was to be administered by the Office of Ordnance and Hydrography, and in March 1863 Cdr. John M. Brooke was given the mission of implementing the new naval school. The task of actually commanding the naval academy fell to the superintendent, Lt. William H. Parker.[24] "The midshipmen of the Confederate States Navy—representing the best blood of the South showed extraordinary aptitude for the naval service," noted Parker, "and on every occasion distinguished themselves in action. They were bold, daring and enterprising to a degree." Of the many midshipmen who were on board the school ship *Patrick Henry* in the two years the school was in operation, he could "hardly recall one who had not the making of a good naval officer."[25]

Subsequent acts of the Confederate Congress authorized the appointment and promotion of more officers and additional midshipmen. An act of April 21, 1862, allowed appointment of all of the admirals, 4 of the captains, 5 of the commanders, 22 of the lieutenants, and 5 of the second lieutenants to be made solely for "gallant or meritorious conduct during the war." This same act allowed for 20 passed midshipmen and 106 acting midshipmen. The legislation authorized congressmen to appoint 106 acting midshipmen from their respective districts and by the president at large. The rank of acting midshipman was a temporary rank, and that of "passed midshipman" signified that they had successfully passed their examinations for midshipman.[26]

On May 1, 1863, the Confederate Congress authorized Secretary Mallory to promote his officers based on merit rather than seniority. The new act created a provisional navy of the Confederate States while retaining the old navy. Confederate warrant officers fit for active service and all petty officers, seamen, ordinary seamen, landsmen, boys, firemen, and coal heavers were transferred into the provisional navy, but officers had to be transferred by presidential appointment "with the advice and consent of the Senate." This new law allowed Mallory to promote younger, more energetic officers into the provisional navy while assigning senior officers to duty in Richmond with the bureaus or to shore facilities. The act specified that "all officers appointed from the Regular Navy shall have, at its formation, the same relative position and rank they held in the Regular Navy."[27]

In addition to officers and engineers, the Confederate navy also sought experienced coast and river pilots. So valuable were these pilots that the Confederate navy accepted qualified pilots, black or white, and compensated them well. Pilots were civilian employees of the navy, not technically commissioned officers, but ship captains often reported them on their muster rolls as officers. Although issued rations and uniforms, navy pilots were not required to stand watches or other duties performed by officers, nor were they subject to navy rules and regulations.[28]

Although the Confederate navy declined to recruit African Americans as sailors or appoint persons of color as officers, those with skills as pilots were welcomed. In the Savannah Squadron more than 40 percent of pilots were African Americans, all of them slaves as the state of Georgia barred free men of color from being pilots. Black pilots, historian Maurice Melton notes, "enjoyed a career of responsibility, respect, and quasi freedom." Their owners hired them out, but many were allowed to keep a substantial amount of their income.[29]

One of the best pilots in the Savannah area was Moses Dallas, who served with the Savannah Squadron from 1862 to 1864. He was killed during the expedition that captured the *Water Witch* on June 3–4, 1864. Dallas' servant, Edward Walden, enlisted in the Confederate States Navy and served as a landsman on CSS *Savannah* with the unusual proviso that if Harriet Dallas needed his help at home, he would be permitted to leave the ship and do her bidding.[30]

In addition to midshipmen, pilots, and commissioned officers, the Confederacy also established a marine corps. In 1861 the Confederate States Marine Corps had sixty-three officers. The commandant, John Harris, had a general staff that included Maj. M. B. Tyler Sr. as adjutant and inspector; Maj. W. W. Russell, paymaster; Maj. William B. Stark, quartermaster; and Capt. M. A. T. Maddox. The marine corps also had 1 assistant quartermaster, 1 lieutenant colonel, 4 majors, 13 captains, 20 first lieutenants, and 20 second lieutenants. Soon the demand for Marines increased, and in his report of April 28, 1861, Mallory suggested another second lieutenant be added to each company of Marines. Subsequently the Confederate Congress enacted an amendatory act for the corps that increased its size to 18 captains, 10 first lieutenants, 20 second lieutenants, 40 sergeants, 40 corporals, 840 privates, 10 drummers, 10 fifes, and 2 musicians. This table of organization remained in place for the remainder of the war.[31]

Enlisted Men

Early in the war, mariners and seamen in Southern ports found enlisting in the Confederate States Navy an attractive option. Manning the new ironclad CSS *Virginia*, for example, took little effort. As E. A. Jack recalled, "There was no difficulty in finding men, for here were many old salts around Norfolk and Portsmouth ready and glad to go in the great ironclad, and of landsmen there were many volunteers from the military companies garrisoned around. Many of the United Artillery were among these and they were very desirable men because of their military training."[32]

In the South, a young man had to have parental consent to join the Confederate navy if he was under twenty-one years of age. The minimum age requirement for enlistment was fourteen, and the height requirement was four feet eight inches. An inexperienced man with a trade could join the navy if he was between twenty-five and thirty-five, inexperienced men without a trade were shipped as landsmen or coal heavers.

By July 1861 the navy had successfully recruited the five hundred enlisted men originally authorized by the act of March 25, 1861. However, determining a need for more men for an expanding fleet, Navy Secretary Mallory asked for authorization for "an additional 500 of the same classes, who will be principally occupied on the coasts of North Carolina, South Carolina, Georgia, Alabama, and Louisiana." The Confederate Congress granted his request and allowed the navy to hire civilian agents to scour for seamen, paying each agent one or two dollars per head for those men enrolled.[33]

Navy agents and civilian recruiters recruited an increasing number of sailors for the Confederate navy's burgeoning fleet. With only some 500,000 tons of merchant shipping, the South lacked a pool of skilled personnel for noncommissioned officers and enlisted men. Initially, the navy's recruiting efforts were undermined by the Confederate army's successful campaign to enroll almost any Southerner capable of naval duties, forcing Mallory to reclaim them, "facing the ill-will of army officers who, themselves hard-pressed by lack of men, declined to give them back."[34]

To recruit sailors for new vessels or to replace men whose terms of service had expired or had fallen ill, the Confederate States Navy established naval "rendezvous" or recruiting depots in cities in the South such as Richmond, Norfolk, Raleigh, Savannah, Macon, Mobile, and New Orleans. In Richmond, these rendezvous were situated in rooms rented by the month.[35] A sea officer, surgeon, and several junior officers staffed each naval rendezvous. The Confederate Navy Department also had agents to assist in shipping men for the navy. For example, on February 10, 1862, Capt. Franklin Buchanan of the Office of Orders and Detail appointed William M. Wilson to be an agent and to report to Lt. John H. Parker, commanding the rendezvous at Richmond. His compensation was to be forty dollars per month. Wilson actively sought recruits and in mid-May reported that he had to date shipped seventy-six men for naval service at an allowance of five dollars for each man mustered into service. Agent Wilson's compensation was $380.[36]

To entice potential recruits, the officer in charge of the rendezvous would place advertisements in local newspapers. "Men wanted for the Navy!" one poster read: "All able bodied men not in the employment of the Army will be enlisted in the Navy upon application at the Naval Rendezvous on Craven Street next door to the Printing Office. H K Davenport, Comdr & Senior Naval Officer, New Berne NC Nov. 24, 1863." Recruiters resorted as well to enticements to encourage men to enlist. In 1861 Lt. William H. Parker advertised for "Ordinary seamen and landsmen. Apply on board the steamer Jamestown . . . Good wages given." Recruiting Officer Lt. J. N. Barney's advertisement specified the rates of men he needed: "Wanted. Seamen and Landsmen for the C.S. Naval Service, also a Cabin Cook and Steward and a few firemen and coal heavers. Apply on board C.S. steamer Jamestown, at Rocketts."[37]

In an attempt to recruit sailors for the newly created Savannah Squadron in May and June of 1861, Commo. Josiah Tattnall sent Lt. Manigault Morris ashore to the naval rendezvous. Morris advertised for "200 able-bodied seamen" in the *Evening Mail*, offering what he hoped would be considered good wages, better than that offered by the Confederate army: "$18 per month for able-bodied seamen, $14 per month for ordinary seamen, and $12 per month for landsmen." In addition to their wages, recruits would be given an initial uniform allowance and a daily grog ration. The army paid privates just eleven dollars per month.[38] Morris' advertisements must have attracted some recruits, and during the first summer of the war, a civilian contractor or agent, Christopher Hussey, also enticed several hundred men to join the Savannah Squadron.

Morris accepted 131 of these men, many of them foreign seamen, especially Danes, Irish, and English.[39]

The Confederate raiders *Alabama*, *Shenandoah*, and *Florida*, however, had less difficulty filling out their crews, for they regularly recruited seamen from prize vessels. Commerce raiders' commanding officers often called upon men from prizes to join their ships, offering them the lure of excitement and prize money. On one notable occasion, the second mate of the whaler *Abigail*, taken prize by the CSS *Shenandoah*, convinced many of his fellows to join him on the Confederate raider. When his ship fell to the *Shenandoah*, the second mate, Thomas Manning, asked Captain Waddell if in exchange for telling Waddell the location of the arctic whaling fleet, he might have a job as an officer on the raider. Unpleasant as it might have been, Waddell could not pass up the opportunity and enrolled Manning as ship's corporal.

"These poor devils," said Mason of the largely Hawaiian crew. "They have never been on any other ship than a Yankee whaler, where they are hard worked, maltreated, poorly fed, and worse paid, [and] seem to think this a sort of paradise." Manning told *Abigail*'s men they could expect a more luxurious life on the rebel raider and enticed them with the promise of grog twice a day, coffee four times, and tea at regular intervals. They would also have four hours on, four hours off instead of around-the-clock duty. Manning did not mention they would be searching for whalers manned by their friends, for the whaling community was a small one.[40]

The CSS *Winslow*'s crew was also composed mainly of foreigners. William Parker made up a crew principally of men who had been in the prizes captured by the *Winslow*. "I had but one American in the crew—a green hand who shipped as a coal heaver." His crew included Englishmen, Danes, and Swedes. Two of the Englishmen were "splendid specimens of man-o'-war's men," he noted. "I never sailed with a better one, and I never knew them to fail in their duty; indeed I used to wonder at their eagerness to go into battle considering the fact that they knew nothing at all about the cause of the war; but a sailor is a sailor all the world over."[41]

As the war went into its second year, navy recruiters resorted to more specific advertisements. In June 1863, for example, the Richmond rendezvous submitted an advertisement asking for men with very specific skills.

"Wanted—For the C S Ship Patrick Henry a DRUMMER and BUGLER. Apply to the Naval Rendezvous on 9th street between Main and Cary. Also, a STEWARD competent to take charge of a large mess."[42]

In early 1862 the Confederacy finally resorted to offering a bounty to men shipping in the Confederate States Navy. On January 16 the Confederate Congress passed legislation allowing the navy to begin offering a bounty to recruits who signed on for three years or for the duration. Navy Secretary Mallory sent Congress an estimate of $100,000 needed "to pay the bounty of fifty dollars to two thousand seamen, ordinary seamen, landsmen, and boys and firemen and coal-heavers."[43]

Anxious to find sailors to man the growing number of vessels in his squadron, Josiah Tattnall welcomed a message from Mallory informing him that the bounty had enticed thirty sailors at Apalachicola, Florida, to join the navy. "Send an officer to ship them for your command," Mallory wrote, "it would be well I think to pay the bounty allowed at Savannah, but pursue the course you deem best." Tattnall had his paymaster draw one thousand dollars to cover the bounties and then sent Marine lieutenant David Raney and Acting Master Isaac Holcombe to Florida to bring back the recruits.[44]

The bounty offered to recruits seems to have varied. In April 1862 an advertisement placed at Richmond read: "Wanted. S Men for the naval services of the Confederate Station the iron-sided and other vessels. . . . The bounty of $40 will be paid immediately on enlistment." Another offered a bounty of fifty dollars. The Confederate States Marine Corps was also authorized to offer a bounty to men joining the corps. An advertisement posted in March 1863 at Mobile read: "$50 Bounty! Prize Money! Computation Money! Pay from $15 to $25 per month. Wanted for the Marine Corps: able-bodied men between the ages of 16 and 45. Prize money guaranteed to every Marine belonging to the vessels in sight of the enemy, for all craft either captured or sunk." This advertisement added additional inducements: "Drummers, Buglers, and Fifers will receive higher pay. Marines are soldiers on board men-of-war, or at Naval Stations, and are not required to perform sailors' duties."[45]

In an effort to recruit more sailors, the Confederate navy looked to free blacks who could enlist in the navy if they had special permission of the navy department or the local squadron commander. Slaves enlisted with owners' consent, and some served as officers' servants as well as coal heavers and pilots. The number of free blacks or slaves in the Savannah Squadron was capped at 5 percent of the strength of the squadron.[46] The precise number of blacks serving in the Confederate navy remains unknown. Confederate naval regulations allowed a ship's captain a ratio of one black seaman to five white seamen. The captain could, however, file an exemption and ship a higher percentage of black seamen.[47]

Pension records and other sources offer glimpses of African Americans serving in the Confederate navy. For example, Randall Polk served as a landsman on the ironclad ram *Georgia* from September 1861 to December 21, 1864, when the vessel was destroyed to avoid capture by Gen. William Tecumseh Sherman's army. James Duncan Moore enlisted in the navy on September 1, 1864, and served with Randall Polk on board the *Georgia*. On the *Macon*, Charles B. Stiles served as landsman and George Snowden as first-class boy. Persons of color serving in the James River Squadron included James Price and Robert Cole, a slave owned by President Davis and assigned to the *Patrick Henry*. David Green and Henry Leonard transferred from Drewry's Bluff to the ironclad *Virginia II* at Richmond. Both were rated as landsmen. At least two black seamen served on the *Shenandoah*, one of whom was Edward Weeks. David White served on the *Alabama* and went down with the ship in the battle with the *Kearsarge*.[48]

Ongoing Recruitment

As the war went on, the Confederate navy continued to strain to man a growing number of vessels. "Where we will get officers for the ironclads is beyond my ken," Lt. R. D. Minor lamented. "Tidall says we will have to organize the Provisional Navy, but this will hardly officer the ships. There is no talk of promotion, and very few officers seem either to think of or care for it."[49] As the war went into its second and third years and many sailors' terms of enlistment expired or they fell ill or deserted, the Confederate navy experienced serious manpower shortages.[50] Without enough men, the navy department grew increasingly desperate. Experienced firemen were given the opportunity to become third assistant engineers, and recruiters fanned out to small towns and army and prison camps.[51] The need for men also prompted Secretary Mallory to have men transferred from army units to the navy.[52]

The Confederate navy's manpower shortage resulted in part because when their terms of enlistment expired Confederate sailors were eligible to leave the service. Knowing the difficulty of replacing these sailors, commanders often made efforts to retain the men. Facing the expiration of the *Georgia*'s well-drilled, disciplined crew on July 4, 1863, the squadron flag officer, W. W. Hunter, boarded the *Georgia* and endeavored to whip up patriotic enthusiasm among them for reenlistment. Most of the men were conscripts from the army, and Hunter failed to convince them to reenlist. Believing he needed these sailors for the defense of Savannah, Hunter ordered the *Georgia*'s captain, Lt. Thomas Pelot, to retain the men on board. None of the crew, Pelot explained, would voluntarily reenlist for the war under the department's terms. After several offers, on August 6, 1863, Hunter asked Mallory if he might offer the men bounty of fifty dollars to return to the *Georgia*. With the secretary's permission, Hunter then had the men reshipped for two weeks' furlough and the bounty.[53]

As the war went into its second and third years, procuring crews for vessels under construction grew more and more difficult. In 1863 Lt. Jonathan H. Carter, the officer supervising the construction of the gunboat *Missouri* at Shreveport, Louisiana, informed Secretary Mallory that the vessel would be launched on the 14th of April but wrote, "I find that it will be difficult for me to ship a crew at this place. I learn that men can be procured at Galveston, and I have consequently written to Cap. Barney of the Str. 'Harriet Lane' to ship me a crew. As soon as I can get a reliable officer I will send there to get men."[54]

In May Lieutenant Carter received men from the *Harriet Lane*, but by November, Carter lamented, the new sailors "have been greatly reduced by sickness, death, and desertion, and those remaining on the 'Webb' are very much debilitated." The commander of the department had promised to detail men from the army, but Carter cautioned Mallory, "I may find it necessary to employ negroes as firemen and deck hands on board the boat that will act as a tender for the 'Missouri.'"[55]

Determined to man the *Missouri*, Carter turned to the Texas Army for seamen who would be willing to volunteer. The *Missouri* would need sixty seamen, ordinary seamen, and landsmen; twelve firemen; one carpenter; and one blacksmith. The *Webb* would require twenty seamen, eight firemen, and a carpenter and blacksmith. He suggested that volunteers be called for and the number of men required be selected from these volunteers.

In early January 1864, however, with *Missouri* ready for service with three guns mounted, Carter still awaited a crew for the vessel. Hoping to find army volunteers, he sent Acting Master Musgrave to Texas with permission to recruit men from an artillery company, but told him, "There are men in Genl Taylor's Army better suited for our service; sailors and river men. If there are any men in the Army that will volunteer as firemen, I would rather have them than negroes."[56]

Master Musgrave succeeded in recruiting thirty-two men, but General Magruder refused to allow them to leave Texas. Maj. Gen. R. Taylor, commanding at Alexandria, Louisiana, also refused to allow men for the *Missouri* to be transferred until the vessel reached Alexandria, prompting Carter to explain that he wished to get the men soon, "so they could be trained at the guns and become acquainted with their duties on board the vessel. You must know that raw hands, unaccustomed to heavy guns would be of but little service if called on to go into action." Then, obviously at the end of his rope, Carter wrote, "If I cannot get men for the vessel, I had as well take the officers under my command and cross the Mississippi, where I can do something."[57]

Other Confederate navy commanders struggled to find officers and seamen and shared Lieutenant Carter's frustration, for by 1863 a lack of manpower had become a serious issue for the Confederate navy. In April 1863, for example, William F. Lynch, commanding the naval defenses of North Carolina, wrote to a member of the Confederate States Senate urging him to use his influence to enable him to obtain the men necessary to man the ironclad gunboats building at Wilmington. "There are many men in the Army, who from having been fishermen, pilots and navigators of Sounds and rivers admirably adapted to our purpose and many such have applied to me for transfer to the Navy," Lynch noted, but added the War Department's order, General Order No. 77 of the War Department, requires the commanding officer, in all cases of transfers, "to certify whether the applicant is or is not a 'sea-faring person,' which term precludes them, as their voyages, have been mostly limited to inland navigation." Clearly, the captains of army companies were averse to transferring men.[58]

Hoping to alleviate the manpower shortage, Secretary Mallory had convinced the Confederate government to enact a series of laws to deal with the navy's manpower issue. The passage of the first draft legislation on April 16, 1862, specified that trained seamen serving in the Confederate army might transfer to the Confederate navy. On October 2, 1862, the Confederate Congress authorized draftees to select the Confederate navy or marine corps. On May 1, 1863, another piece of legislation authorized the navy department to order the transfer of seamen or ordinary seamen from the army to the navy.

This latter legislation was widely ignored, so on March 22, 1864, a law was passed to transfer to naval service twelve hundred men from the army, of whom nine hundred were to come from departments east of the Mississippi River. The head of the Office of Orders and Detail lamented that the number of experienced seamen to be found in the South was small before the war, "and they have been almost entirely absorbed by the conscript law of February 17, 1864, placing in the military service all white men, residents of the Confederacy, between the ages of seventeen and fifty." Many of the soldiers diverted into naval duty were not pleased by the assignment. Some became disciplinary problems and others deserted, but a number adjusted and gave a good account of themselves.[59]

Confederate naval officers, eager to fill out the complements of their crews, welcomed the new legislation, and army units proved a promising source of potential recruits. Robert Watson, recently transferred into the navy from the 7th Florida Infantry, noted one request in his diary: "Lieut. Carnes who was officer of the deck last night while I was on watch asked me if I knew of any seamen in Johnston's army. I told him I would give him a list of names in the morning."[60] The following day, April 2, 1864, Watson eagerly gave the lieutenant a list of names, including seven men in Company K "so there is some hopes of the poor fellows getting out of the army at last."[61] Two weeks later, he wrote, "At night 7 men from Johnston's army came on board with our doctor and more are coming in the morning with Lieut. Carnes."[62] One man from Company K was among the number.

In September twenty-four North Carolina conscripts came on board. "They are a fine looking lot of men and it is a shame that such able bodied men have kept out of the service so long." They were stationed at the forward and after pivot guns. Several days later, however, Watson lamented that conscripts had come on board. "I can't imagine why they send them to the navy when the army was so much in need of men."[63]

Vouchers give some indication of the efforts made by the Confederate States Navy to recruit men from the army. In early 1863 the Richmond rendezvous ordered Acting Master Hudgins "to proceed to the army up north near Fredericksburg to take charge and bring to this office John G. C. Kruse and Wm. H. Dennison of Co. A 2nd Florida Regt.," soldiers who had transferred to the navy. The following month Hudgins was sent to Lynchburg to the surgeon of the hospital there to bring back a man from a company of the 3rd North Carolina regiment.[64]

At Savannah Commodore Tattnall was also sending out men to find soldier recruits. In early February 1863, Graves journeyed to Savannah where he was to join a new vessel, the CSS *Savannah*, about to be launched. "In the meantime I am to go out and enlist myself a crew or guard," he told Mrs. Sarah Graves. "We have already about 12 or 13 and I shall want 35 or 40 more. I shall go to the conscript camps, and am writing now only for written authority from the Sec of War to enlist conscripts for which Capt. Tattnall has written." In February, March, June, and July, Graves dutifully went to register recruits at Decatur, Georgia, a total of thirteen men.[65]

In March Commodore Tattnall ordered an officer from the *Savannah* to assist Lt. Pembroke Jones in getting conscripts for the navy from camps of instruction near Macon and Decatur, Georgia. As soon as Jones had collected them, he was to inform the officer, who explained, "I will send Dr. Sandford to examine them and all those that pass his examination you will send or accompany them to this station." Passed Assistant Surgeon J. W. Sandford Jr. did, in fact, travel to Atlanta and back to Savannah in late March to examine recruits.[66]

In May Midn. W. F. Clayton received very specific orders to proceed to the conscript camp near Raleigh and "endeavor to procure as many recruits possible for the Navy." He was instructed to show the commanding officer of the camp the circular order from the Bureau of Conscription and was given a navy register to display to the conscripts to assure them of navy pay. "Allow seamen's pay to all able bodied, active men, and promise petty officer berths to the intelligent on condition of good behaviour," Lynch told him. If the recruits came forward to enlist slowly, Clayton was to send them on in detachments of eight or ten in charge of Acting Master C. Burr.[67]

By 1864 the pool of potential recruits for the James River Squadron had shrunk so significantly that, with two new ironclads to man, the navy also resorted to recruiting men from army units. Shipboard life promised better food and accommodation, but army transfers also discovered it could mean monotony and hardship. "We get plenty to eat and of that which is tolerably good we get very near twice as much to eat as we did in camp," Oliver Hamilton wrote to his father in 1864. "I can't say yet how I like my transfer though I hope I shall be well pleased after I get used to it." Hamilton had transferred from the 38th North Carolina Regiment to the navy for service on the ironclad CSS *Fredericksburg*.[68]

Early in the war, the navy department had sought army men with specific naval skills but now resorted to even offering soldiers and civilians in Richmond jails the opportunity to shorten their sentences by transferring to the navy. "I am anxious to join the Navy," William Jones told the provost marshal. He had been arrested for selling a captured pistol. Others had gone absent without leave from the army but figured life in the navy better than prison. These were hardly the best sort of recruits, many of them lacking any maritime skills or experience. "The conscripts are not supposed to be very good fighting men, as the balance of the crew kick them around," one deserter explained.[69]

Total enlisted strength in the Confederate States Navy during the Civil War probably never exceeded 4,966 men, one-tenth of the number of sailors who served in the Union navy. The officers and men of the Confederate States Marine Corps numbered over the course of the war 59 officers and more than 1,200 men, who served on approximately 34 naval vessels in addition to duty in small detachments at navy yards and stations.[70]

The Confederate Navy Department's initial task was to recruit and train enlisted men to man the navy's vessels and to find assignments for a wealth of officers, many of them Southern born, who out of loyalty to their states had resigned their commissions in the U.S. Navy. Manning the Confederate States Navy proved a challenge because the South lacked a pool of skilled personnel for noncommissioned officers and enlisted men. The navy hired agents and established naval rendezvous and even resorted to offering a bounty to men willing to enlist, but it still could not ship enough men to man the vessels being acquired or constructed. Commanding officers of Confederate commerce raiders often shipped mariners from the prize vessels they captured or recruited seamen in foreign ports such as Liverpool, England, or Melbourne, Australia. Many of these sailors were foreign nationals lured by the prospect of adventure, prize money, or continued employment.

Manpower shortages brought on by terms of enlistment expiring, illness, death, and desertion continued to be a problem for the navy, compounded by Confederate army officials who waged a successful campaign to enroll almost any Southerner capable of naval duties. Secretary Mallory's subsequent efforts to recruit men from army units proved only partially successful.

2

Shipboard Routine

You're in the Navy Now!

Indoctrination and Training

RECRUITING SAILORS TO MAN the navy's vessels was just the beginning. The navy had to provide new sailors with a physical exam; issue them clothing, hammocks, and mess kits; and assign them to a ship or shore station where they would be divided into messes and indoctrinated as to shipboard routine. Most receiving ships also began training the new men in the rudiments of seamanship and began exercising them at the guns. Commanders were especially concerned that new recruits should be drilled at the guns and exercised in small arms and should be trained to repel boarders.

Before being sent off to a receiving ship, new recruits at each rendezvous were examined by a surgeon. Young midshipmen reporting to the school ship had usually undergone an earlier physical examination by a naval surgeon, possibly using the form provided by the navy for examining recruits, which included a medical history with such questions as "Have you ever had fits?"; "Are you in the habit of drinking?"; and "Have you any difficulty urinating?" If they had not been previously examined, newly appointed midshipmen reported to the school ship, where the surgeon would carefully examine them for vision problems, hearing problems, lameness, and infirmities such as extra toes.[1]

After signing the shipping articles and passing a physical examination at the rendezvous, most Confederate naval recruits went first to a receiving ship, often an old frigate or sailing vessel stationed at a navy yard. In the South, the navy had receiving ships at Richmond, Virginia, and other major ports. Typically, a new recruit reported to the officer of the deck (OOD); gave his name and details, which went into ship's book; and went forward to be given a number for his hammock and one for his canvas clothes bag.

In most cases, the recruits shed their civilian clothes and were issued uniforms and given an allowance for replacements. In 1861 regulations called for a gray cloth jacket and trousers or a woolen frock coat with white duck cuffs and collars and black caps. In summer the sailors might don white frock coats, trousers, and white or black caps. Neckerchiefs and shoes seemed to have been black in color.

Officers' uniforms and allowances differed. Dawson, who had been promoted to the rank of master's mate after leaving the *Nashville*, provided himself with a gray uniform such as an officer would have worn and the insignia described by Confederate States Navy uniform regulations.[2] Regulations prescribed a frock coat of steel gray cloth, faced with the same and lined with black silk serge, double breasted, with two rows of large navy buttons on the breast, nine in each row, spaced four inches and a half apart from eye to eye at the top, and two inches and a half at the bottom. Regulations called for a rolling collar with skirts to be full, commencing at the top of the hip bone and descending four-fifths toward the knee, with one button behind on each hip and one near the bottom of each fold. The insignia of rank was to be displayed on the sleeves and cuffs. All officers were to wear pantaloons of steel gray cloth or white drill "made loose to spread well over the foot and to be worn over boats or shoes."[3]

Officers' caps were to be made also of steel gray cloth, not less than three and a half inches nor more than four inches in height, between nine and ten inches, the top with a patent leather visor. Jackets were allowed to be worn while at sea and were to be made of steel gray cloth or white drill linen with a double-breasted, rolling collar, small buttons on the breast, and shoulder straps for appropriate grades. In summer or tropical climates, officers might wear frock coats and pantaloons of steel gray summer cloth of the style and pattern for service uniforms with medium-size navy buttons. They could also, except at general muster, choose straw hats, the body of which was to be six inches in height and the rim three and half inches in width.

The gray officer's uniform did not prove popular with many Confederate naval officers. "Who had ever seen a gray sailor, no matter what nationality he served," Jimmy Morgan asked in his memoirs. Many chose to don the traditional navy blue or even wore black uniforms.[4]

Although the Confederate navy and marine corps issued men uniforms when they enlisted, over time sailors and marines had to keep up their appearance by having clothing made for them. In November 1863, Iverson Graves sent his mother, Sarah Graves, patterns for a duty coat and pants and included eighteen buttons. She was making him an overcoat, but he wished for a sack coat and a pair of pants. "If you have the cloth to spare and will send it in the same bundle I will get it cut and made here."[5]

"I am very much obliged to you for the cloth," Graves wrote from the steamer *Savannah* to Sarah on June 13, 1864, "I am having it made up and it is all ready except the buttons. The pants are too small at the foot, except that they fit very nicely. Jeans is so seldom worn here that I will be alone in my glory." Graves told her that he hoped the department would get some material "after a while," but he must have had doubts. "The coat costs fifty dollars—a pretty good price for making only. I would like to have some white pants if you can get the material, and two or three white vests."[6] In February 1862 Graves rented a room in Savannah. He wrote to his mother, "Last night I had my cap stolen from the rack at the house where I eat. Unfortunate in the cap line, ain't I? Common gray caps are worth 12 to 14 dollars here. I got one this morning, a simple glazed cap worth 30 cents, and paid $2.50 for it."[7]

Confederate Navy regulations called for midshipmen to be in uniform when on shipboard or on liberty. The regulation undress uniform for Confederate midshipman was similar to that of officers, a gray, double-breasted, frock coat with two rows of navy buttons down the front and a row of three buttons at the bottom of the cuffs. As midshipmen at the

Confederate navy's floating academy did not receive uniforms from the navy, most looked to tailors in Richmond to fashion the regulation undress uniform for them. Midn. Hubbard Minor, for example, provided the cloth and the buttons designed by Cdr. John Mercer Brooke, with "a ship under sail seen from the bow surrounded by stars in an arch over the sea" sailing over letters "CSN." General duty uniforms were made from "the coarsest materials" and might consist of gray flannel jumpers and trousers, straw hats, and white jackets. For sea duty, the navy regulations called for a thick, flat, round gray cap without a visor. The school ship also required midshipmen to provide their own drawers, two pairs of boots, mattress, pillow, two blankets, sheets, towels, hair brush, combs, and needle-and-thread case. The midshipmen were divided into messes of twelve to fifteen men, and each mess had to buy a looking glass, wash basin, water pail, and ship bucket. Acting Midn. James O. Harrison shelled out more than fifty dollars for just his bedding and tableware.[8]

Crewmen of the CSS *Sumter* were issued clothing and small stores by the paymaster on the first of the month, Raphael Semmes explained. "The paymaster's steward is the shopman, on occasion, and he is serving a jacket to one, a shirt to another, and a pair of shoes to a third. His assortment is quite varied, for besides the requisite clothing, he has tobacco, and pepper, and mustard; needles, thimbles, thread, and spool-cotton; ribbons, buttons, jack-knives, &c. Jack is not allowed to indulge in all these luxuries ad lib. He is like a school-boy, under the care of his preceptor, he must have his wants approved by the officer of the division to which be belongs." Once a month, "Jack spreads out his wardrobe before him. . . . If he is deficient a shirt, or a pair of trousers, he is permitted to draw them; if he has plenty, and still desires more, his extravagance is checked. These articles are all charged to him, at cost, with the addition of a small percentage, to save the Government from loss." However, Semmes noted, "Much of the clothing, which the sailor wears, is made up with his own hands. He is entirely independent of the other sex, in this respect, and soon becomes very expert with the needle."[9]

Not all new enlisted recruits received a uniform, hammock, and other items immediately. When Robert Watson and sixteen members of his 7th Florida Infantry company transferred to the Confederate States Navy on

March 9, 1864, they joined the complement of the CSS *Savannah*. After a fitful night's sleep on the berth deck, Watson and the others had breakfast and were set to work getting a cannon out that had burst at the muzzle. "Got it in shore after a great deal of hard work and humbugging and then got dinner, after which turned to and cleaned up decks, etc. We then drew some small stores consisting of tin cups, pans, thread, and soap. The soap is $7.30 per bar." Five days later, he wrote, "Worked hard all day. I drew a hammock and clothes bag today."[10]

Duties

Depending on needs of the navy, new recruits spent a few days or a few weeks on a receiving ship where they may have received some basic training. Here recruits learned how to address and respect officers, petty officers, and shipmates and took part in drills designed to teach them skills at handling sails and rigging, pulling boats, and using cutlasses. Instructors would also if possible drill recruits on large and small guns. Depending on the inclination of the receiving ship's officers and petty officers, new men might also pick up some understanding of naval discipline, lore, and customs.

From the receiving ship, men were sent to join a ship's crew as the complement of a new vessel or as replacements for men lost to death, illness, or desertion. Sailing ships needed a crew of more than 200 men to work the rigging and yard arms and to man the guns. The CSS *Virginia*, for example, had a complement of 230 officers and men. Ironclads, lacking sails and rigging, needed fewer men but also needed more engineers, coal heavers, and firemen.

Naval tradition spelled out the duties of the ships' commissioned officers, midshipmen, master's mates, and petty officers. The senior or commanding officer commanded the vessel and was usually referred to as the captain, regardless of his actual naval grade. He could be any grade from master to captain and was responsible "for the whole conduct and good government of the officers and others belonging to the vessel . . . and must himself set an example of respect and obedience to his superiors, and of unremitting attention to his duties."[11]

The first lieutenant or executive officer, known in naval circles as the "luff," was held responsible for the day-to-day running of the vessel or the superintendence of the general duties to be performed under the captain's direction. The luff was expected to know the capabilities of his men; inspect the ship daily; receive reports from the master, boatswain, gunner, and carpenter's mate; superintend the OOD; maintain order; and ensure the sick and wounded were properly cared for and a host of other duties.

The ship's commanding officer or executive officer might be on deck during a watch but usually gave orders through the OOD. In the event a lookout sighted an enemy ship or other possible threats, the OOD would order the drums on board to beat and send the crew to general quarters' stations. His duties included recording in the ship's log the ship's direction, any ship or land sighted, changes in the weather, steaming or sailing conditions, or any notable occurrences.

Depending on their complement, Confederate vessels usually had a number of commissioned line officers in the grade of lieutenant and ensign. They also had a chief engineer and engineering assistants, a surgeon or assistant surgeon, and a paymaster. These officers were commissioned officers who had either resigned from the U.S. Navy or been recruited from various civilian professions. The paymaster was to keep the ship's books, pay out funds to the crew, and account for and issue food and clothing and "small stores." He kept a pay ledger marked with entries for each sailor's wages and any amounts subtracted for the purchase of items from the ship's store such as needles, tobacco, spices, or jackknives. Sailors going ashore on liberty appreciated getting a few dollars from the paymaster; in emergencies such as sickness, death, or destitution at home, a sailor might appeal to the paymaster for extra funds. The paymaster was also required to keep his funds safe in a strong box and, during general quarters, be ready to open storerooms for supplies needed to make repairs. All of this could keep a navy paymaster busy, as one paymaster serving on the Union navy ship noted, "Then a hundred times a day I am applied for 'a little money, sir. I've got liberty ashore . . . a pair of shoes, sir, mine are all to pieces . . . a cap, sir, mine has blown overboard' & a thousand wants like these."[12] As the Union blockade of the South tightened, his Confederate navy counterparts had to deal with increasing shortages of food, furnishings, toiletries, and other supplies. Sailors in both navies complained about a lack of money, kept a close eye on their accounts, and were suspicious that the paymasters might be cheating them. In the absence of naval agents, paymasters had to settle accounts with naval contractors, and in one instance the CSS *Alabama*'s paymaster was beseeched by sailor landlords coming on board with bills against crew members.[13]

Paymasters were in theory carefully selected for trustworthiness and competence. They had to submit character references, pass examinations, and be at least twenty-one years old. The navy ranked paymasters as lieutenants; their clerks had to be at least eighteen years of age, be appointed not commissioned, and were ranked as midshipmen.

The importance of the chief engineer, assistant engineers, firemen, and coal heavers on board ships of the Civil War era cannot be overstated given that most naval vessels were steam driven, but the engineer's status was less defined by naval tradition. Navy vessels had just one chief engineer who held a commission and was assisted by three warrant officers rated as first, second, and third assistant engineers. Their duty was to design, acquire, install, operate, and maintain engines on board vessels or those on stations ashore.

When the war began, some career engineers in the U.S. Navy resigned their commissions and went South. Winfield Scott Thompson, for example, was a Maryland native who resigned as third assistant engineer in the U.S. Navy in December 1861. Five months later he obtained a commission as a second assistant engineer in the Confederate States Navy and served the Richmond Naval Station, CSS *Georgia*, and CSS *Tuscaloosa*. While on board the *Florida* he was captured off Bahia, Brazil, but was paroled.

George Washington Tennett, who was born in Philadelphia, resigned his commission as a first assistant engineer in the U.S. Navy and joined the Oglethorpe Light Infantry; he was captured at Fort Pulaski in April 1862. After being exchanged, he served on board the CSS *Huntress*, gained appointment as first assistant engineer on the *Georgia*, and served as an assistant engineer on the *Atlanta* and then on two vessels of the James River squadron. Tennett's career followed a similar pattern to many of his fellow U.S. Navy engineers who resigned to support the Confederacy's war effort by first enlisting in local army units, including George

A. Bowe, who served with the Thomas Artillery before being detailed to government work and, in 1863, finally being appointed a third assistant engineer at the Richmond Naval Station.

With fewer engineers to choose from the ranks of the old navy, the Confederate navy recruited most of its engineers from civilian life. Some men appointed engineers in the Confederate navy were machinists. Take, for example, Joseph Stanhope West, a North Carolina native who was employed by the Tredegar Iron works in Norfolk in early 1861, then enlisted in the Norfolk Light Artillery Blues in 1861. He was discharged and appointed third assistant engineer from Virginia, then transferred to the Confederate navy and served on board the CSS *Savannah* and was promoted and assigned to the *Atlanta*. While a prisoner of war at Fort Warren, West received a promotion to second assistant engineer and went on to serve on the CSS *Hampton* and the CSS *Fredericksburg* and, at war's end, with the Semmes Brigade.[14]

Most Confederate vessels had at least one midshipman; the *Nashville* had seven. To direct the powder division, passed midshipmen were preferred to those who had not passed their examinations, but all could be found on the quarterdeck as the captain's aide or could be ordered to assist the engineers or surgeons during general quarters. Some were assigned to assist the lieutenants in charge of the guns, and on smaller vessels or those lacking enough officers, they might rate even more responsible duties such as commanding a prize vessel or temporarily commanding a ship.

Confederate enlisted men were rated as petty officers, seamen, ordinary seamen, coal heavers, firemen second class, landsmen, and boys. They had little if any social interaction with senior officers, who were usually of a different social class and often from a different cultural background. Officers generally avoided physical labor, and naval tradition banned petty officers and seamen from areas of the ship reserved for officers, the quarterdeck, officers' quarters, and the wardroom. In extenuating circumstances on a ship that had a shortage of men, however, officers did pitch in. When men were needed to transfer weapons equipment and provisions from the *Laurel* to the *Sea King*, Midshipman Mason recalled that the officers soon "took our coats & vests off, rolled up our sleeves," and labored alongside the seamen.[15]

The duties of petty officers varied and were arranged by priority. The first was the master's mate, who was not a commissioned officer but received a warrant from the secretary of the navy. Warrant officers ranked just below midshipmen and were assigned duties at divisional quarters, on the quarterdeck, and on the forecastle. They had a responsible position on board ships of the Confederate States Navy and, in a departure from prewar tradition in the U.S. Navy, could look forward to promotion to ensign or to master. When on watch, a master's mate served as an assistant to the OOD. He was often the mustering officer of the division and of the watch, helping to prepare his division for inspection and drills. He posted lookouts and checked on their alertness, saw that the ship's boats that might be employed as a messenger were properly fitted out and manned. It was with pride that George Townley Fullam wrote on August 23, 1862: "Was this day appointed 'Acting Master's Mate' to the C.S. Str. Alabama." In 1864 Fullam would be just one of ninety-six acting master's mates serving in the Confederate States Navy.[16]

Then came the master at arms, who was responsible for discipline and securing prisoners. The yeoman took charge of stores, the surgeon's steward assisted the surgeon, and the ship's corporal assisted the master at arms. Most vessels had an armorer, a cooper, and a ship's cook. The boatswain's mate handled the ships rigging; the gunner's mate, the guns; and the carpenter's mate, the repairs. A painter mixed paints, and the sailmaker made and repaired the sails. The coxswain handled the ship's boats, the quartermaster assisted the master's mate, the quarter gunner assisted the gunner's mate, and a captain of the tops and holds supervised the rigging and store rooms. In addition to these men, steam vessels had a fireman first class. Other petty officers were the armor's mate, cabin steward, wardroom steward, cabin cook, and wardroom cook. To be rated a seaman, a recruit had to have two years' experience at sea; a landsman, only one year. Those who shipped as boys were typically youngsters between the ages of fourteen and seventeen.[17]

Accommodations

On most Confederate ships, officers had commodious or at least comfortable accommodations and at day's end or following their watch might retire to their individual cabins equipped with a bed or cot. On sailing ships and raiders such as the *Shenandoah*, the officers' quarters were aft near the stern and under the raised quarterdeck. The captain had his own cabin on this ship, bathed in light from "elegant stern windows." Forward of the cabins was the wardroom illuminated by skylights where the officers took their meals.[18]

Living on shipboard in tight quarters proved trying for some sailors. Officers, lieutenants, and above often had the luxury of a private stateroom, but warrant officers and lower-ranking officers shared accommodations. Appointed a master's mate and assigned to the CSS *Savannah*, nineteen-year-old Iverson Dutton Graves found the *Savannah* "rather crowded." He asked his mother to "just think of five living in a room not a sixth part as large as yours with bunks trunks stools lockers and a dining table where we sleep eat and live and you can understand the disadvantage of letter writing and but two being allowed to leave the ship the others are dancing singing or tustling [sic] all the time."[19]

Confederate midshipmen at the South's floating naval academy, the CSS *Patrick Henry*, slept in hammocks "slung as closely together as sardines in a box." Confederate navy petty officers and seamen had little privacy and slept on the berth deck in hammocks strung from overhanging beams or on some vessels in wooden bunks built into the forecastle. In his diary, reefer Hubbard Minor noted, "My sleep was a little interrupted last night for the boys tied ropes to my hammock & swung me all night nearly."[20]

Francis Dawson, determined to go to America to fight for the Confederacy, boarded the CSS *Nashville* at Southampton, England, on New Year's Eve 1862. "I reported to the officer of the deck, and told him that I had been ordered by Captain Pegram to come aboard for duty. I was turned over to the boatswain, who told me to go down into the 'foksle.'" Dawson dutifully tumbled down the "companion" and he recalled, "found myself in as pleasant a place for being uncomfortable, as any one could desire. The foksle, or forecastle, was about ten feet long, about five feet six inches high, and about ten feet broad aft, and six feet forward. The lack of height was an advantage to me, as when the vessel rolled I could hold on with my head and have my hands at liberty." On each side of the forecastle "were bunks or 'rabbit hutches' for the crew. In the centre was a small table supported against the windlass bitt, a heavy piece of timber which passed through the forecastle. Around the bitt were hung a number of one-pronged forks, notched knives, and battered spoons, matching each other for only one thing—dirt."[21]

About a week after the ship sailed from Southampton, Dawson and another man, Lussen, were given a stateroom on the hurricane deck with, as he told his mother in a letter, "two bunks and a toilet stand, and is very prettily painted. Through the windows we can see the open sea." His new accommodations gave him a welcome separation from the unfriendly crew who "lost no opportunity of showing their spite and their disgust." When the *Nashville* sailed from Southampton, Dawson explained, "the crew were mustered into the service of the Confederate States and signed the articles. I was rated as a 'landsman' or a 'boy.'"[22]

On most naval vessels, the ship's crew answered calls of nature on the "head," a toilet platform extending from the base of the ship's bowsprit, or they used buckets. The floor of the platform had a grate allowing the sea to wash it clean. The men were expected to use the lee side of the "heads" so all the effluent should fall into the sea. The raider CSS *Shenandoah*, however, boasted three water closets equipped with patent flush toilets, most of them located aft for the use of the senior officers.[23]

Officers and men found serving on monitors and some ironclads especially onerous. "The quarters were cramped," Engineer E. A. Jack recalled of the CSS *Arkansas*, "hot and badly ventilated." Jack preferred not to sleep in the officers' quarters but in a hammock. "The hammock was swung just outside of the fencing around the engine room aft, and near the gangway ladder which led to the deck of the shield." With their ship moored below the guns of Vicksburg, the crew of the *Arkansas* suffered from the heat. "In the engine room, which was petitioned from the ward-room access only by a rough board fencing about four or five feet high, the thermometer indicated over 100. Such a temperature when the engines were at rest and the fires low gave promise of trying and exhausting duty when underway or in action."[24]

A few days after Jack joined the crew of the CSS *Arkansas*, the ironclad engaged two Union vessels, the *Essex* and *Queen of the West*. "Then the heat in the engine room was almost unbearable and in the fire-room the glowing red furnace doors shot out such heat that the men had to be frequently relieved and would gladly take a turn to rest on the quarter-deck where shot were flying around in preference to staying below where they were better protected."[25]

Officers serving on vessels under construction or stationed in rivers or harbors occasionally enjoyed more comfortable quarters ashore. Unable to attack Union forces without infantry support, in the spring of 1864 the gunboat CSS *Neuse* remained in the Neuse River near Kinston, North Carolina. The *Neuse's* enlisted men slept on the boat or nearby, but the gunboat's seven officers were quartered in a "small house" at the western end of the terminus "of Col. Washington Avenue," Lt. R. H. Bacot wrote, a quarter mile from the ship.[26]

Daily Routines

Once assigned to a ship, new recruits were assigned to various stations and set about learning shipboard routine. On a man-o-war, men were stationed by number at the guns, in the tops, in a boat, at a mess, and in a hammock. At first, most new seamen found remembering their number for so many stations difficult but could consult the watch and station bill. On board the CSS *Nashville*, like most navy vessels and men-o-war, the ship's day was divided into five four-hour watches, plus two two-hour dog watches during the dinner hours. "The crew was divided into two watches," Dawson explained. "I found that I had twelve hours on duty out of every twenty-four, and at no time more than four consecutive hours to call my own." Each watch had an OOD, usually a lieutenant or senior ranking master, who supervised the running of the ship on behalf of the first lieutenant and recorded details in the ship's log. Assisted by the quartermaster and a midshipman or on some vessels by the sailing master, the OOD's primary duty was the safe navigation of the vessel if under way. When leaving or entering port, navigation fell to the pilot, who might also be consulted especially when steaming in unfamiliar waters or on narrow obstacle-ridden rivers and sounds. In addition to his primary duty, the OOD also supervised drills and exercises, but the first lieutenant or executive officer was responsible for training the midshipmen in navigation and seamanship.[27]

On a typical day, a trill from the boatswain's pipe woke sailors at or before daybreak, and the boatswain's mate strode through the berth deck shaking hammocks and shouting orders to "Rise and shine! Lash up and Stow!" The sleepy tars had to roll out of their hammocks, stretch, take a quick wash from a bucket, and lash up and stow their hammocks and bedding into a tight bundle before reporting to the weather deck. Here the hammocks were stored behind heavy rope nets, called nettings, along the bulwarks to protect against gunshots and wood splinter or to hamper enemy boarders. On many ships, these tasks were expected to be completed in eleven minutes or less. Although the routine might vary on Confederate vessels, most followed naval custom of delaying breakfast for an hour so the decks might be swabbed or "holystoned"; brightwork polished; rigging, if any, attended to; and necessary repairs made. Learning this new routine on *Nashville* came as a rude awakening to Dawson. "This was rather hard work for one who was fond of comfort and late breakfasts, but I speedily learned not to lose any time in going to sleep, and undressing appeared a useless indulgence."[28]

Swabbing the ship's deck with a mop and salt water to clean off dirt, garbage, or coal dust was a daily and time-honored, necessary task, but one less arduous than "holystoning." To remove grime from the decks, sailors used large flat stones or wooden blocks tied to ropes to work back and forth across the wooden deck planks. Barefooted, with their bell-bottomed trousers rolled up to keep them dry, they mopped or scrubbed the often cold, wet decks—a hard, boring job most sailors heartily disliked, one that "swabbies" endured whatever the weather. As Robert Watson noted in his diary one March day, "Blowing a stiff breeze from the W.S.W., all hands at work holystoning the decks, scrubbing paint work and hammocks." On board his ironclad vessel, the ram *Savannah*, Sundays were no exception. "Washed and scrubbed decks, ladders, etc. in the morning," he wrote.[29] The origin of the name "holystone" is obscure. Some suggest the term was first used by mariners because the decks were scrubbed on Sundays, thus "holy" stone. The term may also have come from the method used to procure a supply of stones—robbing churchyards for headstones.[30]

The duties of landsmen and seamen on most Confederate vessels varied, but many spent hours scrubbing the decks or polishing the ship's brightwork or brass fittings. Both tasks consumed the early morning hours and might be detailed after the noonday meal as well. When Dawson asked the boatswain for something to do, "he furnished me with a bucket and some soap, and told me to go to work and scour the paint. When I had amused myself with this for some hours, I was given a rag and told to polish up the brass-work. This ended, I occupied myself in sweeping the decks and cleaning out the spittoons. This was about the daily routine of my life on the *Nashville*."[31]

After performing these cleaning duties, all hands were typically mustered for an on-deck morning inspection followed by the shrill call of the boatswain's pipe announcing breakfast. The ship's commanding officer typically dined alone in his stateroom, with the officers in the wardroom served by a wardroom steward. Warrant officers, marines, and midshipmen gathered for meals in separate messes, and petty officers shared their own mess. Sometimes members of a gun crew, coal heavers and firemen, and topmen would have their own mess. Seamen were divided into messes, usually eight men to twelve men to a mess and, unless a man hired one of the sailors, took turns as the orderly or cook. The tableware and cooking utensils would be kept in a mess chest as well as the food allotted weekly to each mess by the ship's cook. Typically, each man had his own knife, fork, spoon, and mug, which were cleaned and stowed away after the meal in the mess chest.[32]

When breakfast was over, all hands would "turn to" a variety of shipboard tasks. On some ships, hands were called to quarters after breakfast to have the guns inspected, cleaned, and the metal gun carriages burnished and secured. Maintaining the ship's woodwork, hull, and masts was a daily task supervised by the carpenter's mate. The boatswain's mate handled the training of landsmen and oversaw the daily maintenance of the ship's lines, small boats, and anchor. The paymaster and his clerk, if he had one, were kept occupied handling the accounts. In the engineering department the engineers attended to the machinery, a job that required competence and attention for engines of Southern-built warships had an uncanny ability to break down at the worst possible moment.

Journals and diaries kept by Confederate and Union officers and sailors also offer glimpses of the numerous tasks performed to keep their vessels running. During the first two weeks of March, for example, CSS *Savannah*'s sailors worked "getting a cannon out that had been busted at the muzzle," overhauling the bow gun "to make it run easy," washing clothes, fixing hammocks, spreading awnings, or taking them in when it rained.[33]

In the engineering spaces below deck (the engine room, fire room, and boiler rooms), the engineer and his assistant engineers, firemen, and coal heavers also stood regular watches. The exact number of assistant engineers varied, but on the ram *Arkansas*, for example, the chief engineer, George W. City, had one second assistant engineer, Ellison Covert, and five third assistant engineers: Eugene Brown, James Gettis, William Jackson, John Dupuy, and James Doland. None other than City evidently had previous experience with naval machinery, especially screw propulsion.[34]

The April 1865 muster roll of CSS *Webb* lists one second assistant engineer, William Smith; three third assistant engineers, Harry S. Lewis, George R. Marsh, and Joseph E. Walters; five firemen; and five coal heavers. The firemen and coal heavers were about 10 percent of the ship's fifty-one enlisted men. The CSS *Virginia* went into the Battle of Hampton Roads with chief engineer H. A. Ramsay, first assistant engineer Loudon Campbell, second assistant engineer Benjamin Herring, and two third assistant engineers, E. A. Jack and E. V. White. "I think that Mr. E. V. White and myself . . . were the only ones who were from civil life," Jack recalled. Ramsay had been an engineer in the U.S. Navy since 1853 before resigning his commission to join the Confederate States Navy. Loudon Campbell had been a second assistant engineer in the U.S. Navy, and Benjamin Herring had served on the USS *Richmond* as a third assistant engineer.[35]

The engineering spaces were usually just below the quarterdeck and connected by a speaking tube that allowed the officers on the quarterdeck to speak directly or ring a bell to relay orders to the engineers. If the captain wished the ship to steam at full speed, he would order four bells be made and the OOD would ring the bell four times to signal full speed ahead. The chief engineer was responsible for reporting any stress on the ship's machinery, and regulations called for him to report each day at noon the quantity of coal consumed, the amount remaining in the coal bunkers, and the average revolutions per minute of the engine over the past twenty-four hours.[36]

Firemen supervised the operation of the boilers and controlled fires in the boilers, duties that required they be able to use different types of fuel and be prepared to repair steam machinery. Coal heavers had the most arduous and unpopular duties on board steam-driven vessels. They had to scoop the coal from cavernous coal bunkers and shovel the dusty, dirty coal into the boilers, with a typical first-class steam frigate with four boilers consuming 3,400 pounds of coal per hour and a *Cairo*-class river gunboat almost 2,000 pounds of coal per hour at six knots. Fire-room temperatures might climb to over 120 degrees, causing the walls to sweat and making any metal fixtures impossible to touch without wearing canvas gloves or mittens. One Union navy fireman wrote that his fire room was so hot "you can imagine how a crab would feel in a pot of hot water."[37]

Starting the engines was a laborious process, beginning with shoveling coal, then lighting the fires, and watching to see when the gauge showed enough steam to engage the cylinders. Typically, in most engine rooms, smoke and steam diminished the visibility to a few yards, and the engine room gang had to shout to be heard above the hiss of steam and racket of pounding rods and pistons. Some of the men wore red bandanas to absorb the sweat from the heat. Working in the engine rooms as firemen and coal heavers was hot, noisy, dirty work, and because most gunboats kept their boilers at half steam, the engine room crew were on duty at night. During combat, coal heavers, often stripped half naked, shoved coal into the boilers to keep the ship under full steam, and when it was time to shut the engines down, it was the firemen's job to "haul" the fires and have the boilers blown.

Engineer James Tomb was assigned to the newly constructed ironclad CSS *Chicora*. "The engine was single acting and was taken from a tug," he wrote. "While the engine was lacking in power, she was a good ship, after so many tinder boxes and cook shops we had had. She was thought to be able to make eight knots without forced drafts, but when completed could not under the most favorable circumstances make over seven."[38]

On board the CSS *Chicora*, the engineers messed and shared quarters together. "I was elected caterer for her Engineer's Mess, it was up to me to see about the arrangement of our quarters," Tomb recalled. "After stating the condition of our finances to Mr. Eason, he generously gave me the authority to go ahead and fix up our steerage to suit myself." Tomb industriously set about to procure furnishing, even damask curtains, spreads, and a pantry. The midshipmen and wardroom officers on the *Chicora* had separate quarters.[39]

Dawson stood watch with the other seamen on the *Nashville* and found it reasonably pleasant, "as I could ensconce myself in the pilothouse and read a novel to pass away the time, when I was not required on deck." This constituted his routine when the ship remained in port, but not once she had sailed. Like most new sailors, when his ship left port and reached the open ocean, Dawson succumbed quickly to seasickness. "I suppose I ought to say at this point that I was very seasick on the first day out, but, as Bo'sun Sawyer was constantly after me to do some of the drudgery he had in mind for me, I had no time to indulge in the pleasures of sea-sickness and recovered entirely in less than twenty-four hours."[40]

Afternoons on shipboard meant time spent in cleaning or repairing tasks or drills. The new crewmen on the *Savannah* drilled with small arms with, Watson noted, "Mansard rifles which came very awkward to us at first for they are very short, but soon got used to them and drilled very well." Days later the men drilled on the broadside guns despite a cold rain that fell all day long.[41]

A single 9-inch gun required a crew of seventeen men and a 6.4-inch gun only eleven, but the larger pivot guns needed as many as twenty-seven in a gun crew. An officer, usually a lieutenant, assisted by midshipmen commanded each gun division, and a lieutenant, gunner's mate, and mates were in charge of the powder division. Gunners supplied boarding parties and could be called upon to assist carpenter's mates in manning the pumps. Young boys, dubbed "powder monkeys," carried the powder from the magazine to the guns, and men from the powder division assisted the carpenter in combat making repairs, supplied men for boarding parties, and assisted in carrying the wounded to the surgeon.[42]

Navy crews also drilled at repelling boarders, small arms, and loading and firing the ship's guns. Frequent gun drills were necessary to train the often-inexperienced gun crews on Confederate naval vessels. J. W. Cooke, commanding the CSS *Albemarle*, drilled his gun crews by shouting commands at both crews. Sailors on other Confederate gunboats recalled gun drills twice each day.[43]

For sailors assigned to the 8 p.m. to 12 midnight watch, night duty might also mean manning a picket guard boat. On March 29 Robert Watson pulled picket duty: "We had to pull 4 miles and got on shore several times," Watson wrote. A stiff breeze came up at 10 p.m. and blew hard and "very cold" prompting the boat to pull on shore where there was a picket guard. They built a fire and "remained there until 5 a.m. when we started for the ram."[44]

Messes served a light supper about 4 p.m. Although shipboard routine might vary, commerce raiders and floating batteries or gunboats in proximity to the enemy would customarily call the men to quarters at 5:30 p.m. or near sundown to have the guns inspected and all in order for the night. The boatswain would then announce that hammocks could be removed and readied for the evening. Following supper, those sailors not on watch had free time. "Fiddling and dancing all night," Watson penned in his diary on several occasions. Taps sounded at 10 p.m., and those sailors not on watch turned to and swung into their hammocks to catch as much sleep as possible. After a time, new recruits grew accustomed to the gentle rocking of their hammocks and the unchanging naval sounds— the faint bells in succession, the cry of "All's well" around the ship, and the trampling of bare feet at the changing of the watch.[45]

On a typical day on board ship, the crew kept to their routine, which might be interrupted by a sudden squall that called for all hands to take in awnings or, on ships under sail, to reef or take in sails. When a ship ran into foul weather or a gale, men were sent aloft or required to stand their four-hour watch on deck in wet clothing, tossed about as the ship pitched and rolled and water gushed over the rails. If the hatch combings weren't tight or were too shallow, sea water might wash into the berth deck or drip through leaks into the officers' cabins, leaving men to sleep in wet hammocks. In violent storms huge waves pounding a vessel could make it shudder from stem to stern; during one storm a wave slammed into a ship's starboard side, carrying away the "head" with all its fixtures.[46]

Coaling a ship altered the routine as well, for on many steam-driven vessels all hands might be roused at 4 a.m. to begin the arduous, dirty task of filling the ship's coal bunkers from coal barges brought alongside, which was not a task looked forward to by most sailors. The coal dust coated everything. As one sailor quipped, "why is the coal so hard if it was soft coal?" Coaling a ship could take twelve hours or more and continued until it finished, regardless of what time it began. In some instances, the coaling detail had to load the coal from a wharf onto a collier and then bring the collier alongside the ship. For example, one December day a work party of men under Midshipman Williamson from the CSS *Atlanta* had to first pull their boat from the ship to Lamar's Wharf, spend the day loading thirty tons of coal on to the *Sampson*, then row back to the ship in the dark. The next morning Lt. Sidney Smith Lee and two midshipmen left the *Atlanta* at 5 a.m. with sailors to finish loading sixty more tons of coal. After being diverted to other tasks, they did not get the *Sampson* alongside the ship until 10:30 p.m. and were relieved when told stowing the coal could wait until morning.[47]

Mess on Naval Vessels

On most Confederate navy ships, dinner was served at midday after the morning chores were done. "Twelve o'clock or 'eight bells' rang, and the crew came down for dinner," Dawson explained. "One thing they insisted on, and that was that we should go down to the forecastle for our meals." The *Nashville*'s seamen ate on small tables in the center of the forecastle supported against the windlass bitt. "Around the bitt were hung a number of one-pronged forks, notched knives, and battered spoons, matching each other in only one thing—dirt."[48]

Dawson described the crew's usual diet and behavior: "First, there was a scramble for the knives, forks, and spoons; then a greasy boy brought down a large dish containing roast beef and potatoes, and dumped it on the deck. The men clustered around the dish. One of them seized the meat with his left hand, hacked off a large piece with the dull knife in his right, clutched a handful of potatoes out of the dish, and then retired to a quiet corner with his prey." Each of the others did the same. "A favorite dish once or twice a week was plum-duff, but the plums were so scarce that one of the men said that he could hear one plum singing this little song to another: 'Here am I! where are you? Tell me where to find you.'" Although Dawson admitted he had little appetite, the "food was good in itself, and there was plenty of it, but it was wretchedly served, as I have mentioned."[49]

Dawson enjoyed the food on CSS *Nashville*, but in general the sailor's diet could be monotonous and unappetizing. Yankee sailors complained as well about their fare. "Oh but I wish I had something good to eat," yeoman John Pugh wrote. "Our grub is very hard. Nothing for breakfast but sea brad sconce and coffee that is half beans or something els burnt to give it the colar. Supper, hard tack and something that looks like ea. Dinner sometimes middling good."[50]

Some seamen found navy fare more appealing and plentiful than that of the army. In his diary, Watson briefly described their noon deal. "Got through at 12 1/2 P.M.—got dinner, pork, peas and hard bread, good living to what we've been used to in the army." On most Confederate vessels, the men also looked forward to the twice daily issuing of the grog ration. Custom dictated that sailors receive a gill, about four ounces, of this grog, a mixture of rum and water.[51]

The daily routine and mess on the Confederate navy's "floating academy" varied somewhat from the routine of naval vessels. The day began with the firing of a morning gun at 7 a.m., which rousted midshipmen out of their hammocks. When the hammocks had been rolled up and stowed, at 8 a.m., a drummer playing "Dixie" announced breakfast. Midn. James Morgan recalled that breakfast was usually hardtack "generally infested with weevils and worms" accompanied by ersatz coffee, "a cup of hot water flavored with chicory or burnt grains of ground corn." The reefers' "scanty and unappetizing" diet consisted largely of corn meal and salt-junk beef. Morgan and others suspected the tough, salted beef had "been carved from very close to the horns of some half-starved animal."[52]

To break the monotony of the midshipmen's diet, a special dessert was served. "I feel ... fin ... today," James "Olly" Harrison wrote. "It is what the sailors call 'duff day' we draw 11 oz. of flour dried fruit enough to make 'duff' and molasses to the amount of a half pint to sweeten said 'duff' with."[53] For those lucky midshipmen with means, delicacies like oysters, fine Havana cigars, ale, or whiskey could be purchased from Richmond restaurants, but none came cheap. The Oriental Restaurant charged five dollars for a plate of oysters and twelve dollars for a bottle of ale, well beyond the means of a reefer's annual pay of five hundred dollars. As the Union blockade tightened and armies from both sides foraged in the countryside, food became scarcer and more expensive in Southern cities such as Richmond. In March and April 1863, angry women and men in Richmond blaming the government for inflation and protesting exorbitant food prices began breaking into various grocery shops and stores in the city.[54]

Men serving on Confederate raiders like the *Nashville* suffered when their supplies ran low but often took advantage of their prizes' larders to supplement their diets. "I had only my ship's ration of salt-horse and hard tack to eat," Midn. Jimmy Morgan recalled, "but it must have been a healthful regimen as I had grown wonderfully in height and strength—and my sobriquet of 'Little Morgan' had become a misnomer." When the CSS *Georgia* overhauled a ship from London bound for Australia, Morgan boarded the ship and, "after perfunctorily looking at the ship's papers the captain offered me a glass of sherry. . . . One of the passengers made particular inquiries about my age, and when I was about to get into our boat he presented me with a brown paper bag full of most delicious cakes, a luxury I had not tasted for many a long day."[55]

When at sea, many sailors attempted to catch fish. Observing that albacore and bonito were closely following their ship, the men of the *Georgia* threw a grange or three-pronged harpoon at them. "The fish were so close together that it was impossible to miss and we had quantities of fresh fish for all hands for ten or twelve days before they left us."[56] The crew of the brig *Clarence* had less luck. "Yesterday afternoon we had some little excitement trying to catch dolphin," A. L. Drayton wrote in his diary, "but not having any hooks we were unable to procure the treat of fish." Lawson made a harpoon out of sheet copper "and cut one in two. They remained close along side the ship as long as we could see them." The dolphins would jump at anything, he noted, even pieces of biscuit.[57]

On occasion, fish actually jumped on board Confederate vessels and were naturally quickly cooked and eaten. When Raphael Semmes sat down to breakfast one morning on "a very tempting looking dish of fried fish," he asked his Malay steward on the CSS *Sumter*, "to what good fortune was he indebted, for the prize, his little black eyes twinkled, as he said, 'Him jump aboard last night!'"[58]

When Confederate raiders or blockade runners managed to make a foreign port, they were usually greeted by the arrival of bumboats. Recalling his ship's arrival at Curaçao, Semmes wrote, "The *Sumter* had scarcely swung to her anchors, in the small land-locked harbor, before she was surrounded by a fleet of bum-boats, laden with a profusion of tropical fruits, and filed with men and women, indifferently—the women rather preponderating." The women were admitted freely on board the *Sumter* "and pretty soon Jack was on capital terms with them, converting his small change into fragrant bananas, and blood-red oranges, and replenishing his tobacco-pouch for the next cruise. As Jack is a gallant fellow, a little flirtation was going on too with the purchasing, and I was occasionally amused at these joint efforts at trade and love-making."[59]

Drilling and Gun Batteries

Naval tradition called for the ship's executive officer to take charge of all of the gun batteries, but Henry Stevens, the executive officer of the CSS *Arkansas*, chose to assign actual gunnery duties to his officers. Lieutenants commanded each of the ram's five gun divisions. Lieutenant Grimball had charge of the forward starboard battery; Lieutenant Gift, the forward port battery; and Lt. Charles Read, the two rifled 32-pounders at the stern. The two broadside batteries, port and starboard, were commanded by Lt. A. D. Wharton and Lt. Alphonso Barbot. Stevens assigned as assistant gunnery officers the *Arkansas*'s three midshipmen who served as gun captains. Twelve to fourteen men with one powder boy manned each gun crew. Two master's mates, assisted by quartermasters, were in charge of the ship's fore and aft powder magazines, which fed the guns with a steady stream of shells and powder. The sailors under these men could also be called upon to carry the wounded below to the surgeon.[60]

John McIntosh Kell also noted the importance of drilling sailors unfamiliar with naval guns. He recounts that on June 18 they steamed down to the barracks below the city to take on powder. "Here we remained several days, exercising our crew with the battery." As he explained, "Although our crew were most of them fine sailors, they were not 'men-o-war's men,' and had to be drilled at the guns. The crew consisted of 92 men, 20 of whom were marines."[61]

Drilling the crew of the almost-completed gunboat CSS *Neuse* proved difficult as well for 2nd Lt. Richard Bacot. "Our guns are mounted and we drill the crew every morning at 5:30 o'clock. We have one or two good men . . . but I am afraid the others can never learn anything about a gunboat."[62] Initially, *Neuse*'s commanding officer, Lieutenant Sharp, had twenty-eight men, for the most part sailors, but Lt. Robert Minor reported in February 1864, "he will make up the whole number of men allowed the vessel from those in the army who are accustomed to a seafaring life and have volunteered."[63] Cdr. Benjamin P. Loyall told Minor, sent to hasten completion of the *Neuse*, "I got some very good men—only a few sailors, but good soldiers, inured to hard service."[64] Sharp's attempts to find trained seamen to man the ironclad proved less successful. Describing the inexperienced crewmen, Bacot wrote, "You ought to see them in the boats! It is too ridiculous. They are all legs & arms & while working at the guns their legs get 'Tangled' in the tackles. . . . They are always in the wrong place & in each others way."[65]

Most commanding officers drilled their men in small arms and in the use of cutlasses and pikes used in boarding parties. "When the weather grew fine, the crew were ordered out for drill," Dawson wrote, "and from the recesses of our hold our hidden armament was produced. It consisted of about twenty rusty smoothbore muskets. The muskets were given to the sailors and firemen, who were then drilled in the manual of arms by one of the officers." According to Dawson, they disagreed on what the commands meant, "and the whole affair was very much of a burlesque, as every now and then a sudden lurch of the vessel would send three or four of the squad staggering down to leeward." The command "Ready! Aim!" "brought every musket levelled at our instructor's head, the startled officer called out hastily: 'For Heaven's sake, men, don't point your guns at me! They're loaded!' The warning was not given too soon, for, as they were dismissed, two of the men rolled into the scuppers, their pieces going off with a very ugly report. That was the first and last of the drilling."[66]

Other Confederate naval commanders took drills more seriously. In the journal he kept of the cruise of the CSS *Sumter*, Semmes noted on June 19, 1861, the importance of drilling a new crew at the guns. "The object of my stopping here for a few days is to station my crew and drill them at the guns, they being entirely green and having been called to quarters to-day for the first time." The following day Semmes drilled them again and in the afternoon held target practice. On "Mon. Nov. 25: Exercised crew with small arms, and fired off loaded muskets and overhauled and cleaned pistols, firing of such of them as had been some time loaded."[67]

A quarterly inspection of CSS *Drewry* by Flag Officer Mitchell commanding the James River squadron in July 1864 offers some idea of the type of training and the extent of the gunboat's preparation for combat. The *Drewry*'s commanding officer, William H. Wall, responded to a number of questions about training, target practice, small arms and battalion drill, and the condition of the magazine and shell room. He stated that opportunities for the ship to hold exercises and target practice was "tolerably good." The ship's last target practice had been on June 21. Nonetheless, Wall had to admit the gun divisions had not been properly prepared. "Spare implements not on deck. No brackets to cutlasses." His men were not well skilled, he wrote, "in the exercise of the great guns including working both sides at once, and in pointing and firing," He was indifferent to the condition of *Drewry*'s magazine. "Grape and canister in it. Torpedo stored there also, and also rockets and blue lights." These were, however, "liable to accident at any time." On the plus side, the shell room and shot lockers were in good condition, and the crew was well trained in repairing injuries to the steering apparatus and getting springs on cables. In a response to a question about arrangements for boarding and repelling boarders, Wall wrote that the vessel had no boarding netting, and the crew was not well trained in the use of small arms, leading him to admit, we "could be carried away very easily by boarding."[68]

Inspecting shell rooms and magazines was essential for safety's sake, for explosions and fires posed a serious threat to naval vessels. "There are two things that I dislike aboard a vessel," Landsman A. L. Drayton wrote in his diary, "that is the cry of fire and [of] man overboard." On one occasion a cry of "man overboard" rang out on the brig *Clarence* and, according to

Drayton, "as soon as Mr R [Read] heard the word he was on deck in an instant to cry false and . . . if this crew ever gets ashore I think there will [be] some scores to settle."[69]

Many Confederate warships or raiders devoted time for lessons. Semmes, describing life on board CSS *Sumter*, wrote, "The boys of the ship are taking lessons, in knotting and spicing, and listening to the 'yarn' of some old salt, as he indoctrinates them in these mysteries. The midshipmen have their books of navigation spread out before them, and slate in hand, are discussing sine and tangent, base, and hypotenuse." When informed it was time to "look out for the sun," the commander came on deck with his sextant. "See, he gathers the midshipmen around him, each also with his instrument, and, from time to time, asks them what 'altitude they have on,' and compares the altitude which they give him with his own, to see if they are making satisfactory progress as observers."[70]

Shortages

As the war went into its third year, shortages of rations and clothing appeared. Semmes' paymaster was fortunate in being able to procure "a supply of pea-jackets, whalers' boots, and flannel over-shirts" in the West Indies, but other commanders began to face shortages.[71] Issuing proper clothing for the winter proved taxing to the Navy Department's Office of Provisions and Clothing. "Adequate supply of winter clothing is all important at this time to make the men comfortable," Captain Mitchell advised the *Richmond* paymaster.[72] "And unless they are made, so they must become discontented and unreliable in health and loyalty." Without "cheerful fires and exercise," sailors on shipboard suffered more than their soldier counterparts.[73]

In some cases, uniforms were still available to those officers or reefers who had the means. "I went to town to have my cloth made up. I will get two pair [of] pants & jacket made for $100. as every thing [is] furnished but the buttons & cloth by the tailor," Midn. Hubbard Minor noted in his diary entry for February 11, 1865. When he returned for the clothes, he wrote, "My Jacket fits me quite well but my pants were both pair ruined as they were cut badly."[74]

When Midn. James Morgan returned to Wilmington in 1864, he shared a cottage with several other naval officers stationed in the town but found shortages abounded. "I thought our condition in the Confederacy was bad enough when I had left its shores two years before, but these officers had literally nothing in the way of clothing besides their shabby uniforms, threadbare and patched. I felt ashamed of my new uniform, made by a fashionable London tailor, and my well-laundered white shirt."[75]

By the final year of the war the Union blockade had become more effective, creating wartime shortages and reduced rations for men of the James River Squadron as well. CSS *Richmond*'s commanding officer, William Parker, recalled rations were "pretty short" during the summer of 1864, but Squadron Commander Mitchell noted that by autumn the shortage was mostly in fresh vegetables. Officers and men serving on Confederate vessels stationed up rivers near farms or plantations had a more reliable source of fresh produce. The men of the CSS *Neuse* obtained food from farms near Kinston. "The crops here are all looking fine since the rain," wrote Bacot in mid-July 1864. "Watermelons & Roasting ears are coming on." Taking advantage of their station on the river, *Neuse*'s sailors took to fishing and Commander Loyall explained to Robert Minor, "now and then a stray shad comes into our hand." Nonetheless, the fare on board the *Neuse* was "nothing extra," one sailor noted in February 1864. They received one pound of meat every three days, in addition to "bread, corn, etc."[76]

One morning in December 1864 Hubbard Minor came off watch "& seeing a stray wild goose floating about on the other shore, I got in a boat & pulled towards him." Knowing it would be advantageous to shoot the goose in the wing, Minor made up his mind to wait, but when the goose moved near him, he cocked his gun "& left him have it & down he came." The next day, Minor noted, "My goose went splendidly for dinner. We had plenty of stuffing & he was well cooked. I carved him & helped my messmates, all of whom were present."[77]

On occasion Confederate sailors foraging for local produce had close calls with the enemy. While serving on board the CSS *Arkansas* off Vicksburg, Engineer Jack recalled, "It was the practice to allow a portion of the crew and officers liberty to go ashore during the day, but they were all to be aboard at night, and never out of signal distance of the vessel. I found much diversion and no little excitement at these excursions, for they were at all times perilous." One such excursion to pick ripe fruit from several fig tees behind a deserted house on the bluff above Vicksburg proved especially exciting. "About this time the enemy opened their mortar fire, and some proposed we return to the ship, but I, who had not yet gotten as much fruit as I wanted, dissented and said we were safe here, for look above at the corner of the house, a shot had already cut the eaves off there and fallen down somewhere, so as two shot don't strike the same place we could not be safer than where we are." They stayed awhile longer, but "we had gotten but a short way off when we heard the whistling of another shell and looking back saw it take of another piece of the house top and plunge into the trees which we had just left."[78]

Conclusion

Learning shipboard routine—how to sleep in a hammock or use the "head," how to be part of a mess and a station during general quarters, how to make or repair one's uniforms, and how to man a gun battery or use small arms—was all part of becoming a sailor in the Confederate States Navy. The navy initially provided recruits with uniforms, but over time most sailors learned to sew, decorate, or repair their clothing, and officers often resorted to purchasing uniforms from tailors ashore. When the Union blockade tightened, clothing shortages, especially a lack of winter clothing like pea jackets, developed. Many Confederate ships also began to experience food shortages, and commanding officers were forced to cut rations, prompting many sailors to find opportunities to go hunting or fishing.

On the receiving ship or after joining their first ship, new Confederate recruits were also indoctrinated as to the different ranks held by enlisted men—petty officers, seamen, ordinary seamen, coal heavers, firemen second class, landsmen, and boys. They soon learned not to interact socially with the ship's officers, who generally avoided physical labor, and it never took long for recruits to adhere to naval tradition, which banned petty officers and seamen from the quarterdeck, officers' quarters, and wardroom.

The indoctrination and training, equipping, and gun and small-arms drills were necessary not just to transform raw recruits into sailors but to make them "men-o-war's men."

3

Entertainment, the Sabbath, and Liberty

I N ADDITION TO THE REGULAR shipboard routine, standing watches, conducting gun and small-arms drills, and enforcing discipline, Confederate States Navy commanding officers were charged with maintaining morale on board Confederate naval vessels. Shipboard entertainment, mail delivery, regular worship services, and the opportunity to go ashore on liberty all contributed to morale. Sailors serving on vessels in ports, on rivers, or near the coast found diversion as well in boating parties, fishing or hunting, visiting families in town, or—even in wartime—attending the theater or fancy balls.

Entertainment

Confederate navy officers and crew stood regular watches, but when not on watch sailors might pass the time writing or reading letters, playing checkers or dominos, or sewing. In fine weather, the crews of Confederate raiders enjoyed being on deck to relax and mend their clothes. "With the fore-castle, and quarter deck awnings spread, we do not feel the heat," Raphael Semmes recalled. "Jack is overhauling his clothes-bag, and busy with his needle and thread, stopping, now and then, to have a 'lark' with his monkey or listen to the prattle of his parrot."[1]

If they had carpentry skills, sailors might also make items for their own use. "I was at work all day making a little chest to keep my books, papers, etc. in," Robert Watson wrote one July day in 1864. Playing cards and engaging in any form of gambling was against regulations, but the Confederate navy did not forbid men from enjoying a smoke. Smoking was permitted when the smoking lamp was lit and was usually confined to the galley or forward part of the vessel. To avoid setting fires, matches were not used; sailors lit cigars or pipes from a whale-oil lamp.[2]

For amusement during their time off duty, many sailors enjoyed music. "After hours, those who desired amusement collected in the gangways and gave themselves up to dancing, jumping, singing, or spinning yarns, in which the narrator was the hero," wrote the CSS *Shenandoah*'s captain, James Waddell.[3] No matter how hard the days' work, CSS *Alabama*'s John McIntosh Kell recalled, "the crew would gather around the forecastle and enliven the evening air with amusing nautical ditties, often of their own improvisation, but generally closed the evening's entertainment with the national songs of our beloved Southland."[4]

Most ships had at least one fiddler or banjo player. "Cloudy in the forenoon and raining in the afternoon, Fiddling and dancing at night," Watson noted in his diary in March 1862. Two nights later, he wrote, "I did not close my eyes all night it being too cold to sleep. Fiddling and dancing all night."[5] The men of the *Shenandoah* enjoyed an evening of singing and dancing by three of the Pacific Islanders, "some of the songs were very sweet, but the dancing was excellent," Surgeon Lining recalled. A few nights later, "'Lee' got all the dancers among the men by the main hatch & by a little whiskey set them dancing until after nine o'clock."[6] Navy commanders also encouraged their men to make music. Semmes provided his sailors with a violin and tambourine.[7] Theatricals and minstrel shows were also popular.

Others lent their skills to teaching. In what free time he enjoyed, Francis Dawson gave lessons to some of the *Nashville*'s seven midshipmen. Midn. Clarence Cary, appointed acting midshipman from Virginia in August 1861, was one of his pupils. "Cary was anxious to improve himself in French, and I gave him a lesson nearly every day," Dawson wrote. Being versatile, he "gave some lessons in music" as well.[8]

Confederate vessels also had their share of pets and mascots. "Jack has a great fondness for pets," Semmes recounted, "and no wonder, poor fellow, debarred as he is, from family ties, and with no place he can call home, but his ship; and pretty soon my good-natured first lieutenant had been seduced into giving him leave to bring sundry monkeys and parrots on board, the former of which were now gamboling about the rigging, and the latter waking the echoes of the harbor with their squalling."[9] One of the most unusual pets taken on board a Confederate vessel was a penguin adopted by the crew of the *Shenandoah*. "They are covered with gray down, are unable to fly, and walk with military erectness," the cruiser's captain explained. One of the sailors pinned a rag resembling a shawl around the penguin's neck, which provided much merriment for the men.[10]

Officers and men alike eagerly looked forward to the arrival of mail, a sure antidote to the boredom of shipboard routine. While serving as officer of the deck on the CSS *Savannah* one day, Iverson Dutton Graves found time to write to his mother. "I was walking on the deck thinking of Home when the mail boy came with your letter. I was very glad to get it and it called up so many pleasant thoughts that the hours passed away so quickly I could scarcely believe the quartermaster when he reported eight bells and time to be relieved."[11]

Almost all Confederate navy men looked forward to hearing news from their hometowns and reports of the war effort. They welcomed the arrival of newspapers, even old ones, and relished rumors that circulated freely. "A pleasant day. Good news from Virginia, our army still victorious," Watson wrote on May 22, 1864.[12] Newspapers were more readily available to those officers and men serving ashore or on vessels stationed in or near ports. "The examiner has had some splendid Editorials in it lately, which I have enjoyed very much," Lt. R. H. Bacot told his sister in a letter dated April 28, 1864. "I'd give anything to be able to write like that Editor; he can almost make a man run mad if he gets down on him. . . . He makes Mr Memminger and Gen Bragg appear very ridiculous in a late issue which you'd probably see by this time."[13]

In addition to newspapers, the telegraph carried news from the front. Midn. Willie Wilson noted in his diary that he had received news by telegraph that the Union forces had succeeded in passing the forts below New Orleans and had captured the city. "If this is so it is the gravest miss [*sic*] fortune that had happened to us yet. it would have been better for a hundred thousand of our men to have been killed than this to happen if so Gen Lovell should be shot for a coward."[14]

Sending letters out, however, proved difficult for many Confederate sailors. In the fall of 1864 Watson noted, "Wrote three letters to go by a blockade runner, but after writing them I found that he had left early in the morning."[15] Letters from home could—and often did, as the war went on—bring sad news or word of families struggling at home. On October 4, 1864, a sailor returned from a furlough to Florida and brought Watson two letters and two neckerchiefs from an old friend. "My poor friend sees pretty hard times of it, can't buy anything for Confederate money and has to live on cornmeal and water. His family has lately been increased by the birth of a son."[16]

Elections proved a source of discussion, entertainment, and even amusement. "Everyone expects a lively time about here," Lieutenant Bacot wrote to his sister in July 1864, "when the elections come off in August. A secret, treasonable league has been discovered in the state called the HOAs (Heroes of America) they are in league with the enemy & are all Holdenites. Since the disclosures, made by some members who became disgusted with the society, the remainder have kept remarkably quiet." William W. Holden, a publisher, was the leader of the North Carolina peace movement in 1864 and an outspoken critic of the Confederate government. Bacot, one of CSS *Neuse*'s officers, expressed a blunt opinion on the movement. "I wish President Davis would have Holden and his entire clan taken up & hung; that would stop such rascals quicker than any conciliatory measures."[17]

Despite the diversions of mail and news from home, the navy kept many ships on station with little to relieve the boredom. "We are living the same monotonous sort of life here as usual, nothing to eat scarcely, and no amusements," Master James Long wrote to his friend Hubbard Minor from CSS *Albemarle*.[18] "I find it exceedingly dull here as the town is completely deserted by all of its respectable inhabitants & I know none of these living in the country around," lamented Bacot.[19]

Bacot took advantage of the gunboat *Neuse*'s station on the Neuse River by taking a boat out on night rides, noting that these excursions were a highly pleasurable experience. "The Gunboats (as we are called here) have concluded to have as nice a time as possible and find plenty of amusements. We have the exclusive use of a tin pan alley, where we exercise our 'muscles' every morning." The *Neuse's* officers pursued other forms of entertainment in their leisure time. "We pitch & Quoits after dinner & have various diversions for the evening; such as . . . visiting, walking, &tc."[20]

When there were no enemy merchantmen to pursue, officers and men serving on Confederate raiders also suffered from boredom. One of *Shenandoah's* midshipmen, Francis Chew, noted that the drill routine "is repeated from day to day with dreadful monotony." He read Germaine de Staël's romantic novel *Corrine* for the second time and began Jean-Jacques Rousseau's *Confessions*. Midshipman Mason delved into Charles Dickens' *Martin Chuzzlewit* but penned, "I don't think much of the first chapter, but intend to wade through at all hazards." Mason, like many sailors, was war weary and had bouts of homesickness. "What a blessed thing it would be! and how pleasant it would be to steam into a Confederate port in the 'Shenandoah.'"[21]

Vermin and insects also tormented many Confederate sailors in their spare time or during the night. Midshipman Wilson, serving on CSS *Savannah*, labeled his quarters "the damndest place" and wrote, "a person cannot sleep for the mosquitoes and cockroaches."[22]

Time spent off the ships on liberty helped raise morale, but as the Union blockade began to tighten, liberty men in Southern ports like Savannah found fewer and fewer items to purchase. The fall of Fort Pulaski in April 1862, for example, closed Savannah to most blockade runners, who went on to Charleston and Wilmington, leaving local businesses short on wares. Wilson went into Savannah to shop, but the joy he felt over his pay check of $54.26 may have quickly dissipated when he discovered so little to buy. Shops had no new clothes to offer, not even an abundance of the usual staples of coffee, tea, or flour.[23]

By the spring of 1864, the availability of goods to buy in Kinston, North Carolina, had dwindled as well. As young Richard Bacot complained to his sister in a letter, "Our Paymaster has just arrived & will leave again tomorrow he has no money & will not pay off. We couldn't spend it if he did (as ther's nothing to buy) so will wait." By July 1864 prices in Kinston had risen alarmingly. "Everything is enormously high & of course that is very unsatisfactory to a man living on a salary which doesn't rise with the prices of provisions," Bacot noted. "Butter alone is $7 per lb."[24]

On the other hand, Southerners could readily purchase tobacco. "The Union soldiers craved tobacco of which the Southerners had an abundance," Midn. James Morgan explained, "and the 'graybacks' longed for coffee or sugar." On the line of men defending Richmond, "trading in these commodities went on briskly without the knowledge of the officers." A Confederate soldier would creep outside the works on Drewry's Bluff and place a few large plugs of tobacco on a certain stump, then return to his companions. When he went back to the stump, he would find his tobacco gone "but in its place was a small quantity of longed-for coffee and sugar." Morgan said they always carried plugs of tobacco in their breast pockets, "as it was a common belief that if a man was captured and had tobacco it would insure him of good treatment."[25]

In his memoirs, Morgan related the story of being on duty and visiting one of the rebel outposts. He heard oars slapping the water and then a boat rammed into the mud at his feet. Fearing he might be shot, Morgan pulled his pistol out, but a voice said, "For the love of Mike, Johnny, give me a chew of tobacco." He handed the man a plug of tobacco and received in return a canteen full of whiskey. "We entered into conversation, and discovered that he was an old classmate of mine at Annapolis who had 'bilged' and was now a master's mate in charge of a picket boat whose duty was to give warning if our ironclads descended the river."[26]

The Sabbath, Holidays, and Other Celebrations

Ships of the Confederate States Navy observed Sundays in the typical naval fashion, mustering the crew for inspection and holding divine services. If possible, when in port a local pastor would be summoned to conduct the worship service, but at sea in the absence of a chaplain on board, the captain or one of the officers read the service or offered prayers. The CSS *Savannah* brought a Methodist minister on board to preach on September 4, 1864. "Preaching in the afternoon by Mr. Fairfax, the sailing master," CSS *Savannah* sailor Robert Watson wrote on March 28, 1864. A week later, however, he noted, "No preaching today."[27]

"Sunday on board a ship depends very much on the temperament of the person if it be a day of enjoyment," John Kell recalled. "Of course there is the usual routine-muster, inspection of quarters, reading of the Articles of War, etc. If there is no chaplain, the captain, if he is a religious man or desires it, usually reads the service, the crew attend if they wish and the officers almost without exception do; but the men without work or duty find light reading, or gather in groups and spin yarns for the general amusement of their fellow-sailors."[28]

Custom dictated that the crew don their dress or white uniforms for Sunday services and inspection, and on the first Sunday of the month they removed their caps to hear the Articles of War read. Wartime conditions occasionally made this impractical or impossible, but the letters and diaries of many officers and sailors record the observance of the custom.[29]

As the *Sumter* passed the mouth of the Surinam River, Semmes noted in his diary: "This being Sunday, as we were running along the coast, we mustered and inspected the crew, and caused the clerk to read the articles 'for the better government of the Navy' to them—the same old articles, though not read under the same old flag, as formerly." This was his practice on Sundays, Semmes wrote: "It broke in, pleasantly, and agreeably, upon the routine duties of the week, pretty much as church-going does, on shore, and had a capital effect, besides, upon discipline, reminding the sailor of his responsibility to the laws, and that there were such merciless tribunals, as Courts-Martial, for their enforcement." Semmes felt that "the very shaving, and washing, and dressing of a Sunday morning, contributed to the sailor's self-respect." Furthermore, he explained, "The 'muster' gratified, too, one of his passions, as it gave him the opportunity of displaying all those anchors and stars, which he had so industriously embroidered, in floss silk, on his ample shirt-collar, and on the sleeve of his jacket." The *Sumter* had some dandies on board, he recalled, "and it was amusing to witness the self-complacent air with which these gentlemen would move around the capstan, with the blackest, and most carefully polished of pumps and the whitest, and finest sinnott hats, from which would be streaming yards enough of ribbon, to make a ship a pennant."[30]

The Confederate States Navy faithfully observed other naval traditions, especially crossing-the-line ceremonies. Crossing the line, an initiation ceremony in many navies, commemorated a sailor's first crossing of the equator. Those crewmen who had crossed the line were termed "shell-backs" and the sailors who had not were called "pollywogs." "On the 17th of November we crossed the line and old Neptune with his wife and barber, came on board and found most of his victims among the officers," James Waddell recalled. "Lieutenant Lee, always gay and happy, was the only officer who had crossed the line and he enjoyed arraigning his messmates before the court of the god of the sea, and participated in the preparations for their admission to his favor." As he explained, "Tar and soap for the barber's use and water from the donkey engine which threw a stream two inches in diameter over the unlucky victim is the ordeal through which each one passed upon his introduction to the line where Neptune is supposed to hold his court." One officer felt certain of escape. "I took charge of the deck and Grimball was carried off to his stateroom, where he prepared himself for his immersion and submitted with a good grace."[31]

Holidays brought celebration and appropriate merriment as well. On April 1, 1864, Robert Watson explained, "All fools day and many a trick was played by the men on each other."[32] Most Confederate vessels attempted to provide holiday festivities for the officers and crew during the Christmas and New Year's season, but not always successfully. "Christmas dinner had been prepared of the captured supplies," Waddell recalled, "but it was quite impossible to sit long enough to enjoy it, except under dinner difficulties. Most of the dishes left the table for the deck, and notwithstanding the disappointment at the loss of a good dinner, there was still life enough among us to record it as an incident in the sailor's life." The CSS *Shenandoah* had run into a gale, and Waddell vowed that if he ever again made a trip to Australia, he "would go very little south of the howling forties."[33]

In his journal, Semmes lamented the *Sumter*'s less than merry Christmas Day 1861: "Wednesday Christmas Day: Christmas day! bringing with it away here in mid-ocean all the kindly recollections of the season and home, and church and friends. Alas! How great the contrast between these things and our present condition. A leaky ship, filled with prisoners of war, striving to make a port through the almost constantly recurring gales of the North Atlantic, in midwinter!"[34]

A year later, Semmes' journal entry recorded a far more festive holiday: "Thursday, December 25: Christmas day, the second Christmas since we left our homes in the Sumter. . . . Our crew is keeping Christmas by a run on shore, which they all seem to enjoy exceedingly." Of his own mood that day, Semmes wrote, "My thoughts naturally turn this quiet Christmas day, in this lonely island, to my dear family. I can only hope, and trust them to the protection of a merciful Providence." The *Sumter* was in the Caribbean. Semmes lamented that he had been ashore only but one week in five months. "The only sign of a holiday on board to-night is the usual 'splicing of the main brace,' *anglice*, giving Jack an extra allowance of grog."[35]

For navy men fortunate enough to be in port or stationed ashore, local churches offered worship services on Christmas Day. "Yesterday morn (Christmas day) I went up to Savannah attended service at Bishop Elliott's church which was beautifully decorated for the day," Graves wrote to Cora Graves, "and heard a fine sermon from the Bishop." On the way he met a gentleman friend who invited him to come around and take dinner at his house. Graves accepted this invitation and "got an elegant dinner.—at least it so seemed to me, who had eaten beef and ship biscuit or 'hard tack' as we call it, for weeks without change."[36]

Christmas 1861 found Midn. Willie Wilson at the Pulaski Hotel in Savannah. In his entry for December 25, he lamented, "Today is Christmas and instead of the Joyous day of old how different are my circumstances changed this day one year ago I was in the midst of friends at home now I am far away in the midst of strangers and our beloved country is convulsed with the struggle of civil war." Then Wilson concluded his entry on a more festive note: "Had an eggnog."[37]

Wilson had just turned seventeen on December 3, 1861, but as the New Year approached felt he had little to celebrate. "Went up to the city today and came back at night nothing of interest stirring." Savannah seemed very quiet for New Year's Eve. On a philosophical note, Wilson wrote: "Today is the last of 1861 the year that will ever be remembered as the war for the liberty of thousands of freemen which will brand the yankees as a nation void of all the better principals of the human race." The young reefer remained hopeful for the Southern cause. "My prayer is that when the sun rises on the first of Jan 62 it finds us a free people and our soil rid of the rascally Yankees."[38]

Liberty

When ships came into port, most sailors eagerly awaited the opportunity to go ashore on liberty. "Every day or two I was allowed to go ashore in the evening," Francis Dawson recalled, "and leaving my sailor garb behind me, I led, for a few hours, a pleasant life in town." When his ship the *Nashville* remained in port, Dawson also appreciated being granted liberty to go ashore.[39]

Most of the crewmen from the *Nashville* also managed to enjoy liberty. "The men went ashore as often as they could obtain leave, or steal off unobserved," Dawson recalled, "and the *Tuscarora*'s men did the same." Dawson looked forward to sightseeing. "I had a great desire to go ashore and see what Bermuda looked like, but the privilege was denied me as Bo'sun Sawyer found abundant occupation for the whole of us in shoveling coal and then scrubbing the paint." Although he was unable to obtain permission to go ashore as one of the Sunday boat's crew who went to the landing to bring off Captain Pegram, who had gone to church, he had, "the satisfaction of waiting there in the sun for two or three hours and of being roundly abused, by the rest of the crew, for 'catching crabs' in the most awkward manner as we rowed back to the *Nashville*."[40]

Liberty calls often resulted in bouts of drinking and fighting. "I and my chum Alfred Lowe went on shore after hours and I am sorry to say we got most gloriously drunk," Robert Watson wrote in his wartime journal on March 16, 1864. "When we went on shore we met our 1st Boatswain's Mate and our Yeoman, both very fine men and we went to a bar room and took several drinks together, each treating several times, then we took a cruise about the city, went into several houses of doubtful character and then got to drinking again." With liquor in Savannah costing $2 a drink, Watson spent $55, all the money he had, and woke up the next day with a hangover. "Felt sick all day from the effects of the bad liquor that I drank yesterday and most certainly say I feel heartily ashamed of myself for making such an ass of myself. Luckily I had sense enough left in me to go on aboard in time and turn in. We had leave of absence til 10 P.M., and got on board just in time."[41] Watson made it back to his ship in time, but more often than not inebriated sailors staggered or were carried on board too late. In the spring of 1862, however, a jump in the price of whiskey in Savannah to as high as $10 a gallon discouraged many sailors from imbibing too much.[42]

Although the Union navy abolished the "grog" ration in September 1862, the Confederate States Navy continued the tradition. A mixture of one-half pint of rum in a quart of water, grog had been a staple in the navy from its adoption by the Royal Navy in 1740. The term "grog" is thought to have been chosen to honor the British officer, Adm. Edward Vernon, who introduced the beverage. Vernon wore a cape woven from grogram cloth. Describing a typical day at sea on the *Sumter*, Raphael Semmes explained that the boatswain had just piped the crew to dinner. "The drum has rolled, 'to grog' and the master's mate of the spirit-room, muster-book in hand, is calling over the names of the crew, each man as his name is called, waddling up to the tub, and taking the 'tot' that is handed to him, by the 'Jack-of-the-dust,' who is the masters mate's assistant."[43]

In November 1863, however, Cdr. John Mitchell of the Office of Orders and Detail issued a general order temporarily banning the grog ration because rum had become so scarce. The issuing of liquor to sailors now became the purview of the ship's surgeon, who usually kept a supply of liquor on board "for medicinal purposes." A ship's store of liquor could prove too tempting to these physicians. A volunteer surgeon or army officer who had been ordered on board the CSS *Arkansas* just before the ironclad left Vicksburg drank heavily, Engineer E. A. Jack remembered. "The poor fellow was very much disturbed all the time he was on board. He would go about the ship exclaiming 'oh my poor wife and children!' and drank incessantly and after his whiskey was gone, drank peppermint. He would dip his glass into the water tank until at last the water had a combination flavor of both whiskey and peppermint that made it almost unpalatable."[44] Officers continued to be allowed to purchase wine and spirits for the ship's wardrooms, a privilege that was naturally resented by crewmen deprived of their grog rations.[45]

Midshipmen at the Confederate Naval Academy were forbidden to have liquor on board, but some of these young men certainly enjoyed a pint or a glass or two of wine when ashore visiting friends and family in Richmond. The considerable stress of taking the required examination to advance to another class or become passed midshipmen could prompt "ungentlemanly conduct," as it did for Acting Midn. James Wilson in April 1863. Following the examination, he and his fellow reefers went on a "Bust." Ralph J. Deas "got very drunk, & smashed the crockery in Pizzini's confectionary store. After raising things generally we turned in," Wilson wrote.[46]

Officers and midshipmen serving afloat enjoyed time away from their ships almost as much as the enlisted men did. When his ship arrived at Simon's Town, South Africa, Midn. James Morgan recalled, "Having been cooped up in very restricted quarters for more than four months, I longed once more to throw my leg over a horse and get a little congenial exercise." He obtained leave and found a horse in a livery and started out for Cape Town. On his journey across country he met only one Dutch boy, "who either could not or would not talk English, and a kaffir negro with whom I did not care to fraternize on account of his color." Morgan did "see what interested me greatly—geraniums in profusion growing wild and called weeds, and everlasting flowers, which when plucked may be laid away in a drawer for months and when taken out and placed in water will regain their freshness in very little time."[47]

When the *Sumter* put into Martinique in November 1861, Semmes allowed his men to go ashore. On Sunday he too ventured ashore to attend a governor's mass. "The interior of the church is very pleasing, with some valuable paintings. The congregation was very small. A detachment of soldiers entered the main aisle and formed in double lines a few minutes before the commencement of the service." The governor and his staff entered punctually, and the worshippers enjoyed "fine music from a band in the orchestra. The blacks and whites occupy pews indiscriminately, though there is no social mixture of the races."[48]

Although Semmes did not go ashore on November 12, he jotted: "We have gotten on board all our liberty men, no one of them having shown disposition to desert." At 9 p.m., however, "a drunken fireman jumped overboard and swam ashore, in spite of efforts of a boat to catch him. He thus braved the discipline of the ship solely for a glass of grog, so strong upon him was the desire for drink." Semmes sent an officer for the man and caught him in a grog shop.[49]

When blockade runners managed to run the Union blockade to reach a distant port, their officers and men gladly went ashore to find amusements or visit. After reaching Bermuda safely from New Inlet, the blockade runner *Cornubia* arrived at St. George, discharged her cargo, and the next day paid off the crew. In a notebook he kept on board the *Cornubia*, J. T. Gordon wrote, "Finished discharging. Spent evening very pleasantly with Com. Barron, Prof. Bledsoe, and Lieut. Wittle." On Sunday, Gordon went to church and dined with his fellow officers. He evidently enjoyed his time in Bermuda, writing in his journal "November 2nd: Had a dinner and dancing party on board."[50]

For the officers of vessels stationed in ports such as Savannah, Charleston, Richmond, or Mobile, entertainment also came in the guise of parties or visits to local families ashore. Midshipman Morgan spent thoroughly enjoyable evenings as a guest of the Trenholm family in Charleston. "In the evenings the family and their friends used to sit on the big porch where tea, cakes, and ice cream were served, and the gentlemen could smoke if they felt so inclined." He and one of the Trenholm daughters also had the opportunity to ride two of the family's fine horses. "In the afternoons I would accompany the young ladies in a landau drawn by a superb pair of bays with two men in the box. Just at that time the life of a Confederate midshipman did not seem to be one of great hardship to me; but my life of ease and luxury was fast drawing to an end."[51]

Young Richard Bacot also enjoyed calling on a few select families in Kinston. "I only associate with two or three private families here & they are nice people who seem to care for me & with whom I spend many a pleasant evening." Undoubtedly, twenty-three-year-old Bacot, a bachelor, sought the company of eligible young ladies and from his letters we learn that he courted one young lady five years his junior in nearby New Bern.[52]

The separations and travel restrictions of wartime did not entirely discourage young bachelor naval officers like Bacot from courting or marrying. Hoping to move out west after the war, Bacot explained to his sister, "I might find a 'young lady' just suited to my mind—Marriages seem to be 'all the go' now. I hear constantly of some friend or acquaintance being 'Captured,' 'Taking the Oath of allegiance' to the fair creatures who had made the capture."[53]

While serving on the CSS *Savannah*, Midn. Hubbard T. Minor courted a young woman, Miss Annie Lamar, "one of the wealthiest [ladies] of Savannah." They strolled in Central Park and he walked her home from services at the Presbyterian church. By early December 1864 Annie seems to have welcomed Minor's attention, for he wrote, "After quarters, went to see Miss Annie Lamar & came away in quite good spirits." Minor paid her daily visits that month, she gifted him with a Bible, and he was reluctant to leave her. On December 21 he jotted in his journal, "Slept all night on an empty stomach & dreamed of my Annie. I should like to know what she thinks of me, whether she will always love me." They corresponded throughout the war and in 1867 were married.[54]

Although sailors as well as officers occasionally enjoyed dinners, dances, and festivities ashore, in one instance these amusements may have proven disastrous. On the evening of October 27, 1864, following a "grand bacchanalian feast and dance" in Plymouth, North Carolina, the watch on the CSS *Albemarle* failed to detect the approach of a Yankee raiding party. The sentry, lulled perhaps by rich food and drink, may have been dozing. Alerted finally by a barking dog, the officer of the deck spotted the approaching enemy boats and rang the bell. The ironclad's crew sprang to quarters, loaded the Brooke with grape but were unable to prevent a Yankee party in a launch commanded by William Cushing from exploding a torpedo against the *Albemarle*'s casemate. From the gun deck, Lt. Warley called for the ship's carpenter to examine the hull and report. "He soon reported 'a hole in her bottom big enough to drive a wagon in.' I found her resting on the bottom in eight feet of water, her upper works above water," he recalled. Fortuitously, the crew of the ironclad suffered only one injury. A hatch dislodged by the explosion fell on Acting Master's Mate James C. Hill, injuring the seventeen-year-old. Asked why he was on board the *Albemarle* and had not attended the dance that evening, he replied, "he had taken a few julips too many and didn't feel inclined to take a boat."[55]

The city of New Orleans also offered Southern hospitality to the men of Confederate vessels. "There were balls and dinners ashore, and the ship was constantly filled with visitors," Morgan wrote. Captain Huger, a "very handsome man and a widower," was at this time engaged to "one of the most beautiful girls in New Orleans, so it was not strange, that when lying off the city he always found it convenient to anchor the *McRae* in front of Jackson Square because the Pontalba buildings faced the park, and in one of them, near the old Cathedral of St. Louis, his sweetheart dwelt." As Morgan explained, "I knew all about their courtship because I carried so many notes from the captain, and the young lady made such a pet of me."[56]

The fair ladies of Savannah enjoyed the company of young naval officers of the Savannah Squadron as well. Boating on the river proved a relaxing pastime for the officers but a tedious chore for the enlisted men who had to row the boats. "It is very fine for them to be pulled about for miles but very hard work for us," Robert Watson lamented.[57]

Sudden changes in weather could quickly dampen the enthusiasm of such boating parties. On one occasion, Lt. Taylor Minor and three other lieutenants took some Southern belles out on the river, but a downpour caught them before the sailors pulling the oars could get the boat to the *Savannah*. Soaked but not discouraged, the party went below and, Minor wrote, "enjoyed themselves hugely for we danced & talked & in fact some of us were carried away with joy."[58]

In addition to boating parties, officers and men serving with the Savannah Squadron took advantage of the local waterways for sailing, fishing, or hunting. The inactivity of the squadron left many with free time and little entertainment. On January 4, 1862, for example, Midn. Willie Wilson jotted in his journal, "dull, dull dull." His ship, the steamer *Sampson*, lay off Fort Jackson. To pass the time on what he often described as monotonous duty, Wilson and his friend Wright went sailing. "Went and sailed up to the Floating Battery this morning with Wright and had one of the nicest times in the world besides being well pleased with the battery," he wrote in his diary on May 15, 1862. Days before, he jotted, "Also went in a'bathing. Shot an alligator."[59]

To enjoy his free time and perhaps procure some fresh meat, Wilson often took a boat and went out "ducking." "Fixing to go hunting today this day is one more like spring than the winter the weather is delightful but how could it be otherwise in my own loved South," he wrote in his journal one January day. Several times these excursions turned out to be less than relaxing. "Went out ducking today and had to hail the 'Ship' to get back the wind blowing so hard as to blow this little boat so much that there was danger of capsizing. 'Oh Lord,'" he penned.[60]

With perhaps the exuberance and naivety of youth, Wilson continued to take a boat out to go hunting. Less than a week later, he confided to his journal that he had had "a very disagreeable day." He had taken "a notion to go hunting this evening and a gentleman that was with me went off and left me on the Island after which I borrowed a boat and attempted to cross the river to the vessel instead of which I brought up on the other shore wet and nearly frozen." Wilson had to go to the fort "and after being stopped by the sentinel and carried before Capt Anderson the Commander of the fort I was furnished with dry clothing by his son Lieut Anderson and stayed all night there."[61]

As the war went into its second year, midshipmen or "reefers" assigned to the school ship *Patrick Henry* in the James River just below Drewry's Bluff found studying increasingly difficult. Many professors called midshipmen to the blackboard during recitations, but, Jimmy Morgan recalled, the professor "frequently got no further before a crashing of great guns aroused his curiosity and he would request one of the young gentlemen to step outside and see which one of the batteries was using a particular rifle gun or smoothbore." No sooner had he resumed the lesson than a message would arrive "to send two or three of the midshipmen to assist in working the guns of some battery short of officers. After the artillery duel was over the boys would return to the ship and continue their studies."[62]

At least these Confederate midshipmen saw some action, an opportunity denied others serving in the Savannah Squadron. With little wartime activity, the officers of the Savannah Squadron complained of boredom. "Everything goes on in a treadmill style here," Lieutenant Graves lamented, "the very same yesterday today and tomorrow." Only the proliferation of spring flowers lifted his spirits. "Savannah is a beautiful city with its trees and parks and gardens," he wrote.[63] The squadron's officers spent their leisure time sailing, swimming, and shooting an occasional alligator.

Occasionally these excursions led to more excitement than intended. Driven by boredom, on February 26, 1862, Lt. James Thurston and Mid. Willie Wilson went out sailing. "Blowing very hard to day and raining," Wilson wrote. "I and Liut Thurston went sailing capsised the boat and lost it came very near getting drowned." They had to swim to shore.[64]

The city of Savannah did provide officers and men of the squadron diversions. The *Sampson*, *Ida*, *Habersham*, and *General Lee* made round-trips to town from Exchange Wharf to accommodate officers and men going into the city. In Savannah Lt. Philip Porcher and his fellow officers favored public lectures or plays, games of billiards, and enjoyed meals in homes or hotels like Pulaski House, where shrimp, crab, and fresh fish were still available.

While serving in the Savannah Squadron, Robert Watson had the opportunity to go ashore to the theater and enjoy a drink at a local hotel. Although he spent several evenings in July at the theater, he never mentioned what was featured, but he did write that Captain Coste asked to see him at the Planter's Hotel. "We drank a bottle of fine old Cognac brandy with Capt. C and then left him at 1 P.M."[65]

Venturing out to inspect the defenses also provided a diversion for Midshipman Wilson and his fellow reefer, Wright, who took time to go out to see Colonel Gordon's battery or to visit Fort Boggs, where ten new guns were being mounted. On May 1, he and Wright went to Causton's Bluff "and saw the battery which is there it is a tolerable good one of five guns of small calabras. There I saw the fragment of a fine rifle cannon which had bursted in fireing some time since."[66]

The federals had been blockading Savannah for some time. In late February, the young midshipman went down to the "Beacons" and noted in his diary that the federals were throwing up batteries. A week later he wrote, "Today the yankees fired several shots at the 'Emma' as she went down the river and I could see the shell burst plainly it was a beautiful sight to see them at the distance I was from them although I can say it would not be so at close distance."[67]

Wilson and his fellows on board No. 2 gunboat longed for action with the enemy. On April 19, 1862, he confided his frustration to his diary: "I am of the opinion that some of us on these 'tubs' will die in this marsh this summer. I wish this darn station wood break up and order us to some other station." Just one day later, however, he made the following entry: "Today we had a little excitement in the way of a 'Federal Gun Boat' ascending the Savannah river she came within two miles of where we lay but did not honor us with a shot. We cleared the decks for action and supposed that she would come on and give us fight. I wish she would for I believe we could whip one of their boats."[68] To Wilson's regret, the federal gunboats did not offer battle as a Yankee gunboat came up and anchored off one of their batteries in the Savannah River. "Here we lay eyeing each other like a cat ready to spring on the prey they are afraid to attack us and we cant them and so we lay within two or three miles of each other and doing nothing."[69]

Conclusion

Confederate naval officers endeavored to maintain morale on shipboard by allowing their men to go ashore when possible on liberty, issuing the grog ration until in some squadrons it was discontinued, holding divine services on Sundays, and encouraging musical entertainment. Confederate sailors learned to while away their off-duty hours playing games, smoking, mending or sewing their clothes, and spinning yarns. When possible, they also amused themselves and augmented their navy diet by fishing or hunting. Although liberty did often result in bouts of drinking and fighting, many sailors took advantage of opportunities to go sight-seeing, to visit and dine with families ashore, or to enjoy boating parties. Officers especially attended the theater and balls and other civilian entertainments ashore.

4

Discipline and Desertion

Discipline

THE CONFEDERATE STATES NAVY adopted regulations similar to those of the U.S. Navy, prohibiting, among other activities, gambling and drunkenness as well as flogging. Maintaining discipline was the responsibility of the commanding officer of a vessel or naval station who was bound to follow the navy's regulations but was in turn subject to the orders of the secretary of the navy.[1]

On shipboard, however, the master-at-arms performed many of the duties associated with enforcing ship's rules and navy regulations. He and his assistant, a petty officer with the rank of ship's corporal, made note of the names of violators and reported them to the commanding officer, who determined the appropriate punishment. Most Confederate naval vessels also had a contingent of Marines to deal with serious disturbances or the threat of a mutiny on shipboard.[2]

Discipline on board Confederate naval vessels might vary depending on the leadership of the commanding officer and the first officer. Some captains were strict disciplinarians; others more lenient. Strict discipline could bring results, Raphael Semmes concluded. "It has taken me three or four months to accomplish this, but when it is considered that my little kingdom consisted of 110 of the most reckless sailors from the groggeries and brothels of Liverpool, that is not much."[3]

Breaches of discipline by Confederate naval personnel varied from minor offenses to more serious cases such as desertion plots or threatened mutinies. Not all poor or dishonorable behavior merited punishment, however. Confederate sailors were not above stealing from one another, but stealing seems to have been tolerated by some commanders. As Francis Dawson quickly discovered, his shipmates on CSS *Nashville* could not always be trusted. "The second day after we left Southampton my trunk was broken open and nearly everything I had in it was stolen by the sailors." Dawson complained but was told that he ought to have expected it "and should have been careful to keep my trunk securely locked, or to have had in it nothing that was worth stealing."[4]

Overstaying one's liberty or leave could get a sailor or a midshipman in trouble, as did choosing not to mind the time of the liberty boat's departure. In June 1862 Midn. Willie Wilson went into the city but missed his boat back to his ship and "went home with Eddy Postell and stayed all night with him." The following morning, Wilson came down on the *Ida* and "went aboard and Liut Pelot politely informed me that I was quarantined for over staying my time." He justified it by writing, "This is the first time I have ever been punished since I have been in the Navy but as Shakespeare says 'Man invested with a little brief authority etc.'"[5]

Problems with alcohol often led to breaches of discipline. Article 26 of the *Confederate States Navy Regulations* prohibited gambling and drunkenness, but sailors often indulged in both. Granting sailors liberty ashore almost always led to drunkenness and discipline problems, a fact well known to naval officers and midshipmen. After escorting Cdr. William Parker and his wife to Richmond in October 1863, a confident Midn. Hubbard Minor noted in his diary that he had allowed his six-man boat crew to go ashore, "well knowing that they would be well intoxicated but determined never the less to gratify them knowing I could easily control them no matter in what state they were."[6]

Citizens of Richmond exhibited less confidence in controlling seamen in their town. Sailors ashore in Richmond often got drunk and ended up in fights with one another or in altercations with police. Officers who imbibed too freely of liquor in Richmond occasionally found themselves in trouble as well. For example, Samuel Keene, a master's mate on the CSS *Beaufort*, went ashore in early February 1864 to search for a deserter, but he "indulged too freely in spiritous liquors" and was escorted back to his ship. At 10 p.m., Keene left the ship again and promptly arrested as a deserter an Irishman in no manner connected with the steamer, prompting police to chase and catch him behind Castle Thunder. Cornered by the police, Keene drew his cutlass but was subdued. When the authorities released him, Keene again drew his cutlass, forcing the police to shoot and kill him.[7]

Enjoying the attractions of Richmond cost another sailor his life. James Kelley, a seaman on the *Patrick Henry*, was attending a ball in Richmond on the evening of February 15, 1864, when someone stole his gold ring and two hundred dollars in Confederate money. The following night Kelly returned to the capital to confront the robber, whom he knew at "the house of two white women of easy virtue." The robber stabbed Kelley in the left breast and nearly cut out his left eye. Although rushed to the Confederate Marine Hospital on Governor Street, Kelley succumbed to his wounds within the hour.[8]

In other Southern port cities such as Savannah, intoxicated sailors as well as officers and midshipmen often found themselves in trouble. The captain of the CSS *Sampson*, Lt. Philip Porcher, noted that one young man, Midn. Leroy Washington, habitually went to town, got drunk, and overstayed his leave by days. "Mr. Washington has been seen in uniform under the influence of liquor, on two different occasions by officers of the squadron," Porcher told Captain Kennard. Finally, exasperated, Porcher put Washington on report for intoxication and neglect of duty.[9]

Incidents of drunkenness were not confined to shore excursions but might occur on shipboard. Lt. Henry Graves of the Confederate States Marine Corps wrote to Cora Graves describing one such incident on the CSS *Savannah*. "Christmas Eve myself and two or three of the officers were sitting in the Ward room. . . . The men all stay on deck above us and no one but the officers are allowed in the wardroom." They were sitting quietly "but busily making an egg-nogg when a man came down and said the Captain wanted me on deck immediately. I went up and found about 20 sailors, drunk and like so many wild beasts." Graves called out his Marine guard and had them fix bayonets and form around the sailors "and one after the other were dragged out and ironed. It was two o'clock before we got them all secured." The sailors had broken into the spirit room and stolen several gallons of whiskey from the surgeon's supply, he explained. "I suppose two or three of the men will be court martialed and shot."[10]

Confederate squadron commanders did have the authority to issue general orders, portions of which might deal with instructions regarding discipline. When Richard L. Page assumed command of the Savannah Squadron in April 1863, he promptly issued a general order calling for his commanders to enforce the regulations of the Confederate States issued by the secretary of the navy in 1862. He specified that the first and second in command of each vessel not be absent on liberty at the same time, that only the commanding officer give midshipmen and masters' mates permission to leave the ship on liberty, and that all officers be on board at 9 a.m. ready for general duties. Page's requirement included the furnishing of a pass from the commanding officer to liberty men and instruction that only four men from each ironclad vessel and two from other vessels be allowed liberty every afternoon until the next morning at eight o'clock. "This indulgence will only be extended to those who behave themselves and return promptly at the time specified."[11]

On board rebel raiders at sea for months at a time, discipline could erode. According to one officer of a prize taken by the *Alabama*, by late November 1863, conditions—"no prize money, no liberty, and no prospect of getting any"—had led to much dissatisfaction among her crew. Some Yankees captured by the raider *Alabama* who may not have shared sympathy with the Southern cause described conditions on the ship. One man wrote, "So little discipline was there that the Alabama's men were smoking segars [*sic*] in the boat that took the Captain on aboard the Alabama's decks. The men were lying about aft, as well as forward, smoking pipe and segars. . . . The ship is very dirty, and everything looking in disorder." An English sailor who hated *Alabama*'s executive officer, John McIntosh Kell, said, "There is no principle among the men, and very little enthusiasm in the cause." The sailor later told a reporter, "Whenever we took a prize the officers always made a rush for all the good eatables and drinkables, while the men were not allowed a single article, and severely punished if they touched anything."[12]

Recalling one incident on the CSS *Georgia* in 1863, Midn. James Morgan wrote, "The discipline of the ship needed as much repairing as the vessel did herself." As he noted, "The discipline of the ship also missed the iron hand of Lieutenant Chapman. Lieutenant Evans, who had succeeded Chapman, as executive officer, was a most charming and accomplished gentleman, but he was not a strict disciplinarian." Things went from bad to worse until one day some of the stokers discovered that a coal bunker was only separated from the spirit room, where their grog rations were stored, by a thin bulkhead. The sailors bored through the bulkhead and headed straight for one particular barrel of whiskey, bored through it and "inserting a piece of lead pipe into the hold they got all the liquor they (temporarily) wanted." The liquor was distributed among the crew and "soon there was battle royal going on the berth deck which the master-at-arms was unable to stop." The first lieutenant went below and persuaded the ringleaders to go on deck and appear at the mainmast, which Morgan described as the court-house on the old-time man-of-war. Several of the men were sentenced to be placed in irons and confined in the brig (ship's jail) on a diet of bread and water.[13]

Smuggling liquor on board Confederate naval vessels led to a number of incidents of drunken sailors becoming involved in fights or other infractions requiring punishment. Confederate sailors sent over to man prizes could also fall victim to the temptation of liberating the prize vessel's liquor stores. When thirty men from the CSS *Shenandoah* began emptying a hold on the prize ship *Abigail*, they discovered barrels of rum, whiskey, and gin as well as champagne. The seamen wasted little time imbibing the spirits, and before their officers realized it they were all drunk. "As soon as this was discovered," Acting Master's Mate C. E. Hunt recalled, "the inebriates were shut into the *Abigail*'s forecastle, and the more obstreperous placed in irons." Captain Waddell sent a squad of Marines over to the *Abigail* to squelch the wanton drinking, but they too joined in as did a second squad. "It was the most general and stupendous spree I have ever witnessed," laughed Hunt. "There were not a dozen sober men on board except the prisoners, and had these not been ironed it might have proved a dearly bought frolic."[14]

Surgeon Lining took a boat over to the prize ship, pilfered a few curios, and went back to the *Shenandoah* in a boat filled with inebriated sailors. One man jumped overboard but was hauled back with a boat hook. The ship's carpenter, Lynch, was so unruly he had to be handcuffed to his bunk, and when he broke free Waddell ordered him gagged and triced up in the propeller well.

The aftermath of this drunken spree lasted for three days, the *Shenandoah*'s men all drunk, sick, or hung over. The cook, Hopkins, was found out cold that morning, and the steward "a basket case," and Lining wrote that things were "getting worse and worse." The captain reacted by cracking down on even small infractions. He suspended Lt. Dabney Scales from duty when a beaker of whiskey was found in his room, and he threw his clerk out of his cabin, banishing him to steerage after blaming him for a box of liquor that turned up in the cook's quarters. He disrated the boatswain's mate, then banned smoking in the engine room, alienating the lower ranks who found great pleasure in smoking a pipe.

As difficult as seamen could be to discipline, Confederate soldiers could prove even more of a challenge to a vessel's commanding officer. Manpower shortages, which became more serious as the war went on, prompted Confederate navy commanders to ask for men to transfer to the navy from the Confederate States Army or for volunteers from army regiments to serve temporarily on naval vessels. Many of these former soldiers who had transferred to the Confederate States Navy required strict disciplinary measures.

Several Confederate naval vessels added soldiers to their crew, but one example serves to illustrate the situation faced by many captains. The CSS *Arkansas*, stationed off Vicksburg, had a number of soldiers on board. "As a general thing, soldiers are not much use on board ship," Lt. Charles Read recalled, "particularly volunteers, who are not accustomed to the discipline and routine of a man-of-war." He offered an illustration. "We were engaged hauling the ship into a position near one of our batteries; but having but few sailors to haul on the wharf we were progressing slowly, when Lieutenant Stevens, the executive officer, came on deck, and perceiving a crowd of volunteers sitting on deck playing cards, he said, rather sharply, 'Come, volunteers, that won't do; get up from there and give us a pull.'" According to Read, one of the players looked up at Lieutenant Stevens and replied, "'Oh! hell! we aint no deck hands'; and eyeing the man sitting opposite to him, was heard to say, 'I go you two better!'"[15]

On occasion sea captains or mates taken prisoner by Confederate raiders made observations about rebel crews and the state of discipline on board. One fellow observed, "there was no discipline on board the steamer excepting when Capt. Semmes or Lieut. Kell was on deck." Semmes did not disagree about the difficulty of maintaining discipline on the *Alabama* as many of the hands "thought they were shipping in a sort of privateer where they would have a jolly time and plenty of license." The key was keeping the men busy. "My crew were never so happy as when they had plenty to do, and but little to think about. Indeed, as to the thinking, I allowed them to do very little of that."[16] As first lieutenant on the *Alabama*, it was Kell's duty to drill and discipline the crew—no easy task with some fifty of the men recruited from the slums of Liverpool. Thirty of the men, Kell wrote, were "very fine, adventurous seamen"; the rest "looked as if they would need some man-of-war discipline to make anything of them."[17]

Confederate Marines had their share of discipline problems as well. One January night, a wardman in the city of Savannah confronted a group of loud, inebriated Marines of the Savannah Squadron who were "using abusive and indecent language." The wardman, Peter Smith, "advised them to discontinue their conduct," but as they walked away, one of the Marines threw a rock at Smith and another jumped on him and stabbed him in the back. Smith recovered but could not identify his attackers.[18]

Raphael Semmes also had the benefit of a contingent of Marines but did not find them trustworthy. In his diary, he wrote on December 16: "A marine having been found asleep last night at his post over the prisoners, I have ordered a general court martial for his trial. The marines being mostly foreigners, Germans, are the most indifferent set of men I have in the ship. It is very difficult to lick them into shape."[19]

Punishment

Sailors breaking the navy's rules and regulations were brought to justice before their commanding officer at what was termed a captain's mast or, in the case of grave offenses, before a court-martial. To handle infractions of discipline too grave to be punished, for officers, by suspension of duty or confinement to quarters or, for enlisted men, by being placed in irons, confined on bread and water, disrated, forfeit prize money, or other punishments, the navy convened courts-martial. The captain of any ship might convene a court-martial composed of five to thirteen officers who sat and heard evidence, rendered a verdict, and handed out punishments. The secretary of the navy might also call into existence a court-martial as Secretary Mallory did in late June 1862 in the case of Flag Officer Josiah Tattnall following the loss of the CSS *Virginia*.

Punishments varied. Reducing a man in rank was a popular punishment, and the captains of raiding vessels often punished violators by ordering their prize money forfeited. Liberty men who overstayed their time ashore or, inebriated, staggered back on board might be thrown in the brig. Clapping men in double irons or having them triced up was also a common punishment. Other punishments included being vigorously scrubbed with hickory brooms until clean and then sent "halfway up the main rigging of the ship, spread eagled and left to dry."[20]

The antics of one of the *Alabama*'s boys, or "powder monkeys," could also lead to what was then considered an appropriate form of punishment. When Robert Egan, one of the ship's toughest boys with a reputation for mischief, was accused of stealing the *Alabama*'s beloved pet cat, he was hauled up the mast and charged with knowing or abetting the disappearance of the cat. To prod his memory, Egan was spread eagled in the mizzen rigging barefooted, a common punishment for "powder monkeys." He steadfastly denied any knowledge about the missing cat. But suddenly a sail was sighted, the after pivot gun run out, and tampion removed from its muzzle. Out jumped the cat. Asked why he put the kitty in the gun, Egan replied, "Oh, to see what effect the firing would have on the cat!" Egan later deserted at the Cape of Good Hope.[21]

These breaches of discipline were often referred to by naval officers and men in letters home or in diaries kept during the Civil War. "My code was like that of the Medes and Persians—it was never relaxed," Semmes, of the CSS *Alabama*, wrote. "The moment a man offended, he was seized and confined in irons, and, if the offense was a grave one, a court-martial was sitting on his case in less than twenty four hours." Semmes did not mince words: "The willing and obedient were treated with humanity and kindness; the turbulent were jerked down, with a strong hand, and made submissive to discipline."[22]

In his journal, George Townley Fullam made note of several of the men court-martialed on the CSS *Alabama*. On August 23, 1863, he made a detailed entry: "Court-Martial sentenced chief boatswains mate, Johnston [Brent Johnson], to lose all pay and prize money due him, be confined in irons three months, and disgraced by a discharge from the ship." Fullam wrote that the captain issued an order expressing his regret at having to confirm the sentences but "stated further that the plea of drunkenness should not protect any offender from punishment; he, believing that intoxication was a crime in itself. The charge was resisting, and drawing a knife upon his superior officer, whilst in the execution of his duty." The sentence of the court-martial disrated Johnson, one of the very senior enlisted men in the crew, to a seaman.[23]

A list of four Confederate Marines under sentence of court-martial at Mobile offers some idea of their sentences. Pvt. John Carson "looses [*sic*] all pay due him that date [November 25, 1863] and 2/3 of what may become due for 9 months; Private Frances Byington loses all pay and 2/3 of what is due him for 24 months." John Adams and William Johnson also lost all pay due them and two-thirds of what become due for twelve months.[24]

One general court-martial that sat for weeks to consider minor and major offenses committed by men of the Savannah Squadron offers a few examples of punishments meted out to sailors and Marines. Second-class fireman Patrick Curran, for example, was sentenced to two years' hard labor for "raising, provoking, and mutinous words." Savannah Squadron's chronic offenders included a Marine private named Conway. After serving several months in detention for a minor offense, he joined a group of sailors from the *Resolute* in a plot to desert. Conway was arrested, but because he had not actually deserted, Captain Tattnall had only limited options as to his punishment.[25]

A few of the sailors convicted by a court-martial escaped punishment. Accused of striking an officer during a drunken Christmas Eve riot on the ram *Savannah*, Quartermaster Harry Burns faced a court-martial for what was a capital offense. When the crew assembled on the spar deck to hear the Burns sentence, they learned that he would be put to death by firing squad. The punishment was never carried out because Confederate president Jefferson Davis commuted his sentence.[26]

Although not all sailors who were court-martialed faced confinement in irons or days on a bread and water diet, a few chose to leave their ship. After being sentenced, James Adams, ordinary seaman, asked to be put ashore. In his journal, George Fullam wrote: "30th Strong southerly wind. Put a man ashore at his own request, in accordance with sentence of Court Martial." The sentence had merely been to forfeit his pay ($19.36 per month) and all prize money, but Adams asked to be allowed to leave and was put ashore at Luderitz Bay.[27]

Confederate naval officers and midshipmen who disobeyed the regulations did not escape punishment either. A court-martial on board the CSS *Sumter* suspended Chief Engineer Miles J. Freeman as well for disobeying orders and using "improper language" to John McIntosh Kell. The superintendent of the Confederate navy's floating school ship enforced discipline and meted out punishments to midshipmen for most infractions of the regulations. He awarded demerits for lesser offenses, and those midshipmen who accumulated two hundred demerits in an academic year could be dismissed from the academy and the naval service. More serious offenses called for stiffer punishments. A first-class violation of the rules might mean confinement to the ship, reprimands, and suspension from recitation and from all drills and exercises. A second-class offense could result in "confinement in a guard room," but the superintendent might dismiss a third-class punishment unless the offender "resigned if given the opportunity."[28]

Those midshipmen found guilty of "highly insubordinate, riotous or mutinous conduct" merited confinement, referred to by the midshipmen as "quarantine," in the guard room. The duration of confinement varied. For fighting, Hubbard Minor spent one day in confinement, but William F. Clayton and his classmates received thirty days' confinement for making fun of the accent of a Prussian army officer assigned to the school ship to instruct the reefers in swordsmanship.[29]

Desertion

Desertion was commonplace in both the Union navy and Confederate States Navy. In the Confederate States Navy, men deserted for a variety of reasons: dissatisfaction with the lack of food, pay, or proper clothing; chronic sea sickness or illness; distrust of their officers or the inability to adjust to harsh navy discipline; or war weariness. A sailors' concern for the welfare of his family at home, the need to help out at home around harvest time, boredom, defeatism, and pro-union sentiment also prompted some to desert. Many men deserted because they had been conscripted into the army and then detailed to the navy and were not committed to the Southern cause.

The exact number of Confederate States Navy officers and men who deserted during the Civil War remains unknown but was far fewer than the number of desertions from the Confederate army—1,028 officers and 103,400 enlisted men. An estimated 4,469 sailors, or 6 percent, of all Union navy enlistees deserted during the Civil War, an average of 1,000 men a year from an enlisted force that stood at 7,600 at the beginning of the war but rapidly increased to a total of 55,200 sailors by 1865.[30]

A list of Confederate sailors and officers from Maryland and Virginia compiled by Robert J. Driver provides some idea of the number of naval personnel from those states who deserted. Of the 278 officers and men with names beginning with "M," 31 deserted. Three of the 66 officers (captains, commanders lieutenants, masters or master's mates, paymasters, midshipmen, engineers, surgeons) listed deserted. Twenty-nine of the 212 enlisted men with names beginning with "M" deserted, or 7.4 percent. Driver lists 354 names of men in the Confederate navy with names beginning with "S." Of these, 64 were officers and 290 were enlisted men. Twenty-five of these men deserted, or 14 percent of officers and 11.5 percent of enlisted personnel. The majority of these desertions took place in 1864 (10) and 1865 (11), with 14 of them to the Army of the James.[31]

Desertion among Confederate States Marines was not uncommon, but in a muster roll for August 1864, just 2 Marines were listed as deserters from the 106 men serving at Camp Beall near Richmond. Sailors and

Marines deserted or went absent without leave for a variety of reasons, finding the opportunity to slip away during port calls, leaves of absence, liberty, or picket duty. Marines who returned after a brief absence or "a spell" were required "to wear a band shirt marked 'deserter' for two hours daily for 30 days and forfeit liberty for three months."[32]

Confederate sailors on liberty often took advantage to slip away and never return to duty. Sailors manning small boats or picket boats in Southern harbors, creeks, or sounds sometimes deserted, endangering other loyal members of the crew. In December 1861, for example, James Bulloch ordered an eight-oared boat "with good sails" furnished to him by Kennard of the CSS *Sampson* "to examine the bar and the coast north and south of the point of Wassaw Island, and to report to me as quickly as possible, so that if all was clear we might go to sea on the afternoon tide." They set out with Pilot Craig; John Low, an officer; two midshipmen, Eddy Anderson and Raphael Moses; and eight men from the *Fingal*. Intending to desert to the Yankees, however, two crewmen from the CSS *Sampson* seized the boat, leaving the other sailors stranded. Fearful that Union crews on three federal gunboats anchored just opposite the main passage might look for them, the abandoned sailors hid out. Deprived of water and rations for days, the men ate raw oysters and drank putrid water. They finally sent Pilot Craig off to find help, but in the meantime Bulloch had organized a search party to look for the missing sailors. On Christmas Day, guided by an African American fisherman, they went down the channels of the Wassaw looking for signs of the missing men and any enemy patrols. Two oars lying on the beach caught their eye. "My heart sickened within me for I at once inferred that the boat had been capsized and everybody on board drowned," Major Anderson explained, "and that these two oars had drifted on shore." Anderson had not realized the oars lay above the high-water mark. The searchers found tracks on the beach, followed them, and discovered the missing sailors, who told them that they had sailed briskly along, almost running into three Yankee gunboats, and had put about and run up a creek to hide. The enemy gunboats had passed them by, cutting them off. That night two of the men had deserted, leaving the rest without a boat, hoping not to be discovered and taken prisoner by the Yankees. Relieved to have been found and fortified by rations, the sailors piled into Bulloch's boat, which nearly sank with the weight of twenty-six men. Happily, the overloaded boat eluded enemy patrols and pulled safely to Adam's Landing.[33]

One of the most detailed descriptions of desertion from the Confederate navy came from a correspondent to the *New York Sunday Mercury*. E. L. B., of the independent battalion New York Volunteers, wrote from Morris Island, South Carolina, on January 18, 1864: "During the evening of the 6th ins't. seven deserters, belonging to the Confederate navy, landed at Gregg. They were from the large three-masted vessel lying behind Castle Pinckney that is being iron-plated, but used at the present as a receiving ship. These men were detailed for picket, and while near Fort Johnston, the officer in command concluded to quarter himself within the fort, where he would be more comfortable, for the night—the weather being very cold and stormy, leaving the tars to do the picketing in the harbor." As soon as the lieutenant was out of sight, they pulled their boats for Morris Island shore. Upon landing they were blindfolded and taken into Wagner, and from there escorted to the provost marshal's, where they were provided with safe lodging. "Their song is the same old tune, so often heard and repeated, dissatisfaction and starvation and, since the proclamation of Jeff Davis, compelling soldiers and marines to remain in the Rebel service until the end of the war, their howl of dissatisfaction has been almost mutinous and hundred would accept the pardon offered by President Lincoln, and desert to the bosom of Abraham, if they could not but get the chance."[34]

Many Confederate sailors deserted so they could return home to visit or assist their families. Men who went home on furlough or sick leaves or who spent time in hospitals were often tempted not to return to duty. Because many sailors and soldiers were not escorted back to their ships or units by guards, they found desertion a relatively easy option. Some returned after a while to face punishment; others never came back.

Not all of the deserters who returned or were apprehended offered an explanation for their absence, but in early 1865 two rebel runaway pilots did give their reasons for deserting. John Russell, a pilot on the *Macon*, had disappeared with *Sampson*'s pilot, George Clark, a black pilot named Billy Bugg, and Clark's son, Charlie, a first-class boy. Russell, fifty-four years old, had served the Confederate army and navy for three years without even one leave of absence and insisted he had deserted to see his starving family. In a statement to the squadron commander, William Hunter, Russell lamented: "I am truly sorry that I ever left the ship." George Clark also appealed to Hunter to be released from prison, insisting he had only deserted to help his destitute family. He confessed that Russell had put him up to it. Hunter stoutly refused to release either man, but Billy Bugg, considered one of Savannah's better pilots, had just gone home to see if his family was safe. Reassured, Bugg had returned. He had gone off with Russell and Clark, claiming that he had assumed both were on leave. Desertions continued, however, and in January another five men left the *Macon*.[35]

Many sailors, suffering from the monotony, poor food, close quarters, and the harsh discipline of navy life deserted, but a few bolted for simpler reasons, including lack of action with the enemy, war weariness, and a desire for adventure. Following the fall of Fort Fisher, Robert Watson and his shipmates marched to Wilmington and were assigned to Fort Campbell, where he wrote, "Officers all drunk and drilling us for their amusement. If these things continue much longer I shall certainly desert and go to some other command, for I am heartily sick of it."[36]

Deserters did seek passage on outgoing ships running the blockade, but so did young boys running away from home eager for the high adventure of going to sea. "A little boy came aboard today, who ran away from his parents in Halifax to join the *Tallahassee*," one woman wrote. He may have hidden among the cotton bales. "The Capt. did not know he was on board but the boatswain concealed him until they had left port. He is to be carried home on the *Arkansas* whenever that goes, which is to be hoped it will do at some future time."[37]

In his memoirs, William Parker related the story of a young, fourteen-year-old cabin boy taken on board the CSS *Beaufort* in 1861 as a cook and steward. The boy told Parker he had been "raised in the neighborhood." The first time the boy came into Parker's cabin to announce dinner, "he stuck his head suddenly into my very small state room and, as I was sitting in my bunk, this brought his face within six inches of mine; this seemed so to startle him that he could only open his eyes and mouth: 'Well!' I said, 'what do you want?' 'The vittles is up,' he gasped and evaporated. That night he deserted, and I saw him no more."[38]

Following the capture of the CSS *Atlanta*, seventy-nine paroled members of the crew returned to the South. About thirty remained and took the oath of allegiance to the Union, saying "their families resided in the north." At Camp Lee in Richmond, officers managed to muster in seventy-four of the men who had returned, the other five having gone to the Richmond hospital. Before these paroled prisoners could be taken back to Savannah, however, ten disappeared. When the group reached Savannah, another thirty slipped away, undoubtedly to find and reunite with their families.[39]

Although many sailors quietly deserted during periods of routine duty or lulls, some stole away in the midst of action with the enemy. In October 1864, Flag Officer J. K. Mitchell reported that over a dozen men had deserted from ships of the James River Squadron, which was then engaged in fending off a serious threat to the Confederate defenses at Chaffin's Bluff. "Six of our men took a boat from alongside the forecastle and deserted to the north shore, no doubt going to the enemy; three more have deserted from us since we have been picketing the north bank in front of the enemy," Mitchell wrote on October 13. Battery Semmes had lost two men a fortnight before this incident, "and the *Richmond*, a boat party of six men went off 'bout a week ago, all doubtless to the enemy, carrying some information of all our movements, doings, etc. This enabled the enemy to direct his fire in the afternoon to-day, so much to the annoyance and danger of our vessels at Bishop's Bluff; one soldier was instantly killed by a shot."[40]

The prevalence of desertion in the squadron at this critical time prompted Mitchell to call the problem to the attention of the navy department. "About four days since two men, one a Dutchmen and another French by birth, and both last from New Orleans, deserted from the naval battery at Bishop's with enemy by taking the skiff crossing to the north bank of the river during the night." Mitchell pointed out that nearly all the men sent to the squadron as Yankee deserters and those who had volunteered for navy service as prisoners "have alike proved traitors to us by again going back to the enemy. The opportunities now afforded for easy escape will, I fear, be taken advantage of by many to leave our service, particularly now that their duties are more severe and dangerous." He begged the department not to send him any more Yankee deserters, not only because they might desert but because they would "induce others to do so who might otherwise continue loyal."[41]

Not unexpectedly, desertions increased as the war wound down. By 1865 Confederate soldiers were deserting by the hundreds, whole companies or regiments deserting and disappearing or crossing over into Union lines. From January 21 to May 31, 1865, for example, the Nashville and Chattanooga Union offices administered the oath of allegiance to 5,203 army deserters. The Confederate States Navy also saw an increase in men deserting. In December 1864 the Savannah Squadron reported as deserted or missing three assistant engineers, Master's Mate E. W. Skinner of the *Firefly*, and twenty-one crew men from the *Georgia*. Another twenty-three men also went missing from the *Savannah*, a small number of deserters considering that by then demoralization, short rations, and war weariness had set in.[42]

"Affairs were looking very badly about this time—the winter of 1865," William Parker wrote in his memoirs. "Men were deserting in large numbers from General Lee's army and from the James river squadron." Many soldiers deserted out of concern for the fate of their families at the hands of General Sherman's army marching through Georgia and South Carolina. "The letters received by the soldiers from their wives and families describing their sufferings, maddened these poor fellows and they could not resist their appeals to return for the protection." Sailors, he explained, often deserted that winter of 1865 because of the scanty rations. "A man shut up in an iron-clad with nothing to do after morning drill, broods over his hunger—it is not like being on shore, where a man can move about and forage a little."[43]

Rear Adm. Raphael Semmes, who assumed command of the James River Squadron from Mitchell in February 1865, also recalled the poor conditions on the squadron's vessels. "Both men and officers were crowded into close and uncomfortable quarters, without requisite space of exercise." Semmes sent squads of men ashore to drill and march on the river bank but could do little to increase their rations or supply them with clothing. "Great discontent and restlessness prevailed. Constant applications were coming to me for leaves of absence—almost every one having some story to tell of a sick or destitute family." He had to refuse to grant these appeals. "'The enemy was thundering the gates,' and no man could be spared. Desertion was the consequence. Sometimes an entire boat's crew would run off, leaving the officer to find his way on board as best he might." With the collapse of the Confederacy at hand, Semmes explained, "some reasoned that their desertion would be but an anticipation of the event by a few weeks."[44] Indeed, just prior to his arrival, the crew of a picket boat from the *Virginia II* mutinied, seized the boat from its two officers, and took it to the north bank. The dozen-man crew then promptly deserted to the Union army.[45]

When the Confederates abandoned their capital at Richmond in early April 1865, five hundred sailors and Marines belonging to Semmes' brigade boarded a train for Danville. "On the trip from Richmond to Danville the men who lived in the vicinity we passed through left the train and went home," recalled John Gardner, a gunner on the *Richmond* who subsequently served as a crewman at Battery Semmes.

According to Marine lieutenant Crenshaw, by early April 1865 the problem of men deserting at Danville had become so alarming that "all the officers were required to stand guard duty around the cars to keep our men together." Crenshaw's sergeant had deserted the day before, and he had spent the evening walking a sentry post at Danville.[46]

If apprehended or returned, deserters could be court-martialed and be sentenced to various punishments, including being deprived of pay, sent to public works, imprisonment, or execution. In ordering the sentence of the court-martial of Marine private Patrick Gerlan carried out, Adm. Franklin Buchanan wrote, "As there are no public works upon which he can be employed he was directed to clean arms in the yards." Noting that Gerlan was "an old offender and a mutinous bad character," Buchanan told Secretary Mallory, "it is important that an example should be made of him to secure the efficiency and discipline of the marines."[47]

Union authorities welcomed deserters not only because they might join the Union army or navy but because many brought valuable information about rebel activities. For example, five men who deserted from the paddle-wheeler *Savannah* while on picket duty in March 1863 offered valuable information to a Union naval officer, John Rodgers. As the boat crew of Commodore Tattnall's barge, they had overheard Tattnall say "that when the ironclads move upon Charleston he would take this place." Rodgers sent the deserters' statements to Adm. Samuel F. DuPont, who was at that time assembling ironclads for an attack on Charleston. One of the deserters said, "This was said to his son, who was formerly in the Marine Corps, and to another officer of the *Fingal* who accompanied him. Another one has heard him say that he would destroy the vessels in Wassaw Sound if the ironclads were to leave that place."[48]

The temptation to go absent without leave or desert was not confined to enlisted men; officers on occasion also deserted the service. Joseph Minchener, a second assistant engineer who served on board the CSS *Hampton*, slipped away on February 26, 1865, to the Army of the James and within days took the oath of allegiance to the Union. Adam Neill Baker, a lieutenant in the Confederate States Marine Corps, deserted to the Union in November 1861 at Pensacola. He had resigned from the U.S. Marine Corps in April and accepted an appointment as a captain in the Virginia Marine Corps, then as a first lieutenant in the Confederate States Marine Corps, appointed from Florida.[49]

When desertion became a serious problem, some Confederate naval officers like the commander of the Savannah Squadron, Flag Officer Richard L. Page, took measures to discourage men from deserting the service. In April 1863 Page told Lt. Cdr. J. S. Kennard of the *Isondiga* to proceed down to the Thunderbolt to watch for enemy movements. He gave Kennard specific instructions to have picket boats commanded by well-armed officers and to keep them inside signaling distance. "Boats should be well guarded and hoisted each evening by dark," he told Kennard, presumably to prevent men from using them to desert.[50]

Measures taken by the Confederate army to deal with possible enemy attacks and deserters at Savannah had unfortunate and perhaps unintended consequences for naval vessels stationed there. Orders were issued in the summer of 1863 to army sentries not to hail strange boats at night but to "shoot first and ask questions later." One summer evening, about three o'clock in the morning, the *Isondiga*'s surgeon, Dr. T. Barrow Ford, an assistant engineer, and a cabin boy were out in a boat fishing in a creek. Without warning, an army sentry fired a musket at the boat, the ball whizzing though Ford's hair and striking the cabin boy's leg. "The moon was shining brightly at the time & our proximity to the picket made it well nigh impossible for him to have mistaken our boat or business." The *Isondiga*'s captain, J. Kennard, protested to the army major in charge who merely responded that the sentry had done his duty. Following that incident, the army did belatedly send the navy their watchwords and countersigns.[51]

The navy pursued deserters when possible, and the Confederate States Marine Corps regularly advertised in local papers such as the *Richmond Examiner* or *Richmond Dispatch* for men who had deserted from their units. A notice in the *Richmond Dispatch* of June 11, 1862, read: "$30. reward will be paid for the apprehension and delivery at the Quartermaster's Office, 11 Broad Street, or at the Marine Camp, near Drewry's Bluff, of any one of the following described deserters from the Marine Corps." A list of fifteen deserters followed. Four of the men were over thirty years of age, but ten were in their twenties, and one, Kieran Mullen, was just eighteen years old. Although records do not reveal if these deserters were apprehended, another report states that a thirty-dollar reward was paid to Lafayette Moore in September 1863 for "service rendered in apprehending deserter Jack Williams of the Marine Corps Mobile Ala."[52]

Sailors who deserted from the Confederate States Navy were on occasion discovered among Confederate army deserters. For example, a notice in the *Richmond Dispatch* of November 18, 1862, stated that forty-eight deserters had been received from Camp Holmes "to be returned to their regiments. John Davis, a member of Rodgers's Manchester Cavalry, put in prison for desertion, was recognized as one of the crew of the steamer *Patrick Henry*, and was taken down and put in custody of her officers."[53]

Confederate soldiers who had deserted occasionally sought refuge as crew on board Confederate navy vessels. In January 1863 the provost marshal caught up to one deserter, Ordinary Seaman Isaac Horton, on the CSS *Atlanta*. A midshipman with a Marine escort took the fellow to Oglethorpe Barracks for confinement, but the seaman's arrest must have made the *Atlanta*'s commanding officer suspicious, for a Marine corporal and three landsmen were later thrown into the ship's brig and then turned over to the army.[54]

Not all pursuits ended favorably for the Confederate navy. In November 1863 a pursuit went terribly awry. One day Master's Mate Samuel A. Brockington and four seamen armed with carbines took a picket boat from the CSS *Savannah* down to the obstructions at Savannah with the intention of deserting. A boatswain's mate in town on liberty learned of the planned desertion and returned to the ship. An officer onboard the *Savannah* quickly had a boat manned and sent it off in pursuit, but before they could stop the picket boat, the four sailors aimed their carbines at Brockington and he was taken prisoner by the Yankees. Attempting to explain the incident, W. W. Hunter told Commander Mitchell that Brockington had served creditably in the army, was of good character and "an enthusiastic Southerner," and must have been overpowered by the boat's crew.[55]

In an attempt to encourage deserters to return to service, on August 1, 1863, President Jefferson Davis issued a proclamation of amnesty "to all who have been accused or who have been convicted and are undergoing sentence for absence without leave, or desertion, excepting only those who have been twice convicted of desertion." His proclamation specified soldiers, but John K. Mitchell, the head of the Confederate States Navy Department's Office of Orders and Detail, informed his flag captains and the Savannah Squadron that amnesty and pardon extended as well to Confederate States Navy personnel.[56]

On at least one occasion a deserter was found on board a prize, apprehended, and sentenced by court-martial to serve on the Confederate raider, only to cause mayhem. In his diary entry for October 7, 1862, George Townley Fullam described boarding the brigantine *Dunkirk.* "Examining the prisoners we found one of them to be a deserter from the C.S. Steamer 'Sumter,' he being one of seven deserting at Cadiz. Immediately upon arrival on board he was placed in double irons." At 10 a.m. on October 9, "a court martial was assembled in the wardroom to try Geo. Forrest, A.B., for desertion from the Sumter."[57]

In his next diary entry Fullam noted: "Oct 10th: Read sentence of court martial to prisoner, and discharged him. The sentence was 'that all pay, prize money, & c due him be forfeited, that he fulfill his term of service and forfeiting of all pay, excepting such as is sufficient to provide necessary clothing and liberty money." Although fortunate to receive a sentence to serve on the *Alabama* without pay and prize money, Forrest— Kell's words, "a worthless sailor"—waited for the chance to get back at the officers on the court-martial.

Within a matter of days Forrest seized an opportunity for trouble on the ship. In a subsequent journal entry on October 19, Fullam explained, "The previous evening a drunken disturbance took place on board, by which was found necessary to call the hands to quarters to quell it. It appeared that the deserter from the 'Sumter' (of whom mention has been made previously) had slipped down the cable, swam to a boat, and returned on board with a great quantity of spirits, and had handed it around to the crew, and all unknown to a single officer, he not tasting a drop himself, thus showing that his aim was to cause a mutiny on board." The men that were "infuriated with liquor, were placed in double irons." With a few exceptions, these in addition to irons were gagged, and bucket after bucket of water thrown over them until they became partially sober. As one man had been stabbed severely in the arm, Fullam noted, "The officers and some of the petty officers were fully armed, the Captain having given orders to that effect, and to cut down the first man that hesitated to obey an order. The scoundrel Forrest was triced up in the mizzen rigging, two hours on and two off."[58]

Conclusion

The Confederate navy charged commanding officers with maintaining "good order and discipline" on board ship at naval stations ashore. The master-at-arms and his assistant performed many of the duties associated with enforcing ship's rules and navy regulations, noting the names of violators and reporting them to the commanding officer, who determined the appropriate punishment. He handed out punishment for minor offenses such as gambling, stealing, and drunkenness, but major offenses such as desertion plots or threatened mutinies required that a court-martial be convened to render a verdict. Punishments included being placed in irons, "triced up," being denied liberty or a grog ration, being disrated, or forfeiting prize money. This harsh discipline, although necessary especially in time of war, prompted hundreds of Confederate sailors, weary as well from the war, poor living conditions, a monotonous diet, or concerned about the fate of their families, to desert. Few deserters were discovered, and those apprehended faced stiff punishment.

Medical Care in the Confederate States Navy

The Confederate States Navy Office of Medicine and Surgery

WITHOUT A SYSTEM OF MILITARY hospitals or an organization to safeguard its military and naval personnel, at war's outbreak in 1861 the Confederacy had to improvise. Although the Confederate States Navy numbered relatively few officers and men in 1861, illness, accidents, and the prospect of casualties from action with the Union navy prompted the Confederate navy to create the Office of Medicine and Surgery, or OMS.[1]

Hastily organized to provide medical care for officers and enlisted men, the navy's new OMS benefited from the expertise and experience of several former U.S. Navy surgeons who resigned their commissions and offered their services to the Confederacy as well as from the advances in medical practices made before the Civil War. This new OMS was tasked to provide medical care for the navy's officers and men, which by 1864 had reached its highest personnel level of 753 commissioned officers and 4,450 men.[2]

The OMS was responsible for establishing and operating naval hospitals, acquiring and producing medicines, obtaining or fabricating medical and surgical supplies, and directing medical personnel and providing physicians for Confederate naval vessels. From a small office adjacent to the secretary of the navy's office on the second floor of the war building in

Richmond, the chief of OMS, assisted by one chief clerk and a purveyor, oversaw the bureau's activities and directed medical personnel.[3]

On March 26, 1861, Dr. William Augustine Spotswood received an appointment as a surgeon in the Confederate States Navy and became the first chief of OMS during the war. Spotswood had enjoyed a long career in the U.S. Navy before resigning his commission in January 1861. When the Civil War broke out, Spotswood had just returned to the Pensacola Naval Hospital from his position as fleet surgeon of the East India Squadron.[4]

All of the early Confederate navy medical staff was, in fact, composed of former U.S. Navy physicians. In 1860 the U.S. Navy had an ample pool of physicians: sixty-nine surgeons, forty-three passed assistant surgeons, and thirty-six assistant surgeons. Thirty-eight of these men resigned or were dismissed, a loss of 26 percent of the federal navy's doctors. At least thirty-five of these former U.S. Navy physicians eventually served in the Confederate States Navy.[5]

The March 16, 1861, legislation authorized OMS to have five surgeons and five assistant surgeons, but in December 1861, wartime demand led to the authorization of thirty temporary physicians. The necessity to appoint more doctors led to legislation in April 1862 to increase levels to one surgeon-general, twenty surgeons, fifteen passed assistant surgeons, and thirty assistant surgeons. A year later, a growing need for more physicians prompted President Jefferson Davis to seek authorization to appoint as many naval officers as needed.[6]

Following the Confederate navy's surrender in 1865, the Association of Medical Officers of the Army and Navy of the Confederacy determined there were 107 medical officers who served at one time or other. Of these 107 medical officers, 26 officers held the rank of surgeon, 13 as passed assistant surgeon, 63 as assistant surgeon, and 5 as assistant surgeon for the war. During the war, the OMS also employed surgeon's stewards (a noncommissioned officer rank) to aid doctors. Hospital stewards had to have a working knowledge of pharmacy and bandaging techniques and be able to perform minor surgery.[7]

Most surgeons in the Confederate States Navy in 1864 were Southern born and hailed from Virginia or Georgia, the exception being Arthur

Lynch, a South Carolinian. Of the ten passed assistant surgeons, four were from Virginia, three from North Carolina, two from Georgia, and one each from Maryland and South Carolina. Assistant surgeons represented the largest number of medical officers serving the Confederate navy during the Civil War, and these men came from a number of Southern states, including Arkansas, Texas, Alabama, Mississippi, Kentucky, Louisiana, Missouri, and Florida.[8]

The Confederate States Navy Department Regulations of 1862 spelled out the duties and responsibilities of both a Confederate naval vessel's commanding officer and navy surgeon. A commanding officer was to personally inspect his vessel daily, accompanied by the executive officer, to "satisfy himself that nothing has been neglected for the efficiency of the vessel or health of the crew." To safeguard the crew's health, he was not to permit men to sleep in wet clothes or bedding or take these items below to the gun deck. Navy regulations called for the commanding officer to have the decks frequently washed or cleaned, and the decks where men slept were to be kept dry. The men's bedding was to be opened, dried, and cleansed as often as once a fortnight or oftener in warm climates. Weather permitting, crewmen were to bathe or wash frequently in warm weather and wear clothing suitable to the weather. The regulations required as well that boat crews have breakfast before leaving the vessel and not be allowed to drink water "until the mud and other impurities have had time to settle." Commanding officers were to issue fresh meat and vegetables to the crew not exceeding four days a week and to "cause every attention to be paid to the comfort of the sick and wounded" by the surgeon and others.[9]

A naval surgeon was required to report daily to the commanding officer the names and conditions of sick officers and sailors and to "suggest measures he may deem important for the health of the crew." Regulations specified that he was to report daily those men on the binnacle list who were to be excused from duty or whose allowance of spirits were temporarily suspended. "He will be attentive to the cleanliness of the sick, their bedding and the sick bay, and will take special care that the sick are supplied at proper times with the medicine and food their condition may require." Among the surgeon's other varied duties were to examine men who joined the ship to determine if they needed any vaccinations, examine bumboats selling food to the ship, and, when practical, be certain that any ill men be accompanied to the hospital by a medical officer. In addition to all these duties, a surgeon was to keep a journal of daily practice, a notebook, and to report petty officers or persons of lesser ratings who have long-term inability to perform duty. To prepare for an engagement with the enemy, he was to have a supply of tourniquets and instruct officers and persons assigned to him in their use.[10]

Disease

Ensuring the health and well-being of a Confederate naval vessel's crew represented a vital responsibility for both a commanding officer and the ship's surgeon. Although accidents and combat wounds did account for some casualties, disease was the real enemy for officers and men of both the Confederate and Union navies during the Civil War. Few statistics survive for Confederate navy personnel who died of wounds or were killed in action compared to those who died of disease. However, a review of a sample of sailors from Virginia and Maryland who died shows that an overwhelming number died from diseases such as typhoid, chronic diarrhea, chronic bronchitis, pneumonia, and dysentery.[11]

Knowing the prevalence of fevers and other diseases that, if contracted on shipboard, might quickly spread, conscientious commanders attempted to keep their crews healthy. "The men were required by our very excellent surgeon Lining to clothe themselves warmly and keep themselves dry," James Waddell recalled. "Extra rations of hot coffee and grog were served at regular hours, and the surgeon, with his efficient assistant Dr. McNulty, inspected the food for the crew before and after it was prepared." Indeed, Waddell wrote, "the surgeon cannot be recommended too highly for his discretion in preserving the sanitary conditions of the Shenandoah."[12]

Although they had fondly nicknamed him "Old Beeswax," Raphael Semmes looked out for his men by having two surgeons on board the

CSS *Sumter*, providing the best food he could obtain, and issuing the daily grog ration. He required the men to have two changes of clothing a day when the ship was in tropical waters and, when the surgeon could obtain them, the use of antiscorbutics to prevent scurvy. On long cruises, however, he could not prevent outbreaks of scurvy brought on by a diet of salt pork with few if any fruits or vegetables. Despite Semmes' best efforts, the *Sumter* experienced some cases of scurvy, and scurvy plagued most of CSS *Alabama*'s crew at the end of its cruise.[13]

Confederate sailors serving on board other navy vessels suffered from scurvy as well during the war, a disease brought on by a lack of vitamin C found in fresh fruits and vegetables. Cases of scurvy were often not immediately diagnosed because the early symptoms of mild vitamin C deficiency are listlessness and fatigue. As the effects of this dietary deficiency increased, however, sailors noticed they bruised easily and the bruises healed slowly. In its later stages, scurvy causes serious bleeding and weakens those suffering from the disease, making them susceptible to other diseases such as yellow fever, tuberculosis, or dysentery.[14]

Shipboard diets were notoriously lacking in fresh produce, but, as the British Royal Navy had discovered, the vitamin C in the juice of limes had a beneficial effect. The defeat of scurvy in the Royal Navy is attributed to an English surgeon named James Lind, who studied the disease and discovered that the juice of oranges and lemons ameliorated the condition of his patients suffering the pain and affliction of scurvy. However, as historian Stephen R. Brown has argued, it was "a trio of individuals in Britain who converged to lift the veil of obscurity from scurvy": James Lind, James Cook, and Gilbert Blane. "They proved that scurvy was a disease of chemistry and food—not vapors and viruses." On a voyage of discovery in 1768–71, Cook is credited with the defeat of scurvy and Blane almost eliminated scurvy in the fleet in 1782, but it took another fifteen years to convince the Royal Navy to issue a daily ration of lemon juice to all sailors. The use of the juice of Mediterranean lemons to prevent scurvy did much to solve the problem but the cause of the disease was not well understood.[15]

The Confederate States Navy did not experience cases of scurvy early in the war because ships stationed in Southern ports, rivers, or near the coast had access to local produce, fish, and oysters. Ships relying at least in part on coal-fired steam plants had to regularly return to port to get coal, giving the crew the opportunity to obtain fresh produce.

For Southerners, however, the availability of fruits and vegetables and other foodstuffs dwindled as the war progressed. The effects of the tightening Union blockade, crops and orchards neglected or ruined by war, and transportation disruptions experienced in the South reduced the food available for military and naval forces. It also curtailed friends, family members, and women volunteers from bringing food to patients in hospitals.[16]

When commerce raiders such as the *Shenandoah, Florida,* and *Alabama* sailed on long cruises, however, the danger of scurvy appearing among the crew was a distinct possibility. Concern about the health of both officers and men prompted commanding officers of these raiders to take advantage of supplies of water and foodstuff on prize ships. When the *Shenandoah* chased and captured the schooner *Charter Oak,* James Waddell appropriated its cargo of preserved fruits and cabin stores. "Two thousand pounds of canned tomatoes were brought on board, with other delicacies intended for cabin use."[17] The ship also received gifts of fruit and fish from the king of a tribe in Lea Harbor who gifted them with "two chickens wrapped in cocoanut leaves and a dozen cocoanuts."[18]

Although preventing scurvy was ideal, those afflicted might be treated with a diet of fresh vegetables, fresh meat, acids, salts of potash, and tinctures of iron. Diarrhea was treated with opiates and astringents.[19]

Fevers

In addition to scurvy, Confederate officers and men suffered throughout the Civil War from what they called "fevers." Naval personnel serving in many regions of the South or visiting foreign ports contracted what they often referred to as "intermittent fever," also known as ague or "the shakes." The men of the Savannah Squadron suffered from what they called "intermittent river fever," which kept doctors T. Barrow Ford and Robert R. Gibbes busy during the late summer and fall of 1862. Mosquitoes, abundant in these areas, carried intermittent fever, or malaria.[20]

Sailors on both sides fought mosquitoes while serving off the coast or on vessels in the Mississippi River, and many came down with fevers, but at this time the transmission of disease by mosquitoes was unknown. Physicians and authorities blamed fevers on miasmas. The climate of New Orleans proved especially conducive to mosquitoes.[21] When the CSS *Jackson* entered service and steamed down river to the Head of the Passes, 3rd Assistant Engineer James H. Tomb recalled, "Our duty consisted in watching out for the Yankees and fighting mosquitoes—the largest I ever saw or felt."[22]

Officers and men plagued by these pesky insects employed mosquito netting, if available, but most resorted to lathering themselves with homemade salves composed of grease and even turpentine. Despite these efforts to protect themselves from mosquito bites, several navy men succumbed to malaria or intermittent fever. In October, November, and December of 1861, for example, the CSS *McRae* sent nineteen men suffering from intermittent fever to the hospital ship *St. Philip*. The *General Polk* sent four cases; *Mobile* and *Pickens*, three. In the first three months of 1862, intermittent fever continued to represent the largest number of cases admitted to the hospital ship, followed closely by nine cases of rheumatism, seven of venereal disease, and just four cases of diarrhea or dysentery. Medical professionals treated these sick sailors with the usual remedies of the era, prescribing quinine and medicinal whiskey, sometimes mixed with barks.[23]

Officers were not exempt from the ravages of the fever. For example, Lt. Isaac Brown, commanding the CSS *Arkansas*, was afflicted, as was his counterpart in the federal squadron, Capt. Henry Walke. Confederate troops garrisoned at Vicksburg and African Americans laboring on the defenses fell victim to the fever as well.[24]

Confederate navy personnel serving in other locations also succumbed to fevers. In the fall of 1861, Lt. Augustus McLaughlin, CSN, negotiated a contract with David S. Johnson at Saffold, Georgia, a steamboat landing 140 miles north of Apalachicola, Florida, as a site to construct a new gunboat, to be named the *Chattahoochee*. Although convenient to the Columbus Naval Works in Georgia, Saffold suffered from a debilitating climate that worsened in late summer, the peak of the fever season. The heat, humidity, and numerous mosquitoes proved to have an adverse effect on the officers and men assigned to the *Chattahoochee*. Lt. William Whittle reported in late September that he had sent three officers and twenty-two men to hospitals in Columbus. A few weeks later he noted that he had only two of his thirty-eight men well enough to work on the gunboat.[25] "I never saw men so afraid of chills. They think down here is the sickliest place on earth," Horry Dent told his father in a letter from Saffold. Suffering from "the shakes" was a common experience for the men working on the gunboat. Taken in late November by one of the severest chills he had ever felt, Dent wrote, "I have never had an attack weaken me so. I could scarcely move about. And with any exertion it makes me dreadfully sick at my stomach." With forty or fifty of the men now invalids, Dent despaired and tendered his resignation. "I never saw a set of Officers as sick of a Boat in my life," he wrote.[26]

With so many officers and men ill with fever and unable to work on the gunboat, McLaughlin sent to a pharmacy for quinine, and Whittle sought to expedite an order for a barrel of whiskey from Montgomery. The custom was to soak Peruvian bark, a source of quinine, in whiskey to make it more palatable. In October, when the gunboat's new ship's surgeon, Marcellus Ford, arrived on board, there was little he could do to prevent additional cases of fever other than the usual doses of quinine.[27]

Chief Surgeon Spotswood noted that fevers would always occur on certain stations and acknowledged that no means of prevention existed except strict attention by officers "to the comfort of the crews, in regard to clothing, food, and a regimen that will strengthen and fortify the system against attack."[28] Spotswood also recommended the "issuing of a spirit ration, and allowing the crews their breakfast with hot coffee, at an early hour in every morning . . . as a means of counteracting the effects of the damp and chilling draughts, so prevalent on all fresh water courses and malarial regions at the dawn of day."[29]

In his November 1863 report Spotswood wrote, "The diseases most prevailing are bilious, remittent and intermittent fevers, many of the latter assuming a congestive type, and the stations suffering most severe forms of fever are Charleston, Savannah, and Mobile." He also called attention to the need to procure a large supply of medical stores abroad and suggested a need for an apothecary and chemist with a liberal salary to be sent abroad to select and purchase them and ship them to an agent in Bermuda. The contractors employed, Spotswood noted, "are not competent to make proper selection and have generally more lucrative interests involved."[30]

In this same report, Spotswood wrote, "From the reports of medical officers at all stations, especially in the southern dept, the amount of sickness has been very great especially at Mobile where officers and crews of vessels have suffered exceedingly from exposure to the malarial causes that exist there during the summer and fall months, producing bilious and remitting and intermitting fevers of a virulent character, tending not only to affect their immediate but their future efficiency and usefulness by laying the foundation of chronic disease." He suggested the department adopt some plan to avoid exposure to such causes and recommended that a board of officers be appointed to select healthy locations for temporary use during the hot summer and fall months on those stations most subjected to the influence of these causes. The fleet at Mobile might be moved from the marshes in front of the city to the opposite side of the bay, which was free from malaria and enjoyed good water and healthful sea breezes. This would "be a wise precaution and cause the government less expense than the renting of houses in the city for the crew where they would still be exposed to the same causes which prevail at the fleet anchorage."[31]

A year later Spotswood called attention to the fact that "much sickness of a severe character" had been prevalent at many stations in the southern department, particularly at Savannah and Charleston. Crews on vessels of the Savannah Squadron had suffered unusually severe cases of fever, he explained, after being exposed to "the malaria of the fresh water rivers and swamps bordering the rice fields," but moving the vessels had lessened the severity of such cases.[32]

Yellow Fever

Preventing outbreaks of yellow fever presented a more difficult challenge for Confederate commanders than preventing malaria. Before the Civil War, Southern cities had experienced frequent outbreaks of the disease almost every summer. New Orleans, for example, endured epidemics of yellow fever in 1853, 1854, and 1855 as well as a most severe one in 1858 that affected 18,000 people, 5,000 of whom died. Spread by mosquitoes, yellow fever is a form of fulminating viral hepatitis that causes jaundice, hemorrhages, and, in the nineteenth century, killed from 20–50 percent of its victims. Initial outbreaks during the antebellum period originated from infected passengers debarking in a port from areas prone to the disease, particularly islands in the West Indies. The natives of Southern port cities such as New Orleans often developed a sort of immunity to what they called "yellow jack," but the immigrant population did not.[33]

Cargo ships and warships from the Caribbean and South America carried yellow fever to the shores of the Confederate States to towns such as Galveston, Texas; New Bern, North Carolina; and Mobile, Alabama. The official records offer examples of vessels entering Southern ports with cases of yellow fever on board. In July 1864, Maj. Gen. Dabney H. Maury, commanding at Mobile, reported that the *Ivanhoe*, "a fine ship owned by the cotton bondholders," had run aground near Fort Morgan trying to get into the harbor. Although her cargo was saved, the vessel brought in a case of yellow fever and her crew had to be quarantined.[34]

Most ships experiencing an outbreak of yellow fever headed north to better climes, but anxiety that their men might contract yellow fever in foreign ports influenced the sailing plans of both Union and Confederate navy commanders. The experience of the USS *R. R. Cuyler* offers one such example. *R. R. Cuyler*'s commanding officer, Cdr. John Downes, had been ordered to sea on August 14, 1864, to search for the Confederate raider CSS *Tallahassee*, but when the *R. R. Cuyler* arrived off Bermuda four days later, the U.S. consul at Bermuda "reported yellow fever raging with great violence on shore, many deaths occurring daily." From the consul, Downes learned that the *Tallahassee* had been fitted out for war at Bermuda but had sailed for Wilmington. "On account of the ravages of yellow fever, the consul declared the blockade running business from Bermuda to be at an end for the season," Downes wrote. Rebel blockade runners had, the consul declared, fled to Halifax, Nova Scotia.[35]

Two years earlier, Lt. John Newland Maffitt had experienced an outbreak of yellow fever among the crew of the CSS *Florida*. Maffitt had skillfully eluded federal blockaders including the *R. R. Cuyler* and had anchored off Green Key some ninety miles south of New Providence to transfer stores and arms from a tender. With just five firemen and fourteen deckhands, the task of hoisting on board six-inch guns and two seven-inch pivots had taken over a week of strenuous labor in the hot summer sun.[36] When the wardroom steward, C. Worrell, died on August 15, Maffitt suspected the man had contracted yellow fever in Nassau as Maffitt had himself nursed a young friend at a hotel there when the yellow fever outbreak began on July 20. Brown, "a high-toned gentleman as ever lived," died there.[37]

Initially, Maffitt thought the cases of fever that developed were "but ordinary cases, originating from hard work and exposure to the sun, but in twenty hours the unpalatable fact was impressed upon me that yellow fever was added to our annoyances." In a letter to Commander Bulloch dated August 20, 1862, Maffitt explained, "No doctor, no paymaster. I have now 3 cases of yellow fever; have had 7. Am doing well in that line. You remember my fondness for doctoring the crew."[38]

The tireless Maffitt gathered the sick sailors on the quarterdeck, tending to them night and day. Yellow fever had reduced his crew to only a few working hands, so Maffitt put into Cardenas, Cuba. The Confederate agent Charles J. Helm received permission for the *Florida* to come to Havana, but he wrote, "By this time, unfortunately, the captain, several of his officers, and eight of his crew were prostrated by yellow fever, and it was not possible for him to move." Helm sent a physician to the *Florida* to tend the ill sailors, including Maffitt.

At first thinking he had caught a chill in a thunderstorm on August 22, Maffitt had continued to care for his sick men, but two hours later was "seized with a heavy chill, pain in the back and loins, dimness of vision, and a disposition to vomit." Realizing he had the fever, Maffitt took a mustard bath, some injections, and then changed his undergarments and sheets. Before slipping into delirium, he issued orders and instructions for the care of the vessel and crew. For a week, Maffitt suffered the ravages of the disease, and his description is one of the best by any naval officer or sailor. In addition to throbbing pulsations in his head, Maffitt said it was as if his "bones had been converted into red-hot tubes of iron and the marrow in them boiling with the fervent heat." He vomited, had chills, and his mouth felt as if he had consumed molten lead. Finally, he lost consciousness. One young officer, the third assistant engineer, John Seely, and three men died from the yellow fever, as well as Maffitt's stepson, Laurens, but Maffitt survived and regained consciousness on August 29. Midns. George Terry Sinclair Jr., Floyd, and Wyman also came down with the fever, the latter being taken to shore to convalesce.[39]

When he regained consciousness, Maffitt decided to run for Mobile, but additional cases of yellow fever occurred every day. When the *Florida* approached the blockade line off Mobile, Maffitt had only his officers and four hands out of a crew of one hundred to man the ship. Fortunately, the federals that day had only one blockader able to contest his entering Mobile Bay, the USS *Winona*, and although Maffitt could not man his guns, the *Florida's* speed allowed her to quickly outrun the slow federal gunboat.[40]

Smallpox

Although less common than intermittent fever or yellow fever, one of the most serious illnesses contracted by Confederate naval personnel was varioloid, or smallpox. Reports of Confederate naval personnel suffering from smallpox are scarce, but in December of 1862, James F. Harrison at Richmond Naval Hospital reported that he had sent three men with varioloid—Roderick Currie, ordinary seaman; James Brown, ship's cook; and Howard Thompson, first-class boy—to General Hospital No. 21.[41]

That same month, James E. Lindsay, an assistant navy surgeon at Drewry's Bluff, requested that the surgeon receive in the hospital under his charge Humphrey Hodder, who was, he explained, affected with smallpox. "Humphrey Hodder presented himself Dec 5 with fever & co. nausea-complains much of pain in his back & liver. Yesterday an eruption made its appearance which has not sufficiently developed itself to duly confirm my suspicions. I deem it best to send him to the hospital under your charge, hoping that he will be received on the same footing as a soldier."[42]

Dr. Lindsay's caution in diagnosing smallpox may indicate that the disease was often misdiagnosed, the eruptions being, in fact, from chickenpox and measles. Both of these childhood diseases as well as cases of mumps were common among soldiers, and although few statistics survive, Civil War sailors may have also contracted these illnesses. A misdiagnosis of smallpox by Dr. Ford in Savannah prompted the local health officer to put a seaman on the *Savannah City*, John Sheehan, on a rice flat in the river and quarantine the ship's crew. When Dr. Gibbes returned from leave and examined the patient, he pronounced him suffering not from smallpox but psoriasis. Nonetheless, Josiah Tattnall ordered Sheehan moved to isolation at the local pest house, a move protested by Gibbes, who had him brought back and treated with the usual remedies for psoriasis.[43]

Other Illnesses

Considerable numbers of Confederate naval personnel suffered from illnesses such as malaria, yellow fever, and smallpox but also from a variety of other complaints. A register of Confederate naval patients in the Confederate States hospital ship *St. Philip* at New Orleans, Louisiana, 1861–62, listed 130 entries, with some admitted more than once. These entries indicate patients suffered from the following illnesses or conditions: "intermittent fever, Burns, Dysentery, Contusion, inflammation of brain, syphilis, gonaorrhea, catarhus, rheumatism, diarrhea, toncilitus, buboe, dropsy, cold, pleurisy, paralysis, fracture, delirium trems., orchitus, sprain, neuralgia B., mercurial stoma, incised wound, ulcer, disease of heart, cystitis, epilepsy, opthalmia, injury of hip, hernia, incontinence, gunshot wound, ulcer of ankle, hemoptisis from injury, and varicose veins."[44] Although diphtheria is not included in this list of patients on board the *St. Philip*, this disease could prove fatal, as it did for Capt. William McBlair Sr., who fell ill after getting wet and catching a chill bringing the *Atlanta* into Causton's Bluff. Too sick to continue in command, McBlair left the ship for home. Savannah Squadron Surgeon Gibbes hoped "the home attention and comforts will restore him to us," but on February 16 he took a turn for the worse and died.[45]

Confederate soldiers and sailors also suffered from respiratory ailments, the most serious of which was pneumonia. Confederate army personnel experiencing constant exposure and privation fell victim to pneumonia in large numbers, but sailors serving ashore and on shipboard also contracted pneumonia. Patients suffering from other pulmonary complaints, including tuberculosis, received treatments that focused on nourishing food, tonics, and stimulants. Those thought to have tuberculosis were often discharged from the service.[46]

For colds and coughs, one physician preferred the juice of horehound sweetened, but others used lobelia, the leaves of bene, the bark of holly root, and button snakeroot. In May 1862 Osborne Inglehart had three patients suffering from respiratory ailments. He treated Seaman John Peterson for bronchitis, James Kelly for a cough, and Edward Taylor for asthma. When Peterson suffered a severe attack, he gave him expectorant mixtures and quinine and then a mustard plaster, but the patient continued to be very weak. Inglehart added Dover's powder at bedtime for Peterson, but on May 7 the sailor's cough was "very troublesome" and expectorant "abundant." The next day the fellow spiked a high fever, and on May 9 the surgeon sent him to the receiving ship, presumably for better care.[47]

Sexually Transmitted Diseases

Sexually transmitted diseases afflicted soldiers on both sides in the Civil War, and although no statistics survive, Confederate navy surgeons' journals and anecdotal evidence suggest many sailors suffered from and were treated for syphilis and gonorrhea. Unaware in this period that over time syphilis affects the nervous and cardiovascular systems, physicians diagnosed most cases of primary and secondary syphilis from observing superficial lesions and glandular enlargement. Civil War doctors tended to diagnose all forms of urethral discharge as "gonorrhea."[48]

Confederate sailors on liberty in Southern port towns or foreign ports often contracted venereal diseases from the local prostitutes. Records show a number of sailor patients on board the *St. Philip* at New Orleans were suffering from syphilis. The largest incidences of men being admitted to the hospital ship for symptoms of syphilis came from the *Pickens*: six in a three-month period in 1861, two from the *McRae*, and one from the *Florida*. Before departing Savannah, Georgia, three tars from the CSS *Atlanta* who had visited a brothel reported sick to doctors Freeman and Gibbes, who treated them for syphilis. Venereal disease claimed other sailors in the James River Squadron as victims. For example, eighteen-year-old Jones A. Ottley, of the 4th Battalion (Naval), suffered from syphilis, and Patrick O'Connor, a blacksmith in the 4th Battalion, was admitted with gonorrhea in November 1864.[49]

CSS *Gaines*' surgeon, Inglehart, also treated several men for syphilis and gonorrhea, including Thomas Woods for gonorrhea and Philip Clarke and Andrew Banks for syphilis. For the latter two sailors, the doctor prescribed potassium iodide and two days later added magnesium supplements for Clarke. He discharged twenty-four-year-old seaman Banks on May 4, 1862. Clarke, a forty-year-old Irish seaman, continued to improve on his regimen of potassium iodide and was well enough to be discharged on May 7.[50]

Accidents

Injuries incurred while serving on shipboard were not uncommon. On July 10, 1861, for example, Raphael Semmes was ascending a companion ladder to give direction to *Sumter*'s officer of the deck "and while doing so, I felt a sudden sickness of the stomach and reeling of the brain. I laid my head on my arm, thinking the sensation would soon pass off, but in a moment more I lost consciousness and tumbled from the top to the bottom of the ladder upon the cabin floor, where I remained senseless for a moment." Semmes, who suffered bruises and a concussion, spent time confined to his cabin ill with nausea and confusion.[51]

Incidents of sailors suffering from accidental or even deliberate gunshot wounds were not unheard of. Doctors Freeman and Gibbes in Savannah successfully removed a bullet from Quartermaster Coppell of the CSS *Atlanta*, who had been shot in the right shoulder in February by a Colt revolver. In May a musket discharged, grazing the forehead of Quarter Gunner Thomas Cannahan.[52]

Drowning

Although statistics have not survived, numerous cases of naval officers and enlisted men drowning occurred during the war, both from injuries suffered and from the fact that many sailors were unable to swim. When Engineer E. A. Jack reported for duty on board the CSS *Arkansas* moored off Vicksburg, he wrote that she "looked now like a thing deserted. Not a sign of life upon her decks when I first saw her, but before I had reached her a sailor came out of the forward hatch. Poor fellow, he had only made a few steps away toward the side of the ship when he fell forward into the river." Jack hurried toward him, "but he never reappeared. Whether he was shot by the enemy or was accidentally drowned was never known."[53]

Among the more notable cases of officers drowning was that of Dr. David Herbert Llewellyn of the CSS *Alabama*. Bested in a fight with the USS *Kearsarge*, the raider *Alabama* lowered its flag and, with water rushing in, the *Alabama*'s captain, Raphael Semmes, loaded his wounded, accompanied by surgeon Francis Galt, into the only two undamaged boats. Many of the crew jumped overboard and some of the men drowned, but others swam to safety. Although Semmes and most of his officers, including Surgeon Galt and a young English physician from Charing Cross Hospital, made it to a British yacht, Surgeon Llewellyn had remained on deck, unable to swim. Finally, donning two makeshift life preservers fashioned from shell casings, the doctor jumped into the water, but when one of the life preservers came loose, he drowned.[54]

Dr. Llewellyn was not the only officer who drowned during the war. In November 1864 the navy department received news of the death at sea of Midn. William B. Sinclair of the CSS *Florida* in July 1864. In passing from a prize ship to the *Florida*, Sinclair's boat was swamped, and he perished rescuing a seaman who could not swim. "On this, as on many previous occasions, this young officer displayed that courage, coolness, and conscientious devotion to duty and to right, which ever marked his brief career," Navy Secretary Mallory wrote.[55]

Treatments

Confederate navy physicians endeavored to alleviate their patients' suffering and, if possible, effect a cure using a variety of available medicines and medical procedures. In the 1860s physicians had several drugs or remedies to choose from, but they knew little about infectious illnesses or bacteria and had no transfusions, x-rays, or antibiotics. In some instances, they continued the practice of bloodletting. To treat combat wounds or injuries resulting from accidents or action with the enemy, Confederate surgeons followed medical procedures of the day, which included wound dressing and operative surgery to amputate or resection wounds to extremities. Gunshot wounds to abdomens often proved fatal, however.

Confederate surgeons had a variety of drugs at their disposal and most did not hesitate to use them to alleviate their patients' suffering. "Among the more prominent drugs," Dr. Charles B. Johnson wrote after the war, "were morphine, for alleviating pain, chloroform and ether for producing anesthesia (insensibility to suffering), brandy, wine, whiskey and quinine for exhaustion, and perchloride of iron, a powerful styptic, to stop bleeding."[56]

Fortunately for historians, Assistant Surgeon Osborn Inglehart, CSN, kept a journal while serving on board the CSS *Gaines* in the Mobile Squadron. His journal has survived and offers a detailed record of his patients along with their names, ranks, ages, countries of origin, and symptoms as well as his treatments of them. Inglehart carefully noted which medicines and dosage he prescribed, including many of the common medicines of that era: opium, morphine, Dover's powder, quinine, rhubarb, Rochelle salts, castor oil, sugar of lead, tannin, sulphate of copper, sulphate of zinc, camphor, tincture of opium, tinc of iron, tinc opic, syrup of squills, alcohol, and whiskey. Most of these came in powder form to be mixed with water or in some form of liquid. Pills were less common in the Civil War era.[57]

Inglehart's notes, for example, include this record of his nineteenth patient, thirty-year-old seaman Charles Brown, who was admitted to his sick bay with intermittent fever on May 13, 1862. Brown had suffered a chill the previous day, followed by a high fever. Inglehart prescribed quinine, potassium iodide, and rest, but on May 20 Brown complained of "quite severe" pain in his limbs. Quinine continued to be administered, but the next day the surgeon noted Brown showing symptoms of scorbutus (scurvy). He prescribed morph sulphate for his patient at bedtime, and over the next few days the man's pain lessened. On May 27 Brown was discharged to the receiving ship.[58]

Quinine was frequently prescribed by Civil War doctors treating patients suffering from malaria and other intermittent fevers. French chemists had isolated quinine from cinchona in the early 1800s, and it soon became a favorite remedy of Southern physicians. The usual dose was 15–25 grains followed by half a dram or 30 grains.[59] Mercury was a mainstay—the basis of "blue pills" (*hydrargyri pilulae*), calomel, antisepsis including potassium iodide, potassium permanganate, and later in the war bromides and liquid iodine. Colchicine was used to treat what physicians then called rheumatism (which was actually arthritis). Iodide of potassium also enjoyed "very fair success" for treatment of rheumatism. Physicians also prescribed colchicine for diarrhea, despite the fact that diarrhea is a side effect of colchicine. Dr. Inglehart—in just one month, May 1863—treated eight sailors suffering from either diarrhea or dysentery. For one of these patients he prescribed rest and Dover's powder every two hours for the first day, then morph sulphate the next day. Unfortunately, the man's condition weakened and Inglehart had him sent to the receiving ship.[60]

Many navy physicians also used belladonna to treat intestinal cramps and Dover's powder, which is a combination of ipecac and opium. Potassium nitrate was used to induce sweating; tartar emetic, to reduce fever and induce vomiting. Some Civil War doctors treated fever patients with digitalis, which unfortunately made them worse.[61]

Treatments for venereal diseases varied. For the skin lesions typical of syphilis, treatments included application of compounds made from mercury or home remedies made from poke roots or berries, wild sarsaparilla, sassafras, and jessamine.[62]

Confederate surgeons ashore and afloat were called upon to treat officers and men suffering from injuries incurred by falling from yardarms or rigging or from accidents using carpenters' tools, working in engine rooms, mishandling gun tackles or carriages, or carrying powder bags or shot.[63] Naval engagements with federal warships also inflicted a variety of injuries on officers and men. Exploding shells, spewing out lethal splinters, caused numerous casualties, as did shrapnel and small-arms fire. In hand-to-hand fighting, sabers, cutlasses, pikes, and pistol shots inflicted serious, sometimes fatal, wounds.

During the battle of New Orleans, for example, the *McRae* was badly riddled, some of the shells going in on one side and out on the other, "leaving holes above the water line large enough to crawl through," Third Assistant Engineer James Tomb recalled. One 11-inch shell passed through the engine room; another burst overhead, "taking off about half of First Class Fireman Kendrick's head. He was standing a few feet from me."[64]

Senior officers were not exempt from injury either. "Another portion of a shell nearly amputated Captain Huger's leg. He was directing the fight and the ship's course from a position just above the engine room." Thomas Huger was badly wounded by shell fragments that tore through his groin area and gouged a wound on the side of his head. He was carried below deck but, Tomb wrote, "He died a few days later in New Orleans."[65]

In the March 1862 battle of Hampton Roads, casualties on the CSS *Virginia* included Flag Officer Buchanan, who was struck in the left thigh, a minié ball passing entirely through the fleshy portion, grazing his femoral artery, and inflicting a serious wound. The surgeon of flagship, D. B. Phillips, reported "that Lt. R. Minor was wounded in left side (not dangerously), Midshipman Marmaduke suffered a slight wound of arm. Two men killed (names not known) and five men were wounded, one losing an eye."[66]

The destructive force of just one shell would cause most Confederate sailors to take cover when they heard or saw one coming. Their healthy respect for this danger led to an amusing incident in October 1861 when a Confederate squadron went down from Head of the Passes to chase off the Union blockaders. The CSS *Manassas* ran for the USS *Richmond*, ramming the federal vessel. Ordered to signal that his ship had struck the enemy, one of *Manassas*'s midshipmen climbed onto the shield to light a rocket. The midshipman held the rocket incorrectly, scorching his hands and causing him to drop the rocket, which fell down an open hatch "hissing and sputtering like some angry demon." Panicked by the noise that they assumed was an incoming shell, the *Manassas*'s sailors fell over one another trying to get out of the way. The embarrassed midshipman then correctly lit a second rocket, signaling the Confederate squadron.[67]

Small-arms fire and hand-to-hand combat could inflict serious injuries, sometimes fatal, on naval officers and men alike. In what became known as the Battle of Elizabeth City, the USS *Ceres* grappled with the *Ellis* and boarded the vessel. Most of the *Ellis*'s crew jumped over the side, but Lt. J. W. Cooke, cutlass and pistol in hand, stood firm. In the melee that followed, Cooke was seriously wounded, and seventeen-year-old midshipman William C. Jackson tried to swim away from the boat but was hit in his back by a pistol shot. Although the Yankees fished him out, Jackson died of his wound that evening. Also in this battle, the *Beaufort* managed to flee but the *Appomattox* had to be scuttled and burned, and enemy gunfire drove the *Fanny* aground. The Confederates lost four men killed, six wounded, and thirty-four captured.[68]

In June 1864 Confederate sailors and Marines suffered a number of casualties in fierce hand-to-hand fighting during a cutting-out expedition led by Lt. Thomas Postell Pelot. In the lead boat piloted by Moses Dallas, Pelot planned to stealthily come along the port side of the federal blockader USS *Water Witch* while Lt. Joseph Price of the CSS *Sampson* pulled alongside the starboard side. They would then board the enemy vessel, overwhelm the crew, and take the vessel as a prize. When twenty-one volunteers from his ship returned from Pelot's cutting-out expedition, Robert Watson learned details of the action. "The expedition consisted of 7 boats and 120 men and officers and started at 3 P.M. and towed by the steamer *Fire Fly* to Beulah [Beaulieu] battery, at which place they arrived at 10 ½ P.M. Hauled up the boats and camped for the night."[69]

"Next morning, June 1st," Watson wrote, "Lieut. Pelot went out reconnoitering and saw the steamer *Water Witch* lying in Ossabaw Sound. He returned at 2 P.M. and at 3 P.M. all the boats started and went down until they heard the steamer blowing off steam, but it was so very calm and clear it was not deemed prudent to tempt to board her, so they turned back and arrived at Beulah at 6 A.M." The party laid low until the following night when they approached the enemy steamer again and were "about 150 yards of the steamer when the boats were hailed by the Yankees. They received a defiant answer of 'rebels give way boys.' They then gave way on their boats with a regular Confederate yell. The Yankees then opened fire on them with small arms, they being too near for their cannon to bear on the boats, who were soon alongside." Pelot's rebels boarded the *Water Witch* on the starboard side, port bow, and starboard and port quarters. "The boarding nettings being up and our cutlasses being very dull they had considerable trouble getting on board, but they soon succeeded in gaining the decks but not until several of our men were killed or wounded," Watson explained. "A desperate hand to hand fight then took place, our men yelling like fiends all the time. The fight lasted only but five minutes after our boys gained the decks when the Yankees surrendered."[70]

The *Water Witch*'s paymaster, Luther Billings, encountered one of the first rebel boarders, who struck him with his saber. Billings took his pistol, placed the muzzle into the rebel sailor's side and pulled the trigger. One after the other, boarders came at Billings and Ensign Stover. One rebel "climbed over the rail, reached in and pressed his pistol against my breast, pulling the trigger—once, twice and three times—but no explosion followed. With curse he struck me using the treacherous weapon as a club. Dodging the blow, I grabbed one of my revolvers and shot him through the head. As his body appeared, a grinning Negro face appeared at the port opening." Billings leveled his pistol at the face only inches way. "Again the deadly flash and Moses, the only pilot the invaders had to depend upon, also passed away."[71]

In his diary on June 3, 1864, Watson wrote that a dispatch had arrived reporting the attack: "the Yankee had killed and wounded all our men except 30 who had made their escape. When I heard the news I felt as if I had lost every friend that I had, for I never felt so bad in my life." An hour later another dispatch came in stating that "our men had captured the *Water Witch* with small loss on our side."[72]

That evening a sailor came from the naval hospital "where several of our own men and wounded Yankees were. They both belong to our ship. They state Jules Chabert is badly wounded in the bowels and that he is not expected to live. He is so bad off that they could not bring him up in the ambulances." Watson noted that Patrick Loftus, one of the gunners, and

"Whiskey Bill" (Fireman William Crosby), were killed; "also old Moses, our Negro pilot was killed. These men belonged to our ship and their death is very much regretted by all the officers and crew for they were good and brave men."[73] Coxswain Wright Jones and Ordinary Seaman James M. Stapleton of the CSS *Georgia* were also killed in the cutting-out expedition, and Lt. Joseph Price, Midn. H. T. Minor, and six men were wounded. One man was killed and seven wounded in Master's Mate Rosler and Boatswain Seymour's boats, which got adrift and did not succeed in getting their men on board the Union vessel.[74]

According to Union navy surgeon W. H. Pierson, the rebels took the wounded of both sides in ambulances to Savannah, where he was allowed on parole to take professional charge of his wounded. Pierson's patients went to Savannah Naval Hospital under his care. "The hospital was devoid of some of the luxuries which may be found in Northern hospitals, but was airy and comfortable, and the patients there received every care and comfort which the somewhat limited resources of the country permitted. I myself was treated with gentlemanly consideration by Dr. Jeffrey and the assistant surgeons, as well as by the numerous rebel officers who frequently called there."[75]

Confederate naval officers serving ashore in gun batteries, forts, or entrenchments risked injury or death as well. During an attack on Fort Fisher in January 1865, Lt. Thomas K. Dornin, CSN, was severely wounded by a piece of shell from the federal fleet. Dornin, a lieutenant on the CSS *Chickamauga*, had volunteered to defend the fort "and worked like a private soldier, sponging one of the two 7-inch rifle Brooke guns until it burst. He transferred his sponge to the other and served until that burst also."[76]

Wounds were usually dressed using bandages made from osnaburg, lint, or old sheets, spreads, and clothing donated by Southern women. Surgeons used both cold- or warm-water applications for these wound dressings and debated the advantages of either. Cold water might be directly applied or dripped on the dressing or covered to prevent evaporation. This procedure, given three or four times a day, was generally adopted by the medical service, and one surgeon recalled that in a "fair proportion" of gunshot wounds involving joints it brought about recovery without surgery.[77]

Confederate navy surgeons did perform surgery on patients, especially amputations and resections to avoid infection. Patients during the
war ran a risk of developing infections because physicians of that time
were unaware of the doctrine of sepsis and the proper use of antisep-
tics. They thought an inflammatory reaction would help repair tissue
and welcomed the appearance of a creamy pus, called "laudable pus," in
wounds on the third or fourth day.[78]

The use of minié balls fired from rifled muskets created a new challenge for Civil War military surgeons, for the conical ball caused fractures
of the extremities and made infection more likely. Surgeons thought that
operative surgery for these wounds should be done as soon as possible,
preferably within the first twenty-four hours, a more likely outcome for
naval personnel wounded on shipboard or ashore near hospital facilities
than for large numbers of soldiers lying in fields after land engagements.

Military surgeons performed most operative surgery on patients in
complete anesthesia. Southern physicians used chloroform almost exclu-
sively as it had been proven safe and effective by British surgeons during
the Crimean War. "In every case of operation in this division," one Winder
Hospital surgeon wrote, "chloroform has been used and with invariable
good effect." It was administered by being dropped on a sponge or handkerchief until complete anesthesia had been produced for all manner of
operations. Although chloroform was commonly used as anesthesia, on
occasion patients were given beer, whiskey, or alcohol to deaden the pain. As
Midn. James Morgan discovered, patients were not always given something
to relieve their suffering. In September 1864 Morgan and several of his fellow
midshipmen went ashore to witness the battle for Fort Harrison. "After the
battle a surgeon pressed me into his service," Morgan recalled, "and made me
hold a soldier's shattered leg while he amputated it. I would have preferred
to be shot myself. Medicines were scarce in the South and that particular
surgeon had neither chloroform nor ether in his medicinal kit."[79]

Amputation saved the lives of many soldiers and sailors during the war,
but patients still ran the risk of wound infection following surgery. Surgical fevers—tetanus, erysipelas, hospital gangrene, and pyemia—afflicted
many of the injured or wounded and were the chief cause of mortality
among postsurgery patients. Those soldiers or sailors in hospitals ashore

suffering from erysipelas, or what is now termed contagious streptococcal infection, were often isolated and given a nourishing diet of soup, eggs, milk and butter, and alcoholic stimulants as well as internal medication like sesquichloride of iron and quinine for fever. Medical officers also prescribed cathartics to keep bowels open and opiates for pain. The treatment for hospital gangrene, which appeared in June of 1862 and caused terrible suffering among its victims, was similar.[80]

Any wound, abrasion, or burn might, of course, become infected and require treatment. In his practice on board the CSS *Gaines*, Surgeon Inglehart attended sailors who had been injured in performing their duties. Twenty-nine-year-old landsman Daniel Ahern suffered a puncture wound in his hand that became "much inflamed." On May 1, 1862, Inglehart prescribed a poultice and two days later discharged his patient.[81]

Confederate medical officers had a variety medicines to choose from, but as the Union blockade of Southern ports tightened, the Confederate Navy Department experienced difficulty obtaining medicine and medical supplies from foreign sources. Shortages must have affected Dr. Inglehart's ability to care for his patients, especially those suffering from diarrhea, for on May 26, 1862, he wrote, "The difficulty of treating these cases is owing to the want of proper medicine."[82]

In his report in 1864, Chief Spotswood noted that the purveyor's department had an ample supply of medicines, instruments, and everything to meet the wants of the sick, but owing to the strict blockade of the seacoast and harbors of the Confederacy, he could no longer get medical supplies from abroad.[83] For some time, the Confederate navy had been receiving medical supplies from Cuba brought into Southern ports such as Mobile. The variety of these supplies for the navy department can be ascertained from an invoice of stores shipped from C. J. Helm Esq. on board the British steamer *Denhigh* from Havana on June 1, 1864, to Captain Godfrey in Mobile. The invoice included oil of almond, 10 bottles of quinine pelletine, 5 gallons of alcohol, 12½ oz of morphine, a case of chloroform, cod liver oil, 1 case of dissecting instruments, mosquito netting, 208 pounds of sugar, and a sack of coffee, for a total $810.69.[84]

The Confederate navy also established a medical laboratory in Richmond to manufacture numerous standard-issue medicines "at a cost considerably lower than what was being paid for products delivered by blockade runners." Spotswood credited pharmacist Robert Lecky for important contributions to the facility's success. Army laboratories produced a wide variety of drugs in large quantities as well, the most useful of which were opiates, ether, and chloroform.[85]

In addition to wounds received from enemy fire, boiler explosions and bursting guns caused numerous casualties on board Confederate naval vessels during the Civil War. For example, Levi Balance was killed by the bursting of a shell in the mouth of a gun on board the sidewheel riverboat CSS *Sea Bird* during the action near Elizabeth City, North Carolina, in February 1862.[86] The only casualties on board the little Confederate gunboat *Josiah H. Bell* during the Civil War resulted from a gun explosion that killed two sailors in April 1863 and a boiler explosion in October that cost the lives of four more men. Boiler explosions could inflict a large number of casualties. In May 1863 a boiler explosion on the CSS *Chattahoochee* caused serious injuries. The ship's commanding officer, Lt. John J. Guthrie, had decided to leave Chattahoochee, Florida, and proceed downstream to aid the *Fashion*, a Confederate vessel under attack. Unable to get over the bar, Guthrie anchored for the night and when the river rose the next morning ordered steam up. As Lt. Augustus McLaughlin, CSN, explained, "The relief watch was coming down when the boiler exploded which accounts for so many injured or killed." The explosion took place as Mr. Fagan senior engineer was coming to see. He had been in his bunk "with a chill" but was concerned about the length of time since the fires had been started. "The explosion was instantaneous with the starting of the pump." Sixteen crewmen were killed, one mortally wounded and two seriously wounded, four men only slightly.[87]

Dr. Marcellus Ford did his best to tend to the wounded on deck, and Guthrie began baptizing those crewmen who had been wounded and were about to die. When a gunner warned "that an explosion of the magazine was imminent," a panic ensued among the crew, and some abandoned ship. "Three I believe, were drowned in trying to reach the shore," McLaughlin wrote.[88]

"No description, I am told, could possibly be given of the scene on the deck of the *Chattahoochee*, men running about frantic with pain, leaving the impression of their bleeding feet, and sometimes the entire flesh, nails and all, remain behind them," McLaughlin recalled. "The dead and wounded were taken on shore, where they remained until the next afternoon, most of the time a terrible storm raging." They were finally taken on board the steamer *William H. Young* and reached Columbus on Sunday night, he wrote, five days after the accident. "No attempt was made to dress the wounds until their arrival here, which could not be avoided."[89]

Hearing about the explosion, George Gift went down river to meet the *Young* and in a letter wrote, "Mr. Fagan, Mr. Hodges & my asst Engineers Mr. Henderson and the Pilot were instantly killed, making five officers. My boy Bill Moore was also killed. Mr. Mallory is badly scalded on the face & feet but the Doctor thinks there is hope. A number of men were scalded to death or downed—in all nineteen."[90]

McLaughlin was shaken by Midn. Charles K. Mallory's condition. "Poor Mallory! I shall never forget his appearance. I would not have known him had he not spoken. His face, hands, and feet were scalded in the most terrible manner; he plead piteously to have his wounds attended to. I urged the doctor, who, by the way, was almost used up himself, to pay Mallory some attention. He then told me that he would have to wait for some assistance." The doctor told him that Mallory could not live. "When they first commenced to remove the cloths he was talking cheerfully, but the nervous system could not stand the shock. He commenced sinking and was a corpse before they had gotten half through."[91] Cornelius Duffy, the fireman, died the next day, but Midshipman Craig and Master's Mate Hamilton Golder were only slightly injured. "They all received all the attention that could possibly have been bestowed. The Home was literally besieged with ladies." They placed the four worst cases in the home in a room upstairs. Although McLaughlin had difficulty remaining long in the room because "the atmosphere was so unpleasant," the ladies "did not seem to notice it and remained at their post till the last."[92]

Hospitals and Hospital Boats

Confederate naval officers and sailors who could not be treated on ship-board, or who fell ill or were injured ashore, were sent to naval hospitals or floating hospital boats. By January 1864 the Confederate Navy Department had established hospitals at Richmond, Charleston, Savannah, Charlotte, Selma, St. Mark's, Chattahoochee, Wilmington, and Mobile.[93]

Chief Spotswood's quarterly report of the sick at several naval hospitals during the period October 1, 1863 to October 1, 1864, offers a record of the number of patients admitted and discharged as well as the mortality rate of Confederate sailors cared for in these facilities. A total of 1,860 men were admitted during this period to the naval hospitals at Richmond, Charleston, Savannah, and Mobile. Sixty-six of these patients died, or 20.8 percent of those admitted. By the end of the quarter, 1,320 men were discharged, leaving 4,784 in the hospital.[94]

In the spring of 1862 one of the military hospital encampments in the vicinity of Richmond underwent conversion as a hospital for the accommodation of ailing seamen and Marines of the Confederate States Navy. Known also as Marine Hospital, the naval hospital was established in Richmond on Thirteenth street near Main in a warehouse formerly occupied by a Mr. Harwood.[95]

Richmond Naval Hospital was conveniently located near the James River. The hospital served sailors and officers of the James River Squadron or those who manned naval gun batteries ashore battling not only Yankee shot and shell but fevers and other illnesses. At one time, the James River Squadron was so plagued with cases of malaria as to be "very much impaired." Mosquitoes were to blame for many of these afflictions, and the time spent anchored near the marshes along the James River only increased a sailor's exposure to the pesky bugs. During the summer of 1864, so many men fell ill, most with malaria, that one midshipman on the school ship *Patrick Henry* wrote, "There is but a few of my class on board as most of them have been sent to the hospital."[96]

Confederates stationed at the gun batteries along the river at Howlett's and Drewry's Bluff fell victim to "malarial fevers of every type." In Richmond, Constance Cary recalled, "Funerals by night were common. My uncle who had commanded a battery on the James, was prostrated by malarial fever and taken to Richmond, where he died at the Clifton House, tenderly nursed by his sister. He was to my brother and me a second father."[97]

"The James River furnished a capital article of chills and fever," James Morgan noted, "not malaria, but the good old-fashioned kind with the shivers which made the teeth chatter and burning fever to follow." Morgan estimated about half of the midshipmen experienced these symptoms "every other day. No one was allowed to go on the sick-list on account of chills and fever; one was, however, allowed to lie down on the bare deck while the chill was on, but had to return to duty as soon as the paroxysm was over."[98]

On August 9, 1864, Flag Officer Mitchell informed Secretary Mallory that he had 150 men ill on board the squadron's vessels or in the naval hospital. He noted that CSS *Fredericksburg*'s Marine officer, Lieutenant Bradford, was in the hospital and all the ships' lieutenants and masters were sick. The *Richmond*'s commanding officer had fallen ill as well, and the *Virginia*'s chief engineer was in the hospital. Mitchell requested additional medical officers be sent to the squadron and reported to Mallory that the James River Squadron's crews were so reduced by sickness that he had decided to discontinue certain picket patrols to "enable us to man our batteries, in order that we may act against the enemy." By August, 226 sailors from the squadron had fallen ill and 157 had been sent to Richmond hospitals. Over the course of the summer, Richmond Naval Hospital admitted a total of 464 men, of whom 13 died.[99]

Richmond area hospitals served the sick and wounded from Confederate naval vessels on duty in the James River as well as men from the 4th Battalion (Naval) Local Defense Troops. Although most enlisted men admitted to Richmond hospitals were soldiers in Confederate States Amy units, in local defense forces, or in the 4th Battalion (Naval), Confederate navy sailors were also admitted to Jackson Hospital or other hospitals in the capitol.[100]

Confederate navy physicians and hospital stewards tended patients at these naval hospitals assisted by hired nurses, matrons, ward masters, druggists, porters, and sundry helpers including convalescent soldiers and even children.[101] The majority of the attendants caring for soldiers and for Confederate navy officers and men hospitalized in Jackson Hospital were male, but the hospital also employed twenty-seven female nurses, in addition to thirty-six cooks and forty-one laundresses. Most, if not all, of these nurses, cooks, and laundresses were African Americans or persons of color. Naval officers and sailors admitted as patients in these hospitals would have been attended to by black nurses, their dietary needs taken care of by black cooks, and their bed linens and perhaps even clothing washed by black laundresses or washer women.[102] Thousands of African Americans, men and women, slaves or free, served in Confederate medical facilities. "Their services are obviously not the whole of Confederate medical history, but they served a cause, performed a job, and played an active role, doing no more and no less than others," one historian noted.[103]

Confederate hospitals also welcomed women volunteers to care for the sick and wounded. During the Seven Days' Battle in June 1862, wagons filled with wounded soldiers were often met by the patriotic women of Richmond who greeted them "with saddened hearts but cheerful words." These ladies carried camphor in their pockets to ward off the smell of the dead piled on wagons. Many women may have taken wounded soldiers or sailors into their homes, now converted to makeshift hospitals.[104]

Not all patients welcomed the attention paid them by devoted women volunteers. When Midn. James Morgan went to visit his seriously wounded friend, Capt. Francis W. Dawson, in a tobacco warehouse being used as a hospital, Dawson whispered, "Jimmie, for God's sake, make them move my cot in the back of the building." Morgan recalled, "I assured him that he had been placed in the choicest spot in the hospital, where he could get any little air that might be stirring, but he insisted that he wanted to be moved, giving as a reason that every lady who entered the place washed his face and fed him with jelly." His face was sore, he was stuffed with jelly, and the women would not listen to his protestations.[105]

Some patients in Richmond hospitals were furloughed; others simply left the hospital. Although regulations required ward masters to call the roll twice daily and medical officers to visit wards at least once a day and turn in morning reports, Richmond area hospitals were essentially unguarded. Being a patient in one of these hospitals offered some war-weary men a golden opportunity to escape poor conditions or to desert and go home to be cared for by family members. In 1865 a number of those men who deserted probably left the hospital to learn if their families were even alive.[106]

To accommodate or transport sick and wounded sailors, the Confederates employed hospital boats, usually steamers impressed for emergencies or converted to provide long-term care for seriously ill patients. Initially these hospital boats were improvised. In April 1861, for example, Confederate authorities attached a barge with a capacity for eight to ten beds to a floating battery at Fort Sumter. The Confederates also employed the 147-ton sternwheeler CSS *Kanawah Valley* as a hospital boat, but she was burned at Island No. 10 on April 6, 1862. When the rebel steamer *General Rusk* seized the 1,172-ton sidewheel steamer *Star of the West* off Texas on April 17, 1861, they remodeled the ship as the hospital ship *St. Philip* with the capacity to care for 130 patients. The new floating hospital served on the lower Mississippi River from September 18, 1861 to April 20, 1862.[107]

The Confederacy employed other hospital boats as well to care for sick and wounded soldiers. Following the capitulation of Fort Henry to Union forces in February 1862, the Confederate hospital ship *Patton* surrendered with sixty patients, but the rebels destroyed the *Samuel Orr* to prevent the vessel from being taken. The 179-ton sternwheel steamer was burned and blown up at the mouth of the Duck River on February 7, 1862.[108]

Unfortunately for some very ill sailors, the journey to a hospital or hospital ship proved too arduous. Confederate records of such transfers are relatively scarce, but from a receipt dated March 17, 1862, we learn that in the spring of 1862, A. M. Summers, Third Assistant Engineer, CSN, was put in charge of three ill sailors from the CSS steamer *Pontchartrain* at New Madrid, Missouri. Summers was to accompany the men, Morris Lane, William McCarty, and Nicholas.

Despite shortages and disruptions caused by the war, the overall record of Confederate naval hospitals was commendable. As Iverson Graves wrote to Cora Graves in August 1864, "I was taken ill very suddenly and in a few hours was delirious, continuing for several days when I was sent to the Hospital, which is a very nice place. Navy Hospitals are much better attended than the Army as they have fewer patients and better Surgeons."[109]

The OMS, guided throughout the war by Spotswood, managed to appoint for the most part competent surgeons and assistant surgeons, procure needed medicine and supplies despite an increasingly effective Union blockade, and supervise naval hospitals caring for injured and ill naval personnel. In addition to these hospitals ashore, the Confederate navy employed hospital boats to evacuate and transport patients along the coast or on Southern rivers and sounds to hospitals or to provide care for sailors unable to be cared for on board ship.

6

Naval Combat along the Coast

FROM THE FIRST SHOTS FIRED at Fort Sumter, the Confederate States endeavored to keep open ports such as Charleston, South Carolina; Brunswick and Savannah, Georgia; Beaufort and Wilmington, North Carolina; Mobile, Alabama; and Jacksonville, St. Augustine, and Fernandina, Florida. In May 1861 U.S. president Abraham Lincoln had proclaimed a Union blockade of the Southern coastline from Virginia to Texas. Navy Secretary Gideon Welles' subsequent creation of the Atlantic Blockading Squadron and the Gulf Blockading Squadron presented the Confederacy the considerable challenge of keeping Southern ports, especially those with railroad connections, open so that blockade runners might carry cotton and cargoes for export. Other blockade runners attempted, at first with considerable success, to elude federal blockaders and dash into Southern ports with Enfield rifles, cartridges, ammunition, shoes, blankets, dry goods, drugs, and other supplies for the Confederate war effort. With almost two hundred harbors and coves to blockade, the Union navy was able to capture or destroy only a tenth of the blockade runners in 1861, prompting one officer to call the blockade "a farce."[1]

The First Ship-to-Ship Battle

When the war began, individual states armed and converted vessels into warships to guard their major ports of entry and to protect their coastline from invasion. These initial efforts were hastily conceived to buy time while the Confederacy converted other vessels into warships and acquired or constructed casemate ironclads and ironclad rams. The first ship-to-ship battle of the Civil War was fought in 1861 by a motley group of farmers, fishermen, and soldiers from North Carolina who were "hurriedly taught to fire a gun." Among the first Confederate sailors to see action during the Civil War, they did so from the decks of five small, shallow-draft, lightly armed vessels dubbed the "mosquito fleet." The little flotilla's name came not only from the size and armament of the five ships but from the plagues of mosquitoes that tormented the soldiers and laborers who were erecting fortifications and manning batteries along the coast, especially at Hatteras.[2]

To protect North Carolina's coastline, Gov. John W. Ellis ordered the purchase and arming of the vessels and directed that batteries be erected at the Hatteras, Oregon, and Ocracoke inlets. The North Carolina Squadron (NCS) *Winslow*, the largest vessel, carried a 32-pound forward and a smaller rifled brass 6-pound cannon on the afterdeck, but the other four, *Oregon, Ellis, Beaufort*, and *Raleigh*, boasted just one small cannon each. Even Governor Ellis considered the "mosquito fleet" a hollow threat to any federal offensives along the coast. "Their fuses were uncertain and their guns liable to burst after a few rounds. If the stakes had not been life and the issues desperation, blood, [and] death, the laugh of the satirist would have driven the 'mosquito fleet' ... from the waters."[3]

The inexperienced crews of three of the mosquito fleet's vessels, the *Winslow, Raleigh*, and *Beaufort*, began their wartime service as privateers. The NCS *Beaufort* was not a proper warship but an 85-ton gunboat converted from a tugboat working on the Dismal Swamp Canal before the war. Lt. R. C. Duvall of the North Carolina Navy put the NCS *Beaufort* into commission on July 9, 1861, at Norfolk. Some of her green crew may have had experience on the tugboat, but when they came on board and discovered the *Beaufort* had been shored up to carry a 32-pounder but had her powder magazine and boiler above the waterline, even the new hands could see the little gunboat would be vulnerable to enemy shot.[4]

Loaded with three hundred pounds of powder in her magazine, the *Beaufort* hoisted anchor, stood out from Norfolk, and headed down the coast through the Dismal Swamp Canal into Pamlico Sound. Lieutenant Duvall's mission was to guard the entrance into Pamlico Sound from the Atlantic Ocean at Oregon Inlet. The *Beaufort*'s new skipper may have explained to her crew that, situated just south of Nags Head, Oregon Inlet was a strategic entrance into both Albemarle and Pamlico Sounds, and the *Beaufort* was needed to augment the gun batteries being erected there.[5]

The little gunboat did not arrive too soon, for early on July 12, 1861, the engineer in charge of the defenses of Oregon Inlet informed Duvall that the previous morning three enemy steamers had appeared off the entrance to the inlet. Two had shelled the works. Undoubtedly, on a vessel of that diminutive size, the crew must have heard the engineer disparage the conduct of the Confederate officers during this brief bombardment, which was "such as to completely demoralize their men, and a general stampede took place." Word also would have spread that the engineer had also told Duvall that 130 blacks, four dozen of them slaves, had fled into the marshes and had not been heard from since.[6]

On July 16 Brig. Gen. Walter Gwynn and his staff came on board the *Beaufort*. Gwynn, who commanded the coastal defenses from the Virginia border south to New River, informed Duvall he had given command of Oregon Inlet's shore defenses to Col. Elwood Morris. A civil engineer employed before the war by the Cape Fear and Navigation Company, Elwood had designed the forts at Oregon Inlet, Hatteras, and Ocracoke. The general ordered Duvall to assist Morris and stressed the importance of guarding the entrance to the sound. Three days later the *Beaufort* found a narrow channel and made it over the bulkhead, but Duvall's men struggled to secure the little vessel in the strong 6–8 mph tides.[7]

When Duvall went ashore to examine the works that had been thrown up, he found them "a complete abortion for the purpose designed. They had just placed a gun in position without any rigging, and had another ready." *Beaufort's* sailors may have overheard Colonel Morris tell Duvall "that this was the first work (to-day) performed by the volunteers. They had previously refused to do any work." The engineer in charge of construction had just been relieved and replaced by Capt. C. R. Barney, who had to begin from scratch. Expecting a night attack by the enemy, Duvall established a set of signals and sent a man to the lighthouse to look out for vessels.[8]

The next morning the gunboat's crew saw one of the signalmen wave from the lighthouse "man of war steamer in sight to the northward." Duvall ordered the men to clear for action, sending the sailors scurrying, placing tarps over the hatches; unstowing sidearms; boarding hatchets, revolvers, and cutlasses; and opening the powder magazine below deck. Up came the shot and gun powder in canvas bags, and the gun crews stood their guns. Duvall then sent Master's Mate Young in a boat ashore with a note for Morris, informing him that a man-of-war was bearing down on him from northward and asking him what he intended doing. The enemy vessel was a large, three-masted propeller with a crew of at least 175 men, Duvall explained, and carried a battery of eight guns, and one rifled cannon forward and one aft that worked on pivots.[9]

At 9:25 a.m., the *Currituck* came by towing the schooner *Hugh Chisholm* with a company of one hundred men from Roanoke Island. As they passed the *Beaufort*, her crew gave them three hearty cheers, which were returned with great enthusiasm by the soldiers. "This was the kind of feeling I wished to inspire before the enemy opened fire on us," Duvall recalled.

When Colonel Morris and engineer Barney came alongside on shore, Duvall urged the colonel to employ his two guns at the fort to draw the enemy's fire and give his men a better opportunity of working their guns to their advantage. Morris replied that the guns were not in proper position, and he had no gunners to serve them. "I offered to supply him, and told him that the *Beaufort* was entirely at his service. He remarked that it would do no good." Duvall replied, "Then I will do what I can with my one gun and as long as I can."[10]

The reaction of *Beaufort's* 32-pound smoothbore gun crew is unknown, but their anxiety about being outgunned by the Yankee ship can only be imagined. The gunboat's gun crew had loaded the 32-pounder with solid shot, swung the piece around, and suddenly saw a puff of blue smoke erupt from the Yankee's forward pivot rifle. Showing no flag, the Union ship *Albatross* had closed and opened fire on the little *Beaufort*, but the shot passed overhead. The smoke had barely cleared away from the gun before the rebel gunboat's gun captain cried "Fire." He pulled the firing lanyard, sending a shot toward the enemy hoping that they had elevated the cannon sufficiently to graze the top of the sand hill. The *Beaufort's* gunners thought the shot had struck the enemy vessel between her main and mizzen mast. The firing became general, and the Yankee ship threw rifle cannon shot and shell at the *Beaufort*. "We answered with every shot as long as we could get our gun elevated to graze the sand hill, throwing the shot beautifully in line." In the ensuing engagement, Duvall noted that he personally sighted or adjusted the sight of his one gun, but he did acknowledge the coolness and judgment of his gun captain, who was also the chief boatswain's mate.[11]

The *Albatross* then dropped to the southward behind a higher sand bank, preventing the *Beaufort* from returning fire. One initial shot from the Yankee warship passed near the *Beaufort*'s smokestack and the second between the captain of the gun and the man next to him and struck the water about twenty feet from *Beaufort*'s port bow. Under fire from the enemy's eight guns throwing 32-pound shells and rifled cannon throwing shot and shell, and facing a ship with a crew of not less than 175–200 men to work her guns "against our little vessel of one gun and 26 men, only 13 of whom were the gun on deck," Duvall wisely decided to cast loose and heave off out of range.[12]

Thus ended the first, if brief, ship-to-ship engagement of the Civil War. The *Beaufort* had fired just eight shots and the *Albatross*, thirteen. No damage had been done to the little gunboat save a burning cylinder blown from the gun on to the hurricane deck, which set fire to some hammocks, cots, tents, and sails. The crew quickly threw them overboard and extinguished the fire. Claiming a victory for the *Beaufort*, Duvall argued: "The enemy with all his superior force and choice of position was compelled to draw off and drop behind a sand hill, where he knew it would be impossible for us to injure him, and from which position he could throw his heavy shot and shell into us unanswered." The *Beaufort*'s success against the Union was a morale booster for the Confederates trying to defend their coastline against the newly established Union blockade. Over the course of the three next years, however, as the Yankees tightened the blockade, Confederate attempts to break the blockade had little success.[13]

Iron Ships, Iron Hearts: Confederate Ironclads

The mosquito fleet was merely an improvised solution to protecting the vulnerable Southern coastline from attacks by combined federal forces.

The mission of the newly established Confederate States Navy required modern warships if the Confederacy was to break the Union blockade, a realization that prompted Navy Secretary Stephen Mallory to take advantage of the latest naval technology. In May 1861 he managed to convince the Confederate Congress to appropriate funds to purchase ironclads in Europe. He then sent an officer off to arrange to buy the *Gloire* or a similar warship while he met with John M. Brooke, John L. Porter, and William P. Williamson to study possible ironclad ship designs.[14]

Over the course of the war, the Confederacy converted, ordered, or constructed a number of casemate ironclads: the CSS *Virginia*, converted from the old frigate *Merrimack*; two casemate ironclads with rams, the CSS *Arkansas* and CSS *Tennessee*; the CSS *Manassas*, converted from a towboat; the CSS *Atlanta*, converted from the blockade runner *Fingal*; the *Eastport*; two of the *Albemarle* class, the CSS *Albemarle* and CSS *Neuse*; the ironclad steamer *Mississippi*, never finished; and six *Richmond*-class ironclad rams, *Chicora, North Carolina, Palmetto State, Raleigh, Richmond*, and *Savannah*. In addition, the *Missouri* served on the Red River, and the "ladies' gunboat" or ironclad ram *Charleston* served to defend that harbor. The navy also ordered the *Louisiana*, a floating battery; the *Brandywine, Huntsville*, and *Tuscaloosa*, never completed; and the *Jackson, Columbia, Texas, Tennessee II, Fredericksburg, Virginia II*, and *Nashville*.[15]

The first of these ironclad vessels was converted from the former U.S. Navy frigate *Merrimack* after the frigate's partial destruction at Gosport Navy Yard, which had left her lower hull and steam machinery intact. The screw frigate was renamed the CSS *Virginia* and went abruptly into battle, barely completed and manned by crewmen with little or no training. "The crew, numbering 320 men, had been hard to obtain. They were made up mostly of volunteers from the various regiments stationed round Norfolk," Lt. John R. Eggleston recalled. "I think the Georgians among them were in the majority. There was a sprinkling of old man-of-war's men, whose value at the time could not be over estimated." Most of the crew had never even seen a great gun like the one they were soon to handle in battle.[16]

While the *Merrimack* was undergoing conversion, Eggleston recalled that they drilled her crew at the guns of the old frigate *United States* every day for two weeks. "The first and only practice of these men behind the guns of the *Merrimack* herself was in actual battle."[17]

Surgeon Dinwiddie Phillips recalled that most of CSS *Virginia*'s crew were volunteers from the army and were unused to ship life, noting that about 20 percent of the men were usually ashore at the hospital, and their effective force on March 8, 1862, was about 250 or 260 men.[18] The ironclad's gun captain, Lt. John Taylor Wood, had chosen 80 sailors from a pool of 200 volunteers from a New Orleans regiment at Yorktown. Another 120 men came from army batteries in the Tidewater and a few other men who had escaped from the Confederate flotilla in Pamlico Sound. Among the junior officers were eight midshipmen: Barron Carter, William J. Craig, Franklin D. Dorain, Robert Chester Foute, Hardin Beverly Littlepage, James Cozby Long, Henry Hungerford Marmaduke, and Lawrence M. Rootes.[19]

As Wood recalled, "It should be remembered that the ship was an experiment in naval architecture, differing from any then afloat. The officers and crew were strangers to each other. Up until the hour of sailing the ship was crowded with workmen. Not a gun had been fired, hardly a revolution of the engines had been made, when we cast off from the dock and started on what many thought was an ordinary trial trip, but which proved to be a trial such as no vessel that ever floated had undergone up to that time." The new ironclad drew twenty-five feet, which, Wood explained, confined her to a comparatively narrow channel in Hampton Roads. He freely admitted that the *Virginia* was slow, and her engines were a weak point.[20]

Blue-water sailors scoffed at the ugly steamboats, which had no sails, and complained that they had "no sailoring to do." When, for example, an old sailor looked out a porthole toward the Union monitor *Nahant*, George Greer recalled, "He brought out a stream of profane abuse of 'bloody old tub' as he called her, and he declared, 'Them new-fangled iron ships ain't fit for hogs to go to sea in, let alone honest sailors! You'll all go to the bottom in her, youngster, there's where you'll go!'"[21]

Furthermore, ironclads were powered by steam machinery, which was subject to mechanical breakdowns. Steam-powered ships required regular maintenance. Pumps, cylinders, and injectors that supplied water to the boilers and blow-off and safety valves had to be kept in good working order lest the vessel suffer boiler failures. Keeping boilers in order in ships where steam was kept up month after month was especially difficult. If cleaning and repairs were neglected, then sediments, salts, and minerals (known as scale) could build up on the boilers' walls and render them less efficient. Of more concern for their crews was the possibility of boiler explosions, when cracks of thin spots appeared in boilers and soldered joints broke, causing the boiler to explode, sending fragments and scalding steam that would kill or inflict hideous burns on its victims.[22]

Steam-powered ships also required regular replenishment of their coal supply, and most sailors detested the laborious, messy job of coaling the ship. Coaling a ship might consume as many as twelve hours for the crew to carry bags of coal and dump them onto a chute that would transport it to the ship's coal bunker. The process tended to create coal dust, which settled over the ship and had to be mopped up. Coal dust and methane gas in the darkened bunkers rendered this job an unpleasant and dangerous one.[23]

Living conditions on most ironclads were poor, and officers and men serving on these vessels suffered terribly in both the winter and summer months. In warm weather, the casemates of ironclads like the *Albemarle* absorbed the heat and dampness, making them insufferable hotboxes. Ventilation in these ironclads was inadequate, and none were fitted with forced-air blowers, which meant noxious engine fumes fouled the air. Many of the sailors on the CSS *Tennessee*, for example, crept "out of the ports on the after deck to get a little fresh air." Tight spaces, poor ventilation, and oppressive heat led many ironclad sailors in both navies to take refuge on deck, even cooking their meals on deck.[24] Those ironclads stationed in harbors or in rivers and sounds during the winter months became stuffy and damp. The CSS *Atlanta* leaked constantly and was notoriously "dark, wet, and unventilated below decks," conditions that promoted respiratory illnesses.[25]

Lt. Richard Bacot was assigned to the CSS *Neuse*, of a similar design to *Albemarle*. "The vessel herself will be very close & warm this summer," he wrote to his sister from Kinston, North Carolina, in March 1864, "but we will be richly repaid for all inconveniences if we are permitted to succeed in capturing Newbern & Roanoke island."[26] Perhaps to Bacot's surprise, the onset of summer weather proved less uncomfortable than he expected. "The weather is very warm—equally as warm as it was in Louisiana the August I was there," he admitted in a letter written in May 1864. "Our quarters are very close and warm although better ventilated than some others."[27]

The living spaces on these shallow-draft ironclads were often cramped, but except for the damp cold in winter or heat in summertime, belowdecks were often healthier than in wooden warships. The metal construction prevented the growth of bacteria found in wooden vessels, and several ironclads had distilling equipment to provide the men with clean drinking water. Sailors on both sides seem to have put a good deal of faith in the vessels' iron plating. After being conveyed down the Chickahominy River past enemy batteries on a wooden gunboat, *Monitor* sailor William Keeler wrote, "I am free to say that the sensation of standing behind slight wooden bulwarks & impenetrable iron ones to be fired at somewhat different."[28] Some Union bluejackets serving on ironclads said the iron had "mythical powers" and boasted their vessel could be hit repeatedly without suffering significant damage.[29]

One of the best descriptions of a Confederate ironclad was penned by Thomas Conolly, who toured the *Virginia II* with Adm. Raphael Semmes in March 1865. Conolly entered through a small iron porthole "where we saw the thickness of her iron-sides lined with oak about 4 feet." When they went inside, "the great guns one astern of gigantic proportion d[itto] for' ad & 3 at either side with light & air coming into thick iron bars a top sloping inwards garnished with all the gun requisites tower tier filled with long steel soled shot about 12 inches each." Conolly then went down a hatchway to the mess quarters to find a cooking stove full of excellent dinner surrounded by mess boxes that "when opened had their tin plates, cups, knives salt pepper &c in good array with the n[umber]of rations for each mess in middle." The engine room, Conolly wrote, was at the other end of the ship. "Then wardroom & quarters. Ad[miral] sleeping room all dark but bright and clean when lighted up."[30]

The *Virginia*'s sailors slept on the berth deck and among the guns on hammocks, suffering intensely during the summer from the heat. "The heat and slow air are almost unbearable," Robert Minor told his wife in a letter written in July 1864. In an attempt to provide shade for the ironclad's flush decks and material to make tents so the men might sleep ashore, the James River Squadron's commanding officer, Mitchell, asked Secretary Mallory for a supply of canvas.[31]

The *Virginia*'s sailors also complained that their quarters were "very cold and uncomfortable" during the winter months. Warm clothing might have mitigated the frigid temperatures, but when the Union blockade closed many Southern ports to blockade runners, the squadron experienced a shortage of English-made fabric. Captain Mitchell appealed to the Office of Provisions and Clothing for pea jackets and blankets.[32]

In 1864 warehouses in nearby Richmond provided adequate allotments of food, small stores, and clothing to the James River Squadron's sailors. The CSS *Richmond*'s crew enjoyed a wide variety of regular rations, although by autumn of that year Mitchell was complaining about a shortage of vegetables. Deficiencies in the sailors' diet and the climate, especially "the heated atmosphere of the ironclads," contributed to several cases of illness among the squadron's personnel. Crew members on the James River ironclads also complained of drudgery and the dull routine of life on board the cramped vessels.[33]

The monotony of life on an ironclad was occasionally broken when these uncomfortable, ungainly but heavily armed vessels engaged the enemy. The first of these naval battles was the now famous "duel of the ironclads," the USS *Monitor* versus the CSS *Virginia*. Under the command of Capt. Franklin Buchanan, at 11 o'clock in the morning on March 8, 1862, the *Virginia* left the navy yard at Norfolk accompanied by the steam tugs *Beaufort* and *Raleigh* and steamed down the Elizabeth River to engage three Union frigates, the *Minnesota*, *Roanoke*, and *St. Lawrence*, as well as several gunboats. Off Newport News, the Union navy had anchored the 50-gun frigate *Congress* and 30-gun sloop *Cumberland*. As surgeon Phillips recalled, the *Virginia* had never been tested before, and many who watched the scene predicted failure. As he candidly wrote, "others suggested that the *Virginia* was an enormous metallic burial case, and that we were conducting our own funeral."[34] After an hour of slow progress, the *Virginia* passed through the obstructions at Craney Island and on toward Newport News. "Our crew was called to quarters and buckled on their side arms all ready and anxious to fight, no one can appreciate this position unless he was there," *Virginia* sailor Richard Curtis recalled. Curtis belonged to the first division stationed at the bow gun, and from the bow port he had a good view of the action.[35]

The *Virginia*'s gun captain, John Taylor Wood, also had a view of the federal warships. "The day was calm, and the last two ships were swinging lazily by their anchors," he recalled. "Boats were hanging to the lower booms, washed clothes in the rigging. Nothing indicated the rebel iron-clad was expected; but when she came within three-quarters of a mile, the federal ships dropped their boats astern, got booms alongside, and the *Cumberland* opened fire with her heavy pivots." The *Congress*, the gunboats, and the shore batteries followed.[36]

Buchanan had ordered the *Virginia* to attack the *Cumberland* and *Congress*, then turn westward and aim for the *Minnesota* and *Roanoke* anchored nearer to Fortress Monroe. "I commanded the two hot-shot guns directly under the main hatch, and just over the furnace," Eggleston explained. From his station, Eggleston could see through the gun port out to the wide bay. Then, suddenly, "the port became the frame of the picture of a great ship. It was the *Congress* only about a hundred yards distant."[37]

The *Virginia* came within about fifty yards of the *Congress* and, according to one young sailor on the *Congress*, the captain of the *Virginia* demanded that they surrender "but our captain replied that he would see them in Hades first." On receiving this reply, the *Virginia* opened fire. A shell from the *Virginia* entered the port hole of gun No. 7, striking the gun carriage, dismounting the gun, and "sweeping men about it back into a heap, bruised and bleeding."[38]

The *Congress* returned fire, but after a short time she hauled off and steamed toward *Cumberland*. The rebel ironclad then headed directly for the *Cumberland*. "We were getting close down to the Cumberland and all the ships battering hard," Richard Curtis of the *Virginia* remembered. "I heard the voice of Capt. Buchanan, say 'lookout men, I am going to ram that ship,' meaning the Cumberland, when I heard that like a flash I looked out of the port just as we rammed her."[39] The *Virginia* rammed the *Cumberland*, striking her almost at right angles under the fore-rigging on the starboard side. The blow opened a hole in the Yankee ship "wide enough to drive in a horse and cart," Wood recalled. "Soon she listed to port and filled rapidly."[40]

Although Buchanan ordered the *Virginia* to back clear of the listing *Cumberland*, the ram's feeble engines failed to free the ship until, in the nick of time, a tidal current swept *Virginia* sideways, breaking off the ram. They were now exposed to heavy fire at close quarters from the broadsides of the *Cumberland* and *Congress* as well as the Newport News batteries only a few cables' lengths off. Sharp-shooters "were spiking off every visible man," Chief Engineer Ashton Ramsay recalled.[41] The *Cumberland*'s crew, however, refused to give up. According to Lieutenant Wood, "No ship fought more gallantly." The crew were driven by the advancing water to the spar deck and here worked the pivot guns until the ship went down with a roar, the colors still flying. When one of *Virginia*'s crew came out of a port to the outside of her iron-plate roof, "a ball from one of our guns instantly cut him in two."[42]

Although the *Cumberland*'s gunners tried their best to hit the *Virginia*, the damage to the armor was slight. The *Virginia*'s sloping, greased sides had deflected the shots, creating a crackling, popping noise from the heat and flames. The ironclad seemed to be "frying from one end to the other," Midn. Hardin Littlepage remembered.[43] "The Virginia piled shot after shot at the frigates," George Weber, a sailor on the *Patrick Henry*, wrote to his brother. "Suddenly, one of the frigates, the Cumberland, was seen to topple and then sink. Cheer after cheer was given on our ships."[44] Lt. George Morris, *Cumberland*'s executive officer, now in command, gave the order to abandon ship at 3:35 p.m. "She went down bravely, with her colors flying."[45]

The *Congress* stayed in the battle for an hour after the sinking of the *Cumberland*. She kept up a steady fire on the *Virginia*, but the shot merely struck the Confederate vessel and glanced off into the water beyond. A shell exploded in the *Congress*'s wardroom close to the after magazine, starting a fire, which made it necessary to flood the magazine. Finally, the *Congress* ran up the white flag. The order came to cease firing, and she struck her colors. "My gun was loaded at the time," Frederick Curtis recalled, "and, although the order had been given to cease firing, I pulled the lanyard and fired what proved to be the last shot ever fired on board the fated 'Congress.'"[46] The CSS *Virginia* went on the next day to engage John Ericsson's *Monitor*, and although the battle is regarded as a draw, this duel of the ironclads initiated an ambitious ironclad construction program for both sides.

By January 1863 *Chicora* and *Palmetto State*, two of the six *Richmond*-class ironclad rams (*Chicora, North Carolina, Palmetto State, Raleigh, Richmond,* and *Savannah*) were completed, armed, manned, and ready to serve as harbor defense vessels at Charleston. The *Palmetto State* was an ironclad based on the plan of the *Merrimack*, except that her ends were not submerged and her side plating was turned down at the water's edge, making what the vessel's executive officer, William H. Parker, called a knuckle. The *Palmetto State* had four-and-a-half-inch iron plating and a four-gun battery that included an 80-pounder Brooke rifle gun forward, a 60-pounder rifle gun aft, and two 8-inch shell-guns in broadside. The ram's engines gave it a speed of seven knots per hour, and the ram "worked well and steered well." The *Palmetto State* was launched first, followed by *Chicora* armed with six guns. Unlike the newly converted CSS *Virginia*, both of these ironclads had experienced, well-trained crews. Parker noted the *Palmetto State* was "well officered and manned. Their drill at both great guns and small arms was excellent, and the discipline perfect."[47]

When the *Chicora* and *Palmetto State* were ready, Parker recalled, "it was decided to attack the fleet off Charleston on the night of the 30th." Lying off that port at the time were the federal blockaders *Housatonic, Mercedita, Keystone State, Quaker City, Augusta, Flag, Memphis, Settin, Ottawa,* and *Unadilla*. Although he had anticipated an attack by rebel ironclads, the South Atlantic Blockading Squadron commander, Adm. Samuel F. DuPont, had gone to Port Royal, leaving Captain Taylor in command of the squadron off Charleston. DuPont's fears were confirmed when word came that the two Confederate ironclads *Chicora* and *Palmetto State* had left Charleston clearly intending to attack the Union blockaders.[48] "To-night we had steam, and it looked like we were going to do something," the *Chicora*'s second assistant engineer, James H. Tomb, wrote. "The intention is to ram the first ship we come to."[49]

As Parker, the *Palmetto State*'s executive officer, recalled, about 10 p.m. on January 30 Commo. Duncan N. Ingraham came on board the *Palmetto State*, and ninety minutes later the two vessels quietly cast off and got under way. They steamed very slowly in order to reach the bar eleven miles from the city at 4 a.m., which would be high water. About midnight, after some entertainment, the crew began to drop off to sleep. In his memoirs, Parker painted a vivid picture of the ironclad's crew just prior to the attack. "Visiting the lower deck, forward, I found it covered with men sleeping in their pea-jackets peacefully and calmly; on the gun-deck few of the more thoughtful seamen were pacing quietly to and fro, with folded arms, in the pilot-house stood the Commodore and Captain, with the two pilots; the midshipmen were quiet in their quarters (for a wonder), and aft, I found the lieutenants smoking their pipes, but not conversing." In the wardroom the surgeon was preparing his instruments on the large mess-table and the paymaster was "lending him a hand."[50]

The *Chicora* and *Palmetto State* steamed across the bar with a foot and a half to spare, and headed toward a Union blockade ship, the *Mercedita*, lying at anchor just off the bar. In his report of the attack, Capt. H. S. Stellwagon, commanding the USS *Mercedita*, noted that "at 4:25 this morning the two ironclad rams from Charleston, . . . succeeded in passing the bar near Ship Channel." The moon had set and, cloaked in a thick haze, the two rebel rams were not perceived by the squadron. That the Yankee ship's lookouts failed to see the *Palmetto State* approaching must have puzzled Parker, the ram's first lieutenant, who later noted that the night was very clear, with nearly a full moon, so it seemed to him "that our smoke, which trailed after us like a huge black serpent, *must* be visible for miles off."[51]

The *Palmetto State*'s crew went silently to quarters an hour before crossing the bar, and Parker remembered that the men stood silently at their guns. The port shutters were closed, and the few battle lanterns lit cast a pale light in the gun deck. Parker's friend and fellow officer Phil Porcher, who commanded the bow gun, was equipped with a pair of white kid gloves and had an unlit cigar in his mouth. Next to Parker sat the little powder boy of the broadside guns, sitting on the match tub with his powder pouch slung over his shoulder, fast asleep. "He was in this condition when we rammed the *Mercedita*."[52]

Flag Officer Ingraham had ordered the *Palmetto State*'s commanding officer, Lt. Cdr. John Rutledge, to strike the federal vessel with his vessel's prow. When the *Mercedita* finally spotted the ram, Stellwagon hailed the *Palmetto State* and ordered her to keep off or he would fire. When the ram made no reply, Stellwagon called out, "You will be into me." Stellwagon was informed that it was the Confederate steamer *Palmetto State* and then, Ingraham wrote, "we struck her and fired the 7-inch gun into her as he gave an order to fire."[53]

The *Mercedita*'s lookouts did sight one of the approaching rebel rams, but her guns were unable to train on it as the ram approached on the quarter. The shell from *Palmetto State*'s bow gun struck the *Mercedita*'s aftermost 32-pounder gun, diagonally penetrating the starboard side, through the Normandy condenser, the steam drum of the port boiler, and exploded against the port side of the ship, blowing a hole in its exit some four or five feet square. Without power and unable to bring any weapons but muskets to bear against the ironclad enemy ship, *Mercedita* was all but helpless. So when the Confederate ram asked *Mercedita*, "Do you surrender?" Stellwagon replied, "Yes." Captain Rutledge then directed the *Mercedita*'s captain to send a boat alongside.[54] After some delay, the executive officer, Lt. Cdr. T. Abbot, came on board and informed Ingraham "that she was in a sinking condition and had a crew of 158, all told, and wished to be relieved; that all his boats were lowered without the plugs being in and were full of water."[55]

Meanwhile, the second Confederate ironclad, *Chicora*, had been searching for a target, and her commanding officer, John R. Tucker, turned his attention to the gunboat *Keystone State*. A 1,364-ton side-wheel steamer originally built for the coastal trade, the *Keystone State* had been chartered by the Union navy in April 1861, commissioned several months later, and assigned to the blockade in early 1862. She had taken several prizes and, but for her slow speed, might have taken more.[56]

The *Keystone State*'s lookouts sighted the rebel ironclad *Chicora* that fateful day about five o'clock in the morning but were unable to identify the ship, which Cdr. William E. LeRoy supposed was either a tug out from Charleston or a strange vessel passing along. When LeRoy sighted another column of smoke to the north and east of *Mercedita*, he became suspicious and took *Keystone State* alongside the approaching vessel and hailed her. Dissatisfied with the rebel ship's reply of "Hallo," and by now able to see through his looking glass that the vessel was a ram, LeRoy ordered the starboard bow gun fired, "which was at once responded to by a shot from the stranger."[57]

Keystone State's executive officer, Lt. Cdr. Thomas H. Eastman, describing the engagement with the *Chicora*, wrote, "I fired into him seven guns, one after the other, hitting him at the distance of 50 yards, without hurting him." The *Chicora* returned fire and tried to ram the Yankee, which evaded her. The rebel ram's shot, however, set the *Keystone State* on fire and she had to run before the wind to put it out.[58]

According to the *Chicora's* second assistant engineer, Tomb, the Yankee "was heading away from us when a shot from our bow gun, under the command of Lieutenant W. T. Glassell, struck her engine pipe or drum and another her wheel."[59] The shot came through both the *Keystone State's* boilers and, Eastman explained in a letter to his wife, "blew us up. Then we were done. The ship fell on her side, she had four large holes in her bottom, we could not move any more, and one-fourth of our strong crew were killed or wounded—hors du combat."[60]

Struck by ten enemy shells, with power lost and the forehold on fire, the *Keystone State* began to take on water. "Captain LeRoy (God bless him), out of pity for the dying and the dead, hauled down our flag, the ironclad fired two more shots into us." Then, suddenly, Eastman decided to keep fighting. It is said that when LeRoy hauled down the colors, Eastman threw down his sword and cried, "God D___ it. I will have nothing to do with it." When LeRoy asked him if he would take responsibility and Eastman agreed, they ran the flag back up and continued to fight the ship. Fortunately for the men of the battered *Keystone State*, the federal side-wheelers *Augusta* and *Quaker City* arrived on the scene and opened fire on the assailants.[61]

Engineer Tomb was ordered to take his crew of firemen and accompany the officer detailed to take charge of the *Keystone State* as prize and man the engine department. As they readied the second cutter, Tomb recalled, Lieutenant Glassell requested permission to fire on her again, as she was passing out of range. Captain Tucker said, "No, she has lowered her flag and surrendered." When he realized that the Union blockader was getting away and had no intention of surrendering, Captain Tucker ordered Glassell to open on her again, "but she had got well down to the southeast and well out of range."[62]

The *Housatonic* gave chase, but both the *Chicora* and *Palmetto State* retired northward, under fire, and took refuge in the swash channel behind the shoals. Prior to this, Flag Officer Ingraham had sent Lieutenant Commander Abbot back to the *Mercedita* to render assistance, provided that officers and crew promised not to serve the Confederate States until exchanged. "This he did—it was a verbal parole. He then returned to his ship," William Parker explained. The *Palmetto State* steamed off, discovered another steamer, and fired several shots, but the vessel was soon out of range. At daybreak the two rebel rams sighted a pair of steamers, but they too made off at full speed, firing shots at *Chicora* some distance astern. When the federal steamers sped away, Ingraham ordered his two to the entrance of Beach Channel to wait for high tide so they could cross the bar.[63]

The *Mercedita* and *Keystone State* were the only two ships to suffer casualties in the attack. *Mercedita* had 4 men killed and 3 wounded, but LeRoy reported his casualties were very large, some 20 killed and 20 wounded. From *Keystone State*'s complement of around 163 men, about one-fourth of her crew were killed and wounded. Among the former was the medical officer of the ship, Assistant Surgeon Jacob H. Gotwald, scalded to death while rendering surgical aid to one of the wounded men.[64]

"The upshot of the engagement was a good bit of glory, but not a prize or ship destroyed, and when we passed back over the bar and back to Charleston, we all felt disappointed at the night's work," Second Assistant Engineer Tomb noted.[65] Confederate newspapers reported that the ironclad raid on the blockading squadron off Charleston had resulted "in two vessels sunk, 4 set on fire, and remainder driven way." Gen. P. T. Beauregard went even further, claiming that the *Chicora* and *Palmetto State*'s attacks had dispersed the Union blockading squadron and raised the blockade.[66]

Naturally, Admiral DuPont defended the Union blockade. DuPont argued that with the *New Ironsides, Powhatan,* and *Canandaigua* now stationed off Charleston, that port was more stringently blockaded than prior to the rebel ironclads' raid. Union commanders also maintained that no Confederate vessels were able to run the blockade after the rams went back inside the bar and that, although two were damaged, no Union vessels had been sunk or seriously set on fire.

Oddly, *Chicora's* engineer, Tomb, agreed with the Union assessment of the ironclads' attack. The Confederate naval officer wrote, "We did not accomplish as much as our sister ship, the *Palmetto State.* They say we raised the blockade, but we all felt we would rather have raised hell and sunk the ships."[67]

The Battle of Mobile Bay

The *Chicora* and *Palmetto State* had failed to raise the Union blockade, which by the summer of 1864 had tightened a noose around the Southern coastline. Only Wilmington, Charleston, Savannah, Mobile, and Galveston remained in Confederate hands. Defending these few remaining open ports considered so vital to the war effort were the Confederate ironclads *Chicora* and *Palmetto State, Charleston* and *Columbia* at Charleston, the floating battery *North Carolina* at Wilmington, the *Georgia* at Savannah, and the *Tennessee* at Mobile. In the spring of 1864 the ironclad *Raleigh* had been grounded and lost and, until sunk by the Yankees in a daring raid, the *Albemarle* had remained in the river. The *Atlanta* had been damaged by federal gunfire and run aground in June 1863.[68]

The Confederacy continued to value the city and port of Mobile, Alabama, as an entry point for blockade runners bringing supplies into the Confederacy. For Confederate officers and men guarding the Mobile Bay, eternal vigilance was the word. For three years they had manned the city's defenses, anticipating a major attack by Adm. David Glasgow Farragut's Union forces. Except for a minor effort in February, no attack had materialized on the "Queen of the Gulf," but the Confederate army continued to improve the three forts guarding the entrance to Mobile Bay: Fort Gaines, Fort Powell, and Fort Morgan. In addition to these forts, Adm. Franklin Buchanan's naval squadron stood ready to repel any attempt by Farragut's Gulf Blockading Squadron to enter the bay. In the summer of 1864, however, Buchanan's squadron had just four ships, the three side-wheel gunboats *Selma, Gaines,* and *Morgan* and the casemate ironclad ram *Tennessee,* which served as Buchanan's flagship.[69]

The *Tennessee,* completed at Selma in late 1863 and towed to Mobile for completion, was at the time the world's most powerful warship. At 209 feet overall and 1,273 tons, the ironclad ram had 5- and 6-inch armor. Two horsepower engines from the *Alonzo Child* powered the ram with two screws and two side wheels. Commissioned February 16, 1864, and then towed to Mobile to be fitted out, the *Tennessee* was armed with two 7-inch Brooke rifles mounted on pivots and four 6.4-inch Brooke rifles in each broadside. Designed for the navy by John Mercer Brooke, the Brooke 7-inch rifled cannon had become the mainstay of Confederate naval ordnance. Cdr. James D. Johnston, CSN, commanded the ram, which had a complement of 133 officers and men.[70]

A blue-water sailor joining the *Tennessee*'s complement may have at first been impressed by the ram's enormous casemate, its gray paint streaked with rust, but would have quickly noticed that she lacked the graceful lines of a wooden sloop of war and the tall masts of a sailing vessel. The *Tennessee*'s low freeboard gave the impression that the ram was resting barely atop the waves. Approaching the ram in a launch or boat, a new recruit could not have missed seeing the four gun ports piercing the side of her casemate and another one forward and one aft. Thick wrought iron shutters that swung closed when the gun was being reloaded covered the three pivot ports fore and aft.[71]

In 1864 the Confederate States Navy assembled eight vessels to defend Mobile Bay, including the ram *Tennessee II,* rams *Tuscaloosa* and *Huntsville,* ironclads *Baltic* and *Nashville,* and three wooden gunboats. To bolster the bay's defenses, the Confederates had sown 180 mines in three rows to narrow the width of the bay's entrance and sunk pilings across the shallow entrance of the bay near Fort Gaines stretching to some five hundred yards from Fort Morgan. Any Yankee ships attempting to negotiate the bay's narrow entrance while Buchanan's ships moved in to engage them would also face heavy gunfire from the forts' gunners.[72]

Although seizing control of Mobile Bay had long been an object of Union strategy, for the first three years of the war capturing New Orleans and opening the Mississippi River had taken priority. Finally, in January 1864 Farragut made a reconnaissance of Mobile Bay and then moved a powerful federal fleet of four ironclad monitors and fourteen wooden gunboats into position off the entrance to the bay. Attacking Mobile Bay would be a challenging mission, for Farragut's ships would have to avoid mines or "torpedoes" and obstructions in the ship channel. The fleet would also have to pass close to Fort Morgan, aiming the ships' guns at the fort in "a well directed fire." These difficulties forced Farragut to devise a bold plan. Taking advantage of an incoming tide and hoping for a southwest wind to blow smoke back at the fort's defenders, Farragut's ships would steam past Sand Island in two columns and then turn and bear north by east. The plan called for the vessels to run past the forts in couples, lashed side by side, with the flagship *Hartford* in the lead.[73]

Farragut fully intended to run into Mobile Bay on August 3, 1864, the day when federal troops were scheduled to land on Dauphin Island, but the failure of the monitor *Tecumseh* to arrive until the evening of August 4 frustrated this plan. When the monitor finally took up her anchorage in the Sand Island channel, her arrival gave Farragut a total of four monitors, *Tecumseh*, *Winnebago*, *Manhattan*, and *Chickasaw*. The admiral planned to deploy the monitors to shield the wooden vessels from Fort Morgan's fire and then have *Tecumseh* and *Manhattan* attempt to destroy the rebel *Tennessee*.[74]

Early on the morning of August 5, 1864, the Confederate flagship *Tennessee*'s commander, Lieutenant Johnston, observed four ironclad monitors and fourteen wooden vessels standing up the channel into the bay, "with flags flying. They gradually fell into a line, consisting of twenty-three vessels, four of which were monitors."[75] The monitors *Tecumseh*, *Winnebago*, *Manhattan*, and *Chickasaw*, in the lead to shield the wooden warships from Fort Morgan's fire, were followed on their left in a line about three miles long by the other Union frigates and gunboats. In a hastily written letter to his father just after the engagement, Lt. Edward N. Kellogg described the second column that memorable morning, "At 3:30 of the 5th, the vessels with their consorts were lashed together & at 5.00

we headed up the channel in the Oneida with the Galena lashed to our port side bringing up the rear."[76]

At six thirty, the leading federal monitors *Tecumseh* and *Manhattan* let go the first rounds at Fort Morgan. A half hour later the fort's commander, Brigadier General Page, fired the first gun at long range "and soon the firing became general, our fire being briskly returned by the enemy. For a short time the smoke was so dense that the vessels could not be distinguished, but still the firing was incessant."[77] When Farragut's ships neared Fort Morgan and the rebel gun batteries opened fire, Buchanan ordered the *Tennessee* to signal the Confederate squadron to get under way and follow his motions. Moving the ram into the middle channel just inside the line of torpedoes with the four wooden rebel gunboats *Selma*, *Morgan*, and *Gaines*, Johnston ordered the *Tennessee*'s crew to clear for action.[78]

Slowed to only six knots by punctures in her smokestacks, the *Tennessee* crept toward the enemy, now four miles distant. From Fort Morgan's ramparts, rebel soldiers cheered the ironclad. "It was the beginning of a naval combat the likes of which history has not seen," wrote Lt. A. D. Wharton, commanding the ram's bow gun.[79]

Farragut's intention was for his ships to steam past Fort Morgan at intervals of about 240 yards to concentrate their fire on the fort. At 6:47 a.m. the federal monitor *Tecumseh* fired the first shot at the fort, followed at 7:11 by the flagship *Hartford*. Then, disregarding the enemy minefield, *Tecumseh*'s commanding officer, Cdr. Tunis Craven, boldly headed the ironclad straight at the *Tennessee*, hell bent on attacking the rebel ram while the *Chickasaw* and *Winnebago* bombarded the fort's water battery. From the *Tennessee*, Johnston watched the Yankee monitor steaming toward him. *Tennessee*'s bow gun crew kept their gun, loaded with a steel bolt weighing 140 pounds, steadily trained on the monitor as she advanced.[80]

Suddenly, the *Tecumseh* struck a mine. "A few of her crew were observed to leap wildly from her turret," Parker noted, "for an instant her screw was seen revolving in the air—and then there was nothing left to show that the *Tecumseh* had ever formed one of the proud Union fleet, but a small boat washed from her deck, and a number of half-drowned men struggling fiercely for life in the seething waters which had closed over the vessel forever."[81] Four of the *Tecumseh*'s crew swam ashore, seven took to one of the monitor's boats, and ten others were picked up by a cutter from the *Metacomet*, but Captain Craven went down with his ship.[82]

Moments before, *Brooklyn*'s commanding officer, James Alden, confused about his ship's position, had stopped to ask for clarification of his orders. "The monitors are right ahead. We cannot go on without passing them," Alden signaled to the flagship. "What shall we do?" When the *Brooklyn* stopped her engine, Page ordered Fort Morgan's gunners to concentrate on the now motionless vessel. With the enemy's fire increasing and the wooden vessels to *Brooklyn* and *Hartford*'s rear closing in on them, Farragut made a fateful decision. Despite the report of a heavy line of "torpedoes" across the channel, Farragut determined to take a risk and ordered, "Damn the torpedoes. Four bells, Captain Drayton, go ahead!" With the flagship's pilot, Freeman, conning her and giving orders to *Metacomet*, the flagship passed clear of the *Brooklyn*, increased speed and crossed both lines of mines.[83]

As Farragut's ships continued to pass rapidly by the fort, Page could see shot after shot strike and shells explode on or about the Union vessels, but their sides were heavily protected by chain cables, hung along the sides and abreast the engines so no vital blow could be inflicted. Looking back, he added, "The torpedoes in the channel were also harmless; owing to the depth of the water, the strong tides, and the imperfect moorings none exploded."[84]

Observing that the *Hartford* had cleared the minefield, at 8:00 a.m. Franklin Buchanan ordered Johnston to pursue the Yankee flagship into the bay hoping the *Tennessee* might trap and ram her in a small cul-de-sac four miles above Fort Morgan. By now the wooden Confederate gunboats *Gaines*, *Morgan*, and *Selma* had come out ahead of the *Hartford*, with the *Morgan* opening fire on the Yankee flagship followed by the *Selma* and *Gaines*. Fire from the gunboat *Gaines*, directed at first against the bows of the federal ships, now played along their decks with plunging effect.[85]

Soon, however, the tables were turned as the *Brooklyn* and *Richmond* steamed across the minefield and opened fire on the rebel gunboats. "A shell from the *Hartford* burst near the wheel," Midn. George S. Waterman, who commanded the *Gaines*' two 32-pounder broadside guns, wrote, "wounding the two helmsmen most fearfully and [killing] Quarter-Gunner Aherne, while the wheel ropes were cut and helm splintered to pieces." Then a 9-inch shell came through the side forward of Waterman's gun, extinguishing its fuse while passing through the woodwork and lodging on the berth deck. More hits followed, and the *Gaines'* engineers and firemen battled to control flooding. Finally, the *Gaines* had to be beached and burned. The *Morgan* fled to the protection of Fort Morgan.[86]

Meanwhile, the *Tennessee* had gone in pursuit of the *Hartford*. As Farragut's flagship entered Mobile Bay, the rebel ram "dashed out at her," Parker recalled, but failing to overtake her, turned and made for *Brooklyn*, *Richmond*, and *Lackawanna* in succession. She missed them all, "saluting each with a broadside, which did great injury to the vessel, and laid many a brave fellow low, while their fire, in reply, made not the slightest impression on her iron shield."[87]

Passing by *Lackawanna* and *Seminole*, Buchanan turned his attention next to the sloops *Monongahela* and *Kennebec*. With *Tecumseh* gone and *Manhattan* nowhere in sight, the *Monongahela's* skipper had little choice but to use the sloop's iron prow to ram the *Tennessee*. Lt. Oliver A. Batcheller, an officer on the *Monongahela*, recalled that she made a rush at the *Tennessee*. "The shock was terrific, but the ram, not liking the prospect, had taken a broad sheet, and the blow was oblique." The two vessels swung together with the *Kennebec* caught in between, taking a broadside into her lower deck.[88]

When the *Tennessee* straightened out, she headed on down the line toward the *Ossipee*. "Just as we passed the forts," Charles Clark wrote, "the ironclad *Tennessee* came out of the smoke on our starboard bow." As none of the *Ossipee's* guns in his division would bear until the rebel ram came farther aft, Clark focused on the *Tennessee's* "big rifle gun . . . projecting from her bow the hole in it looking ominously large." The projectile raked the *Ossipee's* berth deck, and "we returned it with the muzzles of our guns depressed, but I imagine all our shot simply struck her casemate and bounced off." The *Tennessee* gave the *Ossipee* one more as she passed, but it missed the boilers, going through just forward of them.[89]

After passing the *Ossipee*, the rebel ram *Tennessee* continued on and then bore down on the *Oneida* "just as a shell from the fort exploded in our starboard boiler, which disabled us completely and scalded all our firemen and engineers horribly," Lieutenant Kellogg explained to his father. Men rushed up on deck from below "with their faces and arms scalded in a frightful manner. The steam followed them and drove our men from the guns leaving us helpless."[90]

The *Oneida*'s sailors managed to rally, and as the ram *Tennessee* approached, Kellogg wrote, "they gave a loud cheer of defiance and poured a hot fire at the ugly looking rebel," but the gunboat's solid 9-shot glanced harmlessly from the rebel ram's sides and she moved on firing two broadsides at the *Oneida*.[91] "We were completely at her mercy while her 130 pr. Brookes shell went raking & crashing through us mangling & wounding our men while they had no chance to return her fire. The carnage was awful."[92] Captain Mullany, his arm shot off, was carried below, and Lieutenant Huntington, the executive officer, took command.[93]

The *Tennessee* was now about a half mile astern of the *Oneida* but "again turned, this time bent upon sinking us, but the monitors had been watching her & bore down to our assistance," Kellogg explained to his father. When the *Tennessee*'s acting chief engineer reported the ship leaking badly, Buchanan personally ordered Johnston to steer for Fort Morgan.[94]

Although pummeled by federal shot and shell, the *Tennessee* had suffered little serious damage except for a perforated smokestack. About 8:30 a.m., Dr. Conrad emerged from the cockpit and went topside to discover that "everything had been shot away, smokestack, boat davits, stanchions and, 'fore and aft, our deck had been swept absolutely clean." The ram's crew—rushed into action without breakfast, exhausted and hungry—welcomed an opportunity to wolf down hardtack and coffee.[95]

As the first phase of the battle ended, Buchanan, limping on his wounded leg, paced the flagship's deck. Should he retire to the protection of Fort Morgan's guns or pursue the Yankee fleet? The *Tennessee* had about six hours of coal left, and Buchanan chose to go on the offensive. "I determined by an unexpected dash into the fleet, to attack and do it all the damage in my power," he explained. "Follow them up, Johnston, we can't let them off that way," Buchanan is said to have told the ram's captain.[96]

By 8:35 the flagship *Hartford* and Farragut's other ships had passed Fort Morgan and come to anchor some four miles northwest of the fort. The *Manhattan* had barely come to anchor, Harrie Webster recalled, when a signal came from the *Hartford* to "prepare to engage the enemy." Webster glanced toward Fort Morgan and saw the *Tennessee* slowly steaming from under the fort into the bay, making it evident that the final struggle was about to begin. The *Manhattan* weighed anchor and, before entering the fray, "word was sent below to secure everything for ramming, and we waited for breathless minutes of the attack which never came."[97]

Farragut had decided to take the monitors *Manhattan*, *Winnebago*, and *Chickasaw* and attack the *Tennessee*, but Buchanan beat him to it. Getting under way, the *Tennessee* headed for the Yankee fleet but at such a slow speed it took the rebel ram almost an hour to cover the four miles to where the eight Union wooden gunboats and three monitors had anchored.[98] Watching the *Tennessee* closing the range to the anchorage, Farragut knew his adversary intended to run directly for the flagship *Hartford*, so he ordered, "Run down the enemy's principal vessel at full speed."[99] Hoping to intercept the rebel ram, the *Monongahela*'s commanding officer ordered "full ahead." With colors flying, the ram made directly for the flagship, "ignoring all lesser fry," Lieutenant Batcheller, on *Monongahela*, wrote.[100]

The *Tennessee*'s commander, Johnston, could clearly see the small screw sloop picking up speed and aiming for the *Tennessee*. "Steady yourself when she strikes! Stand by and be ready!"[101] he yelled from the ram's pilot platform. Churning up to ten knots, the *Monongahela* struck the *Tennessee* amidships, but Johnston ordered the helm a-starboard, and the two vessels collided at an acute angle, the ram swinging alongside of the *Monongahela*'s consort, the *Kennebec*, whose sharp cutwater cut her barge in two. To the rebel crew's surprise, the blow did little damage. As the *Monongahela* scraped the rebel ram's side, *Tennessee*'s gunners fired two shots at the ship, piercing her through and through.[102]

No sooner had the *Monongahela* slipped away than a second Yankee ship, the sloop *Lackawanna*, came speeding toward the *Tennessee* at fourteen knots. The *Lackawanna* "was more fortunate and delivered a fair blow . . . just where the iron house joined the mid deck, with a shock that prostrated every man on deck and tore to atoms the solid oak bow for six feet as if it had been paper," *Lackawanna*'s assistant surgeon, W. F. Hutchinson, remembered.[103] The *Lackawanna* backed clear of the *Tennessee*, but the sloop's gunners got off musketry shots into the ram's gun ports. The sloop attempted to make another run at the rebel ram, but the *Lackawanna* turned so slowly it smacked into the flagship.[104]

With Farragut poised in the port mizzen rigging, the flagship steamed in toward the *Tennessee*. "The grand old *Hartford* rushed at her, but the blow was a glancing one, and the broadsides were exchanged with the muzzle of the guns almost touching," Clark remembered. The two vessels were so close, that a man on *Hartford* used his bayonet to jab *Tennessee*'s engineer, William M. Rodgers, standing near a gun port. Another Union sailor aimed his pistol at Rodgers, hitting him in the shoulder.[105]

As the two flagships maneuvered, the Confederate ram sighted the formidable monitor *Manhattan* two hundred yards off the port bow. Peering through *Tennessee*'s gun port and observing the monitor's turret revolve, Wharton shouted, "Stand clear of the port side!" A moment later a thunderous report shook the ship and a blast of dense smoke covered the portholes and the shot penetrated over two feet of solid wood, covered with five inches of solid iron.[106]

The *Manhattan* fired just six shots, Cdr. James W. A. Nicholson claiming that the monitor steered poorly and that dense smoke from his guns interfered with the gunners' aim. The *Chickasaw* had less trouble, closing to within fifty yards of the Confederate ram and firing repeatedly at the *Tennessee* with her two forward 11-inch guns. Shot from the *Chickasaw* jammed one of the *Tennessee*'s gun ports, and another struck the casemate, killing two sailors who were trying to pry the shutter open. Word that the enemy shot had wounded Admiral Buchanan brought Johnston down from the pilothouse. "Well Johnston," Buchanan is reported to have said, "they have got me again. You'll have to look out for her now; it is your fight."[107] Johnston replied that he would do his best, but with the ram's wheel chains shot away, two quarter ports for the after gun jammed, and the riddled smokestack fallen over, he had few options left to continue the fight. When Johnston returned to the berth deck to inform Buchanan on the condition of the vessel, he asked the admiral if he should surrender. "Do the best you can, sir," Buchanan replied, "and when all is done surrender."[108]

The *Tennessee*'s skipper went back to the gun deck, where he could see one of the heaviest Union vessels about to run into the monitor on the port quarter. Shot was "fairly raining upon the after end of the shield, which was now so thoroughly shattered that in a few moments it would have fallen and exposed the gun deck to a raking fire of shell and grape."[109] Seeing another enemy ship bent on ramming him and others closing in, Johnston made a decision. "I concluded that no good object could be accomplished by sacrificing the lives of the officers and men in such a one-sided contest."[110] He then went to the top of the shield and took down the ram's ensign, then descended, "although with an almost bursting heart, to hoist the white flag."[111]

As the *Ossipee* neared the rebel ram, Cdr. William E. LeRoy observed the white flag but could not stop his engines in time to prevent striking the *Tennessee* a glancing blow. He then hailed the ram. "Hello, Johnston, how are you? LeRoy—don't you know me? I'll send a boat alongside for you."[112] "We lowered and sent over a boat for the Confederate captain," Charles Clark recalled. "As he came aboard, he was nervously handling his sword, but LeRoy, ignoring this, shook him warmly by the hand, and said in his cordial way, "'My poor fellow, have a glass of ice water. You see, my steward has it ready for you. Wasn't it fortunate our supply steamer came in a day or two ago?'" Johnston bowed his head "to hide his emotion," Clark said, and taking LeRoy's arm, the two went aft to the cabin.[113]

Commander Johnston confirmed that fifty-three marks were found on the *Tennessee*'s shield, "three of which had penetrated so far as to cause splinters to fly inboard, and the washers over the ends of the bolts wounded several men."[114] The Confederate ram had inflicted numerous casualties on the federal ships as well. "We were struck ten times in the turrets by the *Tennessee*," Schoonmaker had to acknowledge. "The latter is faster than ourselves & had it not been for the shooting 'way of the smoke stack, she might have escaped us."[115]

Confederate gunfire had found its mark on other Yankee ships as well. The *Octorara*, *Metacomet*, and *Richmond* all received numerous damaging hits, five went through *Lackawanna*'s hull, and five penetrated

Monongahela. Ossipee sported five huge holes, and *Galena* was struck by two 10-inch gun shells.[116]

The Confederate navy suffered a total of 12 killed and 20 wounded in the engagement. Of these, *Tennessee* had suffered 1 seaman, William Moore, and 1 fireman, John Silk, killed and 9 wounded, including Admiral Buchanan. The ram's 133 surviving officers and men were taken prisoner, as were 94 of *Selma*'s crew.[117]

Farragut sent Fleet Surgeon James C. Palmer over to the captured *Tennessee* to examine Buchanan's wounded leg. Dr. Palmer concluded that the admiral's broken leg need not be amputated but might be saved. To ensure that the wounded would receive proper care, Farragut requested that General Page allow a boat under a flag of truce to take the casualties from the battle to Pensacola.[118]

Farragut now determined to take the westernmost of the three rebel forts, Fort Powell, in order to control egress to the Mississippi Sound from Mobile Bay. The *Chickasaw* bombarded the little fort from the rear, but, realizing he could not defend the fort, Fort Powell's commander, Lt. Col. J. M. Williams, ordered the guns spiked and demolition charges set, and he evacuated his men. That night the fort exploded.[119]

Two days later, the commander of Fort Gaines sent a message offering to surrender. Captain Drayton and Colonel Myer went to meet with him and that evening signed an unconditional surrender. Fort Morgan, however, held out. Covered by the guns of the *Lackawanna, Itasca*, and *Monongahela*, federal troops landed in the rear of Fort Morgan and, adding insult to injury, Farragut had the captured *Tennessee* towed into position to assist the monitors in shelling the fort. Days of steady bombardment did not break the Confederates' resolve, and an exasperated Farragut told his wife, "Page is surly as a bulldog, and says he will die in the last ditch." Page said "he could hold out six months and that we can't knock his fort down."[120]

On August 22 the army prepared to open with its batteries, and several Union ships took position to assist in the bombardment. They expected to be more severely punished than on August 5, but "to our surprise, the guns of the fort, on this occasion, did comparatively little execution," Clark wrote. By morning, federal infantry had advanced to within two hundred yards of the fort, and wooden gunboats had moved in to support the ironclads in a joint attack. Fort Morgan then hoisted a white flag, and Captain Drayton went to the fort to meet with its commander and negotiate a surrender, with Fort Morgan's four hundred men becoming prisoners of war.[121]

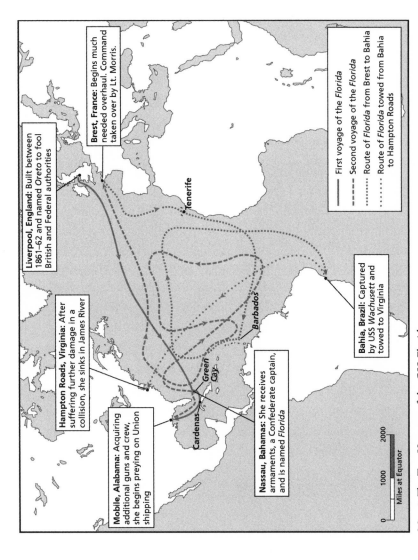

Liverpool, England: Built between 1861–62 and named *Oreto* to fool British and Federal authorities

Brest, France: Begins much needed overhaul. Command taken over by Lt. Morris.

Tenerife

Hampton Roads, Virginia: After suffering further damage in a collision, she sinks in James River

Mobile, Alabama: Acquiring additional guns and crew, she begins preying on Union shipping

Barbados

Nassau, Bahamas: She receives armaments, a Confederate captain, and is named *Florida*

Green Cay

Cardenas

Bahia, Brazil: Captured by USS *Wachusett* and towed to Virginia

First voyage of the *Florida*
Second voyage of the *Florida*
Route of *Florida* from Brest to Bahia
Route of *Florida* towed from Bahia to Hampton Roads

0   1000   2000
Miles at Equator

Map 1. The Two Voyages of the CSS *Florida*

7

Naval Warfare on the High Seas

FINDING THAT PRIVATEERING COULD only go so far to advance the navy's wartime effort, Secretary Mallory turned to a more ambitious strategy: commerce raiding. Mallory hoped to cripple the Northern economy by commissioning Confederate warships to prey on American merchant ships and compel the Northern public to demand that the Union navy dispatch blockade warships to find and pursue them.[1] To implement this strategy, the Confederacy would have to lease or build fast vessels able to remain at sea for long periods of time. These cruisers would be manned by naval officers and, when possible, by Confederate navy seamen who Secretary Mallory counted on to be more loyal to the Southern cause than to the pursuit of riches.[2] The commerce raider's mission was to seek out American-owned vessels with American-registered cargoes, take them as prizes and—after removing the crew, passengers, and useful supplies—burn them. If the cargoes belonged to foreign nationals, the vessels might be released on ransom bond, assuring owners that at the end of the war the Confederacy would pay the value of the vessel.[3]

Over the course of the war and in one instance for months following the end of the conflict, the Confederate cruisers *Sumter, Florida, Tallahassee, Nashville, Georgia, Alabama, Rappahannock, Chickamauga,* and *Shenandoah* implemented Mallory's commerce-raiding strategy. Two prize vessels were also employed as raiders, the *Clarence* and *Tacony.* These raiders captured, destroyed, or sold to foreign owners nearly a million tons of American shipping. They drove up insurance rates, forcing hundreds of vessels to remain in port and sending a substantial number of vessels into permanent foreign registry. One estimate of direct losses in Union ships and cargoes is said to have been $25 million.[4]

Commerce raiding presented Confederate commanders with new challenges: recruiting crewmen, operating within the limits of international law, supplying their vessels with coal and other provisions, dealing with the prisoners taken from prize vessels, and coping with shipboard morale as the war wound down.

Recruiting Crewmen

The CSS *Sumter* had the honor of being the first Confederate commerce raider, converted as a cruiser from the auxiliary screw steamer *Habana,* built in 1859 and purchased by the Confederacy at New Orleans. In addition to four 32-pounders, furnished from the Norfolk navy yard, the *Sumter* carried one 8-inch shell gun placed on a pivot amidships. Chosen as her commanding officer was Raphael Semmes, who had once denounced privateering and commerce raiding, arguing that the crews of these vessels were "little better than licensed pirates."[5]

To recruit sailors for the *Sumter,* a naval rendezvous had been set up in New Orleans attracting more volunteers to ship on Semmes' cruiser than Semmes could receive. "New Orleans was full of seamen discharged from ships that had been laid up," John McIntosh Kell wrote. Kell, who served as the *Sumter*'s first lieutenant or executive officer, had an advantage of picking ninety-two men for the *Sumter*'s crew, but he noted that "although our crew were most of them fine sailors, they were not men-of-war's men and had to be drilled at the guns." The new cruiser's sailors were undoubtedly attracted by the promise of prize money but may also have joined for patriotic reasons. Others were foreigners with no special attachment to the new Confederate States of America. Semmes managed, for example, to ship an English mariner in Curaçao, the first of many foreigners to join the Confederate naval service in foreign ports. The commanders of other Confederate commerce raiders also hoped to convince seamen in foreign ports to join their crews.[6]

Enticing seamen to join Confederate commerce-raiding vessels built or acquired in Britain, however, proved a distinct challenge. Although

Britain's Foreign Enlistment Act of 1819 had been a "vaguely defined law" for forty years, the British government could use this law to protect its neutrality during the American Civil War. The act forbade other foreign powers from recruiting military volunteers including sailors within Britain and forbade its citizens from selling arms and other military hardware to belligerents. Although the Foreign Enlistment Act did not prevent the Confederacy from having vessels built in the British shipyards, it did forbid outfitting these vessels as warships and hampered Confederate efforts to recruit seamen to man the vessels. The limitations imposed by this act led agents like the Confederacy's James Bulloch to turn to secrecy and subterfuge.[7]

The shipyard of William C. Miller & Sons in Liverpool constructed the first of these foreign-built cruisers, the *Florida*. Equipped with a retractable screw propeller to improve her speed and handling under sail, the *Florida* was a schooner-rigged wooden vessel 191 feet long with a beam of 28 feet and a draft of 14 feet.[8] Unlike the American-built and manned *Sumter*, the *Florida* began her commerce-raiding career as an unarmed cruiser named *Oreto* under the command of a merchant captain, James A. Duguid, with an English crew. This was an arrangement conceived by Bulloch to circumnavigate British neutrality laws. On March 22, 1862, the cruiser left for Nassau, where she would take on coal and be joined by her new commanding officer, Lt. John Newland Maffitt, CSN, a consummate navigator known for his skill and courage.[9]

When the *Oreto* arrived in Nassau, the governor balked at allowing her to meet her tender. The *Oreto*'s presence in Cochrane Anchorage caused a good deal of diplomatic maneuvering including prosecution of the vessel in the Vice Admiralty Court of the Bahamas for violation of the Foreign Enlistment Act. A British prize crew manned the cruiser while Maffitt awaited the court's decision. When the court ruled that the *Oreto* had left England unarmed with a merchant crew and thus had not violated the Foreign Enlistment Act, the vessel was released but remained under scrutiny. This naturally hampered Maffitt's endeavors to recruit crewmen or arm and equip the cruiser.[10]

When the *Oreto* finally steamed outside the harbor in Nassau on August 8, 1861, Maffitt took command with just one experienced officer,

Lt. John M. Stribling; a handful of junior officers; and a skeleton crew of five firemen and four deck hands. Once at sea and cruising, Maffitt hoped to entice neutral sailors on Northern ships to fill out his complement, which should have numbered thirteen officers and at least one hundred crewmen.[11]

In April 1862 Raphael Semmes had laid up the CSS *Sumter* in Gibraltar, paid off most of his crew, and sailed for home. Upon reaching Nassau, however, Semmes received orders from Secretary Mallory to go back to England and take command of a new commerce raider being completed in Liverpool, to be named the CSS *Alabama*. Launched on May 15, 1863, as the *Enrica*, she sailed to the Azores where Semmes joined her. The CSS *Alabama*'s crew consisted of about 120 men and 24 officers including Semmes, 5 lieutenants, a surgeon and assistant surgeon, a paymaster, a marine officer, a captain's clerk, and 3 midshipmen. But as Semmes recalled, "None, with the exception of the captain, the surgeon, and myself had even reached the prime of life, . . . they all had the alacrity, enthusiasm and bravery necessary for our haphazardous cruise and steady, ceaseless work."[12]

"As for the crew, they were a mixture," Kell recalled. "With some very fine, adventurous seamen, we had also about fifty picked-up sailors from the streets of Liverpool, that looked as if they would need some man-o-war discipline to make anything of them." Looking back, Kell wrote that he had placed his faith in the adage that "time will show (as time did show), that we had some good material to work upon."[13] By midnight, the CSS *Alabama* had set sail on a cruise that Semmes promised would be "one of excitement and adventure."[14]

As he had done with the *Sumter*, Semmes sought to recruit sailors to fill out his crew from prize vessels. The *Alabama* went on to take many prizes, including the *Thomas B. Wales*, an East Indiaman whose passengers included the former U.S. consul George H. Fairchild, his wife, and three little daughters. The children were made "great pets by the officers and parted from us with regret." The consul's wife was "an Englishwoman of culture and refinement," Kell noted. They gave up their best staterooms to the family, "and they fully appreciated our efforts to make them comfortable."[15] The *Wales* also gave the *Alabama* eleven new men as recruits, several of whom were fine seamen.[16] According to Semmes, they now numbered about 110 men, close to a full complement, which should have been 120. All were rated as ordinary seamen and were the largest number of men shipped from a single prize vessel.[17]

The raider CSS *Shenandoah* needed an even larger crew than the *Alabama*. She started out as the *Sea King* and on October 20,1864,"a day bright and cheering," James Iredell Waddell put the ship in commission as the CSS *Shenandoah*. The new raider had, however, shipped 23 men as petty officers, seamen, and firemen, far fewer than the 150 men needed to properly man her. Waddell hoped that in the absence of Southern recruits, the promise of prize money and adventure would induce British seamen to join the raider. Lt. William C. Whittle joined the new raider as executive officer with lieutenants John Grimball, Francis T. Chew, Sidney Smith Lee, and Dabney Scales. As her surgeon, the *Shenandoah* had Charles Lining and his assistant, Fred J. McNulty.

Waddell informed the crew of the *Sea King*, now named the *Shenandoah*, that she had been sold to the Confederacy and then asked them to step forward to join her. He enticed few volunteers from the vessel's British seamen, who were no doubt exhausted from transferring cannon, powder, shot, and stores from the *Laurel* and probably half drunk on grog. Despite increasing the bounty for joining from ten to fifteen pounds, only one engineer, a fireman, a steward, and two cabin boys took Waddell up on his offer. Five men from the *Laurel* did join the *Shenandoah*, but the rest, fifty men from the *Sea King*, departed.[18]

His officers were all young—Whittle just twenty-four; Chew, Grimball, Lee, and Scales even younger—and with so few crewmen, the *Shenandoah*'s officers had to pitch in. But if caught in a storm or facing an enemy, Waddell feared the raider did not have enough men to cope or even survive. Recalling the fate of the CSS *Florida*—dragged out of a Brazilian port, her men now in Yankee prisons—Lieutenant Whittle advised against putting into Tenerife to recruit more men. They would have to hope to ship seamen from the whalers or merchant ships taken as prizes. Waddell and his officers hotly debated the advisability of setting off on a cruise to the Pacific as a privateer bent on capturing ships of the American whaling fleet with so few crew men. Determined to set off, however, Waddell polled his officers, and all of them voted in favor of carrying on.[19]

After pursuing and overhauling a strange vessel that proved to be British, on October 30 the *Shenandoah* chased and took as her first prize the American bark *Alena* of Searsport, Maine, bound for Buenos Aires with a cargo of railroad iron. A valuable prize, the *Alena* provided the cruiser with gun tackles; a variety of blocks, canvas, and provisions; and five seamen and a coal passer who also shipped, bringing the cruiser's crew to twenty-nine men.[20]

Following repairs, on February 19, 1865, the *Shenandoah* steamed out of Melbourne harbor with additional crewmen, thirty-four American seamen, and eight other foreigners. This gave the cruiser seventy-two men on deck, "all adventurous and accustomed to a hard life." Several were New Englanders, and the men in the group included one sergeant, a corporal, and three privates, a nucleus of a marine guard for the *Shenandoah*.[21]

Operating within the Bounds of International Law

Observing international law hampered Confederate commanders' efforts to recruit seamen and prevented the Confederacy from outfitting and arming vessels built abroad. Confederate commerce-raider captains were also unable to bring prizes into certain ports to sell. For example, on July 24, the *Sumter* departed Curaçao headed for the coast of Venezuela. Within one day they had sighted a sail, the 180-ton schooner *Abby Bradford*, which Semmes forced to heave to and captured, the rebel cruiser's ninth prize. He put a prize crew on board and towed her to Puerto Cabello, but he was forbidden to bring the prize into port and sell her cargo. Learning he was now unable to sell prizes in Spanish or Venezuelan ports, Semmes chose to send the *Abby Bradford* back to a Confederate port. Unfortunately, she was captured near the mouth of the Mississippi River by the USS *Powhatan*.[22]

Meanwhile, the *Sumter* had snatched up her tenth prize, the bark *Joseph Maxwell*. The bark had a neutral cargo, so Semmes sent the prize in charge of Midn. William A. Hicks to Cienfuegos. Unable to take her into Cienfuegos, Hicks headed to sea but sighted what he thought to be a Union warship. In his haste to outrun what was actually a Spanish vessel, he ran the *Joseph Maxwell* aground.[23]

The *Sumter* went on to Port of Spain, Trinidad, the first English port where the governor chose to recognize her as a warship with belligerent rights, eligible to enter port. His refusal to receive Lieutenant Evans annoyed Semmes, as did local press accounts calling his ship a privateer, but the officers and men of the rebel cruiser were undoubtedly pleased by the salute of a British merchant ship.[24]

Obtaining Supplies

Observing international laws also hampered commerce raiders' commanders' ability to procure fresh provisions and replenish their ship's coal supplies. They had to either seize provisions from prize vessels or buy them in foreign ports. But while crews could subsist on a limited amount of food or could fish to supplement their diets, searching for enemy ships and struggling in adverse winds and currents gobbled up the cruisers' coal supply.

Cuba's friendly relations with the Confederacy made that country a haven for Confederate commerce raiders as well as blockade runners. Semmes put into Cienfuegos for coal and when the cruiser *Florida* needed to replenish her coal supply Maffitt, too, headed for Havana, Cuba, where he hoped to obtain the needed coal and winter clothing for his "nearly nude" crew. Enthusiastic crowds greeted the *Florida* the next morning, and "a very strong Southern feeling was exhibited," Maffitt recalled. Anxious to coal and depart before federal blockaders could arrive, he donned his best uniform and went ashore to request from sympathetic authorities the needed supplies. The authorities allowed him to coal his ship, and as soon as the coal bunkers were filled, the eager Maffitt set sail.[25]

Prowling along Cuba's northern coast proved profitable, with the *Florida* snatching up the *Windward*, with a cargo of molasses, and then the *Corris Ann*, carrying timber and barrel staves.

However, a defective supply of coal from Havana forced Maffitt to put into Nassau on January 26. Here, despite vigorous objections from the

U.S. consul, the *Florida* did obtain twenty tons of coal and several new crewmen to replace the twenty-six men, "hard cases," who had deserted.[26]

Maffitt then set off for Green Cay to properly stow supplies, clean the ship, scrape off the whitewash put on at Mobile, and paint her "man-of-war black." Leaving on February 1, however, the *Florida* was sighted and pursued by the USS *Sonoma*. Maffitt ordered two of his broadside guns shifted to the aft-quarter ports and the after-pivot rifle loosed. Then eager gun crews loaded them with shot and fired, the recoil shaking the *Florida* and wreathing her in smoke. Undeterred by near misses, *Sonoma*'s commanding officer, Thomas H. Stevens, doggedly pursued the fleeing rebel cruiser for three hundred miles until on February 2 he lost sight of the *Florida* in the dark. Once again Maffitt had deftly eluded the enemy.[27]

Over the next few months the rebel cruiser, now painted black, continued to elude pursuers and take prizes, one of the largest the *Jacob Bell* with a valuable cargo of "choice tea, camphor, chow chow, etc. valued at $2,000,000 or more."[28] On February 25, 1863, the *Florida* put into Bridgetown, Barbados, where Maffitt appealed to James Walker for permission to coal, stating that the severe wind had damaged the ship and caused her to run entirely out of coal. Although the governor was uneasy about allowing it, he did acquiesce.[29]

In one instance the need to find a supply of coal landed the paymaster of the rebel raider *Sumter* into considerable trouble. Unable to procure coal at Gibraltar, Semmes sent the paymaster, Henry Myers, and a friend, a former consul named Tunstall, in search of a supply. They went across the strait to Tangier but were set upon by a Moorish mob of soldiers, seized, and "placed in double irons and imprisoned at the American Consulate." Semmes tried to have the men released but to no avail, and the men were shipped back to Boston in irons, a harsh treatment that aroused a feeling of righteous indignation among the *Sumter*'s officers and men.[30]

Commerce raiders' officers and men looked forward to entering port to replenish their coal supplies because it meant time ashore. To A. L. Drayton's disappointment, on May 6, 1863, a sail was sighted from the *Florida*'s masthead, squelching Drayton's hope the ship was going to put into Pernambuco to have her engine refitted and bunkers filled with coal.

After a few hours chase that morning, "we made her out to be a brig which we overhauled in fine style and she proved to be the *Clarence* from Rio de Janeiro bound for Baltimore." They took the 253-ton brig with a cargo of coffee as a prize and put her captain and crew on board of the steamer. "Our prize crew was put on board for the purpose of wrecking her and then burning her but for some unknown reason to me Capt Maffit changed his mind and put a large crew aboard of her and bound on an unknown expedition." To Drayton's surprise, his name was called to be among the prize crew, "a very disagreeable development" for he wrote, "it interrupted my calculations as I intended on arriving at Pernambuco Landing [to send] a package of letters to England which should have reached home in the course of time."[31]

Unknown to Drayton, the audacious Charles "Savez" Read had asked Maffitt if he might take the *Clarence* and a crew of twenty men to Hampton Roads and cut out a gunboat or an enemy steamer. With the new men on board, a supply of pistols and rifles, and a 12-pound howitzer mounted on the forward deck, the *Clarence* set sail on her mission. From the *Florida*'s quarterdeck, Maffitt raised his right arm in salute and Read dipped the brig's colors. As the *Clarence* pulled away, Landsman Drayton felt that many sailors on the *Florida* thought "that they had seen the last of us."[32]

On June 9 they captured the brig *Mary Alvina*, loaded with commissary stores consigned to the quartermaster at New Orleans. Read ordered her burned. Three days later, off the Virginia Capes, a lookout sighted a black bark in the dim early light and cried, "Sail ho." "This has been a busy day for us we have captured the Bark *Tacony* from Port Royal," A. L. Drayton wrote in his journal.[33] Deeming the 296-ton *Tacony* a faster, more seaworthy vessel, blessed with a cargo of coal for the fleet, Read transferred his crew to her. Before he had completed the task, a sail appeared, the schooner *M. A. Shindler*, which the rebels pursued, captured, and burned. The flames caught the attention of yet another vessel, the *Kate Stewart*, but this time, with their only howitzer afloat in a boat, Read had to bluff. He ordered the *Clarence*'s gun ports opened with the fake black cannons' gray-clad crews poised beside them, a sight that persuaded the schooner's captain to heave to. Read had the *Clarence* set on fire, prisoners put on board the *Stewart*, and headed north.[34]

In November the *Alabama* took the *Levi Starbuck*, a whaler out of
New Bedford, just in time to provide the raider's crew with cabbages,
turnips, and other antiscorbutic foods. The fresh produce was welcome,
for after seventy days at sea, living mainly on a monotonous diet of salt
pork, navy beans, and dried beef, the men were in danger of developing
scurvy.[35] Cruising the Caribbean, the *Alabama* took a good many prizes
in March and April 1863. From two bound for Liverpool, they took forty
tons of coal and a half a dozen recruits and then burned both ships.

After two years of sailing, the *Alabama* needed a proper refit, so Semmes decided to put into Cherbourg, France, which had a naval base. "She
was like a wearied fox, limping back after a long chase, foot-sore, and
longing for quiet and repose. Her commander, like herself, was well nigh
worn down." On June 11, 1864, a French warship escorted the raider to
the three-mile limit, and a pilot brought her into the harbor. Semmes
promptly paroled all of their prisoners and sent them ashore, and the
following day the ship welcomed a stream of visitors.[36]

Two days later, lookouts on the *Alabama* sighted a steamer standing
in to the harbor flying American colors. Semmes recognized her as the
USS *Kearsarge*, with Capt. John Ancrum Winslow commanding. Winslow
had been alerted to the rebel raider's presence in Cherbourg and had
sailed from the river Scheldt for the French port. Gathering his crew,
Winslow had told them he intended to fight the *Alabama*. The bluejackets
responded with rousing cheers.[37]

On Tuesday, Semmes sent Winslow, his former shipmate during the
Mexican War, a challenge to battle. "All hands expecting an opportunity
to exchange civilities with her," George Townley Fullam jotted in his
journal.[38] By all accounts Raphael Semmes was also anxious to prove to
the world that his ship was not a privateer, intended only for attack on
merchant vessels, but a true man of war.[39] Before engaging the *Kearsarge*,
however, the raider captain took his time to drill his gun crew, take on coal,
and have the men practice boarding procedures. Semmes also advised his
men to write their wills. On Saturday night, June 18, 1864, the *Alabama*'s
officers enjoyed a banquet hosted by pro-Southern sympathizers, and the
crew were feted to farewells in local cafes. Semmes then attended Mass at
a small local Catholic church.[40]

Other Confederate commerce raiders had encountered federal block-aders or warships and exchanged gunfire, but the coming engagement between the *Alabama* and the *Kearsarge* was the most closely fought and ultimately unsuccessful for the Confederate States Navy.[41] Word spread quickly that a duel between the two ships was imminent, drawing a large crowd of curious onlookers. The French frigate *Couronne* came after the *Alabama* to ensure the engagement would take place beyond the three-mile limit and, trailing them, the *Deerhound*, a private yacht owned by a wealthy Englishman. As the *Alabama* steamed out to meet her Yankee opponent, her officers and crew must have been weighing the odds. Although the *Alabama* had heavier guns, her full load of coal and a hull covered in barnacles would undoubtedly give the *Kearsarge* the advantage of speed. Yet, Semmes recalled, "My crew seemed in the right spirit, a quiet spirit of determination, pervading both officer and men."[42]

"We commenced the action about one mile distant, knowing the enemy had the advantage of us in his 11-inch guns," Kell explained, "although we had the advantage of range in our 100-pound (Blakely) and 8-inch solid shot." As the two ships drew near, circled and exchanged fire, the *Kearsarge* did indeed prove faster and her fire more effective. Although Lieutenant Kell is said to have moved about directing the men and assessing the damage to his ship, the gun pointers were evidently left to their own devices and may have fired too high.[43]

One of the *Alabama*'s shots did strike her opponent's sternpost but failed to explode, probably because, after so many months at sea, the powder or fuse was defective. Although the *Kearsarge*'s crew had improvised armor from 120 fathoms of chains hung over her sides to afford some protection as well from shot and shell, a 68-pound Blakely shell passing through the bulwarks exploded on the quarterdeck, wounding three of the gun crew.[44]

Shot and shell from the *Kearsarge*, on the other hand, pummeled the Confederate raider, tearing up the bulwarks and decks, killing or maiming her gun crews, and disabling her steering gear. Semmes kept up the fight, calling for Kell to switch to solid shot, but then Winslow ordered the *Kearsarge*'s gunners to aim for below the enemy ship's waterline. Shortly after this order, two 11-inch shells pierced the *Alabama*'s sides. One shell struck the waterline and exploded in the engine room, and the furnaces went out.[45]

Determined to head to shore, Semmes ordered Kell to clear the decks of the dead. The first lieutenant did his best, but when he informed Semmes that the *Alabama* might remain afloat only for another ten minutes, Semmes responded, "Then, sir, cease firing, shorten sail, and haul down the colors, it will never do in this nineteenth century for us to go down, and the decks covered with our gallant wounded."[46] As the ship settled, the crew were told to take an oar, or a spar, and jump overboard. Concerned for the fate of the wounded and those sailors unable to swim, Kell sent Fullam, Wilson, and Howell in a boat over to the *Kearsarge* with some of the injured men. The Yankee victor lowered boats to assist in the rescue efforts, joined by the English steam yacht *Deerhound* and two French boats. The yacht picked up forty-two men and twelve officers, and the *Kearsarge*'s boats rescued four officers, including Arthur Sinclair. When a boat fished Kell out of the water, to his relief he found Semmes pale but still alive in the stern sheets. They were taken to Southampton and the wounded to the Sailors Home. The *Alabama* suffered nine men killed in action and a dozen drowned.[47]

The *Alabama*'s demise signaled the end for other Confederate raiders as well. Two other Confederate raiders, the CSS *Georgia* and CSS *Rappahannock*, had managed to get to sea but were not successful commerce raiders. The CSS *Tallahassee* made two cruises and the CSS *Chickamauga* just one.[48]

By the time of the *Alabama*'s engagement with the *Kearsarge*, the last Confederate raider had been launched and begun her epic cruise. After enjoying much success with the *Florida*, *Alabama*, and *Fingal*, Bulloch wanted but was unable to arrange construction of a number of the most modern warships, 221-foot rams armed with heavy guns in rotating turrets sheathed in railroad iron and teak. He then purchased a "beautiful ship" for the Confederacy, the *Sea King*, a fast sailer suitable for conversion to a commerce raider.[49] Lt. James Waddell was selected to command the new raider and was instructed to "do the enemy's property the greatest injury in the shortest time." He was to sail on a cruise "to the far distant Pacific, into seas and among the islands frequented by the whaling fleet of

New England, a source of abundant wealth to our cruisers and a nursery for her seamen," Waddell wrote in his memoirs.[50]

By the time the CSS *Shenandoah* set sail, the practice of replenishing commerce raiders from prize vessels had become a standard practice, one endorsed by Confederate agent Bulloch, who told Waddell "to live off the enemy's supplies." The rebel cruiser went on to seize and burn the schooner *Charter Oak*, which was amply supplied with preserved fruits, and a thousand pounds of canned tomatoes.[51]

In mid-June Waddell headed into the North Pacific and discovered five whaling vessels. When one of the captains came on board, he said he had heard the war was over but could not present any solid evidence of the fact. The raider's crew clung to the hope that the war had not ended with a Confederate defeat. After capturing ten more whalers, Waddell finally learned on August 3, 1865, from a British captain that the war had indeed ended. He then decided to sail down and around Cape Horn to Liverpool, a voyage of some 9,000 miles that took the *Shenandoah* three months. On November 5, 1865, the raider anchored at Mersey Bay, and the following day the *Shenandoah* steamed up the Mersey River alongside HMS *Donegal*, and Waddell surrendered the ship to Captain Paynter. The British government released her officers and crew, many of whom were British or from British colonies. The *Shenandoah* had sailed 58,000 miles around the globe, captured or sunk thirty-eight vessels, and taken more than a thousand prisoners without suffering a single crewman killed and only two who died of disease.[52]

Prisoners

One of the most pressing problems faced by captains of commerce raiders was the care and feeding of prisoners taken from prize vessels. By the accepted rules of war, the officers and crew of vessels legitimately taken by these raiders were to be given humane treatment and returned to freedom as soon as possible. The prize vessels were often burned or, if they could be brought into foreign ports, sold, but their crews had to be housed on board the raider, transferred to another vessel, or taken ashore.

The care and disposal of prisoners compelled the raiders' commanding officers to seek creative solutions. For example, on September 5 the rebel cruiser *Alabama* took a Portuguese brigantine and then the *Ocmulgee*, a whaler from Martha's Vineyard. They put the American crew in irons. Although the stores and whaling gear were deemed valuable, Semmes ordered the ship burned. Eager to release prisoners taken from the prize *Ocmulgee*, Semmes closed on a small village on the island of Flores in the Azores, put them into three whaleboats, and sent them to land. He figured the men would sell the whaleboats and use the money to subsist until they contacted the American consul on a neighboring island.[53]

On September 8, 1862, the *Alabama* took the prize *Alert*, which had just left New London. This prize gave them fresh rations, which were a welcome addition to the raider's larder, as well as a good supply of winter clothing, "being just what our crew stood most in need of," Kell recalled. "We paroled the officers and crew and sent them ashore."[54]

With the seizure of the *Elisha Dunbar* on September 18, the raider had taken a total of ten vessels in just two weeks. In addition to the promise of prize money, these captures also yielded chronometers, stores, and prisoners. Taking prizes one after the other, however, meant accommodating an increasing number of prisoners on board the raider, a fact Fullam found "irksome." At first prisoners were housed on the main deck with a tent specially rigged for them, but when the weather turned cold, "the prisoners were put below in the forward fire room, it being vacated for that purpose." Fullam took issue with news reports from New York that the *Alabama*'s treatment of prisoners was "worse than dogs." He penned, "Such gross falsehoods annoyed us considerably, as all our prisoners had been treated with every kindness consistent with safety."[55] As Lt. Arthur Sinclair explained, they made the prisoners as comfortable as possible under the circumstances. The prisoners were allowed "free rations (less the spirit part), and their own cooks had the range of the galley in preparing their food to their taste." Women prisoners were given the officers' own staterooms.[56] In early October, Semmes had the prisoners loaded onto a neutral vessel, the *Emily Farnum*, and told her captain to take them to Liverpool. The practice of placing prisoners on board a prize continued.[57]

On occasion a crewman from one of the raider's prizes agreed to volunteer for duty in the Confederate States Navy and join the *Alabama*'s crew. A notable addition was David White, a seventeen-year-old lad who was a slave traveling with his master to Europe. White became a wardroom mess steward and servant of Dr. Francis Galt, the *Alabama*'s surgeon.[58] When they took the prize *Ariel*, with 500 passengers, 150 Marines, and naval officers going to the Pacific squadron, they held her awhile in hopes of getting a smaller ship to take the prisoners. The ladies on board were alarmed, but Semmes sent the boarding officer, Lieutenant Armstrong, back with a promise that no ill should befall them. The ladies "were so won by his courtesy that the fairest among the prisoners began to ask for his bright Confederate buttons as souvenirs of this occasion, and he came back with very few buttons on his uniform."[59]

Morale

Accommodating and caring for prisoners was an ongoing responsibility for Confederate raider officers and men. As the Civil War wound down, obtaining supplies became even more difficult and weariness, tedium, and homesickness set in and morale plummeted on board some of these commerce raiders. A. L. Drayton was clearly becoming discouraged when he wrote, "the general morale of this crowd is at a heavy discount, wonder if we will ever take a Yank? don't believe we will." He longed for some outward-bound vessel to give them some newspapers so he could hear from "the seat of war."[60]

So long at sea, the *Shenandoah*'s men also became despondent. "To know how I feel would give anyone the blues," Lieutenant Whittle wrote. Midshipman Mason's romantic notion of life at sea had been eroded by the constant confinement, deprivation of the company of females, and the miserable diet. He had found his life unbearable but noted that the common sailor had ten times the privations of an officer.[61] Francis Chew lamented, "Our situation is now very peculiar, and very dangerous. The Powers which extended to us the Rights of Belligerents have withdrawn them and excluded us from their ports." He told the men they were now considered pirates "and will be picked up by any man-o-war that happens to see us."[62]

Conclusion

Although it did not disrupt U.S. trade or break the Union blockade of the Southern coast, Confederate commerce raiding proved effective at driving up insurance rates and forcing a number of vessels into foreign registry. The Confederate commanders of these rebel raiders managed to meet the numerous challenges before them, with the *Alabama* and the other raiders destroying some 257 Union merchant vessels. These rebel captains recruited crewmen, supplied their vessels with coal and other provisions, dealt with the prisoners taken from prize vessels, endeavored to operate within the limits of international law, and coped with shipboard morale as the war wound down.

Manning these commerce raiders did not always prove a simple task for, although a naval rendezvous provided seamen for the *Sumter*, subsequent commanding officers had to entice men to volunteer on their raiders or hope to entice men on prize vessels to join the crews. Many of these men were foreigners, attracted by the promise of adventure and prize money; others joined for patriotic reasons. A large number were foreigners who joined the Confederate naval service in foreign ports and had no special attachment to the new Confederate States of America.

The nationality of these rebel cruisers was unrecognized, and neutrality proclamations limited their ability to make needed repairs and obtain supplies, especially coal. As Maffitt wrote of these Confederate cruisers, "She had to do everything for herself, live upon the enemy, and contend friendless and alone against the world."[63] Indeed, U.S. consuls and other authorities issued vigorous objections to allowing Confederate raiders to enter ports to make repairs or procure supplies. Using diplomacy and an occasional bluff, however, Semmes and other rebel raider captains managed to enter foreign ports and procure what they needed.

They also resorted to living off the enemy, securing from prize vessels not only seamen but valuable supplies, chronometers, tackles, and food stores such as pork, ham, beef, flour, crackers, and even a gaggle of sheep, pigs, and geese. Raiders seeking refits or repairs faced more formidable challenges. In one case this led to a confrontation with the Union navy. After two years of sailing, the *Alabama* needed a proper refit forcing Semmes to put into Cherbourg, which had a naval base, but this led to her famous engagement with the *Kearsarge*.

Semmes, Maffitt, Waddell, Read, and their officers learned as well to deal with the influx of prisoners from prize vessels. Taking prizes one after the other meant accommodating an increasing number of prisoners on board, an "irksome" task that increased crowding and consumed ships' stores. Consequently, most raider commanders preferred to put prisoners on prize ships or when possible debark them ashore.

8

Guns, Mines, and Experimental Craft

Navy Gunners Ashore

CONFEDERATE SAILORS AND MARINES served ashore in gun batteries, at naval stations, or in landing parties, but on occasion Confederate navy officers and men were detailed for special service in what became known as the Torpedo Division or as crew on experimental vessels. In the spring of 1862, for example, Confederate sailors and Marines joined their soldier counterparts manning a fort located on a bluff overlooking a bend in the James River seven miles below Richmond. The position commanded the river for miles in either direction, and with a federal squadron poised to advance up the James River, the Confederates were anxious to strengthen the fort, named Fort Darling. The fort boasted eight cannon, including field artillery pieces and five naval guns salvaged from the former USS *Merrimack*, now renamed CSS *Virginia*. Midn. James M. Morgan was among the navy men assigned to a naval battery at what became known as Drewry's Bluff. "It was manned by sailors principally from the gallant crew of the Merrimac," he recalled. "The river had been barricaded by sinking in the channel ocean-going steamship *Jamestown* and several steamboats besides crates made of logs and filled with stone, leaving only a narrow passageway for our own boats." Additional guns from the CSS *Patrick Henry* had been sited just upriver, and obstructions sunk in the river to discourage federal vessels from passing.[1]

The CSS *Jamestown* had run past the batteries at Newport News to Mulberry Island on the evening of April 18, 1862, and then the side-wheel steamer's crew assisted in removing equipment from the Norfolk Navy Yard and bringing it to Richmond. "We made several trips in this service past New Port News without incident or molestation," Midn. Daniel Trigg recalled. "Of course it was done at night." The *Patrick Henry* towed the unfinished *Richmond*, followed by the *Jamestown* with a brig containing guns and ordnance. Eighteen-year-old Trigg had resigned as a midshipman in the U.S. Navy, and after being appointed a midshipman in the Confederate States Navy, he had drilled artillery at Craney Island, served on the New Orleans and Apalachicola stations, at Fort Fisher and Fort Caswell, before becoming a member of the CSS *Jamestown* in December 1861. Known as the "Southern Gibraltar," Fort Fisher was a formidable coast defense fortification guarding Wilmington, North Carolina, with a mixture of 10-inch Columbiads, rifled 32-pound guns, 8-inch Blakelys, and other heavy artillery. Young Trigg and his sailor mates would have been trained and experienced in handling these heavy guns at a time when most army artillerymen were trained to load and fire the light 12-pound howitzers known as Napoleons. No stranger to combat, Trigg had seen action on board the *Jamestown* during the Battle of Hampton Roads and undoubtedly was familiar with the gunboat's battery of 8-inch cannon and 32-pound guns.[2]

On May 8 orders came to move the heavy guns from Mulberry Island Point and Jamestown to Drewry's Bluff in hopes of delaying the advance of Union general George B. McClellan's troops from Williamsburg up the James River. A career naval officer from Alabama, Ebenezer Farrand, had been appointed to command Confederate forces at Drewry's Bluff, which included eight Virginia heavy-artillery batteries and three infantry regiments. Before this could be accomplished, three Union ships, the *Galena*, *Aroostook*, and *Port Royal*, appeared off Mulberry Island. Observing the Yankees, Trigg and the gun crews of the *Jamestown* and the *Patrick Henry* fired back.[3]

Capt. John R. Tucker, CSN, commanding the Drewry's Bluff position, then ordered the Confederate squadron to pull back and sent the

Jamestown on ahead to deliver news of the federals' advance toward Richmond. At City Point, Lt. Cdr. Joseph N. Barney ordered Trigg ashore with a dispatch. The midshipman hurried to a nearby house and requested a riding horse from a woman who, he later wrote, "understood the whole situation and acted as if she were lending a horse to a neighbor for a ride to town or to church." Trigg sped off to Petersburg, where he learned that a train was about to depart for Richmond. Catching the train, Trigg made it to the Confederate capitol and to the navy department but was at first refused an audience with Secretary Mallory. Using his powers of persuasion, Trigg managed to see Mallory, who ushered him into a meeting. "I found [the room] filled with officers of rank and among them was one of distinction with iron gray hair and mustache and whom without introduction or ever having seen him before I recognized as General Lee. He was giving orders to one or another of the officers present and directions as to the fortification of the river."[4]

Lee issued instructions to the officers present as to the placement of guns on Drewry's Bluff, including guns of the vessels sunk as obstructions in the river. Sailors from the squadron would be detailed to man the captured guns as they had experience and training with heavy guns. "I was struck with General Lee's familiarity with every detail and his accurate knowledge of every resource and accessory for meeting the emergency," Trigg recollected. "We went that night on board the 'Jamestown' and down to Drury's Bluff where she was dismantled and sunk in the river and her crew went ashore to mount the guns and man them."[5]

Officers and men from Tucker's six ships set to work with picks and shovels digging rifle pits at the base of Drewry's Bluff and Chaffin's Bluff across the river. The sailors also hauled five guns from the *Jamestown* and *Patrick Henry* up the steep bluff and, as Lt. James Rochelle explained, the guns "were mounted in pits dug in the brow of the bluff."[6] According to James Morgan, "wooden platforms were built at the bottom of them and the guns were mounted on navy carriages with all their blocks and tackle such as were used on board of the men-of-war of that day." Two companies of Confederate Marines, joined by Capt. A. Van Benthuysen's Company B from Norfolk, then went into rifle pits along the banks of the

James on the Drewry's side, and sailors from CSS *Virginia* and the 56th Virginia Infantry on the Chaffin's side.[7]

As it grew light on May 15, Cdr. John Rodgers' federal gunboats came into view just below Drewry's Bluff with the lightly armored *Galena* in the lead. Capt. Jonathan Simms, of the Confederate States Marine Corps, had stationed his command on the bluffs some two hundred yards from them to act as sharpshooters. "We immediately opened fire upon them, killing three of the crew of the *Galena* certainly, and no doubt many more."[8]

From his station at Drewry's Bluff, Midshipman Morgan and the crew manning the battery saw the *Galena*, *Monitor*, ironclad *Naugatuck*, and two wooden gunboats ascending the river. Morgan recalled, "Our drums beat to quarters while we rushed to our stations at the guns. neither Commander Farrand, who commanded Drewry's Bluff, nor Commander Rodgers, who commanded the federal squadron, seemed in any hurry to open fire." According to Morgan, "We in the battery awaited patiently at our silent guns while the *Galena* came up to within four hundred yards of us accompanied by the *Monitor*, the rest of the squadron remaining below the bend seeking its protection from our plunging fire." The *Galena* let go its anchor, swung across the stream, and "brought her broadside to bear to us."[9]

In a leisurely fashion, Rodgers fired a shot to determine the range. "The gun was a signal for the fun to commence," Morgan explained. "It was not necessary for us to find the range, as from our great height we had only to fire down on him; our guns were depressed to such an extent that we had to put grommets of rope over our round projectiles to keep them from rolling out of the muzzles."[10]

Drewry's Battery opened fire on the federal ironclad, and for three hours "we were at it hammer and tongs," Morgan wrote. "The *Galena* was perforated twenty-two times and without counting the shots which struck her without going through her armor. The riflemen of the river-bank fairly rained bullets at her portholes, one of which became jammed, and when a sailor put his arm outside in an attempt to free it, the limb fell into the river amputated by musket balls." The Confederates also suffered casualties. "Although we were supposed to be safe in our covered gun pits perched so high on the bluff, all had not been cakes and ale with us," Morgan wrote. "Several men had been killed and wounded; among them my classmate at Annapolis, Midshipman Carroll of Maryland, had literally been cut in two by a shell."[11]

The guns at Drewry's were the only obstacles between Richmond and the Union squadron, Morgan explained. "A passage had purposely been left through the obstructions in the river for our own boats and it was sufficiently wide and deep for the Federal vessels to have passed through ... and if Commander Rodgers' squadron had not been stopped by the naval battery there was nothing else to prevent them from going on to Richmond."[12]

The CSS *Nansemond* and the Confederate squadron's smaller wooden vessels had been stationed upriver to make a last-ditch attempt to stop the federal ships, but Midn. George Tucker Brooke, who commanded one of the *Nansemond*'s 8-inch guns, recalled giving the order to "cast loose," but the order to fire never came. "The little fleet never fired a shot," he recalled, "although every man stood at his guns ready for battle."[13] Captain Simms' Marines remained at Drewry's Bluff after the engagement with the *Galena*, but Farrand received orders to surrender his command to Brig. Gen. Sidney Smith Lee, the brother of Confederate army general Robert E. Lee.[14]

As a key defensive position, Drewry's Bluff soon acquired eleven more guns, and Capt. Thomas L. Page, CSN, with the rank of army colonel, assumed charge of both the Drewry's and Chaffin's Bluff batteries. By the fall, the bluff boasted fifteen heavy guns and naval pivot carriages, three in the fort, and another trio in an "iron battery" made of earth protected by railroad iron. Upriver from the fort, the rebels placed another seven guns in a line so as to command that part of the James River.[15]

Troops also arrived to defend the position, and throughout that summer of 1862, three companies of Marines labored to construct a permanent base at Drewry's Bluff, which they dubbed Camp Beall after the Marine Corps commandant Col. Lloyd Beall. By January 1863 the camp boasted barracks and eventually two chapels, walkways, and a flower garden. Remembering his time stationed at Drewry's Bluff, Midshipman Morgan explained, "At Drewry's Bluff we lived in tents and were very comfortable. Parties composed of ladies and gentlemen would frequently visit the Bluff and they made it quite gay; besides, by this time, quite a large number of midshipmen were stationed there and they made it lively for their superior officers as well as for themselves."[16] Marines also went to serve as guards at the Richmond and Manchester navy yards and on board vessels of the James River Squadron.[17]

The Torpedo Service

Gun batteries manned by Confederate sailors, Marines, and soldiers continued to be vital to the land and river defenses of Richmond, but to further impede enemy advances up the James River, beginning in May 1862, the rebels constructed river obstructions composed of sunken vessels and wooden cribs filled with stones. One of the vessels sunk in the river was Midshipman Daniel Trigg's ship, the venerable side-wheel steamer *Jamestown*.[18] To further augment the city's defenses, in October 1862 the Confederate government established the Torpedo Bureau at Richmond commanded by Brig. Gen. Gabriel J. Raines and the Naval Submarine Battery Service headed by Capt. Matthew F. Maury. When the aging Maury was sent to Spain to continue his research, his assistant, a thirty-five-year-old Annapolis graduate, Lt. Hunter Davidson, replaced him as head of the service. Initially, the navy assigned him the little tug CSS *Teaser* as his headquarters. When the lightly armed *Teaser* was captured on July 4, 1862, however, the tugboat *Torpedo* became Davidson's headquarters.[19] Under Davidson's leadership, the Submarine Battery Service endeavored to develop more reliable torpedoes detonated by electricity as an effective means of defending Richmond against advances by federal gunboats up the James River. Davidson had experienced the use of a spar torpedo on the *Virginia* and undoubtedly knew of experiments with the submersibles, dubbed the "Davids." As R. O. Crowley, CSN, an electrician in the Torpedo Division, recalled: "Our headquarters were on board a small but swift steam-tug called the Torpedo, and two Parrott rifles were put aboard of her for emergencies." In the cabin of this little steamer they studied, planned, and experimented for months "with various fuses, galvanic batteries, etc. and finally we determined a system."[20]

In the autumn of 1862 they planted three of these copper torpedoes, each containing 150 pounds of powder, in the Rappahannock, below

Port Royal, with the intention of destroying any federal gunboat passing up. "Our plans, however, were disclosed to the enemy by a negro, and no attempt was made to steam over the torpedoes." In December, anticipating Gen. Ambrose Burnside's attack on Fredericksburg, they abandoned their station near Port Royal to avoid being cut off if the federal army should succeed in making Lee retreat.[21] Crowley was ordered to go to Port Royal to save all the wire and galvanic batteries. He arrived at sunset one evening and prepared to transport the materials. "The galvanic battery was charged and the circuit closed, and a tremendous explosion took place, throwing up large columns of water, and rousing the inhabitants for miles round." Needless to say, Crowley and his fellows beat a hasty retreat and, despite muddy roads, reached Confederate lines near daybreak. "Having our system now perfected, we established a torpedo station, some five or six miles below Richmond, by submerging two iron tanks, containing one thousand pounds of powder each, in twelve feet of water, leading the wires ashore, and connecting them with a galvanic battery concealed in a small hut in a deep ravine," he explained. The wires led to a man stationed nearby to watch for passing federal vessels. Two sticks planted about ten feet apart on the bluff, in a line with each other and the torpedoes, marked their position. The watchman was instructed to explode the mines "by contacting the wire as soon as the enemy's vessel should be on a line with the two pointers."[22]

One beautiful clear day, warned by a telegraph wire that a federal gunboat was approaching, Crowley hastened to the first torpedo station, but to his disappointment the watchman panicked and fired one of the 1,000-pound powder tanks when the gunboat was at least twenty to thirty yards distant. "A great explosion took place, throwing up a large column of water to a considerable height, and the gunboat momentum plunged into the great trough, and caught the downward wave on her forward deck. The blow threw a dozen men overboard and damaged the gunboat, but the vessel turned around, picked up the sailors, and fled." The partial success of this attempt at exploding torpedoes by electricity immediately established the reputation of the Torpedo Division, Crowley asserted, and "created great excitement all over the South."[23]

The Torpedo Division now established other torpedo stations. At the station on Turkey Island Plantation, the rebels erected a one-hundred-foot-high tower from which they could see the federal gunboats at City Point. When the federal squadron advanced up the James River to cover the right wing of Gen. Benjamin Butler's army, Crowley recalled, "the federals began shelling our tower, and it was soon demolished, but no one was hurt, as our men took way the telegraph instruments, and rapidly retreated up the river road." Fortunately for the Confederates, the Union boats, which went well ahead of the fleet dragging for mines and wires, found none. "Their grapnels, however, passed over and over our wires, without producing any damage, our lookout, from his concealed station in the pit, noting all the movements of the men in the boats, and hearing every word of command." After a while the federal commander, satisfied there were no mines, ordered the double-ender gunboat *Commodore Jones* on up to Deep Bottom. The gunboat passed over the torpedoes "but our man in the pit kept cool, and did not explode them, because, as he afterward said, he wanted to destroy the ironclad, recently captured by the federals from us near Savannah, Georgia."[24]

As the *Pequot*'s paymaster, Calvin Hutchinson, recalled, the *Commodore Morris* was the leading boat passing over a torpedo in Turkey Bend but it exploded under the *Commodore Jones* and blew her to pieces. "Most of her officers and crew were killed but some coal heavers and firemen standing on the flat bottom of the boat were thrown out unhurt, picked up in the water and were afterwards part of our crew."[25] Acting Master Peter N. Smith, with two comrades from the Submarine Battery Service, had been hiding onshore at Deep Bottom, patiently waiting for an unsuspecting Yankee vessel to come along. Their turn came on May 6, when Smith crossed the wires leading from the galvanic battery to the mine and watched as the gunboat "absolutely crumbled to pieces."[26]

Mines or, in the parlance of the day, "torpedoes" indeed proved more than an annoyance to federal vessels in the James River. "The river is full of torpedoes & our movements are much delayed thereby," Hutchinson wrote. "Eleven of these devilish engines have been taken up in this reach of the river." Some of the mines were large iron vessels, "similar to a steamer boiler, containing 1500 to 2000 lbs of coarse powder, and fixed by means like a can buoy having 60 to 80 lbs powder, attached to a floating driftwood & fired by percussion on coming in contact with anything."[27]

In his report, the USS *Mackinaw*'s commanding officer, Cdr. J. C. Beaumont, stated that *Mackinaw*, *Commodore Jones*, and *Commodore Morris* had gone upriver preceded by boats dragging for mines. Informed by contrabands about torpedoes, Beaumont anchored within five hundred yards of their reported location. While Beaumont maneuvered his vessel to gain a more convenient berth down the river, the *Jones'* captain, acting volunteer Lt. Thomas F. Wade, disregarded the order not to approach the boats and ran over a mine, which exploded instantly, "absolutely blowing the vessel to splinters," Beaumont explained to Lee.[28] According to Crowley's recollection of the events later, "Our man now concluded that the entire fleet would retire, and he determined to destroy the *Commodore Jones*." As she steamed back, she passed over one of the two mines planted in the river. "All at once a terrific explosion shattered her into fragments, some of the pieces going a hundred feet in the air. Men were thrown overboard and drowned, about forty being killed instantly."[29]

In his memoirs, John Grattan relates that they discovered three men running from a clump of bushes on shore. They captured two of the men who were responsible for the mine that struck the *Commodore Jones*. The two prisoners were Acting Master P. N. Smith and Pvt. Jeffries Johnson. At first Johnson refused to reveal the location of other torpedoes in the river, but, Grattan wrote, "when he was informed he would be placed on board the advance vessel and share her fate if she was destroyed he consented to communicate all the knowledge he possessed."[30]

One day after *Commodore Jones* struck a mine in the James, the *Shawsheen* detonated another while searching for a "torpedo," reported by a friendly contraband to be located near Turkey Bend. Acting Master's Mate William Rushmore explained that the *Shawsheen* had dropped anchor just before midday, and her crew began preparing dinner. Then, "at 11:40 a.m. a field battery of four Napoleon guns and two 24-pounder howitzers, with four companies of infantry, suddenly opened fire on us from the woods on the cliff." All hands went to quarters, but the rebel gunfire drove the gun crews from their guns. "We succeeded in unshackling the chain

20 fathoms, when the captain [Charles Ringot] jumped overboard and swam for the south bank," Rushmore wrote. After Ensign Ringot jumped into the water, Rushmore backed the vessel until nearly out of range of the enemy's guns, but not before a 24-pounder shot penetrated the steam drum. Although wounded in the head, Ringot swam toward the vessel, hailed Rushmore, and ordered him to haul down the ensign and hoist a white flag. "I sent a boat for him, but he sank before it could arrive," Rushmore wrote.[31]

According to *Shawsheen*'s acting second assistant engineer, Richard Anderson, who survived, Charles Ringot had been scalded and jumped overboard only "to be killed in the water by a rifle ball, which entered the right eye." Eight or ten of the crew also jumped overboard, attempting to escape by swimming to the south bank, but, according to Anderson, "doubtless many were killed or wounded." The rebels captured and took *Shawsheen*'s remaining personnel, including four officers and twenty-one men, prisoner.[32] The *Pequot*'s paymaster, Hutchinson, explaining that the *Shawsheen* was destroyed near where his ship now lay, concluded, "If it were not for these confounded torpedoes I think we could run by Fort Darling and take them in the rear with the Monitors."[33]

Experimental Craft

Crowley and the Torpedo Division went on to Wilmington, North Carolina, to defend Forts Fisher and Caswell. "Our force was small. . . . It comprised the officer in charge, the electrician and his assistant, two men at each station, two or three telegraph operators, one or two scouts, and the crew of a tugboat, commanded by an executive officer—in all, about fifty men."[34] When the tug *Torpedo* was captured on July 4, 1862, the navy gave her to Torpedo Division chief Hunter Davidson and armed her with two Parrott rifles. Davidson's mission was to employ mines to assist in the defense of the James River. These mines were iron boilers filled with powder and armed with a simple electronic or galvanic fuse.

In the spring of 1864 Hunter Davidson took the offensive and built a semisubmersible, steam-powered torpedo boat. "Sometime in March, 1864, I was ordered by the Secretary of the Navy to report to Hunter

Davidson, who was in charge of the Torpedo Corps of James River, Virginia," Jonathan Curtis recalled. "I superintended, in part, the completion of the building of the boat." Named the *Squib*, the spar torpedo boat was "built, at Richmond, of wood, about thirty-five feet long, five feet wide, drew three feet of water, two feet freeboard, designed by Hunter Davidson, Lieutenant-commander, C.S.N. The boiler and engine were encased with iron, forward of the boiler was the cockpit, where the crew stood and from where we steered her." The *Squib* was fitted with a single impact detonated spar torpedo.[35]

The *Squib* was similar to the *David*-class torpedo boats but had open decks and lacked the *David* class's ballast tanks. The most famous of the *David* boats had attacked and damaged the USS *New Ironsides* in 1863. "About the first of April she was completed," Curtis wrote. On her bow, at the water line, they fitted an oak spar, about six inches in diameter sixteen foot long. To this was attached a chain for hoisting or lowering the spar, and he explained, "on the end of the spar was a tank made of copper, filled with powder; fifty-three pounds; on the head of the tank were six sensitive tubes, either of these striking any hard substance caused the powder to explode." Electrician Crowley designed the "torpedo."[36]

With his new device, Davidson decided to launch an attack on the flagship of the federal blockading squadron, the frigate USS *Minnesota*. As the largest vessel in the Union navy and an old foe to Davidson, the 47-gun frigate was a prime target. On April 6, the *Squib* left Richmond and went down the James River. The crew included J. A. Curtis, acting master; G. W. Smith, acting master; Thomas Ganley, boatswain; H. A. Wright, first assistant engineer; Charles Blanchard, first class fireman; and William A. Hines, pilot.[37]

"After getting below to City Point, hid away until night, then went slowly and carefully down the river. On the morning of the 8th, just before day, went into Pagan Creek and hid our boat in the marsh." At about eleven o'clock, they fixed the torpedo on the spar, "holding it above the water by the tackle," and proceeded down the river for Newport News. Curtis remembered that it was a dark night with light wind to the eastward, and there was a fleet of some ten or fifteen war vessels of different classes off Newport News.[38]

Slipping down the north side of the river hidden in shadows, the *Squib* "crossed the channel to the south and crossed the Frigate *Minnesota*'s bow, lowered away our torpedo six feet under water, starboard the wheel and turned for the *Minnesota*." The tide being ebb, they drifted down abreast of the frigate and, when about 150 yards off, were hailed by the officer of the deck. "Our commander answered, 'Roanoke.' He ordered us to keep off, and we answered, 'aye, aye sir,' but still going for the ship."[39]

According to the *Minnesota*'s log, "The object by this time was steering straight for the ship and coming rapidly."[40] The officer of the deck, Acting Ensign James Birtwhistle, could not make out any oars but ordered the *Poppy* to "see what she was, hailing her three times, and the third time received an answer."[41] When he discovered the object to be a little steamer, he ordered the *Poppy* to run her down, and endeavored to fire a gun at her. Then Birtwhistle told his men to open fire with small arms, the musket balls peppering Hunter Davidson's coat and cap.[42]

"We were then within twenty feet of the ship," Curtis recalled, "pointing for her main chains on the port side. In a few minutes after they fired, the torpedo exploded against her. I shut my eyes, opening them in about a second, I think. I never beheld such a sight before, nor since." Port shutters and water from the explosion filed the air, he recalled, "and the heavy ship was rolling to the starboard, and the officer of the deck giving orders to save yourselves and cried out, 'Torpedo, Torpedo.' The explosion carried away the spar from the bow, and our boat handled quickly." Although the *Squib*'s torpedo had struck the *Minnesota* some ten feet below the waterline, the damage was confined to the shell and spirit rooms.[43]

As the Minnesota rolled to the starboard, we were sucked under her quarter, then she came back to the port and the pressure of the water shoved us off. The second time she rolled to the starboard, I jumped forward on the Squib deck and put my hand against the Minnesota and gave her a shove, so that the ebb tide would catch her on the starboard bow. Our commander gave orders for me to take charge of the boat. I jumped into the cockpit and gave orders to go ahead and hard a starboard.[44]

The *Poppy* tried to run the *Squib* down but failed. Her pilot, Isaac Miller, explained that he rang for one bell to go ahead, but the engine was not started. In fact, it took a half an hour for steam to be raised to allow the tug to move.[45]

"We ran down towards Craney Island for about one mile, then hauled into Nansemond Ridge Shoal Water," Curtis explained, "and proceeded up the river and at daylight went into Pagan Creek up to Smithville, where we lay all day watching for the enemies' boats, but, none appearing, we left that night and proceeded to Richmond."[46] The torpedo had struck the flagship too near the surface to cause serious damage. Nonetheless, for his "cool daring, professional skill, and judgment . . . in this hazardous operation," Secretary Mallory promoted Davidson to the rank of commander.[47]

The *Squib*'s tasks had included towing a new, experimental craft, the *H. L. Hunley*. Early in the war, the Confederates in New Orleans had built a small, three-man submarine, just nineteen feet long and powered by a crank shaft attached to a four-bladed propeller. The CSS *Pioneer* was commissioned in March 1862 but never had to opportunity to attack the enemy. When the city fell to Union forces, the boat was scuttled. A successor, the *Pioneer II*, was built in Mobile but sank in heavy seas. Horace Hunley and other entrepreneurs in Mobile then made another attempt to produce an effective submersible. To fashion the new craft, workmen cut a cylindrical boiler in two and inserted a 12-inch piece of boiler to give it an oval shape tapered at each end by castings. Ballast tanks fitted at either end allowed the boat to be raised or lowered in the water making her a true submersible. The long, cylinder-shaped craft also featured a bared spike for ramming and a torpedo. A crew of seven manned the *Hunley* and turned a crankshaft to propel her at a speed of three or four knots.[48]

Taken to Charleston, the *Hunley* underwent sea trials, proving only that the submersible was a coffin for the all-volunteer crew of the first two trials. Their fate convinced General Beauregard that the experimental *Hunley* should not be used as a true submersible but should be deployed as a surface gunboat. The newest commander of the boat, Lt. George E. Dixon, CSA, facing the daunting task of recruiting a new crew for the

Hunley, boarded the receiving ship *Indian Chief* and managed to entice four men to volunteer for this dangerous duty: James Wick, Arnold Becker, Joseph Ridgway, and Frank Collins.[49]

The *Hunley*'s presence in Charleston was no secret, for the city was abuzz with speculation about a torpedo boat that could dive. From prisoners and deserters, Rear Adm. John V. Dahlgren, the commander of the Union navy's South Atlantic Blockading Squadron, had obtained very accurate information about the rebel torpedo boat. To defend his ships against attack, he had issued strict orders to his blockade vessels to use nets and fenders to prevent the enemy boat from approaching too near and had instituted nightly patrols and calcium lights to illuminate the harbor entrance.[50]

Lieutenant Dixon diligently trained his new crew and set out to prove Beauregard correct. On the night of February 17, 1864, he guided the *Hunley* out of Breach Inlet on an ebb tide, intent upon exploding her torpedo against the USS *Housatonic*. At 8:45 p.m. Lt. John Crosby, an alert lieutenant on the federal ship, spotted a suspicious object on the starboard beam. He asked the quartermaster to look through his glass at what he thought might be a porpoise, but the man reported seeing only "a tide ripple on the water." Suddenly realizing the object was now bearing rapidly down on the *Housatonic*, Crosby ordered all hands to stations, the anchor slipped, and the engine reversed. Now aroused, the ship's officers came to the rail and started firing revolvers and muskets at the craft, but it was too late to stop the *Hunley*, which fastened her torpedo just forward of the *Housatonic*'s mizzenmast. A deafening blast followed, opening a gaping hole in the ship, and she sank in the harbor's shallow waters. Only five of the ship's sailors died, but the *Housatonic* became a total loss.[51]

The gallant little *Hunley* failed to return, but her fate went unnoticed in the city of Charleston for days. Lieutenant Dixon and her crew were finally reported missing on February 19, followed by Beauregard's brief statement the next day. The *Hunley*'s successful attack on the *Housatonic* had, however, proved the potential of rebel torpedo craft to inflict serious damage on federal blockade vessels and had vindicated Dahlgren's concerns and earlier requests for Union torpedo craft to steam around his monitors at night. The twenty-one men of her three successive crews had demonstrated impressive courage in manning this experimental craft, none more than the last crew, knowing the fate of the first two *Hunley* crews.[52]

Historians have not given as much attention to the wartime service of Confederate sailors and Marines who served ashore in gun batteries, at naval stations, or in landing parties as they have given to commerce raiders and naval engagements. As the war progressed, the loss of ships such as the *Merrimack* sent their officers and crews ashore to man gun batteries at Drewry's Bluff on the James River and other locations. The contribution of Confederate navy officers and men detailed for special service in what became known as the Torpedo Division is also less well known, but the Confederate States Navy's experiments with the *David*, the *Squib*, and the *Hunley* semisubmersibles have been the subject of numerous works. The crews of these experimental craft demonstrated impressive courage and helped prove their effectiveness against the Union blockade.

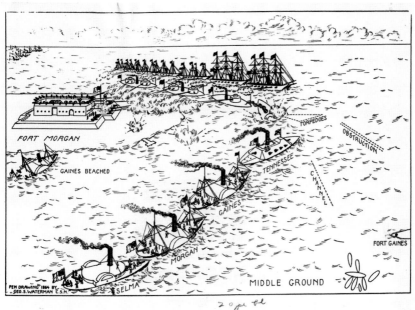

Battle of Mobile Bay, August 5, 1864.

On February 14, 1863, the *Queen of the West*, a side-wheel steamer fitted out as a ram for the Union ram fleet, was taken under fire at Fort DeRussey, forced aground, and captured by the Confederacy.

The explosion of a shell fired from CSS *Ivy* at the USS *Niagara* near the mouth of the Mississippi River on November 3, 1861.

The CSS *Manassas*, a twin-screw towboat converted to an iron ram with an armored convex "turtle back" shield built over her main deck.

Capt. Raphael Semmes and Lt. John M. Kell on the deck of the CSS *Alabama*.

Captain Semmes with his officers on the CSS *Sumter*.

President of the Confederate States of America, Jefferson Davis.

The USS *Tecumseh* hits a torpedo and sinks within sight of Fort Morgan during the Battle of Mobile Bay.

CSS *Manassas* and the USS *Brooklyn* during the battle of Forts Jackson and St. Philip, April 24, 1862.

"THE MANASSES STRUCK US A DIAGONAL BLOW."

The CSS *Manassas* strikes a diagonal blow during the naval battle of Mobile Bay.

The Confederate ram CSS *Arkansas*.

The ironclad *Carondelet*, a *City*-class Union gunboat on the Mississippi River.

Secretary of the
Confederate States Navy
Stephen R. Mallory.

A gun crew firing on a Confederate blockade runner.

9

Naval Warfare on the Rivers

IGHTING THE CIVIL WAR ON western rivers presented the Confederate States Navy with opportunities and challenges. These often narrow, twisting, shallow rivers that were subject to falling water or flooding limited navigation and demanded that the navy's gunboats and ironclads have loyal, qualified pilots. Sandbars and snags in the Mississippi River proved especially hazardous for the larger, deep-draft wooden vessels of both navies. The Mississippi Valley's heat and humidity and the prevalence of fevers proved debilitating for the navy's officers and men, especially sailors serving in fire rooms and engine rooms of the navy's ironclad vessels, who endured temperatures of 120 degrees or more. Furthermore, the pilothouses of these rams and ironclads were particularly vulnerable to enemy shot and shell, inflicting serious injuries and deaths on pilots and officers alike.[1] As illness took its toll, manning these vessels became increasingly difficult, but unlike the Union navy, the Confederates did not resort to enlisting African Americans.[2] Instead, commanders looked to soldiers from the army to fill out their complements and often sought army sharpshooters to help defend their vessels against Yankee attacks.

The Challenge of Opening the Mississippi River

The challenges faced by the Confederate navy meant that Confederate victories on these western rivers were few. Offensively, George N. Hollins' "Mosquito fleet" managed to repulse federal blockaders that attempted to cross the bar and steam up the Mississippi toward New Orleans in October 1861.[3] The following May the Confederate River Defense Fleet's eight rams took the battle to Flag Officer Charles Davis' flotilla as it advanced downstream on Memphis. Engaging the federals at Plum Point Bend, the rebel vessels, called cottonclads because they protected vulnerable parts with cotton bales, inflicted serious damage on the ironclads *Mound City* and *Cincinnati* but took a beating as well. In July 1862 the ram *Arkansas* made a daring attempt to attack the Union fleet, a feat that boosted morale but was actually a defensive measure.[4]

The Confederate States Navy's lack of success in opening the Mississippi River may be attributed in part to the U.S. Navy's greater access to resources and its ability to convert or construct far more timber, ironclad, and tinclad vessels to serve on the Mississippi and other western rivers such as the Tennessee, Cumberland, Arkansas, Yazoo, White, and Red Rivers. Fewer shipyards and a limited supply of raw materials dogged Confederate efforts to construct, convert, and repair their vessels, forcing the navy to fight an uphill battle to maintain control of these waterways and keep the Yankees from splitting the Confederacy in two.

To protect the important port of New Orleans in 1861, the Confederacy did, however, order the construction of several wooden ships, including the twenty-gun *New Orleans*, the eighteen-gun *Memphis*, and the seven-gun *McRae* and *General Polk*. In September 1861 Secretary Mallory authorized the Tift brothers to construct two formidable ironclads to defend Southern harbors, the CSS *Louisiana* and CSS *Mississippi*. The innovative armored warships were to be built in a Jefferson City shipyard a few miles above New Orleans and the *Mississippi*'s engines built by the Paterson Ironworks. The contract for the smaller *Louisiana* went to E. C. Murray, a Kentucky steamboat builder.[5]

Murray and the Tifts managed to find skilled workmen but had to bring timber from Lake Pontchartrain or areas as far away as seven hundred miles, which resulted in numerous delays. To obtain large enough shafts for the *Mississippi*'s engines the Tifts had to bring them in from Tredegar Iron Works in Richmond, Virginia, on a special railroad car. Difficulties in finding materials, engines, shafts, propellers, and other needed items caused further delays, and strikes by laborers and the failure of guns produced in New Orleans compounded delays in the construction of the two warships. Although crews worked night and day to finish the two ironclads, when Adm. David Farragut's fleet steamed up the Mississippi in April to threaten the two forts defending New Orleans, the *Louisiana* and *Mississippi* remained unfinished and not ready to defend the city.[6]

The Confederates had to rely instead on the CSS *Manassas*, commanded by Alexander F. Warley, and the little steamer *McRae*. In September an armed rebel crew under the command of Warley had seized the *Manassas*, which had recently been converted to a powerful ram by the Union navy. Weeks later, in early October 1861, Capt. George Hollins took what became known as his "Mosquito fleet," the *Calhoun, Jackson,* and *Tuscarora,* joined by the newly acquired Confederate ram *Manassas,* down the Mississippi River from New Orleans to attack Union warships, including the twenty-two-gun USS *Richmond* at the Head of the Passes.[7] Blessed with a foggy, moonless night and led by the *Manassas,* they caught the unsuspecting Yankee blockaders by surprise and scored one of the few Confederate victories on the Mississippi River during the war. Warley's ram smashed into the *Richmond,* tearing a hole in her side but also damaging the ram, which then ran aground. By then pandemonium had erupted as the Yankee blockaders fired wildly at their attackers. In what became known as Pope's Run, *Richmond*'s Capt. John Pope panicked and ordered his ships to flee across the bar and into the Gulf of Mexico. Pursued by the Confederate *Preble* and *Water Witch,* Pope's flagship ran aground, as did the *Vincennes,* offering the rebels tempting targets. When Hollins ordered a cease-fire the "Mosquito fleet" all returned to New Orleans and, thinking the *Preble* had been sunk, the attack was declared "a complete success."[8]

The people of New Orleans feted the returning sailors, but Admiral Farragut had not given up his plans to get his large ships across the bar and into the Mississippi and then to run the gauntlet of Forts Jackson and St. Philip. By April 24, 1862, Farragut had accomplished the difficult task of getting his flagship, the *Hartford,* and large wooden warships over the bar and through the mud of the Mississippi. As Farragut, Andrew Hull Foote, Charles Davis, David Porter, and their Confederate counterparts discovered, falling water, sand bars, snags, and debris made navigation on the muddy Mississippi difficult. Western rivers could be shallow, with narrow channels and unpredictable water levels that changed rapidly, stranding gunboats, transports, and steamers. So narrow were some of these rivers that crews occasionally had to uproot trees by their roots so vessels could pass. As one sailor remarked of his gunboat's passage, "It was like traveling thru a woods that had been flooded."[9]

Determined to get his fleet over the bars into the Mississippi and advance on Forts Jackson and St. Philip, Farragut persisted, and on April 24, 1862, his warships steamed up abreast the forts. The first Union ship that Warley saw was the *Mississippi*, which he recalled "was slanting across the river where the *Manassas* was run into her starboard quarter, our little gun being fired at short range, through her cabin and wardroom."[10] The Yankee ship fired over the *Manassas* and "went into the dark." As his ship turned downstream to hit the federal mortar fleet, she passed the forts, which opened fire on her, with "Fort Jackson striking the vessel several times on the bend with the lighter guns." Warley knew the *Manassas* would be sunk if she became the target of the forts' heavy 10-inch guns, so he turned upstream, colliding with an enemy ship in the dark. "We struck her fairly amidships, the gun recoiled and turned over and remained there, the boiler started, slightly jamming the Chief engineer Dearning, but settled back down as the vessel backed off." At daybreak, when the *Manassas* saw the fleet, Warley ran his ship into a bank "as she had nothing to fight with, and no speed to ram with." He and the ram's crew took to the swamps, thus ending their second wartime encounter with the enemy.[11]

Farragut's fleet went on to pass the forts and to wrest the Crescent City from Confederate control. In the meantime, Foote's Western Gunboat Flotilla had been moving down the Mississippi from Cairo, Illinois, seizing key points on the river for the Union. With New Orleans now in Union hands, Farragut's warships began moving up the river to Baton Rouge, intending eventually to meet Foote's flotilla and take control of the river. A Confederate bastion at Island No. 10 temporarily halted Western Gunboat Flotilla's progress, but on April 24, 1862, Foote's ironclad *Carondelet* ran the gauntlet past Island No. 10, which subsequently fell to the federals.[12]

The Confederate Navy Strikes Back

With the remnants of Hollins' fleet, the Confederates had formed a Confederate River Defense Fleet under James Montgomery to defend Memphis. After clashing with Davis' flotilla off Plum Point Bend, on June 6, 1862, the cottonclads tried to fend off an advance by the federal gunboats now reinforced by the rams of Charles Ellet's fleet. In what was deemed one of the hottest naval engagements on the river, the Confederates lost all but one boat, the *Van Dorn*. The Battle of Memphis cost the Confederate Defense Fleet around 100 men killed or wounded and another 150 captured. The most successful of the Confederate rams built in the west was the CSS *Arkansas*. After initial efforts to construct the vessel failed, the ram's new commander, Lt. Isaac N. Brown, had the unfinished vessel towed down the Yazoo River from Greenwood, Mississippi, to Yazoo City. There the twenty-eight-year-old navy veteran from Kentucky pressed ahead with almost superhuman effort to turn the hulk into a powerful ram. "Her condition was not encouraging," he noted later. "The vessel was a mere hull, no gun ports cut, the engines apart, and no visible evidence of construction." With few facilities available in Greenwood and the river falling, a decision was made to take the unfinished gunboat down to Yazoo City.[13]

Soon after reaching Yazoo City, Brown had two hundred men, chiefly from the nearest army detachment, at work on the deck's shield and hull. He also found fourteen blacksmith forges at neighboring plantations and placed them on the bank to speed up the vessel's ironwork. The ram's crew labeled her a "bucket of bolts," in part because Brown had plated the vessel's 18-inch thick wooden casemate, which sloped at a forty-five-degree angle, with railroad iron. The 165-foot *Arkansas* had a lethal sixteen-foot-long ram, and according to Brown, for armament had two 100-pounder Columbiads, two 8-inch 64-pounder cannon forward, two 6-inch rifles in each broadside, and a pair of rifled 32-pounders astern. A pair of unreliable, low-pressure engines salvaged from the sunken *Natchez* powered twin screws, giving the ram an eight-knot speed, but with a twelve-foot draft, even Brown doubted the ram's suitability for the west's shallow, narrow rivers.[14] Brown compared the finishing, armoring, arming, and equipping of the *Arkansas* within five weeks' working time under the hot summer sun to Oliver Hazard Perry's feat in cutting a fine ship from the forest in ninety days.[15]

On the morning of July 1, 1862, Flag Officer Charles Davis' Western Gunboat Flotilla joined David Glasgow Farragut's fleet anchored above Vicksburg, Mississippi. The joining of these two Union flotillas forced Vicksburg's Confederate commander, Maj. Gen. Earl Van Dorn, to reassess the city's defenses. He then made a straightforward choice, ordering the ram *Arkansas* completed, put under his orders, and sent to attack the Yankee fleets. "It was better to die in action," he argued, "than to be buried up at Yazoo City."[16]

On July 14, in the river below the bar at Sataria, the *Arkansas* cast off and began her journey downstream. The ram went only fifteen miles before a gunnery officer discovered powder from its forward magazine had been dampened by steam from her old leaky boilers. The ram stopped a day to dry the powder. Then Brown ordered the *Arkansas* to cast off, and she steamed on down the Yazoo. At midnight, they anchored to give the crew a few hours of much-needed sleep. Most knew the morning would bring action against the federals. As Lt. George W. Gift recalled, "We were in for it—yes, in for one of the most desperate fights of any one ship ever sustained since ships were first made."[17]

The next day, described by one sailor as a "bucolic, warm and calm day" with good visibility, the *Arkansas* approached the Old River channel, which was actually a lake near the Mississippi River. Fortified by coffee and a cold breakfast, the men were ready for action. "The men of the 'Arkansas' were now all at their stations," Read recalled, "the guns were loaded, and cast loose, their tackles in the hands of willing seamen ready to train; primers in the vents, locks thrown back and lanyards in the hands of the gun captains." The decks had been sprinkled with sand, and tourniquets and bandages were at hand; tubs between the guns were filled with fresh water and down in the berth deck were the surgeons "with their bright instruments, stimulants and lint, while along the passageways stood rows of men to pass powder, shell and shot."[18]

Executive Officer Henry Stevens went about the boat offering words of encouragement, especially to the Missouri and Louisiana marksmen.

"Many of the men had stripped off their shirts and were bare to the waist," Read remembered, "with handkerchiefs bound round their heads and some of the officers had removed their coats and stood in their undershirts." The *Arkansas* chugged down the river, Brown and the crew anticipating the enemy would soon be looking for the ram, unaware the timber-clad gunboat *Tyler* and ram *Queen of the West* had begun to ascend the Yazoo.[19]

Late the previous evening, Flag Officer Charles Davis had sent S. Ledyard Phelps with orders to the *Carondelet*'s commanding officer, Henry Walke, to make a reconnaissance up the Yazoo the following morning. Many of Walke's crew suffered with fever, the curse of duty on western rives, and he had only enough men to man one division of guns, but Phelps complained that deserters insisted the rebel ram would come down on the fifteenth of July.[20]

The *Carondelet* departed before dawn the next morning and two hours later entered the Old River. To Walke's surprise, he spotted the faster *Tyler* and *Queen of the West* passing him. Walke later claimed that Phelps had said nothing about other vessels accompanying *Carondelet* on the reconnaissance, nor that the ram *Arkansas* "was expected to attempt a run through our fleets then anchored above Vicksburg."[21]

The *Tyler* and *Queen of the West* steamed on a mile or so ahead of the *Carondelet*. About 7 a.m., the call "Boat in sight" interrupted the crew's meal of coffee and hard biscuits. Observing the mysterious craft, *Tyler*'s pilot exclaimed, "Looks like a 'chocolate brown' house." Lt. William Gwin, *Tyler*'s captain, immediately recognized the vessel as the *Arkansas*. Gwin could clearly see heavy guns through the rebel ram's open gun ports; because the ram was not flying any colors, he ordered a shot fired at her.[22]

The *Arkansas*'s lookout spotted the federals, and Lieutenant Gift observed the enemy "round a point in full view, steaming towards us gallantly and saucily, with colors streaming in the wind." From the ram's shield, Brown also saw the federal timber-clad and, in the light of the rising sun, two more vessels. With only eight guns, *Tyler* posed less of a threat to the *Arkansas* than the city-class ironclad *Carondelet*, with her thirteen heavy guns, or the armored ram *Queen of the West*. Gathering his officers, Brown said, "Gentlemen, in seeking combat as we now do we must win or perish." Admonishing them to fight their way through the enemy fleet and on no account allow the *Arkansas* to be taken by the Yankees, he told them, "Go to your guns!"[23]

A puff of powder followed by a cannonball whizzing over the pilot-house prompted Gwin to order First Master Shaw on the *Tyler*'s forward gun deck to open fire on the rebel ram. The timber-clad's guns took aim on the *Arkansas*, which returned fire from a pair of bow guns. Gwin had stopped *Tyler*'s engines but now called down to Chief Engineer Goble in the engine room for full speed astern. *Tyler* then commenced backing down the river, Gwin hoping that he would have speed enough to keep ahead of the rebel ram and be able to fight most of his battery. As the *Arkansas* rapidly approached, Gwin rounded down the river and took a position about one hundred yards distant on the port bow of the *Carondelet*.[24]

The *Carondelet*'s crew heard the report of a gun. "I looked through a port to see what caused all the commotion," coxswain John G. Morrison wrote, "and I beheld our gunboat and ram retreating from a most formidable-looking monster which was coming down river in style, at the same time keeping up a steady fire on the Tyler."[25] Walke turned to the helmsman and ordered him to back round and go down the river. *Carondelet*'s engines churned and the stern-wheeler sped down the Yazoo as fast as the stokers could feed the boilers. When *Tyler* came near the *Carondelet*, Walke hailed Gwin and ordered him to go and report the approach of the *Arkansas* to Flag Officer Davis. Gwin shook his head and kept the timber-clad's 30-pounder stern rifle blasting away at the *Arkansas*. Occasionally, the *Tyler*'s broadside battery joined in to support the *Carondelet*. "The gunnery of the enemy was excellent," Gift recalled, "and his rifle bolts soon began to ring on our iron front, digging into and warping the bars, but not penetrating." A cannon ball whizzing past the *Arkansas* killed a sixteen-year-old sailor. The first blood was drawn from Gift's division. "An Irishman, with more curiosity than prudence, stuck his head out the broadside port, and was killed by a heavy bolt which passed the ship." The *Arkansas*'s executive officer, Stevens, was standing near Gift at the time and, fearing that the sight of the mangled corpse and blood might demoralize the guns' crew, he sprang forward to throw the body out of the port, and called upon the man nearest him to assist. "'Oh! I can't do it, sir,' the poor fellow replied. 'It's my brother!' The body was thrown overboard."[26]

For the next hour, the *Arkansas* pursued all three federal vessels, pummeling them with fire from her bow guns. The rebel ram was close astern of *Carondelet*, now steadily gaining on her. Brown's intention was to stand for the *Carondelet* and ram the Union gunboat. According to Gift, "Her armor had been pierced four times by Grimball, and we were running after her to use our ram, having the advantage of speed."[27]

When Walke saw the ram headed straight for *Carondelet* raking his boat with her 64-pounder guns, he avoided her prow, and as she came up the two exchanged broadsides. When the ram swept by, *Carondelet*'s bow gunners gave the *Arkansas* a few rounds. "I got several good shots at her," diarist Morrison claimed, "but I imagine without effect, as her iron-cased sides did not look as if they were broached." As the *Arkansas* steamed past, Walke could see two shot holes in the rebel's side and the crew frantically pumping and bailing.[28]

"The stern guns of the *Carondelet* and the *Tyler* were briskly served on us," Lieutenant Brown had to admit. The *Arkansas* kept bearing down on the two federals, zigzagging and firing her guns. As the Union ironclad's captain recalled, "No vessel afloat could long stand rapid raking by 8-inch shot at such short range." The gun duel proved costly to *Arkansas* as well. A shell from the *Carondelet* (Brown said it was from the *Tyler*) landed at Brown's feet on the hurricane deck and then pierced the forward face of the pilothouse, mortally wounding the pilot, John Hodges, and injuring Shacklet, who exclaimed as he was carried below, "Keep in the middle of the river!"[29]

The range closed, and soon *Arkansas* was barely fifty yards from the *Carondelet*. Realizing that the *Carondelet* was disabled, pilot Brady called to Brown warning him the Yankee ironclad was headed for the bank of the channel and, should they continue to pursue her, that the *Arkansas* could also run aground. Brown knew that on western rivers the advice of the pilot was crucial, so he abruptly shouted, "Hard a port and depress the guns!" As Brown later explained, the vessel drew thirteen feet, and he feared getting increasingly aground and so ordered the helm aport, almost touching the side of the *Carondelet* as the *Arkansas* sheered off. The ram slipped close alongside the Yankee ironclad and, Gift recalled, "It would have been easy to have jumped on board."[30]

Hoping that as they slid past the *Carondelet* his guns could fire, Savez Read called for his gun crews to stand by. The *Arkansas* touched the Yankee gunboat's stern and then ranged up on her starboard side. The *Carondelet*'s coxswain, Morrison, fired the last shot he could at the *Arkansas* and "came forward just as she poured her broadside guns into us, which stove in our plating as if it were glass. She then ran across our bows and left us."[31]

The *Arkansas*'s fire had cut the federal gunboat's wheel ropes and destroyed steam gauges and water pipes. Realizing that *Carondelet*'s engine room had been hit, Walke ordered the ironclad run aground and she nosed into the willows and mud of the lake's east bank. In his journal, Morrison recorded the cost of their encounter with *Arkansas*. "I now had time to look around and I found that we had four killed, sixteen wounded (some very severely) and twelve missing, all in one short hour's fight."[32]

From the *Tyler*, Lieutenant Gwin assumed the *Arkansas* would pause to take the Pook turtle as a prize, but instead the ram pressed on downstream. Gwin managed to keep a lead of two hundred or three hundred yards on the *Arkansas* for a time, but then the ram began gaining on *Tyler*, its bow guns raking the timber-clad's stern. Gunner Herman Peters' stern gun crew kept firing on the rebel ironclad, but their shots merely bounced off the ram's sloping sides. Gwin remained grimly determined to outrun the *Arkansas*, but shot and shell from his pursuer began taking its toll. So far *Tyler* had lost thirteen men killed, thirty-four wounded, and ten missing in the fight with *Arkansas*. The sharpshooters gave as good as they got, however, forcing *Arkansas*'s captain, Brown, to take cover below. As he headed for the hatch, however, a minié ball grazed his temple and he collapsed unconscious to the gun deck below. Gift ordered several sailors to carry the captain to sick bay, but he awoke and to everyone's relief discovered neither the minié ball or the fall had caused him serious injuries.[33]

The rebel ram continued to pound *Tyler* with her guns and, as Gwin watched, a rebel shot took pilot John Sebastian's left arm clean off. He crumpled to the deck in a pool of blood as the second pilot, David Hiner, took the wheel. Although struck eleven times by enemy shot and shell and pummeled by grape from the rebel ram, the *Tyler* continued on downstream, her stern gun crew blazing away at the rebel ram.[34]

As the *Arkansas* steamed down river, Brown had the opportunity to inspect the engine and fire rooms, where he found the engineers and firemen had been suffering under temperatures of 120–130 degrees. A relief party assembled by Stevens had allowed the men to rotate in and out every fifteen minutes, but the connection or breechings between the furnace and the smoke stack had been shot away, allowing flames to enter the gun deck, the temperature soaring to 120 degrees. "With the breechings gone and the stack riddled by fragments and minnie-balls, the furnace was losing its draught and steam pressure to the boilers was dropping alarmingly," Brown wrote.[35]

Early that morning, the *Tyler* finally turned out into the Mississippi River at Tuscumbia Bend. Lieutenant Gwin ducked out of *Tyler*'s pilothouse to the welcome sight of the federal fleet, which he supposed would be alerted and give the *Arkansas* "a warm reception," Coleman recalled. "This was not the case."[36] The Union squadrons had been caught by surprise. None of the commanding officers of Farragut's ships, Davis' ironclads, or Ellet's rams had anticipated the *Arkansas*'s arrival. Most had only enough steam up to maintain their engines, and the appearance of the rebel ram had caught them all napping.

Swept along by the Mississippi current, the *Arkansas* approached the federal fleet. "It seemed at a glance as if the whole navy had come to keep me from the heroic city," Brown recalled, "—six or seven rams, four or five ironclads, without including one accounted for an hour ago, and the fleet of Farragut generally behind or inside this fleet."[37]

Hoping to reach the shelter of Confederate batteries on the bluffs, the *Arkansas*'s captain had decided to steam rapidly through the Yankee fleet. As they advanced, the line of fire seemed to grow into a circle constantly closing. "The shock of missiles striking our side was literally continuous, and as we were now surrounded, without room for anything but pushing ahead, and shrapnel shot were coming on our shield deck twelve pounds at a time." Brown then went below to see how the Missouri backwoodsmen were handling their 100-pounder Columbiads. "At this moment I had the most lively realization of having steamed into a real volcano, the *Arkansas* from its center firing rapidly at every point of the circumference, without fear of hitting a friend or missing an enemy."[38]

The *Arkansas*' rifled guns managed to foil a feeble attack by a ram on her stern, but Union infantrymen on the shore began aiming at the *Arkansas*. One bullet knocked Brown off the platform where he stood, breaking a marine glass in his hand. Without flinching, he resumed his place directing the ram's movements. When a seaman called out that the colors had been shot way, Scales dashed past Brown up a ladder, ignoring a hail of fire, to bend on the colors again.[39]

Keeping to midstream, the *Arkansas* ran the gauntlet of broadsides from federal vessels anchored on either side without suffering any damage. The *Hartford*'s gunners eagerly watched for the smoke to lift so they could get a shot at her, but the *Arkansas* passed by the flagship and then turned to.[40]

When the *Arkansas* came to the end of the line of enemy ships, Brown called his officers up to take a look at what they had just come through and to get the fresh air. "As the little group of heroes closed around me with their friendly words of congratulations, a heavy rifle-shot passed close over our heads; it was a parting salutation, and if aimed two feet lower would have been to us the most injurious of the battle." Yet, he noted, although not yet in sight of Vicksburg, none of the Union fleet followed them. With that, and to Farragut's "mortification," the battered and hammered *Arkansas* steamed on to the Vicksburg wharf and the protection of Confederate batteries.[41]

The soldiers and citizens of Vicksburg greeted the *Arkansas*' arrival with shouts of joy. General Van Dorn quickly dashed off a telegram to President Jefferson Davis announcing *Arkansas*' safe arrival and assuring him that the ram would "soon be repaired, and then ho! for New Orleans." When Van Dorn went on board the *Arkansas* to speak to Lieutenant Brown, however, his elation turned to dismay and shock. The ram's smokestack looked like a nutmeg grater, and the sides were peppered with shot and the boats cut away. Much of the ram's gun deck still showed signs of the battle with blood, hair, and brains splattered everywhere and arms, legs, and headless trunks lying about. The exhausted Brown explained that the federals' shot had found weak places in the ram's armor, and their shrapnel and minié balls had come through the portholes.[42]

The *Arkansas'* accomplishment had impressed her adversaries. The rebel ram had "successfully run through a fleet of sixteen men of war, six of them ironclad, and mounting in the aggregate not less than one hundred & sixty guns," Anthony Francis O'Neil commented. "A far more brilliant achievement than that accomplished by the 'Virginia' at Hampton Roads."[43]

The *Underwriter*, February 24, 1864: "One of the most brilliant episodes of the war"

The offensive spirit had taken hold of Confederate sailors and Marines in North Carolina as well. In late February 1864 Cdr. John Taylor Wood led a Confederate boat expedition composed of 15 officers and 100 sailors and Marines up the Neuse River to attack a Yankee gunboat lying close inshore under the protection of two forts at New Bern, North Carolina. Wood's expedition was part of a larger Confederate operation to secure railroad lines and to gather supplies in eastern North Carolina. Gen. George Pickett, in overall command of this operation, had assembled 13,000 troops supported by Wood's naval force of more than a dozen wooden vessels.[44]

"Our object was to attack the gunboats & take them while the army attacked the land forces," Lt. Richard H. Bacot explained.[45] Wooden cutters needed for the expedition arrived by rail from Kinston and two heavier launches from Wilmington, manned by navy volunteers reporting in at Kinston from stations at Richmond, Charleston, and Wilmington. A navy department telegram in January had summoned what surgeon Daniel B. Conrad described "as four boats' crew of picked men and officers, who were to be fully armed, equipped and rationed for six days." Their mission was so perfectly secret and well guarded, he noted, that they did not learn their destination until arriving at Kinston. Knowing they were to report to Commander Wood at Weldon, Surgeon Conrad suspected that it would be "nervous work."[46]

Lt. Benjamin P. Loyall, commandant of midshipmen at the Confederate States Naval Academy, commanded four cutters manned by veteran sailors from the James River Squadron. Confederate midshipmen also participated in this daring raid. Acting midshipmen Richard Slaughter, Paul H. Gibbs, and John B. Northrop were detailed to the expedition, and Parker and Loyall chose William F. Clayton, Henry S. Cooke, J. Thomas Scharf, Daniel Murray Lee, and Palmer Saunders. Each cutter was manned by ten seamen and two officers, warmly dressed in pea coats and armed with cutlasses, revolvers, and a few with axes. This cutting-out expedition also included Confederate Marine Corps captain Thomas S. Wilson commanding the contingent of twenty-five Marines armed with Enfield rifles.[47]

"I have just returned from a long but exciting expedition," Lieutenant Bacot told his sister in a letter written from Charleston shortly after the expedition. "When we left here we didn't know how long we would be gone or where we were going to. We took 75 men & 5 officers to Wilmington NC where we were joined by 35 men and 4 officers where we also shipped 2 launches with Howitzers & two small boats."[48] On a brisk late January morning, Loyall's cutters slipped out of Richmond and headed downstream to Petersburg to meet Wood in the predawn hours the next day. At Kinston, Bacot explained to his sister, they met Wood's ten boats carrying 125 men.[49]

In the meantime, Lt. George W. Gift had assembled a pair of boats and two heavy launches, one armed with a 12-pound howitzer, and set off to meet Lt. Philip Porcher's volunteers from Charleston at Goldsboro. From there the two continued by train to a rendezvous with Wood at Kinston on January 31, 1864. The boats from Wilmington and Charleston were dragged to the river, and Wood departed with the boats to join the James River contingent a few miles downstream at an island camp. When Wood reached the camp, he summoned the 150 sailors and Marines and divided them into two groups. As Surgeon Conrad remembered it, he then issued instructions to each boat crew, stating that the object of the expedition was to board one of the enemy's gunboats supposed to be lying off the city of New Bern, "now nearly sixty miles distant from where we then were by water."[50]

The expedition moved silently to the muffled oars down the river, Midshipman Scharf recalled. The Neuse River broadened, then narrowed until the party could almost touch the trees on either side. "No signs of life appeared, just an occasional flock of wild ducks, and hour by hour, the boats still sped on, the crews cold and weary, but yet cheerful and uncomplaining."[51] Night fell, and they did not reach New Bern until 4 a.m. on February 1. With daylight nearing, Wood led his little flotilla into a backwater stream to allow the men to rest. They had pulled sixty miles almost uninterruptedly and were exhausted. Here Wood communicated with General Pickett and learned that during the day his troops had driven the enemy inside of their works around the town.[52]

All the next day the men rested while Wood and Loyall reconnoitered the harbor where they discovered just one federal gunboat anchored off the town of New Bern, the 325-ton gunboat *Underwriter*. Wood reported that the gunboat carried a battery of two 8-inch shell guns, one 30-pound rifle, and one 12-pounder howitzer as well as a crew of seventy-two men and, according to her watch bill, twelve or fifteen officers. The side-wheel steamer seemed ripe for the picking, so Wood decided to attempt to board and seize the gunboat.[53]

An attack on the unsuspecting Yankee gunboat would have to be made stealthily under the cover of darkness, for the vessel lay just five hundred yards from a Union battery. Wood divided his boats into two divisions, one led by himself and another by Loyall. Each boat had grappling hooks, and Midshipman Scharf's boat sported the small howitzer. They would advance on the enemy vessel in two columns, Loyall's aiming to strike aft of the paddlewheel and Wood's men to aim forward. Gift's launches would bring up the rear as reinforcements.[54]

At sunset Lieutenant Gift joined with the launches and they started down the river again, pulling for the gunboat's position. The two columns of boats rowed downstream and then paused to receive final instructions and a fervent prayer from Wood. A light rain began to fall, and the men could hear the ship's bell from the *Underwriter* striking four bells. Guided by the sound, the boats pulled toward the steamer with, Scharf wrote, "pistols, muskets and cutlasses in readiness." "Suddenly when about three hundred yards from the *Underwriter*, her hull loomed up out of the inky

darkness." A watchman on the Union gunboat hailed "Boat ahoy!" No one
gave a reply. They could hear the sound of the rattle calling the federal
sailors to quarters and could see the dim and shadowy outline of hurrying
figures on deck. Wood shouted, "Give way!" and Loyall repeated, "Give
way, boys, give way!" and the respective boat commanders gave way with
a will.[55]

Now alerted, the Yankees opened fire on the advancing rebel boats
with muskets and pistols, but Wood and Loyall's men bent to their oars
and Marines standing in the bows returned fire with their Enfield rifles.
Surgeon Conrad recalled the dramatic moment. "Our coxswain [in
Woods' boat], a burly, gamy Englishman who by gesture and loud word,
was encouraging the crew, steering by the tiller between his knees, his
hands occupied in holding his pistols, suddenly fell forward on us dead,
a ball having struck him fairly in the forehead."[56] Rudderless, the boat
swerved and hit the wheelhouse instead of the gangway, "so that the next
boat, commanded by Lieutenant Loyall, had the deadly honor of being
first on board."[57]

The rebel boats struck the *Underwriter* just abaft the wheelhouse. The
Underwriter's defenders, which Third Assistant Engineer G. Edgar Allen
claimed numbered only forty men, fired at the attackers with loaded pistols. "It seemed like a sheet of flame, and the very jaws of death," Loyall
wrote. "Our boat struck bow on, and our bow oarsman, James Wilson,
of Norfolk, caught her with his grapnel, and she swung side on with
the tide." Loyall and Engineer Emmet Gill went up over the rail first,
but a hail of bullets felled Gill. Wood's men boarded the *Underwriter*,
and Gift shouted for Scharf to open fire with the 12-pounder howitzer.
The midshipman quickly pulled the lanyard, sending canister into the
gunboat's pilothouse.[58]

"Now the fighting was furious, and at close quarters," Loyall wrote.
"Our men were eager, and as one would fall another came on. No one fal-
tered or fell back. The cracking of firearms and the rattle of cutlasses made
a deafening din."[59] The Yankee sailors began to fall back across the deck,
slippery with blood and rain. Dr. Conrad could hear Wood's stentorian
voice giving orders and encouraging his men. The *Underwriter*'s crew had
gathered in the ways just aft of the wheelhouse and poured volley after

volley of musketry into the attacking Confederates, "each flash of which reddened the waters around."[60]

The *Underwriter's* engineer, Allen, reported that they repelled their assailants successfully for fifteen minutes but were then overpowered. The rebels captured all the men and some of the officers on deck and drove the remainder down into the wardroom, "where they followed with cutlasses and revolvers, demanding us to surrender, which, as nothing could be gained by resistance, we did."[61]

Acting Master Westervelt, the *Underwriter's* commander, was wounded and escaped, as did a number of her crew who jumped overboard and swam ashore. Several others managed to escape in the captain's gig. The Confederates took some of the Yankees prisoners but lost two men, Midshipman Palmer Saunders and Engineer E. J. Gill. They were "most promising young officers and a loss to the service." Two sailors, William Hawkins and Anthony Sullivan, and marine Bell, were killed in the attack, "excellent men, tried and faithful," Wood told secretary Mallory.[62] According to Lieutenant Bacot, "We lost 4 killed—poor Midm Saunders among the number & 16 wounded & 4 missing. We took 26 of the enemy (6 officers and 20 men) the rest killed or jumped overboard."[63] Nineteen years old, a Virginian native, Saunders had accepted an appointment in the Confederate navy as an acting midshipman in 1861; he served at Drewry's Buff and on board CSS *Chicora* before taking part in the *Underwriter* expedition. He was killed by a cutlass blow. "He was a mere boy," William Parker recalled, "but a gallant one. The seaman who killed him—a petty officer of the *Underwriter*, and fine fellow himself—told a friend of mine after the battle that he very much regretted having to do so, seeing his youth; but Saunders and another midshipman attacked him with such impetuosity that he was forced to cut him down in self-defence."[64] First Assistant Engineer Edwin James Gill, a member of the crew of CSS *Richmond*, died of his wounds three days after the attack.[65]

In his report, Wood explained that they had made preparations to get under way and to tow the *Underwriter* off with the launches but were unable to save her. Wood ordered the wounded and prisoners put into the boats, but just as they were boarding, the guns of Fort Stevenson opened fire on the vessel. The first shell went through the port wheelhouse and signal box and burst, wounding several of the enemy. Then, as Gift explained, they were compelled "to abandon and fire her and thread our way back from under the forts."[66] The Confederates returned up the river to their rendezvous, and at 5 a.m. the *Underwriter's* magazine exploded and she burned to the water's edge.[67]

In the meantime, General Pickett's three-pronged offensive at New Bern had come to naught, and by February 4 all his units had fallen back to Kinston. "The army failed to take advantage of this [cutting-out expedition or raid] & attack the front thereby losing the only chance of a fight with land forces unassisted by gunboats," Bacot explained.[68]

The Confederate navy's brown-water sailors could claim only a few victories in the Mississippi Valley campaign, and raids such as the one that captured the *Underwriter* had proved costly to the rebels. Confederate sailors had found that service on the rivers could be arduous duty. Although occasionally boring, duty on board the cramped, noisy, and often damp or uncomfortably hot vessels could tax the most patient sailor. Furthermore, the Southern climate was not conducive to good health, and the men found cotton bales poor protection against enemy shot and shell, especially for those officers and men stationed in vulnerable pilothouses.

10

Prisoners and Prison Camps

A	T THE END OF THE CIVIL WAR, the officers and crew of the CSS *Webb* were taken captive and sent to Northern prisoner of war (POW) camps. Their experience mirrored that of other Confederate naval personnel who risked capture if their ship surrendered, sank, or had to be destroyed. If unable to make their way to shore or be rescued by other Confederate ships, sailors from these vessels were likely to be taken prisoner. Union forces captured several Confederate States Navy vessels during the Civil War including seven ironclad, steam-powered batteries, the *Atlanta, Baltic, Columbia, Eastport, Missouri, Nashville,* and *Tennessee* as well as the unfinished *Texas.*[1]

Confederate naval personnel who became POWs were confined in federal prison camps alongside Confederate army personnel sharing the same regimen, rations, boredom, deprivations, and the possibility of suffering serious, even fatal illnesses. Confederate POWs incarcerated in federal POW camps endured conditions similar to Union POWs confined in Confederate POW camps, who also suffered from overcrowding, poor rations, lack of clothing, and a variety of medical ailments.

Accounts of naval engagements by Confederate sailors during the Civil War are rare, but George Hardcastle, a carpenter's mate, gave the *Savannah Republican* a firsthand report of the capture of CSS *Atlanta* on June 17, 1863. That day the *Atlanta* attacked three federal ships in Wassaw Sound, Georgia, the ironclad monitors *Weehawken* and *Nahant* and the side-wheel steamer *Cimarron*. Hardcastle recalled, "The Weehawken was attacked first. The shot was fired by the Atlanta, from her bow pivot gun,

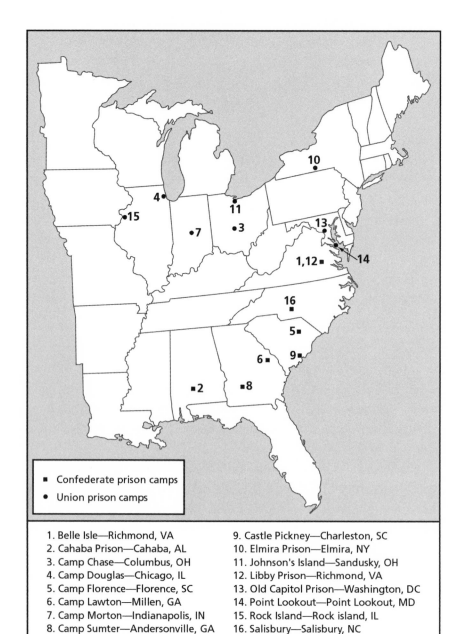

Map 2. Locations of Civil War Prisons

■ Confederate prison camps

● Union prison camps

1. Belle Isle—Richmond, VA
2. Cahaba Prison—Cahaba, AL
3. Camp Chase—Columbus, OH
4. Camp Douglas—Chicago, IL
5. Camp Florence—Florence, SC
6. Camp Lawton—Millen, GA
7. Camp Morton—Indianapolis, IN
8. Camp Sumter—Andersonville, GA

9. Castle Pickney—Charleston, SC
10. Elmira Prison—Elmira, NY
11. Johnson's Island—Sandusky, OH
12. Libby Prison—Richmond, VA
13. Old Capitol Prison—Washington, DC
14. Point Lookout—Point Lookout, MD
15. Rock Island—Rock island, IL
16. Salisbury—Salisbury, NC

followed immediately after by a second." A 15-inch shot from the federal monitor "struck the Atlanta in the starboard side, three feet aft of the pilot house, driving in the iron plates, shattering the woodwork on the inside of the casemate, and wounding 18 men—one of whom (Barrett) died in about two hours from the effects of his injuries." The *Atlanta* fired its broadside gun, and *Weehawken* replied, doing no injury. The two exchanged shots and then the *Weehawken* fired one "which struck the pilothouse, demolishing it and wounding two of the pilots (Austin and Hernandez)."[2]

With the pilothouse broken up and only one pilot uninjured, the *Atlanta* ran aground. Seeing the ship disabled prompted William A. Webb, the *Atlanta*'s captain, to order her colors struck and a white flag to be run up. The *Weehawken* fired another shot, but it did not take effect. "Capt. Webb jumped on the spar deck and hailed the Weehawken, saying 'I surrender.' Capt. Rodgers of the Weehawken stated to Capt. Webb that he would not have fired on the Atlanta after the flag was hauled down but from the fact that he could not make out what our flag was. It was white, and they took it for the blue or black, on account of the smoke." Hardcastle recalled that the *Atlanta* was "in an awful state. . . . The wounded were lying on all sides. It was impossible to get the men from their guns to look after them, until Capt. Webb said to his men, 'I have given up the ship.' The fight lasted about thirty minutes."[3]

Fifty-eight of the *Atlanta*'s men surrendered and became POWs. Placed in handcuffs, they were taken on board the steamer *Cimarron* and divided into two groups. The officers were invited to take breakfast on board the two Union monitors and then the *Cimarron* took all twenty-two officers and the remaining crew on to Port Royal, South Carolina. The *Island City* transported the wounded men to Hilton Head, South Carolina.[4]

By the time the *Atlanta*'s officers and men became POWs, the prisoner exchange and parole system had effectively ceased. After the parole system was abolished, detention in a stockade, military prison, or POW camp was the fate of most Confederate navy officers and crew captured by the Union during the war. Both combatants, Union and Confederate, confined POWs in military prisons, stockades, camps, or pens, of which

150 are known to have existed on both sides during the Civil War. In 1903 Adj. Gen. F. C. Ainsworth estimated that 194,743 Northerners and 214,865 Southerners were captured and confined in these facilities, and that more than 30,218 Union and 25,976 Confederates died in captivity, or about 12 percent held captive in the North and 15.5 percent in the South.[5]

At one time or the other during the Civil War, the U.S. government housed prisoners at camps or prisons in Illinois, Ohio, Delaware, New York, Missouri, Tennessee, Kentucky, Maryland, Virginia, the District of Columbia, and Massachusetts. Studies have been made of the well-known prison camps—Elmira, Camp Chase, Point Lookout, Johnson's Island, and Forts Warren, Lafayette, and Delaware, but historians know little of the experience of prisoners and conditions in most of the other federal prisons and prison camps. Although Confederate States Navy and Marine Corps personnel were held prisoner in some of these camps, no complete listing of individual officers, sailors, and Marines exists.[6]

Arrival

Few firsthand accounts of naval prisoners have survived, but those written by Confederate army prisoners offer glimpses into the typical life of a Confederate prisoner at these camps. One of the first steps taken by the federal government regarding POW camps was to establish strict rules and regulations governing camp administration and the safety of prisoners. Federal prison officials were required by the laws of war to feed, clothe, and provide POWs with the necessities of life. The exact amount and kind of rations, clothing, and living quarters, however, became the provenance of the quartermaster general and, in time, the commanding officers of each POW camp.

Federal POW camps were guarded, and prisoners were not allowed to leave the camps. To ensure the safety of prisoners and those who guarded them, prisoners were required when they entered a camp to hand over their arms, a roll of their names was taken, and officers were separated into different messes from the enlisted men. Prison camp rules allowed prisoners to keep small amounts of money to purchase food and supplies, other than intoxicants, from licensed private merchants called sutlers, who had purchased a commission to sell articles to POWs, but commanding officers administered any larger amounts of money sent to prisoners. In most cases only close relatives were permitted to visit prisoners.[7]

The rules and regulations for Northern prison camps may have varied slightly from camp to camp, but those for Camp Morton in Indianapolis offer specific details of one such facility. Prisoners at Camp Morton were divided into divisions and a chief selected from each division. A prisoner confined at Camp Morton would quickly learn that these chiefs were responsible for the general appearance, policing, and welfare of their divisions. A prisoner would be read a list of crimes and misdemeanors that warned him that prisoners might be punished for counterfeiting a commandant's, doctor's, chaplain's or adjutant's signature for requisitions, or making improper use of premises. Selling to the sutler any article issued to him as clothing, appropriating items belonging to others, or insulting a sentinel might also bring down the wrath of the prison authorities. A newly arrived prisoner would soon realize that life at the camp was strictly regulated. Camp Morton officials set the times for the issuing of tobacco, reading material, and stationery and for mail being given out. The officer of the day conducted a daily inspection to ensure that "facilities will be afforded for sports and athletic exercise also conducive to health as well as bathing by companies." To many a soldier's or sailor's dismay, the rules at Camp Morton forbid cursing and abusive language as well as climbing on fences or trees.[8]

One of the first federal facilities to be designated a POW camp during the Civil War was Fort Warren in Boston Harbor. Built as a coast defense fortification in 1833, Fort Warren was initially used as a training camp and as a place to incarcerate smugglers and political prisoners. Following the fall of Fort Hatteras in 1861, one hundred Confederate POWs arrived at Fort Warren, and more arrived over time. The prison facility there confined a total of 2,307 prisoners during the war, but only a dozen died while confined at the fort.[9]

Among those early POWs at Fort Warren was Engineer James Tomb. Following the Battle of New Orleans, Tomb and six of his engineers with fourteen other naval officers surrendered and were taken on board a newly converted New York ferryboat, the USS *Clifton*. Union navy commander

David Dixon Porter ordered them held in close confinement and allowed the prisoners to go on deck just twice a day "for indispensable visits." Recalling their journey, Tomb wrote, "From New Orleans, we were sent to Fort Warren, Boston Harbor, via Key West, as they would not parole any of the naval officers, after the destruction of what was left of the fleet." They stopped in Pensacola and found things in bad shape, "as the Yankees were in full possession."[10]

Engineer Tomb's reception at Fort Warren may have been similar to that of prisoners arriving at other facilities, such as Fort Lafayette. "On his arrival at Fort Lafayette, he is delivered to the charge of Lieut. Wood commanding the post," the *New York Times* explained to readers. "All the money from his person is taken by the commanding officer, and a receipt is given for the same. He is then introduced to his quarters, which are situated on the ground floor, or one or other of the casemates, in which the prisoners sleep."[11] Men captured on privateer vessels, however, received different treatment, the article claimed. They "are still in shackles, and are confined during the day and night under strict guard. They share the same food as the soldiers of the fort."[12]

Discipline

Federal POW camps were guarded, and disciplinary measures taken by guards at these camps varied. Initially, Camp Chase had few rules. Officers were allowed to take an oath and wander through the nearby city of Columbus, register in hotels, and receive gifts of food and money. By the time John H. King reached Camp Chase in 1864, however, the facility had assumed the appearance of a penitentiary. "The walls surrounding the prison ground were very high, twenty feet at least, and well lighted at night. On a platform near the top, sentinels were pacing to and fro and never out of sight of each other or the prisoners."[13]

Camp Chase and the other prison camps had a proscribed regimen for its POWs. By June of 1864, for example, officials at Fort Delaware had established a strict routine for the camp's ten thousand prisoners. Lights out was called at 9 p.m., but a globe remained lit all night at each division of the prison. A chief superintended the dining room, held meetings, and kept order. A postmaster attended roll call, a postmaster brought the mail, and a money clerk attended money call. Although prisoners were allowed to receive letters, any money enclosed was taken, recorded, and sutlers' checks issued for the cash. Divisions were divided into messes of eight to ten officers each. Fort Delaware's strict rules were enforced by guards, which author Muriel Joslyn argues were "trigger happy" and "most prisoners suffered humiliation and mistreatment at the hands of their captors."[14]

Confederate prisoners confined at Point Lookout, Maryland, also complained of mistreatment by prison guards. On the southern tip of the peninsula, Point Lookout prison, known as "the Point," was the largest federal POW camp. Fourteen-foot-high walls surrounded the forty-acre camp, and African American guards kept watch on a walkway on the top of the walls day and night. One prisoner remembered that these guards were insolent and cruel.[15] Confederate naval personnel detained at Ship Island, Mississippi, also experienced humiliation by African American guards. CSS *Selma* crew member John Bragg recalled the black soldiers "who jeered us with oaths and such remarks as 'Bottom rail on top now.' Some even laid their hands upon us, but were thrust back by our white guards who threatened to run them through with their bayonets if they molested us."[16]

The black guards assigned to the federal Ship Island prison were men of the 74th U.S. Colored Infantry. They are remembered by some prisoners as making the prisoners' lives difficult. "Our wretched condition was aggravated by the brutality and insolence of negro guards," Bragg recalled. He claimed that the white officers accompanying the guards never disciplined them for mistreating prisoners, the exception being an Irish lieutenant named Poilet who "treated the prisoners with humanity."[17]

According to Bragg, overall conditions at the Ship Island camp were miserable. The prison camp administration refused to issue clothing to new arrivals, but "as the Navy men we were better off, in the way of clothing, we did not suffer as much." Fires were not permitted, which only added to their suffering. Bragg recalled they were also tormented by insects: "We could not have water to kill the vermin which swarmed over us and almost ate us up alive. . . . We moped about all during the day and passed the cold nights upon our beds of rush grass."[18]

Often bored, hungry, ill clothed, or concerned about family at home, some prisoners did attempt to escape from federal prison camps, with a few successes. POWs were entitled by military code to try to escape, but guards were expected to prevent such escapes and authorized to shoot anyone caught scaling fences or tunneling out of the prison. One of the most common means of escape for prisoners was to dig their way out, using table knives, large bones, or iron bars to excavate tunnels. Others dressed in Union army uniforms and attempted to slip out when on work or roll-call parties. Only twenty of the ten thousand prisoners held at Johnson's Island in Lake Erie during the war managed to escape. One, Lt. William Triplett, did leave the island but was recaptured on October 31, 1864, and dispatched to another prison.[19]

Rations

The food served to prisoners at these federal POW camps varied. A prisoner at the Old Capitol Prison in Washington, D.C., said they were well treated, "and the rations were all we could wish." At Fort Delaware in May 1864, meals consisted of ordinary bread and coffee for breakfast, bread and meat for dinner, and plain bread for supper. The food was of good quality, they wrote, but not always tempting to a fickle appetite, although one prisoner noted the food was as good as the Confederate army's average ration. Sailors serving on board commerce raiders and other vessels without access to fresh meat and vegetables would have found prison food similar to their meager navy diet.[20]

Others remembered the food at Fort Delaware was badly cooked, of inferior quality, "and scarcely sufficient in quantity to sustain life." Breakfast was at 8 a.m. and dinner at 4 p.m. Breakfast consisted of a cup of water, about four ounces of light bread, and sometimes pork. Dinner was a small amount of bread and meat and a pint of bean soup. One prisoner recalled, "The soup was generally burned, and always made of old beans, altogether, it was the most nefarious stuff I ever tasted."[21]

In July 1864 the expansion of the camp yard at Johnson's Island gave prisoners the opportunity to plant gardens and supplement their diets, but most federal POW camp prisoners did not enjoy such a luxury.[22]

Clothing and Gifts

Prisoners at federal POW camps were issued clothing, and many received gift boxes from family and friends. The clothing issued and the regulations concerning gifts varied from camp to camp over the course of the war. According to Camp Chase prisoner Anderson, "Every Prisoner was issued one blanket, one changing of under clothing and one suit of common grey pants and coat." This proved to be a minimal allotment of clothing given the poor conditions at many federal prison camps and the severity of northern winters. Those prisoners without money to buy clothes suffered at Camp Chase in Columbus, Ohio, and the prison camp at Elmira, New York, from a lack of warm clothing, especially during the bitterly cold winter of 1864–65.[23]

Prisoners with means at the Elmira prison camp, however, could order or purchase additional clothing and buy from the prison supply room "stamps, writing materials, tobacco, cigars, pipes, combs, hair brushes, tooth brushes, clothes brushes, scissors, thread, needles, handkerchiefs, soap, pocket looking glasses and matches." In December 1864 newspapers and candles were added to the list of items that prisoners at Camp Chase were allowed to purchase.[24]

At most camps, prisoners purchased goods from sutlers. Although many unscrupulous sutlers earned a reputation for selling poor-quality items at inflated prices, they were often the only option for prisoners to acquire fresh food and dairy products, since their funds were taken upon arrival and most prisoners in these camps were forced to purchase items only from the sutler. "When we first entered the prison we were allowed to purchase certain articles of food from the prison sutler, and ... we would have to pay several hundred per cent more for what we did get than the same thing could have been bought for with cash elsewhere."[25]

At Johnson's Island prison, a sutler kept a general store and offered to sell fresh fruit, vegetables, butter, milk, writing paper, clothing, tobacco, pipes, and shaving equipment to prisoners who had funds. Prison authorities regulated the prices, and the prisoners kept money at the post headquarters and took orders against their accounts. In the summer of 1864, however, the sutler was removed following accusations of price gouging and was never replaced.[26]

Confederate prisoners could look forward to receiving gift packages from relatives and friends. The commander of the Johnson's Island prison camp allowed prisoners to receive gift packages unless they contained Union uniforms, colored clothing or liquor, but not all prison officials permitted prisoners to receive these much-anticipated gift boxes, which could provide them with needed clothing and food. "They permit vegetables and milk and butter. Clothing, ice, everything but whiskey," Johnson's Island prisoner John Rush recalled, "and I am glad that is forbid to be brought in."[27] Relatives might send prisoners delicacies including fruit cakes, dates, figs, prunes, sugar, boxes of sardines, nuts, lemons, dried beef, cans of blackberries, and tomatoes. Fortunate prisoners might receive a Christmas box with welcome gifts such as blackberry wine, peaches, farina, sardines, shoes, loaf sugar, and candy.[28] Officials at some camps, Johnson's Island in particular, also allowed relatives to send prisoners packages that included reading material. "We are allowed to receive pretty much all kinds of books and magazines," Makely explained to his wife.[29]

Poor Conditions Bring on Illness and Death

Living conditions at federal POW camps varied from year to year or month to month during the war. POWs fared better earlier in the war in some camps, but as time went on overcrowding, inadequate or foul water, reduced rations, and scarcity of clothing took a toll. Most prisoners suffered from dysentery and diarrhea, illnesses not uncommon in army camps and on board ships but rampant in POW facilities, where men often had little access to clean water, nutritious unspoiled food, or proper medical care. The lack of fresh vegetables also contributed to cases of scurvy in these camps, which, while rarely fatal, did tend to weaken prisoners' immune systems and their resistance to other illnesses.

Fort Lafayette, an island fortification in the Narrows of New York harbor, was a convenient location to house political prisoners and Confederate naval prisoners. On September 4, 1861, Fort Lafayette welcomed some Confederate prisoners captured on Hatteras Island.[30] The navy personnel held at Fort Lafayette were fortunate, for prisoners at this facility enjoyed good living conditions. "Fort Lafayette, named by some the American Bastile, is not a bastile at all," explained a report in the *New York Times* on September 24, 1861; "in fact the fort is more like a hotel than anything else, where the proprietor is rather strict and has a wholesome dread of fire, insisting upon all lights being out by 9 o'clock."

Initially, living conditions at Point Lookout were acceptable, although hardly luxurious. However, an influx of rebel prisoners in May 1864 had prompted the camp officials to move the boundary line between the officers' camp and that of the privates, reducing the size of their enclosure. As they were still allowed the privilege of the beach for bathing, at least one prisoner did not find this a serious deprivation, noting "we still have space for tents, streets, mess hall, hospital, etc. without crowding."[31] Among the amenities at Point Lookout was less crowding, more room, punctuality of sending letters, and "good sea bathing."

A prisoner at the Fort Delaware prison camp, describing his quarters, wrote, "We live here in a large barn like barracks, from 75 to 125 in each. The bunks are ranged in here rows like immense shelves, one above the other, on each side, and in some cases across the ends, with some space on the floor between." The "cuddies," as he called them, could be arranged "so as to be quite comfortable."[32] Fort Delaware had an ice cream stand, barracks instead of tents, a decent commander, and less dust. Disadvantages there included "a delay in sending letters, a very rascally sutler who charges triple prices, no opportunity to get 'Copperhead Journals,' no good place to bathe, smaller rations, less room and no opportunity to hire extra cooking done."[33]

This positive picture of prison life at Fort Delaware was not true of all federal prison camps, some of which were overcrowded and the prisoners poorly clothed and ill fed. Over the course of the Civil War, complaints and accusations of poor or inadequate rations and clothing, bad water, incompetent prison officials, squalid, filthy, unhealthy quarters—or none at all—in Union prison camps abounded. Over time, officials and citizens of the Confederacy came to believe that their POWs were being unfairly and cruelly treated. Federal officials ordered inspections of federal prisons, and reports explained much of these accusations as false, but the war of recrimination went on.[34]

Although life as a POW at Camp Chase in Ohio was not especially onerous in the early days, conditions at the camp did deteriorate over time. Poorly built barracks, low muddy ground, open latrines, above-ground cisterns, and overcrowding all contributed to the worsening situation. Most prisoners at Camp Chase were Confederate soldiers, but the prison camp held some Confederate States Navy or Marine personnel, and as the population of the camp grew, rumors about maltreatment of prisoners increased. By 1863 the Camp Chase prison camp housed between seven thousand and eight thousand men. In his study of the prison, Maj. Jack Morris Ivy Jr. states that in January 1865 the camp had been expanded to hold 9,423 prisoners, making it one of the federal government's largest POW camps.[35]

Even in August 1864, when rations were cut, the quality of medical care and sanitation "kept mortality below Union Army deaths from disease." In fact, the disease death rate (in percentages) at the camp was 1.07 in May 1862, 2.77 in December 1864, and 5.30 in February 1865.[36] The most serious challenge for medical personnel at Camp Chase was an outbreak of smallpox in 1863, which spread quickly throughout the prison population. Cold, malnourished prisoners contracted the disease in droves, and 499 died. Although prison officials at this camp gave medical care and sanitation priority, improving hospital facilities, drainage, and waste disposal, prisoners did succumb to pneumonia and to another smallpox epidemic in October 1864.[37] When the first smallpox cases appeared, little could be done to prevent the spread of the disease even among prisoners who had been vaccinated. Prisoners who were discovered to have contracted smallpox were quarantined in what became known as the pest house or "dead house."

For Southern-born prisoners, the cold and snow of an Ohio winter came as a shock at Camp Chase. In late December 1864 a snowstorm brought snow four or five inches deep and then bitter cold. New Year's Eve 1865 was "bright and sunshiny," but more snow fell on January 6; John Wesley Rush noted, "Our prison is full of drifts from two to four feet deep. Such sights as these I have never before seen."[38]

Confederate prisoners at Point Lookout slept in tents until overcrowding became so bad that there were not enough tents to go around.

Extreme overcrowding, freezing temperatures, shortages of firewood for heat, and living in tents led to great suffering and caused many to fall ill or die of exposure. A few of the Confederate States Navy and Marine Corps personnel who died at Point Lookout prison camp are buried in the Confederate Cemetery, including Samuel Bracey, a landsman; George F. Bright, a Marine; Stephen Caul, a Marine; Edwin Cook, a seaman of the North Carolina navy; B. W. Davis, a seaman; W. R. Davis, a seaman; and Ed Dunigan, a navy assistant engineer.[39]

Conditions at Elmira prison camp were also poor. The prisoners lived in houses one hundred by twenty-five feet built of rough lumber and heated by wooden stoves and later by Burnside coal stoves. "Tainted meat appeared more frequently and our pieces of bread was perceptibly smaller," one fellow wrote. Another lamented on December 22, "very cold & dull times among the prisoners suffering much from colds & dying by the dozens per day some freeze."[40]

Fort Warren was a better facility than many prisons. Only a dozen or so men died there, and seven escaped, four of whom were recaptured. Two of the seven escapees were naval officers, Joseph W. Alexander and Charles W. Read, and a third was a Confederate Marine, Lt. James Thurston. Naturally for other prisoners, the death of fellow prisoners caused concern. Thomas L. Wragg, one of the officers captured on CSS *Atlanta*, was sent to Fort Warren. In a letter dated October 29, 1863, he wrote of one death to his father, Dr. John Ashby Wragg, in Savannah: "We lost our Chief Engineer [on the *Atlanta*] Mr. E. Johnston. He died about two weeks ago and was buried on the island."[41]

When overcrowding in the Union prison at New Orleans became a serious problem, federal officials decided to move prisoners to a remote island off the coast. In early October 1864 crowded conditions in the prison coupled with a number of escapes prompted Gen. Edward Canby, commanding the Division of the West, to order all Confederate prisoners except those awaiting exchange or too ill to travel, transferred to Ship Island, Mississippi. The general assigned Capt. Matthew Marston the task of overseeing preparations for the arrival of prisoners on the island, which had no facilities to house them. Four days later, the transport *Warrior* brought the first contingent of prisoners from New Orleans to Ship

Island, without the fifty tents allocated to protect them from the elements. The men spent their first night on the island sleeping in the open on the beach during a raging storm, but a week later their tents arrived, including three hospital tents to accommodate the twenty or so ill prisoners.[42]

On October 21 and 23, 1864, Ship Island received 817 prisoners from New Orleans, and over the next week, 53 noncommissioned officers and privates and 153 petty officers, seamen, and enlisted naval personnel arrived. After the CSS *Tennessee* surrendered on August 5, 1864, 63 enlisted men from the *Tennessee* went to Ship Island, along with 34 of the CSS *Selma*'s crew. By the end of October, Ship Island held a total of 1,292 Confederate prisoners.[43]

The prisoners were confined in a three-square-mile area enclosed on all sides by a two-foot-high embankment "on which negro guards walked and kept watch over us," John A. Bragg, one of the men captured onboard the *Selma* at Mobile Bay wrote in a postwar account. "We were furnished with small A shaped tents but were given no blankets. Most of us, however, had blankets which we spread on the rush grass which we gathered and placed on the ground under our tents."[44] The condition of the Ship Island prison camp improved slightly, but according to the memoirs of a private captured on April 9, 1865, and taken to the prison, "no tents or blankets were issued to us and we had to sleep on the bare ground." Rations issued every morning consisted "of a few crackers and a small piece of beef to each man; occasionally in lieu of crackers, a small amount of corn mush." The water was brackish and undrinkable, and prisoners were not given fuel to make fires to boil their clothes in order to kill the vermin.[45]

Obtaining a reliable water source on Ship Island proved a challenge from the early days when federal troops occupied the sandy island. The Yankees solved the problem easily. "By digging two feet into the sand and setting down a barrel," James Schneider, U.S. Colored Troops, wrote in a letter, "we have a well of sweet water. This white sand is an excellent filter." Although others recalled that they had cool, fresh water, Ship Island was a hot, insect-infested place, and over time living conditions contributed to illness among the Northern troops as well as prisoners. An officer with the U.S. Sanitary Commission sailing with the Union expedition to the island cited "the badness of the food, which was of salt meat (no fresh meat being issued), the badness of the water, and the wretched system of cooking made the presence of the Sanitary commission not undesirable."[46]

More than two hundred Union soldiers, mostly from Maine, Vermont, New Hampshire, and Connecticut, died there and were buried on the island. Of the 4,879 Confederate prisoners who passed through Ship Island, 153 died, a mortality rate of 3 percent.[47]

Entertainment

Surviving life in captivity for Confederate prisoners meant not only securing adequate rations, clothing, and clean water, but also coping with boredom and the lack of exercise and purpose. Most POWs had few duties to perform and sought entertainment to while away the hours. Camp Chase prisoners, for example, spent their time reading, writing, and gaming. Others gambled, fashioned jewelry, or made furniture. As time went on amenities were added to the Johnson's Island prison. A barber shop kept the men's hair and beards shorn, and a theatrical group called the Rebellonians performed a minstrel show charging twenty-five cents admission. A lending library opened in 1864, and prisoners sent the books they had read to the prison librarian. Prisoners with an artistic bent fashioned rings and shell jewelry, and those with carpentry or woodworking skills made canes, stools, chairs, and tables.[48]

Prisoners confined in federal prison camps looked forward to receiving letters from home and endeavored to write encouraging letters to family and friends. However, in 1864 Camp Chase prisoners found the prison censorship frustrating. "Every means was used to prevent our friends outside or at our homes from knowing our real condition," John King claimed. "No letter was allowed to leave the prison that was not read and censored by the superintendent—and his postmaster." He recalled that complaints or appeals to friends for relief were forbidden and nothing that reflected on the management was allowed. To save time reading every letter from hundreds or thousands of prisoners, federal prison camps limited letters to a single page, although some found putting bribes of money in the letters would induce the reader to pass on more pages.[49]

Writing paper and stamps were frequently mentioned and much desired. In their letters to family and friends, prisoners often asked for money or needed items. "When you write send me some postage stamps," Thomas Wragg asked his father. In a response to an unexpected letter from his father in November 1863, he wrote, "I was gratified, however, to hear from you and hope that you will take advantage of every opportunity to write to me, as it is my only pleasure now, to receive letters from home." Wragg did receive postage stamps from his father but in December wrote, "I request that you not make any arrangements for sending me money as we are not allowed (Per Special Order) to purchase any necessaries, therefore, it will be no use to me."[50]

Naturally, prisoners welcomed visits from friends and relatives, although few diaries or letters written by POWs indicate that such visits were permitted or even possible, given wartime travel. However, a letter written by Virginia Dalton in December of 1861 to Commo. Louis Goldsborough has survived. In her letter she implores him to allow her to visit her son, Lieutenant Dalton, who was a prisoner on the *Cumberland*. "I hastened from my far off Mississippi home to see him. He is very dear to me," she said. Hoping the commodore would grant her "a mother's wish" even for a short visit, she penned, "so that I may not have made this long fatiguing trip, having left my younger children at home, without meeting with success." The commodore granted her wish.[51]

Although entertainment was in short supply at the prison camps, the prisoners came up with some creative solutions to the boredom of camp life. Camp Chase prisoners despised the lice that made their lives miserable, but some chose to enliven their prison existence by holding lice races, placing the lice on inverted, heated tin pans "to produce a lively movement of the louse without destroying life." They selected "the most vigorous pedicules" and even named them "Phil Sheridan, Sherman, Pope or Hunter." At a signal the lice were thrown into the middle of the heated pan and the one who reached the edge first was declared the victor in the race. "Surprising thought it may be to you, yet I have seen a room full of grown men thrown into great excitement over these races, at which many an unlucky prisoner would lose a days rations."[52]

One camp held a ball in the open plaza or street of the camp, with the music provided by some of the "graceful and accomplished" prisoner musicians. Some of the prisoners would be selected to represent ladies. "These, to distinguish them from the men, would run strings through the center of their blankets and tie these around the waist." The ball opened with a grand march followed by a graceful waltz and an old Virginia reel "to the infinite delight of the dancers and the entertainment of those who were lookers on. Even our Yankee guards appeared to enjoy the occasion and never interfered to break up the merry dance of our gallant comrades."[53]

Prisoner Exchange

Most Confederate POWs longed to be exchanged. Over time they grew weary of life in a prison camp and with the boredom, cramped quarters, and poor food. Concerned about their families at home and with many of their compatriots ill and suffering as conditions deteriorated, some prisoners became desperate to be exchanged. Thomas Wragg and the officers and men of the CSS *Atlanta*, for example, remained in prison until finally exchanged at Cox's Wharf. During his months of confinement Wragg longed to hear that he would be exchanged. In a letter to his father, he lamented, "There is no prospect of an exchange, and it seems as though we were destined to remain here during the war." In December Wragg told his father, "I see that the officers of the 'Harriet Lane' have all been paroled and are now at Vicksburg, and I think it hard that we should be retained." After learning that Dr. Gibbes from the *Atlanta* had been released and would be in Richmond "so soon," Wragg grew even more desperate. "While I, who was so unfortunate as not to be an M.D. would have to remain behind for an indefinite period. I have serious intentions of devoting myself immediately to the study of 'materia medica' as my only chance, and if that fails, my chances for the war are good."[54]

Prisoner exchanges were effectively discontinued under General Grant in March 1864. With the Union strength increasing and the Confederate war effort dwindling, Grant felt that giving prisoners back to the Confederate army would only prolong the war. On August 10, 1864, the Confederate government proposed to exchange officer for officer and man for man, but Grant refused. He explained that every prisoner released on parole "becomes an active soldier against us at once either directly or indirectly. If we commence a system of exchange which liberates all prisoners taken, we will have to fight on until the whole south is exterminated."[55]

The issue of "negro soldiers" continued to complicate the resumption of prisoner exchanges. On October 1, 1864, a proposal to Grant by Gen. Robert E. Lee for a man-to-man prisoner exchange was met by Grant's asking if the Confederates would deliver "coloured troops the same as white soldiers." Lee refused to agree to the exchange of African American soldiers. Finally, perhaps anticipating the imminent collapse of the Confederacy, Grant accepted on January 24, 1865, another proposal by Lee for a prisoner exchange.[56]

Exchanges of prisoners did not entirely cease when the parole system ended but occurred occasionally throughout the war. As late as November 1864, Confederate prisoners were sent south to be exchanged for Union prisoners. "Last night 1,200 of our exchanged prisoners arrived. They received a warm welcome by our citizens," Robert Watson, serving in the CSS *Savannah*, wrote in his diary. "A fine supper awaited them and I suppose they did it ample justice for the poor fellows have suffered a great deal while in the hands of the Yankees." Three steamers went down the river to bring the rest of the prisoners to Savannah. "These 3,200 men are or were sick when they left the Yankee prisons, and a like number of sick Yankees are to be given in exchange."[57]

Confederate prisoners had the option of taking the oath of allegiance to the Union and being released from prison. The number of men choosing this option varied from prison to prison. An announcement made at Johnson's Island in July 1862 brought only a few officers willing to "swallow the eagle." The following month handbills promoting the offer failed as well to attract oath takers. "Of course we deem the act an insult to the prison," one POW wrote.[58] As Inslee Deaderick explained, "When the men here lose all hope in the success of our cause, and their grit gives out, they apply for the oath and are put in separate barracks, and fed and treated better than the rest of us. We call them 'Calvanized.'"[59]

Enticed by Union army recruiters visiting Point Lookout, Camp Chase, and Camp Morton as well as the Illinois prisons at Rock Island, Alton, and Camp Douglas, thousands of Confederate POWs took the oath of allegiance to the Union and joined regiments designated United States Volunteers. Known as Calvanized Yankees, these men were likely to be posted to duty on the western frontier. A recruiting call at the Rock Island prison camp yielded three hundred men for the Union navy as well. "Their officers all went amongst our men and coaxed, argued, and bribed and commanded all who they could influence to desert the cause of their country and enlist themselves in the ranks of their brutal enemies," William Dillon wrote.[60]

11

Fighting to the Finish

Naval Infantry: Sailors without Ships

As GENERAL SHERMAN'S TROOPS advanced, Confederate naval personnel in Savannah, Charleston, and Wilmington attempted to either defend their ships and shipyards or destroy them to prevent the federals from seizing them. To prevent CSS *Savannah* from being captured by Sherman's bluecoats, the crew was ordered to destroy the ram. Robert Watson's boat crew took the captain and first lieutenant ashore and then set the ram afire. "The Ram blew up at 20 minutes after 11 P.M. We were about 8 miles from the ferry when we heard the explosion. It was terrific. It lit the heavens for miles."[1] Following *Savannah*'s destruction, Watson and his fellow sailors departed *Savannah*.[2]

Days later Lt. James H. Rochelle took command of three hundred sailors, including Watson and Lieutenant Hudgins, and set out for Wilmington. After a journey on board "some dirty old box cars," they arrived in Wilmington and the sailors went by boat to Battery Buchanan, a two-tiered, oval-shaped earthwork commanded by Lt. Robert T. Chapman and located at Confederate Point below Fort Fisher. Lamenting that they had to sleep crowded together on the floor and eat badly cooked food, Watson wrote on December 31, "This day one year ago, I was at Dalton, Ga. and felt confident that the war would be over and I be at home today, but alas am sadly disappointed and God only knows when this cruel and unnatural war will end."[3]

Almost two weeks later, when federal ships opened fire again, Watson received orders to Fort Fisher. "The sailors double quicked up to the fort, the shell bursting around us in large numbers but did us no damage. We manned three guns and commenced firing at 1 P.M. and continued till dark when both parties ceased fire." Despite terrific fire from the Yankee fleet, he explained, "none of our men were hurt except Lieut. Hudgins who was slightly wounded in the mouth with a fragment of shell, and several of us were knocked down with sand bags."[4]

At daylight on January 14, weary from being on lookout all night, the men marched back to Battery Buchanan for a drink of whiskey and breakfast but were sent back to Fort Fisher to man the guns. Watson, posted at a 6.4-inch Brooke rifle, "made some excellent shots." They ceased firing at dark. The federal fleet continued its heavy bombardment on Sunday, "many of their shells exploding near our quarters. One man had a leg cut off and the other broken, he was asleep in the ground tent at the time." At 11 a.m. Watson and his fellow sailors went to the battery but by midafternoon Yankee infantry had advanced on Fort Fisher. They were repulsed three times, but on the fourth charge gained a footing on the left of the works. "Our men fought them bravely until after dark with musketry and contested every inch of ground," Watson wrote. "The slaughter was great."[5]

"As soon as we saw that the enemy had gained a footing and planted their hateful flag on the left of the works we knew that the fort was lost," Watson explained. Chapman chose to abandon it, ordered the sailors to wade out to the boats, but then countermanded the order. "Our battery then opened fire on the left of Fort Fisher with one 11 inch and one 10 inch gun, the other two guns would not bear. Continued shelling until 8 P.M." Finally, two hours later they received orders to cross the river to Battery Lamb. Watson and his fellow shipmates got over safely, but Lt. Hudgins was captured while trying to get into the boat. After a four-mile march toward Wilmington, they halted, built a fire to dry their clothes, and then fell asleep.[6]

At daylight the next morning, January 16, 1865, the sailors resumed marching, but about three o'clock, three of them stopped at a house "and got some corn bread and meat for the small sum of $30.00 from a Negro.

We were very hungry for we left the battery with nothing to eat. This was the fault of the officers who I am sorry to say were all intoxicated." They arrived at the Wilmington navy yard the next day and then were ordered to Fort Campbell, a battery mounting five smoothbore guns.[7]

Robert Watson and his shipmates spent the rest of January at Fort Campbell, moving guns to the battery, drilling, and standing guard at night. On February 17, learning that the Yankees were landing below them, all hands went to quarters, and twenty-seven of the sailors fanned out as pickets. The sailors were poorly trained as infantrymen, Watson explained. "Our officers did not know as much about posting us as a lot of old women, we were scattered all about in the woods and had the Yankees attacked we would have shot our own men."[8]

Two days later Yankee gunboats came up the river and opened fire. "The third shell the Yankees threw came very near killing me and several more." One shell struck the platform, tearing it all to pieces, but sandbags protected the gun crew from injury. The end was drawing near, however, for Watson and his shipmates. In the wee hours of February 22, an officer ordered them to quietly pack up and in the bitter cold the sailors marched through Wilmington, narrowly escaping the Yankees. A train took them to Greensboro.[9]

On the last day of February 1865, they made it to Richmond, boarded a steamboat and went to Drewry's Bluff. "This is a very fine place with plenty of comfortable houses. Our mess was fortunate enough to get a house to ourselves. Fire wood very scarce," he jotted in his journal.[10] After spending the next few days drilling and cutting and carrying firewood in the pouring rain he wrote, "We have nothing to do with the guns in the battery and I begin to think that they intend to put us in the army."[11] The following day, a contingent of officers and 180 men including several of Watson's old shipmates from Charleston joined the other sailors at Drewry's Bluff. With Sherman's forces approaching the city, Charleston had been evacuated on February 17, 1865. Before departing, Engineer E. A. Jack was detailed with a party to set fire to and destroy the *Chicora* to prevent the Yankees from salvaging her. The first ship to explode was the *Charleston*. Her magazine blew up, followed by those of the *Palmetto State* and *Chicora*. Now without a ship, Jack and others of the Charleston squadron took a train out of the city, intending to head for Wilmington, but, he recalled, "before reaching there we learned that that city had fallen too." The men disembarked, and the sailors were organized into a brigade with Commodore Tucker in command. Engineer Jack and his company, jestingly called "Q," took the advance, enabling them to forage and go into camp that night with "chicken, cornbread, and sorgum, delicacies that our superior officers were deprived of."[12]

Company Q's sailors continued on to Fayetteville, North Carolina, where various cars took them to Richmond. Jack was assigned to duty on the ironclad *Richmond*, as senior engineer, but by March 12, he and the other sailors from Charleston were organized into four infantry companies and set to drilling at the Drewry's Bluff battery's guns.[13]

While the sailors practiced being soldiers, Robert Watson went to work in a carpenter's gang building bridges but in his April 6 diary entry wrote they had made a sudden departure: "Heavy firing commenced ahead of us and we found ourselves cut off so we struck through the woods and marched all day in hopes of flanking the Yankees and getting to our command." Soaked by rain and draped in wet blankets, suffering from a severe fever, Watson had halted. Late that afternoon, joined by his friend Alfred Lowe, he crossed the Appomattox River on trees felled across the river, for there were no bridges.

When dawn came the two set out again and marched all day. "Gave pair of shoes to a Negro for as much cornbread as we could get for we were starving." They trudged on and spent that night in a barn. By dark, the heavy firing they had heard ahead of them all day had ceased. On Saturday, April 8, he wrote, "Started at sunrise and traveled about three hours when we fell into the hands of some Yankees who treated us very kindly." For Robert Watson, the war had ended. Just twenty-four hours later, the Army of Northern Virginia surrendered.[14]

The war was winding down as well for other Confederate States Navy officers and sailors serving on board vessels such as the CSS *Neuse* at Kinston, North Carolina. The advance of Union general Sherman's army in March 1865 had forced them to abandon their ship. "My old home the 'Neuse' is gone," Richard Bacot wrote to his sister on March 27, 1865; "all the troops were withdrawn from Kinston & the Yankees 18,000 strong came upon us." With no prospect of being relieved before their provisions gave out, under fire, and unable to work the *Neuse's* guns, "after shelling the Yankee Cavalry for a little while, we removed our powder & stores & burnt the vessel."[15]

Explaining that Sherman was at Goldsboro and that Johnston was trying to force a fight, Bacot lamented, "I have been trying to find out, whether I belong to Navy or Army. I have no ship, live on land, drill at light Artillery & infantry tactics & have been in the trenches at Weldon (that Paradise) which do you think I belong to?"[16] In the final months of the war, many sailors like Bacot, Watson, and Jack found they no longer had ships to serve. In early 1865 Confederate naval personnel from the Charleston, Savannah, and Wilmington squadrons had gone to Richmond to join the naval brigade manning the city's defenses. The James River Squadron, commanded now by Adm. Raphael Semmes, still occupied a stretch of the James River but "were but little better than prison ships," a collection of unserviceable vessels in need of repairs or new torpedo defenses.[17]

In February Semmes' predecessor as James River Squadron commander, J. K. Mitchell, had agreed to a last-ditch breakout attempt to blow up the federal ironclads, clear a passage for the rebel fleet, and force the abandonment of City Point. Battery Wood's commander, Lt. Charles W. Read, led this daring mission, which set out from Drewry's Bluff on February 10 with about a hundred sailors and Marines. The men were carrying torpedo boats on wheels and planned to launch the boats on the James and advance on City Point from below. They hoped to seize any tugs or steamers passing by, arm them with a spar torpedo, and attempt to sink any federal ships, allowing Mitchell's Confederate ironclads to advance to destroy the Yankee gunboats and open the James River to Hampton Roads.[18]

In the only narrative account of the expedition, Master W. F. Shippey explained that the three detachments of the expedition had marched off in freezing weather and for three days traipsed undetected toward City Point. A storm of sleet then forced them to stop, "the sleet being so blinding that our mules could not make headway, besides the road being frozen and slippery." While sheltering in a home near the Blackwater and waiting for the storm to abate, "a young man in a gray uniform came in and informed us that our plan had been betrayed." A regiment of federals was lying in wait for them, "to give us warm reception."[19]

Read then called a council of war and, Shippey explained, "it was decided that we should go back about a mile and find a hiding place in the woods" while Read made a reconnaissance. Read confirmed that the Yankees were planning to ambush them and ordered the men to return to Richmond without accomplishing their objective. "The enemy's cavalry was scouring the countryside in search of us, and every road of retreat was guarded," Shippey noted, but by avoiding the main roads and moving only at night, they managed to elude Yankee patrols and get safely across a ford in the frozen Appomattox River, "our clothes freezing stiff on as we came out of the water." The expedition made its way back toward Confederate lines, which they reached safely, without loss of a man, wagon, or mule.[20]

The advance of Union forces had also sent Midn. Willie Wilson north from Wilmington toward Richmond. After two weeks of marching in the rain, they reached Richmond where they were assigned to duty below Chaffin's and Drewry's Bluffs. Capt. W. B. Ward sent Wilson to a two-gun battery known as Battery Cook about a half mile from the main fort. "Alas, the next morning," he wrote, "the blowing up of war vessels, the smoke from burning Richmond told us it was time to move."[21] They received new orders and, after waiting a few hours, Captain Ward spiked the battery's guns, destroyed the ammunition, and started up the river.[22]

After "a long and tiresome march," Wilson and his fellows came upon the army's rear guard at Amelia Courthouse. The men reported to General Lee's headquarters for orders, and he gave them scant rations out of his commissary wagons. "This is the last time I ever saw our beloved and trusted commander, mounted on 'Traveller,' black broad brim hat, new gauntlet gloves, sack coat with the Col's stars; all the insignia of rank to indicate the commander of the grandest army of heroes that has been seen in modern times," Wilson wrote.[23]

At sundown they set off but then halted "and the harsh roar of field pieces, with the sharp rattle of musketry told us that General Grant was going to dispute our way without waiting for reinforcements for his small army." The rebels formed a skirmish line and marched parallel with the enemy until about the middle of the day, when Sheridan's Yankees charged them "like they were going to ride right over us.... They were in 25 or 30 yards of us when my feet flew up and I fell backwards." Wilson had backed over the rail breastworks.[24]

Midshipman Wilson and his fellows went on a few miles only to find the main Confederate command engaged with the Sixth U.S. Army Corps, "shelling us for a period with 11 guns, charged with grape, canister, and schrapnel [*sic*]. They advanced to the charge. Knee and waist deep in the mud and water of 'Sailor's Creek,' from then until sundown it was one continuous charge. We laying on our faces on the brow of a hill, till they would get close, then rising, we fired in their faces, and they broke and ran." After three of these charges, Wilson heard loud talking, turned and found an enemy soldier pointing a gun at him. "Sheridan's troops had taken us in the rear. That was my last fight in quick order." The Yankees placed the men under guard and marched the prisoners back to Petersburg.[25]

The Naval Brigade

On April 2, 1865, Navy Secretary Mallory had sent Semmes a message informing him that General Lee had advised the government to withdraw from Richmond. With Sherman's army advancing up from Savannah, Semmes had anticipated that the capital would have to be abandoned, but the news still came as a shock. As ordered, Semmes set his men to work preparing to abandon the squadron's ships. Before scuttling or setting fire to the vessels, he decided to move them from Chaffin's upriver to Drewry's Bluff, but the *Richmond* sank passing the obstructions.[26]

Semmes formed his Marines and sailors into a naval brigade. Early on the morning of April 3, 1865, they boarded the remaining wooden vessels and steamed up the James River to Richmond, finding the capital in flames. Semmes managed to get his sailors ashore and ordered them to light the wooden vessels and shove them into the channel. The *Virginia II* had already exploded in grand spectacle, which shook houses in the capital and roused people for forty miles around. PO John T. Chappell, who had served on board *Virginia II*, recalled that after she had been blown up, the crew of the James River Squadron crossed from the north to the south side of the river that night on a bridge hastily built above Drewry's Bluff.[27]

Although ordered to join Lee in the field, Semmes was unable to contact the general. He marched his men to the rail station but discovered the last train had departed. Determined not to fall into the Yankees' hands, they found two abandoned engines, allowing Semmes and the last of the squadron crews to get away just as the federals neared Richmond. "We took an engine out of the Manchester shops of the Richmond & Danville railroad, where it had been sent for repairs," Chappell recalled and "manning it with one of our own engineers—a man by the name of Reams—we coupled up to a number of freight cars and started on one of the most remarkable railroad journeys I ever experienced."[28] After two days, he said, they reached Danville, Virginia, where the ship's crew were formed into batteries of field artillery. President Jefferson Davis and the Confederate cabinet were in Danville. When Semmes' brigade arrived there on April 4, 1865, Semmes was authorized to be a brigadier general in the Confederate States Army, and sailors under his command were transformed into an artillery brigade.[29]

In the meantime, Commodore Tucker's four hundred former sailors and Marines from Charleston and Wilmington had withdrawn from Richmond, forming a rear guard for Gen. G. W. Custis Lee's division. On April 2 Tucker, asking but not receiving orders from Lee, had blown up the batteries' magazine and the following day gone off to join Lee.[30]

Engineer E. A. Jack had spent the night in Richmond, awakening to "ominous sounds of explosions." At the wharves he recalled, "I learned that the fleet had been destroyed & was told that our men were retreating by south bank of the river." Jack started down for Drewry's Bluff but met two other engineers who told him that the main body of crews were marching to Richmond by the North Side. The trio retraced their steps, hoping to catch up to their command. "We could see the smoke and haze of the fires in Richmond, but our hearts were so full of sadness that this did not strike us as being anything unusual." Finding Mayo Bridge in flames and thus unable to rejoin their commands, the men returned to the city only to learn that the naval forces had taken to cars and left the city. "I cannot describe the feeling of desertion that came upon me at this news." Although tempted to stay and surrender to the Yankees, Jack decided to set out to try to find Tucker's naval brigade. A cavalryman who claimed to know the brigade's whereabouts pointed the way, and the men tramped off.[31]

Trudging along muddy roads thronged with refugees and abandoned equipment and harassed by federal cavalry, Tucker's men reached Gen. Richard Ewell's corps at Amelia Courthouse on April 5, 1865. When they joined G. W. Custis Lee's rear guard, Maj. Robert Stiles recalled that his soldiers "were mused by the 'Naval Battalion' as they did not march 'right' and 'left' but to the 'port' and starboard.'" This salty language prompted the army men to dub Tucker's boys the "Aye, Ayes."[32]

On April 6, at Saylor's Creek near Farmville, Virginia, General Ewell deployed his Confederates on the west bank of the creek, the naval battalion taking position to the right of Custis Lee's men. The battle, which was actually three separate actions, opened with an artillery bombardment on the Confederate line behind the creek. When the Yankee bluecoats advanced across the creek, they waved white handkerchiefs at Tucker's sailors, expecting the rebels would surrender, but Tucker barked, "Prepare to repel boarders!" A volley of musketry from the naval battalion broke the Union line and Major Stiles' soldiers charged down the hill, the federals fighting fiercely in what was "one of the fiercest, most hand to hand and literally savage encounters of the war." The soldiers and sailors clubbed their muskets, fired pistols into each other's faces, and used the bayonet "savagely."[33]

Union forces regrouped and made another determined attack, the cavalry cutting through rebel lines, forcing Ewell's Confederates to surrender. Tucker's naval brigade held out and pulled back to thick woods as the battle swirled around them but were finally convinced to lay down their arms. The "Aye, Ayes" fought bravely at Saylor's Creek in the last major engagement between the Southern and Northern armies. As the sailors walked out of the woods, federal troops cheered the men of the naval brigade for their gallantry, then gave them a meal and serenaded them with strains of "The Bonnie Blue Flag" and "Dixie."[34]

Engineer Jack and his fellows had been searching for Tucker's battalion. On the morning of April 6, they had heard the sounds of battle and headed toward it, expecting "to soon find the front of our army and escape from the stragglers." They met an old man who had had a brush with federal cavalry but continued on their journey. "Not long after this I hard some one call Halt! but supposing that it was from my companions I paid no attention to it. Again I heard the command and again was indifferent. Then I caught the sound of saber striking against a saddle. I knew that none of my friends were so equipped." Jack turned to see what was approaching "and to my astonishment saw a Yankee orderly with a pistol pointed at me. He again commanded me to halt, which I did most promptly." Jack and his companions were taken prisoner, and for them the war was over.[35]

Confederates Surrender

Following their defeat at Saylor's Creek on April 6, 1865, the remaining men of Lee's army headed west. The following day under a flag of truce General Grant sent a surrender demand to Lee, but Lee dithered, hoping to make one last, desperate attempt to break out. Two days later, the graycoats lunged at Sheridan's cavalry on a road near Appomattox Courthouse, only to meet a wave of federal infantry. With two Union corps closing on the Confederate rear, Lee reluctantly realized that he was vastly outnumbered and agreed to surrender. Grant's generous terms allowed the rebel soldiers to go home as long as they observed their paroles, and allowed officers and men who owned their own horses to keep their mounts.[36]

Lee's army surrendered, but it took days and weeks for the remainder of Confederate military and naval personnel to learn the war had come to an end and to accept terms. In April and early May 1865, however, as the war came to a close, many Confederate States Navy and Marine Corps officers and enlisted men found themselves faced with the decision of whether to take the oath of allegiance or go to prison. Most went first to federal prison camps or facilities and were then paroled if they took the oath.

Not all of them chose to take the oath of allegiance. Robert Watson, taken prisoner on April 8 by Union troops, refused to "swallow the eagle" or take the oath. At first the Yankees "treated us very kindly," he wrote in his diary. The soldiers marched the prisoners along until sunset and turned them over to the provost marshal. "Remained in lines with many more prisoners until about 8 P.M. when we started with a cavalry guard and marched hungry for I had eaten but one scant meal during the day." The following day they were marched to Burkeville, Virginia, given no rations, and Watson spent a miserable night standing in the rain covered by his blanket.[37] On April 10 the prisoners did receive some beef, which they cooked. "Greet cheering in the Yankee camps, an official dispatch from Grant states that Lee has surrendered. I fear it is too true." At two o'clock on the afternoon of April 14, Watson was paroled and caught a rail car for City Point. Arriving at City Pont, wet and hungry, he had his parole stamped. After waiting three hours in line at the transportation office, Watson obtained passage on a steamer to Fortress Monroe and then to another steamer headed for Washington.[38]

In the capital, Watson wrote, "I went to the Soldiers Rest and got supper. This place is crowded with the Negro and white soldiers all mixed together. There are also many Southern soldiers, the most of them deserters who have taken the oath and waiting for transportation." At 3 a.m. that night he was turned out of the shelter to make room for 1,200 black soldiers. Watson stayed outside in the cold and was told he would have to remain in Washington until authorities brought transportation. The funeral of slain president Lincoln, however, kept delaying it.[39]

"Nearly every man here has taken the Oath of Allegiance," Watson explained. "I don't want to take the Oath but if they send me to prison I will take it for I am satisfied that the South is gone up the spout and it is of no use for me to linger for long time in a prison for no purpose."[40] Still a paroled prisoner, Watson went to the provost marshal under guard, had his parole stamped, and got a pass, but he found he would not receive transportation unless he took the oath. He and his buddy Alfred refused, but they found an old friend who loaned them $25, which enabled them to buy tickets for New York City. There, with another loan from William Pinkney, Watson bought new clothes and passage to Havana, from which he made his way home to Key West.[41]

Confederate naval personnel and Marines captured at Saylor's Creek also briefly became prisoners of war. Midn. Willie Wilson was sent to Washington to the Old Capitol Prison. "We were marched up Penn Ave.

to the old capitol prison. The streets and sidewalks were thick with nicely dressed men and women, who were having lots of fun over our appearance." The mood of Washingtonians changed abruptly, however. "That joy was changed to grief before the next evening. This was the 14th of April and that night Mr. Lincoln was basely murdered. We knew nothing of it and could get no reason for the bells tolling next morning." When the streets began to fill up in front of our prison, the prison commander "told us the mob were going to kill us, and he was powerless to save us. The bricks in the jail yard were up in a few minutes, and we would have [illegible] the cowards with brick bats. Fortunately a regiment of regulars came and dispersed the crowd."[42]

Wilson was sent to Johnson's Island that same month. "Staying in this filthy place 10 days, we were sent to Johnson's Island in Lake Erie, where we swallowed the oath and were turned loose. We were never given as much as we could eat, in Washington or Johnson's Island, and men suffered in both places for food and clothing. And this was after the war was over."[43]

The final months of the Civil War were trying times for most Confederate naval personnel. As the Yankees advanced toward port cities, the Confederates had to destroy their vessels and march off to man forts and gun batteries. In April and early May 1865 many Confederate States Navy and Marine Corps officers and enlisted men found themselves faced with the decision of whether to take the oath of allegiance or go to prison. Some went first to federal prison camps or facilities and, if they took the oath, were paroled, but many of the sailors and Marines in prisoner of war camps suffered from lack of food and poor conditions, and a number refused to take the oath of allegiance.

Epilogue

W HEN PEACE CAME IN MAY of 1865, the Confederacy no longer existed, and the officers and men of the Confederate States Navy said their goodbyes to shipmates and went their separate ways. A large number of the eight thousand sailors in the Confederate navy no longer served on board ship and had seen their vessels burned and destroyed as Union armies advanced. Most had gone ashore to serve as infantry or in land batteries, and others languished in Northern prisoner of war camps or in Southern hospitals.[1]

These Confederate naval officers, Marines, and sailors had served the Southern cause well, many until the very end of the conflict. They had served on board eleven Confederate raiders that together destroyed or captured 252 merchantmen or whalers; endured months of inactivity on ships, bottled up defending Southern harbors and cities like Charleston and Savannah; manned and fought the enemy from land batteries; executed raids; and joined their army counterparts in combined operations. Special units sowed mines or "torpedoes" that sank thirty-one Union vessels. Confederate sailors had endured stifling heat and damp cold serving on ironclad monitors, months of boredom on gunboats blockaded in Southern ports, and marching and fighting with their army counterparts in battles such as Saylor's Creek. Their service left a legacy of courage and innovation.

"The Confederate Navy, minute though it was, won a place for itself in history," John Newland Maffitt wrote. "To the Confederates the credit belongs of testing in battle the invulnerability of ironclads and of revolutionizing the navies of the world. The Merrimack did that."[2] Union admiral David Dixon Porter echoed this testimony and expressed admiration for the Confederate navy, writing, "Though the Confederates had nothing like the resources of the North in naval matters, yet they put forth so much more energy and converted as many ordinary vessels into powerful rams and gunboats, that they made up in that way for what they lacked originally."[3]

Indeed, Navy Secretary Stephen Mallory's navy department had confronted the war's many challenges: establishing the navy's organization and naval stations, leasing or ordering 121 steamships, 20 of them ironclads, and then having them armed and manned. Mallory understood that the birth of the Confederate navy coincided with a new era of naval tactics and technology. Realizing that sea power might have an impact on the war's outcome, he intended to take advantage of the opportunities provided by what many historians consider history's first "modern war." In addition to armies that employed the railroad, the telegraph, and the rifled musket, both navies in the Civil War converted or constructed vessels that were steam powered, many armored with iron, and armed with rifled shell guns.[4]

Secretary Mallory hoped that by deploying proper warships the South might employ "hit and run" tactics against the North's vulnerable merchant marine and, as one historian argued, might disrupt Union economic life, decrease enemy trade, draw Union navy blockaders from off the coast in pursuit of these rebel raiders, and induce war weariness.[5] When privateering failed to produce the desired results, Mallory decided to purchase steamers abroad and convert them to commerce raiders. The first raider, CSS *Sumter*, converted at New Orleans, had proven their worth, so with the ambitious help of agent James Bulloch, the Confederacy acquired the *Florida*, *Alabama*, and *Shenandoah*. Mallory's final plan was to order "a class of specially constructed ironclad rams armed with rifled guns set in revolving turrets to take the war to the enemy, disperse the blockaders, open southern ports to commerce and permit the export of cotton and assure South unlimited access to war material." If these were successful, he hoped the Confederacy might win a negotiated peace with the North and gain recognition of its independence.[6]

With fewer resources to combat the Union navy, the Confederate navy also turned to innovation with the use of mines, the submersible CSS *Hunley*, semisubmersibles, and spar torpedoes, which "forecast combat of the future." The Submarine Battery Service sowed mines or "torpedoes" that hampered Union naval operations in rivers and sounds and sank or damaged several Yankee vessels. In a few weeks in March and April 1865, for example, mines blew up seven Union vessels in Mobile Bay and destroyed two Confederate steamers in Charleston harbor.[7] As forerunners of today's underwater torpedoes, the spar torpedo was a more selective weapon but capable of blowing up a target. The little *Squib* was equipped with a spar torpedo but was not a submersible. The CSS *Hunley* proved to be nearer a true submersible than the *David*. Water tanks allowed her to dive, and lateral fins assisted her diving and surfacing.[8]

Despite these creative weapons and the commerce raiders that roamed the seas, destroying Northern merchant ships, the Confederate navy's efforts did not prove decisive. The Northern public became alarmed by these raiders; ships remained in port or went to foreign registry, but most Union navy blockaders continued to keep vigil off the Southern coast. The Union blockade, although porous, gradually tightened and "contributed to a growing sense of isolation and eventually depression, both economical and psychological, in the South."[9]

Establishing a navy and a navy department, and acquiring and arming men of war, required diligence and effort, but recruiting officers turned out to be less difficult than enticing mariners and seamen to join the new Confederate navy. Many of the U.S. Navy's Southern-born officers resigned their commissions and "went South." A number of those who left the U.S. Navy were midshipmen who preferred to resign and serve with Confederate army units or seek appointments as midshipmen in the Confederate States Navy. Other young Southern gentlemen joined the navy as midshipmen. Realizing a need to train them for their new profession, the Confederacy established a floating naval academy. To recruit sailors and Marines, the Confederate navy opened rendezvous or recruiting stations in major towns and cities, but soon experienced manpower shortages that prompted Mallory to ask the army to transfer men to fill out the complements of the navy's vessels.

Initially with just a handful of ships, the Confederate navy confronted Union navy blockade squadrons, then engaged Yankee gunboats and warships on the high seas, in Southern rivers and sounds, and on the mighty Mississippi River. These rebel gunboats, rams, and ironclads won a few victories or draws, such as the Battle of Hampton Roads, the captures of the *Underwriter* and the *Water Witch*, and the battle off Plum Point. But in engagements with Union forces, they also suffered defeats, including those at Hatteras Inlet, Port Royal, New Orleans, Memphis, and Mobile.

Although Confederate navy secretary Stephen Mallory never penned his memoirs, he did summarize the Confederate navy's contribution to the war: "Our Navy alone kept that of the U.S. from reaching Richmond by the James River, and from reaching Savannah and Charleston, and yet not ten men in ten thousand of the country know or appreciate these facts."[10]

Battling bugs and bullets, rebel sailors suffered not only from combat wounds but fell victim to illness, especially malaria but also dysentery, scurvy, yellow fever, pneumonia, venereal disease, and smallpox. Most Confederate bluejackets injured in accidents or in combat or those who succumbed to fevers and other diseases received adequate medical care from professional physicians assisted by hospital stewards, matrons, and nurses on shipboard and in numerous hospitals in Southern cities.

When their ships were destroyed, however, or when they were captured by the enemy ashore, Confederate sailors and Marines went to Union prisoner of war camps where most languished for months or years, coping with disease, boredom, confinement, poor conditions, and reduced rations. In the last few weeks of the war, as hope for a Southern victory faded, numerous sailors took advantage of being near Union lines and deserted. As war's end came, others took the oath of allegiance to the Union, but many navy men went to prison camps for weeks or months and then were released and returned to civilian life. Most presumably returned home to farms and communities that, if not ravaged, had been greatly affected by the war and by the Union blockade.

In the years following the end of the Civil War, American naval strategy focused on a defensive mission. In case of war, the navy's limited mission would be to defend the U.S. coast and major ports from enemy attack and blockade. As a legacy of the Civil War, U.S. Navy vessels would also strike out against enemy commerce. As one historian notes, "This continentalist tradition was reaffirmed between 1865 and 1875 and not radically revised until 1898."[11]

Peacetime brought new challenges for the Confederate navy's officers. When the war ended, Savez Read finally obtained permission to take the oath of allegiance and went to New Orleans to visit his old friend and former midshipman Jimmy Morgan. He confessed to Morgan that he was now destitute and might have to go to sea as a common sailor, as had many other Confederate naval officers. Morgan lent Read the funds necessary for him to purchase a small brig so he could engage in the fruit trade; with his usual energy, Read had it fitted out and sailed for the Caribbean.[12]

Precluded from service in the U.S. Navy, those former Confederate States Navy officers who could found employment with foreign navies. Beverly Kennon, James "Jimmy" Morgan, and others served with the khedive of Egypt. William H. Parker became the captain of a Pacific Ocean mail steamer, then accepted an appointment as professor at the Maryland Agricultural College.

Alexander Warley returned to civilian life in New Orleans and a career as the clerk of the Board of Liquidation City Debt. He lived three blocks from the city hall with his wife and children in what his obituary described as "the big mansion at the corner of Julia and St. Charles streets, designated as No. 195, that is full of history incidental to the war."[13]

Franklin Buchanan was exchanged on February 19, 1865, and spent the remainder of the war on convalescent leave. After the war, he became the president of the Maryland Agricultural College and then an insurance agent in Mobile, Alabama. John Taylor Wood went to Nova Scotia after the war to pursue a career in marine insurance. Isaac Brown went to Texas and died in 1889. John Randolph Eggleston was paroled at Jackson, Mississippi, on May 14, 1865, and became a farmer in Hinds County, Mississippi. He later wrote an article published in the *Southern Historical Society Papers*.[14]

The skills and experience learned in the engine rooms and fire rooms of navy vessels during the war served some Confederate navy engineers well in peacetime. "When the Civil War ended in 1865, I like many other

Confederates had nothing to start with and little prospects for the future in the South," Engineer James Tomb recalled. He was fortunate to secure from friends in Philadelphia "a position with an oil company in Oil City, Pennsylvania, to sink oil wells on a farm that they paid $25,000 for and was said to have every prospect of oil." However, they never found a drop of oil, and before Tomb left for South America the company went broke.[15]

Most if not all Confederate navy surgeons and assistant surgeons fared well in the years after the Civil War. Although held a prisoner at Fort Warren, when released Richard W. Jeffrey continued to practice medicine in Norfolk and died in 1882. James Francis Harrison was paroled and became a professor of chemistry at the University of Virginia in the decade after the war. Paroled as well, Robert Gibbes practiced medicine in Baltimore and then became a physician for the government at Governor's Island before moving west. Robert E. Lee's family doctor, Alexander Garnett, went on to become a professor of clinical medicine. Others, like George Nolley Halstead, turned to farming and probably private practice in the years following the war.[16]

Confederate navy midshipmen, many just youngsters when the war began, spent the postwar years pursuing a variety of careers. Frank Arthur became a theatrical agent. Andrew Beirne ran the Old Sweet Springs Resort in Union, West Virginia. Louis Bennett was a teacher and then a high school principal in Weston, West Virginia, but in later years practiced law in New York. Daniel Trigg also studied law and then practiced law. Midn. J. Thomas Scharf was released from the Old Capitol Prison in March 1865 and subsequently became a Protestant missionary, then earned a master's degree and a law degree from Georgetown University. He was also a journalist and author of the *History of the Confederate States Navy.*

After the war, Dabney Minor Scales went to Mexico and then returned to practice law in Memphis. He was elected to the Tennessee legislature and served in the Tennessee state senate. Commissioned a lieutenant in the U.S. Navy, he served his country in the Spanish American War.[17]

Willie Wilson moved to Jefferson, Texas, where he was licensed to teach in the local schools. In 1868 he married Sarah Burnside, a Kentucky girl; while supporting himself as a druggist, he "read medicine." He was licensed to practice medicine and surgery in 1874 and for the remainder of his life was a physician and a farmer until his death in 1919.[18]

Admiral Porter summed up the Confederate navy's war effort, writing that their officers and men did not lack courage, energy, and ability. "They were fighting," he noted, "with a cherished object, to gain something new and beyond their reach which they thought would conduce to their happiness, and out of which they thought the North was trying to deprive them."[19]

Notes

Introduction

1. Dawson, *Reminiscences of Confederate Service*, 37.
2. Dawson, 3.
3. Dawson, 4.
4. Dawson, 8.
5. Dawson, 37.
6. Sullivan, "The Marines." McPherson estimates 4,996 (*War on the Waters*, 26). The officers and men of the Confederate Marine Corps numbered over the course of the war 59 officers and more than 1,200 men who served on approximately thirty-four naval vessels in addition to duty in small detachments at navy yards and stations.

Chapter One. Navy Gray

1. Shingleton, "The Officers," 113–15, appendix to chap. 6. McPherson states 259 resigned or were dismissed (*War on the Waters*, 14).
2. Shingleton, "The Officers," 112–13; and Shingleton, "Seamen, Landsmen, Firemen and Coal Heavers," 134–35.
3. Scharf, *History of the Confederate States Navy*, 33–35; see also Lester and Bromwell, *A Digest of the Military*, 127.
4. Shingleton, "The Officers," 115–16.
5. Of those from Southern states, 350 officers remained in the navy; 259 of the other officers were resigned or dismissed from the service. President James Buchanan's secretary of the navy, Isaac Toucey,

accepted their resignations without requiring a reason, and the government released them from any service contracts.

6. Brooke, *John M. Brooke Naval Scientist and Educator*, 224–27. In fact, Brooke submitted his resignation as a lieutenant in the U.S. Navy to Secretary Gideon Welles on April 20, 1861.

7. Brooke, 224–27. The register of the U.S. Naval Academy Graduate Association put it kindly, "Dismissed," with a footnote that read, "resignation not accepted, went South." Brooke was not the only naval officer with twenty or more years of service to make the difficult decision to "go South."

8. Jack, *Memoirs of Eugenius Alexander Jack*, 2, 6.

9. Campbell, *Sea Hawk of the Confederacy*, 11–12.

10. Campbell, 14–15.

11. Waddell, *C.S.S. Shenandoah*, 65–66.

12. Dudley, *Going South*. See also Shingleton, "The Officers," 112.

13. Shingleton, "The Officers," 114; and Shingleton, *High Seas Confederate*, 32–33.

14. Kell, *Recollections of a Naval Life*, 134.

15. Kell, 139.

16. Melton, *Best Station of Them All*, 4. The rank of "passed midshipman" signified that they had successfully passed their examinations for midshipman.

17. Scharf, *History of the Confederate States Navy*, 33–35; Lester and Bromwell, *A Digest of the Military*, 127; and Shingleton, "The Officers," 115–17.

18. Conrad, *Rebel Reefers*, 6.

19. Driver, *Confederate Sailors*, 138, 152, 141, 133; and Trigg, "A Romantic Adventurer Comes of Age," 19–20. Just five months after his appointment as acting midshipman in July 1861, Frank Harris was appointed a master and went on to serve on the CSS *Ellis*. Other men took longer to rise to the rank of master. Samuel S. Gregory, for example, was appointed midshipman in July 1861 but did not obtain the rank of master until January 1864.

20. Trigg, "A Romantic Adventurer," 19–20.

21. Conrad, *Rebel Reefers*, 1.
22. Conrad, 6.
23. Conrad, 6; and Brooke, *John M. Brooke*, 275.
24. Conrad, *Rebel Reefers*, 9; and Thompson and Owsley, "The War Journal of Midshipman Cary." See Cong ser. set, 711–712, Cruise of CSS *Chickamauga*, extract from journal of Midshipman Cary.
25. Evans, *Confederate Military Service*, 12:98.
26. John E. Hart letter, June 7, 1863, Nimitz Library, Box 1, folder 09.
27. Lester and Bromwell, *A Digest of the Military*, Provisional Navy, Appointment of Officers, 220.
28. Melton, *Best Station of Them All*, 53; and Wells, *The Confederate Navy*, 63–64. When Lt. William H. Parker became commandant of the Confederate States Naval Academy at Richmond, Virginia, he put forward a plan to train pilots and have them commissioned as officers, but the plan never materialized.
29. Melton, *Best Station of Them All*, 53.
30. The muster roll of CSS *Savannah* lists Moses Dallas, pilot. U.S. Navy Department, *Official Records*, ser. 11, vol. 11, 30.5 [hereafter, OR]; Melton, *Best Station of Them All*, 54–55; see OR ser. 11, vol. 1, 289. The muster roll of *Isondiga* for January–March lists William Bugg, pilot. Among the black pilots who found employment with the Savannah Squadron was William "Billy" Bugg, who served on the CSS *Isondiga* and the CSS *Sampson* at Savannah. He was appointed from the state of Georgia. Commodore Tattnall's flagship routinely employed several pilots, including one well-known, expert pilot from St. Mary's named Isaac Tattnall. The squadron also found local pilots, two of whom, William W. Austin and Thomas Hernandez, became the senior pilots for the squadron. CSS *Palmetto State* had three pilots listed on her muster roll for October–December 1863 and January–December 1864: George O. Gladden, J. W. Cannon, and Joseph E. Aldert.
31. Gardner, "The Confederate Corps of Marines"; and Sullivan, "The Marines," 148, 153–54.
32. Jack, *Memoirs of E. A. Jack*, 10.

33. S. R. Mallory July 18, 1861, reports on the operations of the Navy Department since 26 April. Enclosure from Sec Navy report to Pres of CSA, July 18, 1861, OR ser. 2, vol. 2, 76–80.
34. Browning, "The Confederate States Navy Department," 26.
35. Shingleton, "Seamen, Landsmen, Firemen and Coal Heavers," 133; and Confederate Navy Subject File [hereafter, CNSF], NR, Misc., 271.
36. CNSF, NR, Misc., 201, 250, 262, 275.
37. CNSF, NR, Misc., 179.
38. Melton, *Best Station of Them All*, 48.
39. Melton, 39.
40. Schooler, *The Last Shot*, 188–89.
41. Parker, *Recollections of a Naval Officer*, 220.
42. CNSF, NR, Misc. 250.
43. CSNSF, NR, 196–97.
44. S. R. Mallory to Hon. A. H. Stephens, February 5, 1862, CNSF, NR, Misc., 197–98; Mallory to Josiah Tattnall, March 5, 1862, CNSF, NR, Misc., 216; Shingleton, "Seamen, Landsmen, Firemen and Coal Heavers," 133; and Melton, *Best Station of Them All*, 118.
45. CNSF, NR, Misc., 181; Donnelly, *The Confederate States Marine Corps*, 11, 48; and CNSF, NR, Misc. 263. A fifty-dollar bounty went also in September 1862 from Ingraham on CSS *Indian Chief*, the receiving ship, to J. Gillan, Charles Wilson, and H. Matters. On August 20, 1862, however, J. H. Ingraham, writing from the CSS *Huntress*, authorized a bounty of fifty dollars paid to John O'Brien, James Doyle, William Buber, and John Brown.
46. Melton, *Best Station of Them All*, 48; Shingleton, "The Officers," 124; and Musicant, *Divided Waters*, 74.
47. Coski, *Capital Navy*, 178.
48. Coski, 176; and Melton, *Best Station of Them All*, 48. Sailors captured during land battles were often listed as privates. The Wilmington Squadron and Charleston Squadron enlisted African Americans as well. Benjamin H. Gray, a twelve-year-old who enlisted in the navy at Wilmington, served as a powder boy on the CSS *Albemarle*. Johnny Robinson enlisted in the Confederate navy in early 1863 and served on the *Chicora*. He was discharged when they discovered he

was a runaway slave. Free blacks who enlisted early on the *Chicora* included Charles Cleaper, James Hicks, and Joe Johnson.

49. Coski, *Capitol Navy*, 175.
50. McPherson, *War on the Waters*, 27; Shingleton, "The Officers," 131; and Shingleton, "Seamen, Landsmen, Firemen and Coal Heavers," 134–35.
51. Bright, Rowland, and Bardon, *C.S.S. Neuse*, 11, 13n60, 154.
52. Shingleton, "The Officers," 118–20.
53. Hunter to Mallory, July 16, 1863; Hunter to Mallory, August 6, 1863; OR, vol. 14, 716; and Melton, *Best Station of Them All*, 238–39.
54. Jeter, *A Man and His Boat*, 31 and note.
55. Jeter, 77.
56. Carter to Crane, February 4, 1864, in Jeter, *A Man and His Boat*, 105. The Shreveport naval commandant's office reported shipping six men in February 1864, and five men in March. CNSF, NR, 398, 400, 406.
57. Jeter, *A Man and His Boat*, 100.
58. CNSF, NR, 325.
59. Shingleton words this differently in "Seamen, Landsmen, Firemen and Coal Heavers," 134. See also Escott, *Military Necessity*.
60. Watson, *Southern Service on Land and Sea*, 97; and Melton, *Best Station of Them All*, 145. He cited Jones to Johnston and Brent to Johnston in Georgia State archives. The archives has two letters, November 16 and December 21, 1862, written by the camp commandant, Lieutenant Colonel Weems.
61. Watson, *Southern Service on Land and Sea*, 107–8, 131.
62. Watson, 108.
63. Watson, 107–8, 131.
64. CNSF, NR, 297, 301.
65. Harwell, *Confederate Marine*, 98–99.
66. CNSF, NR, Misc. 311, 314.
67. CNSF, NR, 339. Lynch sent Midshipman Person to the conscript camp at Columbia, South Carolina, in July to bring back three recruits. See CNSF, NR, 356.
68. Oliver Hamilton to father, Hamilton Fish Papers.

69. Coski, *Capitol Navy*, 178.
70. McPherson, *War on the Waters*, 26. Sullivan estimates 4,500 ("The Marines").

Chapter Two. Shipboard Routine

1. Conrad, *Rebel Reefers*, 15.
2. Dawson, *Reminiscences of Confederate Service*, ix.
3. "Uniform and Dress of the Navy of the Confederate States."
4. Morgan, *Recollections of a Rebel Reefer*, 53; see also Shingleton, "The Officers," 126, 241–42.
5. Iverson Graves letter, November 1863, in Harwell, *A Confederate Marine*, 107.
6. Graves, in Harwell, 120.
7. Graves, in Harwell, 99.
8. Conrad, *Rebel Reefers*, 16–17. The Confederate States Marine Corps issued uniforms to its recruits.
9. Semmes, *Memoirs of Service Afloat*, 273.
10. Watson, *Southern Service on Land and Sea*, 102–3.
11. Conrad, *Rebel Reefers*, 44. See also Shingleton, "Seamen, Landsmen, Firemen and Coal Heavers," 128.
12. Fullam, *The Journal of George Townley Fullam*, 137.
13. Ringle, *Life in Mr. Lincoln's Navy*, 93; and Bennett, *Union Jacks*, 119.
14. Driver, *Confederate Sailors, Marines, and Signalmen*, 332, 328-9, 33, 357–58, 39.
15. Quoted in Chaffin, *Sea of Gray*, 53.
16. Fullam, *The Journal of George Townley Fullam*, 13.
17. Fullam.
18. Chaffin, *Sea of Gray*, 76–77.
19. Quoted in Melton, *Best Station of Them All*, 291.
20. Quoted in Conrad, *Rebel Reefers*, 17.
21. Dawson, *Reminiscences of Confederate Service*, 11.
22. Dawson, 16.
23. Chaffin, *Sea of Gray*, 77.
24. Jack, *Memoirs of E. A. Jack*, 23–24.

25. Jack, 23.
26. Quoted in Bright, Rowland, and Bardon, *CSS Neuse*, app. 3.
27. Dawson, *Reminiscences of Confederate Service*, 16; and Chatelain, *Fought Like Devils*, loc. 497.
28. Dawson, *Reminiscences of Confederate Service*, 31; see also Weeks, "The Civil War Sailor's Life."
29. Watson, *Southern Service on Land and Sea*, 106, 103.
30. Dear and Kemp, *Oxford Companion to Ships and the Sea*, 392.
31. Dawson, *Reminiscences of Confederate Service*, 30.
32. Ringle, *Life in Mr. Lincoln's Navy*, 73–74.
33. Dawson, *Reminiscences of Confederate Service*, 22–23.
34. Smith, *CSS Arkansas*, loc. 2097. Dennis Ringle states that in the Union navy between 20 and 25 percent of the engineering divisions were first-class firemen, another 25 percent, second-class firemen, and the remainder coal heavers. The Union navy did not have third-class firemen. Ringle, *Life in Mr. Lincoln's Navy*, 47.
35. Campbell, *Sea Hawk of the Confederacy*, app. G, 214–16; Jack, *Memoirs of E. A. Jack*, 10, 13; and Quarstein, *The CSS Virginia*, 366.
36. Conrad, *Rebel Reefers*, 46. See Quarstein, *The CSS Virginia*, for Ashton Ramsay's comments on her weak engines.
37. Quoted in Bennett, *Union Jacks*, 35; see also Ringle, *Life in Mr. Lincoln's Navy*, 47.
38. Tomb, *Engineer in Gray*, 54–55.
39. Tomb, 57.
40. Dawson, *Reminiscences of Confederate Service*, 21.
41. Watson, *Southern Service on Land and Sea*, 105.
42. Shingleton, "Seamen, Landsmen, Firemen and Coal Heavers," 138–40.
43. Conrad, *Rebel Reefers*, 22–24; Elliot, *Ironclad of the Roanoke*, 168–69; Jack, *Memoirs of E. A. Jack*, 12–13. Manning the guns on the CSS *Virginia* in 1862 were Lt. C. C. Sims at the 7-inch bow gun, Lt. Hunter Davidson at guns 2 and 3, John Taylor Wood at the 7-inch Brookes, John R. Eggleston at guns 4 and 5, and Walter Butt at guns 6 and 7, assisted by four midshipmen, H. H. Marmaduke, H. B. Littlepage, R. C. Foute, and W. J. Craig. Midn. J. C. Long assisted paymaster James J. Simple, who commanded the powder division.

44. Watson, *Southern Service on Land and Sea*, 106.
45. Watson, 106–7.
46. Marvel, *The Alabama & the Kearsarge*, 25–26.
47. Melton, *Best Station of Them All*, 172.
48. Dawson, *Reminiscences of Confederate Service*, 10, 11.
49. Dawson, 11, 22.
50. John Pugh, June 21, 1862, Pugh family papers, Manuscripts of the American Civil War.
51. Watson, *Southern Service on Land and Sea*, March 14 journal entry, p. 103.
52. Morgan, *Recollections of a Rebel Reefer*, 145.
53. Dear Ellen, October 30, 1864, James O. Harrison Papers, 412, Box 2, Family Correspondence, LOC.
54. Conrad, *Rebel Reefers*, 17–18; Morgan, "A Most Realistic War College"; and Calcutt, *Richmond's Wartime Hospitals*, 49.
55. Morgan, *Recollections of a Rebel Reefer*, 145.
56. Morgan, 154.
57. A. L. Drayton diary, May 29, 1863, Drayton Papers, 265, LOC.
58. Semmes, *Memoirs of Service Afloat*, 225.
59. Semmes, 155.
60. Smith, *CSS Arkansas*, loc. 2082–85; and Master's Mate John Wilson's diary, OR vol. 19, 132–36.
61. Kell, *Recollections of a Naval Life*, 148.
62. Quoted in Bright, Rowland, and Bardon, *CSS Neuse*, 13.
63. Quoted in Bright, Rowland, and Bardon, 11.
64. Campbell, *Storm over Carolina*, 158.
65. Quoted in Bright, Rowland, and Bardon, *CSS Neuse*, 11, 13. Loyall had been sent to replace Sharp as the commanding officer of the *Neuse* at the end of February.
66. Dawson, *Reminiscences of Confederate Service*, 22.
67. Semmes journal, June 19 and 20, 1861, OR ser. 1, vol. 1, Cruisers: 692.
68. Report of Inspection of the CSS *Drewry*, July 5, 1864, CNSF, Misc., 1–5.
69. A. L. Drayton diary, May 21, 1863, Library of Congress.
70. Semmes journal, OR ser. 1, vol. 1, 615.

71. Semmes, *Memoirs of Service Afloat*, 79.
72. Coski, *Capital Navy*, 178–79.
73. Semmes journal, OR ser. 1, vol. 1, 779.
74. Hubbard T. Minor, "Diary of a Confederate Naval Cadet," *Civil War Times Illustrated* 13, no. 8 (December 1974): 128–29.
75. Morgan, *Recollections of a Rebel Reefer*, 197.
76. Quoted in Bright, Rowland, and Barton, *CSS Neuse*, app. 3.
77. Minor, *Confederate Naval Cadet*, 111–12.
78. Jack, *Memoirs of E. A. Jack*, 24.

Chapter Three. Entertainment, the Sabbath, and Liberty

1. Semmes, *Memoirs of Service Afloat*, 191.
2. Langley, "Shipboard Life," 183; Watson, *Southern Service on Land and Sea*, 121; and Conrad, *Rebel Reefers*, 37–38.
3. Waddell, *C.S.S. Shenandoah*, 106.
4. Kell, *Recollections of a Naval Life*, 190.
5. Watson, *Southern Service on Land and Sea*, 107.
6. Chaffin, *Sea of Gray*, 331.
7. Semmes, *Memoirs of Service Afloat*, 453.
8. Dawson, *Reminiscences of Confederate Service*, 18–19; see also Driver, *Confederate Sailors, Marines, and Signalmen*, 57. Cary had originally enlisted in the 17th Virginia Infantry and been at the Battle of Bull Run before being discharged as underage.
9. Semmes, *Memoirs of Service Afloat*, 156.
10. Waddell, *C.S.S. Shenandoah*, 122.
11. Quoted in Melton, *Best Station of Them All*, 291–92.
12. Watson, *Southern Service on Land and Sea*, 113.
13. Bacot to "Sis," April 28, 1864, in R. H. Bacot Letters, State Archives of North Carolina, Raleigh, North Carolina.
14. Wilson, diary entry, April 26, 1862, in Wilson, *Willie Wilson's War*.
15. Watson, *Southern Service on Land and Sea*, 135.
16. Watson, 132.
17. Bacot to "Sis," July 18, 1864, in Bacot Letters.
18. Conrad, *Rebel Reefers*, 39.

19. Bacot to "Sis," March 19, 1864, in Bacot Letters.

20. Bacot to "Sis," March 19, 1864.

21. Quoted in Chaffin, *Sea of Gray*, 218–19.

22. Wilson diary, April 22, 23, 1862, in Wilson, *Willie Wilson's War*, 22.

23. Wilson diary, April 23, 1862, 22.

24. Bacot to "Sis," March 19, 1864; and Bacot to sister, July 18, 1864, in Bacot Papers, State Archives of North Carolina, Raleigh, North Carolina.

25. Morgan, *Recollections of a Rebel Reefer*, 214–15.

26. Morgan, 214–15.

27. Watson, *Southern Service on Land and Sea*, 128, 106, 108.

28. John M. Kell, *Recollections of a Naval Life*, 190, 126.

29. Melton, *Best Station of Them All*, 51; and Conrad, *Rebel Reefers*, 38.

30. Semmes, *Memoirs of Service Afloat*, August 18, 1861, p. 197.

31. Waddell, *C.S.S. Shenandoah*, 112.

32. Watson, *Southern Service on Land and Sea*, 107.

33. Waddell, *C.S.S. Shenandoah*, 118.

34. Extracts from the journal of Commander Semmes, Confederate States Navy, commanding the *CSS Sumter*, from May 24, 1861, to April 11, 1863, hereafter cited as Semmes journal, OR vol. 1, 732.

35. Semmes journal, OR vol. 1, 732.

36. Quoted in Harwell, *Confederate Marine*, 110.

37. Wilson diary, December 25, 1861, in Wilson, *Willie Wilson's War*, 13.

38. Wilson diary, December 31, 1861, in Wilson, *Willie Wilson's War*, 13.

39. Dawson, *Reminiscences of Confederate Service*, 12.

40. Dawson, 12, 25.

41. Watson, *Southern Service on Land and Sea*, 103, 105.

42. Melton, *Best Station of Them All*, 127.

43. Semmes, *Memoirs of Service Afloat*, 191. See also Ringle, *Life in Mr. Lincoln's Navy*, 4–5.

44. Jack, *Memoirs of E. A. Jack*, 27.

45. Melton, *Best Station of Them All*, 269.

46. Quoted in Conrad, *Rebel Reefers*, 56.

47. Morgan, *Recollections of a Rebel Reefer*, 145.

48. Semmes journal, OR vol. 1, 719. When Raphael Semmes did have occasion to go ashore, he enjoyed searching for seashells.
49. Semmes journal, OR vol. 1, 720.
50. Private notebook kept by J. T. Gordon on board the blockade runner *Cornubia*, captured November 8, 1863, by USS *James Adger* and *Niphon* near New Inlet, Wilmington, North Carolina. S. P. Lee, November 4, 1863, OR vol. 9, 277, enclosure, 279.
51. Morgan, *Recollections of a Rebel Reefer*, 95–96.
52. Bright et al., *C.S.S. Neuse*, 142.
53. Bacot to Sister, May 23, 1864, Bacot Papers.
54. Minor, *Confederate Naval Cadet*, 107–10, 112, 117. See also Conrad, *Rebel Reefers*, 39.
55. Elliott, *Ironclad of the Roanoke*, 253, 256–57, 345n1.
56. Morgan, *Recollections of a Rebel Reefer*, 54.
57. Watson, *Southern Service on Land and Sea*, 110.
58. Quoted in Melton, *Best Station of Them All*, 301–2.
59. Wilson diary, January 4, 1862; May 15, 1862; and May 11, 1862, in Wilson, *Willie Wilson's War*, 13, 24.
60. Wilson diary, January 13, 1862, January 9, 1862, 14.
61. Wilson diary, January 23, 1862, in Wilson, *Willie Wilson's War*, 15.
62. Conrad, *Rebel Reefers*, 59, citing James Morgan, "A Most Realistic War College," U.S. Naval Institute *Proceedings*, March–April 1916.
63. Melton, *Best Station of Them All*, 301.
64. Wilson diary, February 27, 1862, in Wilson, *Willie Wilson's War*, 18.
65. Watson, *Southern Service on Land and Sea*, 125. In this incident they got gloriously drunk.
66. Wilson diary, May 1, 1862, in Wilson, *Willie Wilson's War*, 23.
67. Wilson diary, February 27 and March 8, in Wilson, *Willie Wilson's War*, 16, 18. By now midshipmen Wilson and Edward McDermott had been assigned to the No. 2 Gunboat under the command of Lieutenant Porcher. Returning from a visit to the city on April 7, 1862, Wilson wrote: "When I came back found that the enemy had been within about three miles of fort Jackson and tried their guns on it they fell short about 400 yards, the d__n rascals are impudent and need a licking."

68. Wilson diary, April 19, 1862; and April 20, 1862, in Wilson, *Willie Wilson's War*, 22.

69. Wilson diary, April 21, 1862, in Wilson, *Willie Wilson's War*, 22.

Chapter Four. Discipline and Desertion

1. Still, *The Confederate Navy*; Langley, "Shipboard Life," 189; and "Confederate States Navy Department, Regulations for the Navy of the Confederate States, 1862," in *On Deck! The Webzine of the Navy and Marine Living History Association*, http://www.navyandmarine.org /ondeck/1862CSN_Regulations.htm. Flogging had been abolished in 1850. Over the years, naval officers had invented substitutions for flogging, such as tying an offender's wrists to a hammock for four hours.

2. Still, *The Confederate Navy*, 189.

3. Quoted in Delaney, *John McIntosh Kell*, 139.

4. Dawson, *Reminiscences of Confederate Service*, 19.

5. Wilson, *Willie Wilson's War, 1861–1865*, June 10 and 11, 1862, 28.

6. Coski, *Capital Navy*, 183; and Article 26, *Confederate States Navy Regulations*, 1862.

7. Coski, *Capital Navy*, 183–84; and cited in *Daily Dispatch*, February 17, 1864, and *Daily Richmond Examiner*, February 17, 1864. A New Orleans resident, Keene had enlisted in the 1st Louisiana regiment but transferred to the Confederate States Navy.

8. Clayton, *A Narrative of the Confederate States Navy*, 102–3.

9. Melton, *Best Station of Them All*, 109.

10. Henry Graves to Cora, December 26, 1863, in Harwell, *Confederate Marine*, 109–10.

11. General Order No. 1, April 17, 1863, OR vol. 14, 690; and Melton, *Best Station of Them All*, 211. Page turned command over to W. A. Webb on May 13, 1863 and Webb issued an order keeping Page's orders in force, OR vol. 14, 697. The new squadron commander also gave orders specifying that clothes be washed on Mondays, Wednesdays, and Fridays of each week, and the men be exercised

not less than half an hour each day, Sundays excepted, at the great guns and small arms.

12. Delaney, *John McIntosh Kell*, 148. "When the bread was full of maggots and the provisions in the *Alabama* of the very worst description, tons of the very best provisions, taken from prizes, have been sunk rather than given to the men." Delaney, 149.

13. Morgan, *Recollections of a Rebel Reefer*, 163–64.

14. Schooler, *The Last Shot*, 179–80.

15. Read, "Reminiscences of the Confederate Navy," 357.

16. Schooler, *The Last Shot*, 179–80.

17. John M. Kell, *Recollections of a Naval Life*, 187; and Delaney, *John McIntosh Kell*, 131–32.

18. Melton, *Best Station of Them All*, 109.

19. Extracts from Semmes Journal, OR vol. 1, 730.

20. Harold Langley, "Shipboard Life," 190.

21. Sinclair, *Two Years on the Alabama*, 28.

22. Semmes, *Memoirs of Service Afloat*, 420, 427.

23. Fullam, *The Journal of George Townley Fullam*, 176. Johnson was wounded off Cherbourg on the *Alabama* on June 19, 1864.

24. CNSF, Personnel, Marine Corps, Misc. 23; see also CNSF, Personnel, NO Court-martials, 59 and 174.

25. Melton, *Best Station of Them All*, 300.

26. Melton, 273, 298.

27. Fullam, *The Journal of George Townley Fullam*, 143.

28. Conrad, *Rebel Reefers*, 27.

29. Conrad, 28.

30. Lonn, *Desertion during the Civil War*, 3, 7, 13; Melton, *Best Station of Them All*, 404; Still, "The Common Sailor," 39; and Melton, *Best Station of Them All*, chap. 27, n. 42; Bennett, *Union Jacks*, 1, 103; Ringle, *Life in Mr. Lincoln's Navy*, 103; and Lonn, *Desertion during the Civil War*, 231. The Union army lost more, with New York alone suffering 44,913 desertions by war's end and Ohio 18,354 desertions.

31. Driver, *Confederate Sailors, Marines, and Signalmen*, 215–45; 293–324; see also Still, "Common Sailor."

32. Donald Ray Gardner, "The Confederate Corps of Marines," 28.

33. Bulloch to Mallory, December 24, 1861; Bulloch to Mallory, December 26, 1861, in Bulloch, *Secret Service of the Confederate States in Europe*, 1:138–39; and Melton, *Best Station of Them All*, 100–102. Bulloch recommended that John Low be appointed a master in the Confederate States Navy, and he accompanied Bulloch to Europe, as did Midshipman Anderson.

34. Styple, *Writing and Fighting the Civil War*, 235–36.

35. Melton, *Best Station of Them All*, 404, 408, 419–20; and Hunter to Lee, January 5, 1865, OR vol. 16, 498.

36. Watson, *Southern Service on Land and Sea*, 152.

37. Culpepper, *Women of the Civil War South*, 33.

38. Parker, *Recollections of a Naval Officer*, 220.

39. Melton, *Best Station of Them All*, 241–42. He argues desertion was as common in the Union navy during the war as in the Confederate States Navy. But he does not offer any data or cite any sources.

40. Memoranda of Flag-Officer Mitchell, Confederate States Navy, on naval affairs in James River, October 3–14, 1864, OR vol. 10, 769.

41. Mitchell, October 8, 1864, OR vol. 10, 776–77.

42. Lonn, *Desertion during the Civil War*, 23; and Melton, *Best Station of Them All*, 393. Some, like W. McGrath, were reported by Hunter as deserters but were not actually deserters. According to Driver (*Confederate Sailors, Marines, and Signalmen*, 309), E. W. Skinner, age twenty-four, was paroled at Savannah on April 12, 1865.

43. Parker, *Recollections of a Naval Officer*, 347.

44. Quoted in Coski, *Capital Navy*, 213–14.

45. Coski, 213; see also Harwell, "Diary of Captain Edward Crenshaw," part 5.

46. Gardner, "The Confederate Corps of Marines," 20.

47. Gardner, 28.

48. Melton, *Best Station of Them All*, 199; and enclosure to Rodgers to Du Pont, March 20, 1863, OR vol. 13, 766–77.

49. Driver, *Confederate Sailors, Marines, and Signalmen*, 323. Carpenter's Mate Peter Stout deserted to defenses of the Potomac on September 6, 1864, took the oath, and went to New York City.

50. Page to Kennard, April 25, 1863, OR vol. 14, 693. Webb issued similar instructions; see Melton, *Best Station of Them All*, 221.

51. Melton, *Best Station of Them All*, 287.

52. CNSF, Marine Corps, Misc. 40, Personnel NZ Deserters, 38, 58 ,68; and *Richmond Dispatch*, June 1, 1862, available at Civil War Richmond website, www.mdgorman.com.

53. *Richmond Dispatch*, November 18, 1862, available at Civil War Richmond website, www.mdgorman.com.

54. Melton, *Best Station of Them All*, 187, citing the Dabney Scales diary at Duke University.

55. Melton, 266; and W. W. Hunter to Cdr. J. K. Mitchell, November 9 and 28, 1863, OR vol. 15, 107–8. The seamen were from Ireland and Denmark.

56. Melton, *Best Station of Them All*, 266; and W. W. Hunter to Cdr. J. K. Mitchell, November 9 and 28, 1863, OR vol. 15, 107–8.

57. Fullam, *The Journal of George Townley Fullam*, 33–34. The editor noted that the deserter is identified as George Forrest, who jumped ship in Cadiz months earlier from *Sumter*, along with several other men tired of their commerce-hunting cruise.

58. Fullam, *The Journal of George Townley Fullam*, 33–34, 53–54. The note says Forrest was convicted of desertion from the *Sumter* and the maximum penalty was death.

Chapter Five. Medical Care in the Confederate States Navy

1. Browning, "The Confederate States Navy Department," 24.

2. Furer, "Bureau of Medicine and Surgery"; and Langley, *A History of Medicine*.

3. Browning, "The Confederate States Navy Department," 30; and Scharf, *History of the Confederate States Navy*, 28–29, 39. The navy of Virginia was authorized April 27, 1861, to consist of two thousand sailors, Marines, and officers, as needed. The bureau's medical activities on the Confederate States' cruisers were largely independent of any administrative control.

4. Browning, "The Confederate State Navy Department," 30; Bollet, *Civil War Medicine*, 26; and Freemon, *Gangrene and Glory*, 92. Although he attended the University of Virginia medical school for only the first of a two-year program and therefore had no formal medical degree, Spotswood was commissioned an assistant surgeon in the U.S. Navy in December 1828 and a surgeon ten years later.

5. Journal of the Congress of the Confederate States of America 1861– 1865, Provisional Congress, vol. 1, July 30, 1861, pp. 297–98.

6. Lynch, "Confederate Navy Medicine."

7. Report of Office of Medicine and Surgery, November 30, 1863, OR ser. 1, vol. 2, 559–61.

8. Driver, *Confederate Sailors, Marines, and Signalmen.*

9. "Confederate States Navy Department, Regulations for the Navy of the Confederate States, 1862," in *On Deck! The Webzine of the Navy and Marine Living History Association*, http://www.navyandmarine .org/ondeck/1862CSN_Regulations.htm.

10. *The Confederate States Navy Department, Regulations for the Navy of the Confederate States, 1862*, 124–28. The Confederate navy also required naval surgeons to conform to the regulations and allow- ances of medicine, instruments, and stores established by the Bureau of Medicine and Surgery and to take charge of and receipt for all medicines, surgical instruments, and hospital stores. Bollet, *Civil War Medicine*, 25–26; Cunningham, *Doctors in Gray*, loc. 365, 411.

11. "The Medical History of the Confederate Army and Navy," at *Shot- gun's Home of the American Civil War*, http://civilwarhome.com/ csmedicalhistory.html; and Driver, *Confederate Sailors, Marines, and Signalmen*, 5–188. The sample includes men with surnames beginning with A through K. Of these, only seven died of wounds or were missing in action or killed in action. Twenty-four men died of disease or for unknown reasons or drowned.

12. Waddell, *C.S.S. Shenandoah*, 159.

13. Dalzell, *The Flight from the Flag*, 33; and Semmes, *Memoirs of Service Afloat*, 159.

14. Brown, *Scurvy*, 212–13; and Bollet, *Civil War Medicine*, 354–56. Freemon, *Gangrene and Glory*, 94, states that scurvy "did not afflict

Civil War navies. Scurvy remained a problem for armies, but it no longer crippled a ship at sea." This generalization does not appear to be borne out by the evidence.

15. Freemon, *Gangrene and Glory*, 126, 153, 218. For scurvy in the Union navy, see Ringle, *Life in Mr. Lincoln's Navy*, 113–14; and Bollet, *Civil War Medicine*, 345–46; 354–56.
16. Read, "Reminiscences of the Confederate Navy," 357.
17. Waddell, *C.S.S. Shenandoah*, 107.
18. Waddell, 154; see also Humphreys, *Marrow of Tragedy*, 221–24; Denney, *Civil War Medicine*, 9; and Bollet, *Civil War Medicine*, 350–51. Both armies and navies knew that scurvy might be prevented by the use of antiscorbutics and endeavored to provide their men with fresh produce, canned vegetables, or a new dry mixture called desiccated vegetables. The Union navy shipped canned tomatoes to the blockading squadron.
19. Denney, *Civil War Medicine*, 109; U.S. Surgeon General's Office, *The Medical and Surgical History*, 688–96, 713; Freemon, *Gangrene and Glory*, 21, 212, 94; Brown, *Scurvy*, 44–46.
20. Melton, *Best Station of Them All*, 147, 156; and "The Medical History of the Confederate Army and Navy," at *Shotgun's Home of the American Civil War*, http://civilwarhome.com/CS medicalhistory .html.
21. Bollet, *Civil War Medicine*, 51.
22. Tomb, *Engineer in Gray*, 11–12.
23. Register of Confederate Naval Patients in the Charity Hospital at New Orleans, Louisiana, 1861, OR ser 2, vol. 2, 759. The largest incidences of men suffering from syphilis being admitted to the *St. Philip* came from the *Pickens*, six alone in a three-month period in 1861, plus two from the *McRae* and one from the *Florida*.
24. Smith, *C.S.S. Arkansas*, loc. 2027–30. "Nearly ½ of my whole force is on the sick list," Union general Williams wrote.
25. Turner, *Navy Gray*, 71–73.
26. Turner, 71–73.
27. Waddell, *CSS Shenandoah*, 107, 154.
28. Humphreys, *Marrow of Tragedy*, 221–24.

29. Bollet, *Civil War Medicine*, 350–51. See also Denney, *Civil War Medicine*, 9.

30. Spotswood to Mallory, November 30, 1863, OR ser. 2, vol. 2, 559–61.

31. Report on condition of the Medical Department of the CS Navy, Spotswood to Mallory, November 30, 1863, OR ser. 2, vol. 2, 559–61.

32. Register of Confederate Naval Patients in the Charity Hospital at New Orleans, Louisiana, 1861, OR ser. 2, vol. 2, 759.

33. Bolett, *Civil War Medicine*, 51–53, 298–301.

34. Maury to General Cooper, July 7, 1864, OR ser. 1, vol. 21, 904–5; and Freemon, *Gangrene and Glory*, 94. Yellow fever was a major problem for Civil War ships, but Freemon erroneously claims scurvy had disappeared by 1860. Bollet, *Civil War Medicine*, 301; *Medical and Surgical History of the War of the Rebellion*, vol. 3, 678, 682. The steamer *Delaware* brought from Key West the 7th New Hampshire cases who were left sick at Ft. Jefferson. Yellow fever from the *Kate* caused fifteen deaths.

35. Bollet, *Civil War Medicine*, 303; OR ser. 1, vol. 3, 161–63. In his report, Downes stated that a Bermuda newspaper indicated clearance of other vessels or Nassau but no presence of yellow fever there.

36. OR ser 1, vol. 1, 763; Conrad, *Rebel Reefers*, 77; and Register of Confederate Naval Patients in the Charity Hospital at New Orleans, Louisiana, 1861, OR ser 2, vol. 2, 759.

37. Shingleton, *High Seas Confederate*, 47–48.

38. Shingleton, 47–48; Extracts from the journal of Lt. J. N. Maffitt, commanding the C.S.S. *Florida*, May 4–December 31, 1862, OR ser. 1, vol. 1, 760, 764. Note: The Maffitt letter says he had but two firemen and eleven men.

39. Shingleton, *High Seas Confederate*, 49; Extracts from the journal of Lt. J. N. Maffitt, OR ser. 1, vol. 1, 765–66. For symptoms of yellow fever, see also *Medical and Surgical History of the War of the Rebellion*, vol. 3, 667; and OR, ser 2, vol. 2, 759.

40. Dalzell, *The Flight from the Flag*, 99–100.

41. Freemon, *Gangrene and Glory*, 80–81; CNSF Medical, MM, Augusta—Miscellaneous, James F. Harrison, surgeon in charge, December 9, 1862, p. 12; and Bollet, *Civil War Medicine*, 291, 294.

Bollet claims a fatality rate of 20–40 percent. Records show that Union navy physicians attempted to vaccinate sailors and even African American civilians ashore to prevent outbreaks of the dread disease, which had a high fatality rate. Tomblin, *Bluejackets and Contrabands*, 224–5. Confederate army recruits were often vaccinated against smallpox, and vaccination became an official army policy. Despite this precaution, an outbreak of smallpox occurred in the fall of 1862 in Confederate military hospitals in Virginia.

42. CNSF Medical: December 9, 1862, p. 11, 32.
43. Bollet, *Civil War Medicine*, 29; Melton, *Best Station of Them All*, 155–56; and Bennett, *The London Confederates*, 75–76.
44. Register of *St. Philip* at New Orleans, Louisiana, 1861–62, transcribed by Terry Foenander, Lewis Willis Minor Papers, University of Virginia.
45. Melton, *Best Station of Them All*, 195. One patient, James Myers, a seaman, died of paralysis on Christmas Day.
46. Shingleton, *High Seas Confederate*, 48; Bollet, *Civil War Medicine*, 271–72; and Extracts from the journal of Lt. J. N. Maffitt, commanding the CSS *Florida*, May 4–December 31, 1862, OR ser. 1, vol. 1, 760, 764.
47. Shingleton, *High Seas Confederate*, 49; and Extracts from the journal of Lt. J. N. Maffitt, OR ser. 1, vol. 1, 765–66.
48. Bollet, *Civil War Medicine*, 313–14. See also Inglehart Journal, CNSF; and Extracts from the journal of Lt. J. N. Maffitt, OR ser. 1, vol. 1, 760, 765. Melton points out that only two cases in the Savannah Squadron was an unusually low number. Among the USS *Fernandina*'s crew of 110 men, 28 contracted venereal disease during a port call at Portsmouth, New Hampshire. Melton, *Best Station of Them All*, 222, 470n22.
49. Gibbes Diary, 1861–65; and Freeman, *Journal of Medical and Surgical Practice*, Confederate States of America Medical Records, M 217, Manuscript Collection.
50. Journal of Osborn Inglehart, CNSF, subfile ML, frame 109–11.
51. Semmes journal, July 10, 1862, OR vol. 1, 696–97.
52. Melton, *Best Station of Them All*, 222.
53. Jack, *Memoirs of E. A. Jack*, 23.

54. Jones, *Civil War at Sea*, 224–26.
55. CNSF Medical, 41, Confederate States Navy Department, November 7, 1864, General Order.
56. Johnson, *Muskets and Medicine*, 97.
57. Inglehart, journal, frame 109–11.
58. Inglehart journal, 6, 9, 12.
59. Johnson, *Muskets and Medicine*, 44–45.
60. Inglehart journal, 1–14.
61. Cunningham, *Doctors in Gray*, loc. 3067. A brown mixture, named for its color, was Corneau & Diller's concoction for colds and coughs, a patented medicine used in the Civil War. Corneau & Diller was a drug store in Springfield, Illinois, where Mrs. Lincoln shopped.
62. Melton, *Best Station of Them All*, 222, 470n22; Register of Confederate Naval Patients in the Charity Hospital at New Orleans, Louisiana, 1861, OR ser 2, vol. 2, 759; and Bollet, *Civil War Medicine*, 313–14.
63. Ringle, *Life in Mr. Lincoln's Navy*, 120; and Bollet, *Civil War Medicine*, 313–14. See also Inglehart Journal, CNSF; Gibbes Diary, 1861–1865; and Freeman, *Journal of Medical and Surgical Practice*.
64. Tomb, *Engineer in Gray*, 38–39.
65. Tomb, 38–39.
66. Report of D. B. Philips, OR ser. 1, vol. 7, 42. For the naval action at Hampton Roads, see Buchanan to Mallory, March 27, 1862, OR vol. 7, 43–49.
67. Tomb, *Engineer in Gray*, editor's note, 24. The action of the James River Squadron with the Yankees on January 23, 24, and 25, 1865, caused numerous casualties; for a detailed report of those injured, see Report of Fleet Surgeon on Casualties in the James River Squadron, January 26, 1865, W. D. Harrison, OR vol. 11, 688–89.
68. Campbell, *Storm over North Carolina*, 79–80.
69. Watson, Southern Service on Land & Sea, June 7, 1864, 116.
70. Watson, June 7, 1864, 116–17. Midn. Hubbard Minor's account and report are in Minor, *Confederate Naval Cadet*, 90–97.
71. Matthew Young, "Irony Clad: The Remarkable Odyssey of the *U.S.S. Water Witch*," 10–11; and Ass. Paymaster Luther Billings, Manuscript Division, Library of Congress.

72. Watson, *Southern Service on Land and Sea,* June 3, 1864, 115.

73. Watson, 114–16.

74. Melton, *Best Station of Them All,* 327; and Joseph Price to W. W. Hunter, June 3, 1864, OR vol. 15, 495. Price listed Union casualties at one killed and eleven wounded.

75. Pierson to Dahlgren, September 10, 1864, OR 15:481.

76. Porter, A Record of Events, 318.

77. Cunningham, *Doctors in Gray,* loc. 3452.

78. Cunningham, loc. 3445.

79. Morgan, *Recollections of a Rebel Reefer,* 211.

80. Cunningham, *Doctors in Gray,* loc. 3539, 3576.

81. Inglehart journal, 1.

82. Inglehart journal, 1.

83. Spotswood to Mallory, November 1, 1864, OR ser. 2, vol. 2, 759.

84. CNSF, S Merchant ships, SG Illegal services, 103.

85. Hasegawa and Hambrecht, "The Confederate Medical Laboratories." He cites Spotswood to Mallory, OR ser. 2, vol. 2, 559–62.

86. Campbell, *Storm over North Carolina,* 79–80; and Trotter, *Ironclads and Columbiads,* 44, 88–90.

87. Report of Lt. A. McLaughlin, December 2, 1863, Confederate States Navy, OR ser 1, vol. 17, 869–72. Lynch also cites reports of Surgeon John A. Browne, USN, OR ser 1, vol. 3, 69–71; Acting Surgeon Edgar Holden, USN, OR ser 1, vol. 9, 742–43; Lt. McLaughlin CSN, OR ser 1, vol. 17, 871–72; W. D. Harrison, OR ser 1, vol. 11, 688–89; and Commodore Buchanan, OR ser 1, vol 7, 43–49.

88. Report of Lt. A. McLaughlin, Confederate States Navy, December 2, 1863, OR ser 1, vol. 17, Gulf Blockading Squadron, 869–72. Sixteen were killed, one mortally wounded, two seriously wounded, and four slightly wounded. See also Block, "Requiem for a Confederate Gunboat"; "Benjamin Drummond—The First Patient," http://www.oldnavalhospital.org/fpt_main.html; and Turner, *Navy Gray,* 99–100.

89. Report of Lt. A. McLaughlin, Confederate States Navy, December 2, 1863, OR ser. 1, vol. 17, 869–72.

90. Turner, *Navy Gray,* 100. Gift wrote to Ellen Shackelford on May 28, 1863.

91. Report of Lt A. McLaughlin, Confederate States Navy, December 2, 1863, OR ser 1, vol. 17, 869–72.

92. Turner, *Navy Gray*, 100.

93. Shingleton, "The Officers," 132; and Hasegawa and Hambrecht, "The Confederate Medical Laboratories," December 1, 2013. Hasegawa and Hambrecht cite Spotswood to Mallory, OR ser. 2, vol. 2, 559–62. Shingleton says the navy had a hospital at Pensacola and Norfolk.

94. Spotswood, Annual report of receipts, from October 1, 1863, to October 1, 1864, Medical Purveyor's Department, Confederate States Navy, November 1,1864, OR 2, ser 11, vol. 2, 761.

95. Waitt, *Confederate Military Hospitals in Richmond*. Chimborazo opened in the fall of 1861 under the command of Dr. James B. McCaw. *Richmond Dispatch*, May 20, 1862, p. 2.

96. Conrad, *Rebel Reefers*, 76–77.

97. McCallum, "Medicine, Naval," 387. See also Calcutt, *Richmond's Wartime Hospitals*, 49–50; McGuire, *Diary of a Southern Refugee*, 169–70; and the Civil War Richmond website, www.civilwarrichmond.com.

98. Morgan, *Recollections of a Rebel Reefer*, 226.

99. Allison, "Confederate Matrons," 40.

100. Driver, *Confederate Sailors, Marines, and Signalmen*, 257, 297, 299. James Parr, a private with the 4th Battalion (Naval), who was ill with remittent fever and spent most of June 1864 in a Richmond area hospital. Pvt. Charles Schnellenburg spent six weeks in one of the area hospitals in November and December 1864 and January 1865. Men serving with the 4th Battalion (Naval) who fell ill were sent to nearby Richmond. Pvt. L. B. Scruggs spent November and December in a hospital in the capitol.

101. CNSF, Medical, R. W. Jeffrey, surgeon, a receipt for supplies (apples and lemons) for the C. Naval Station at Savannah, March 1 includes $12 paid to Robert Wallace for an ad, which he cut out from paper and included.

102. Brewer, *The Confederate Negro*, 95.

103. CNSF, Personnel, Medical, page 3, following page 78 on strip.

104. Calcutt, *Richmond's Wartime Hospitals*, 64–65.

105. Morgan, *Recollections of a Rebel Reefer*, 226.

106. Driver, *Confederate Sailors, Marines, and Signalmen*, 269, 287. In early January 1865, for example, R. R. Pollard, a corporal with the 4th Battalion (Naval) took off, and that same month 3rd Cpl. George W. Rollinson, sick in a Richmond hospital, also deserted.

107. Silverstone, *Warships of the Civil War Navies*, 247, 213. The source claiming that, following the battle for Vicksburg in 1863, the CSS *Nashville* was also pressed into service to care and transport sick and wounded men must be erroneous. The Union did have a hospital ship, the USS *Nashville*, however.

108. Schroeder-Lein, *The Encyclopedia of Civil War Medicine*, 144–45; Silverstone, *Warships of the Civil War Navies*, 232, 249.

109. Harwell, *Confederate Marine*, 121. Ill or injured Confederate naval personnel in naval hospitals may well have enjoyed better food than their well counterparts on shipboard as hospitals were given food allowances, and surgeons encouraged special diets for patients. See Shingleton, "The Officers," 132.

Chapter Six. Naval Combat along the Coast

1. McPherson, *War on the Waters*, 32; Wise, *Lifeline of the Confederacy*, 51; and Luraghi, "Background," 10–11.

2. Luraghi, "Background," 10–11.

3. Trotter, *Ironclads and Columbiads*, 19–20; see also Campbell, *Storm over North Carolina*, 30–31.

4. Lt. R. C. Duvall to Hon. Warren Winslow, July 22, 1861, OR ser. 1, vol. 6, 21; and Campbell, *Storm over North Carolina*, 16–18. R. C. Duvall was probably Robert C. Duvall, who had been appointed a midshipman in the U.S. Navy in 1841 and had served in Stockton's battalion in California but four years after being promoted to lieutenant in 1855 had been dismissed from the navy.

5. Duvall to Winslow, OR ser. 1, vol. 6, 21–22.

6. Duvall to Winslow.

7. Abstract log of CSS *Beaufort*, OR ser. 1, vol. 6, 790–95; and report of Lieutenant Duvall, commanding steamer *Beaufort*, July 22, 1861, OR ser. 1, vol. 6, 21–22.

8.   Duvall to Winslow, July 22, 1861, OR ser, 1, vol. 6, 21–23.
9.   Duvall to Winslow.
10. Duvall to Winslow.
11. Duvall to Winslow, 22–23; and Trotter, *Ironclads and Columbiads,* 17–18. Lieutenant Parker was ordered to assume command of *Beaufort* at New Berne on September 2, 1861 by F. Forrest, see OR ser. 1, vol. 6: 720. By the end of July 1861, the *Winslow, Beaufort, Ellis,* and *Raleigh* were on station in Pamlico Sound near Roanoke Island.
12. Duvall to Winslow, OR ser. 1, vol. 6, 22–23.
13. Duvall to Winslow.
14. Holcombe, "Types of Ships," 51–52.
15. Silverstone, *Warships of the Civil War Navies,* 202–9. The battle between the *Monitor* and *Merrimac,* the "duel of the ironclads," led to a building spree in ironclad vessels, with the Union navy constructing sixty-two *Monitor*-type vessels during the war.
16. Eggleston, "Captain Eggleston's Narrative," 166–78.
17. Eggleston, 166–78.
18. Phillips, "Surgeon of the 'Merrimac,'" 717.
19. Wood, "First Fight of the Ironclads," 696; and Quarstein, *CSS Virginia,* 116.
20. Wood, "First Fight of the Ironclads," 696.
21. Hunter, *A Year on a Monitor,* 8–9.
22. Barratt, *Farragut's Captain,* chaps. 5 and 7.
23. Ringle, *Life in Mr. Lincoln's Navy,* 51–52.
24. Friend, *West Wind, Flood Tide,* 43–44.
25. Conrad, *Rebel Reefers,* 39.
26. Bacot to sister, March 19, 1864, Bacot Letters and Diaries.
27. Bacot to sister, May 23, 1864, Bacot Letters and Diaries.
28. Keeler, *Aboard the USS Monitor, 1862,* 190–91.
29. Bennett, *Union Jacks,* 125, 184, 206.
30. Quoted in Coski, *Capital Navy,* 180.
31. Coski, 179.
32. Coski, 179.
33. Coski, 178, 181, 184.
34. Phillips, "Surgeon of the 'Merrimac,'" 718.

35. Curtis, "History of the Famous Battle."

36. Wood, "The First Fight."

37. Eggleston, "Captain Eggleston's Narrative," 166–78.

38. Curtis, "The 'Congress' and the 'Merrimac.'" From CSS *Beaufort*, Lieutenant Porcher saw the large white flag as it went up; he wrote, "Midshipman Mallory in charge of our bow guns, waved his cap and exclaimed, I'll swear on the Bible that we fired the last gun!"

39. Curtis, "History of the Famous Battle."

40. Wood, "First Fight of the Ironclads," 698; see also Scharf, *History of the Confederate States Navy*, 158–59. Another source says she listed to starboard. Time-Life Books, *The Blockade*, 55.

41. Ramsey, "Most Famous of Sea Duels," 11–12. The ram stuck in the Yankee's ship "like a stinger of a wasp inside its victim," Ramsey wrote.

42. Wood, "The First Fight," 698n.

43. Curtis, "History of the Famous Battle."

44. George Weber to Louis, March 10, 1862, from Weber Letters, Library of Virginia.

45. Quarstein, *The CSS Virginia*, quoting Catesby Jones, 128; see also F. Buchanan to S. Mallory, March 27, 1862, OR ser. 1, vol. 7, 44–49; Wood, "The First Fight," 696. Captain Marston (USS *Roanoke*, March 9, 1862 report, OR ser. 1, vol. 7, 8–9) stated that he had the aid of two tugs, but *Roanoke*'s bad steerage kept the vessel from getting head "as rapidly as we desired."

46. Curtis, "History of the Famous Battle."

47. Parker, *Recollections of a Naval Officer*, 288–89; see also Tomb, *Engineer in Gray*, 54–56. Johnson (*The Defense of Charleston Harbor*, 32–33) lists the *Palmetto State*'s officers and crew by name.

48. Parker, *Recollections of a Naval Officer*, 288–89.

49. James Tomb, January 30, 1863, OR vol. 13, 622–23.

50. Parker, *Recollections of a Naval Officer*, 294–95. Parker mused, "We knew that when day came the enemy would see they were contending with ironclads, and would refuse battle—and we with our inferior speed could not force it."

51. Parker, 295.

52. Parker, 295.

53. Parker, 295; Ingraham report, OR vol. 13, 618. In his report, Ingraham wrote, "When quite near we were hailed, 'What steamer is that? Drop your anchor or you will be into us.'" "They did not see us until we were very near," Parker explained. "Her captain then hailed us, and ordered us to keep off or he would fire. We did not reply, and he called out, 'You will be into me.'"

54. Stellwagon to DuPont, January 31, 1863, OR vol. 13, 579–80; and Parker, *Recollections of a Naval Officer*, 295.

55. Stellwagon to DuPont. Du Pont report of CSA ironclad attack on February 3, 1863, OR vol. 13, 577–78; and Johnson, *The Defense of Charleston*, 32–33.

56. Browning, *Success Was All That Was Expected*, 140; and Clark, *My Fifty Years in the Navy*, 91.

57. T. H. Eastman to Mrs. T. H. Eastman, February 3, 1863, OR vol. 13, 586; and W. E. LeRoy to DuPont, January 31, 1863, OR vol. 13, 582.

58. Tomblin, *Bluejackets and Contrabands*, 211–12n51. His commanding officer, Commander LeRoy, added details: "Owing to a fire in the forehold, we stood to the northward about ten minutes, and shoaling water kept S.E. about ten minutes to subdue the fire, and then turned around and under full steam proposed attempting to run down the ram."

59. Tomb report, in Tomb, *Engineer in Gray*, 60.

60. T. H. Eastman to Mrs. T. H. Eastman, February 3, 1863, OR vol. 13, 586.

61. T. H. Eastman to Mrs. T. H. Eastman, February 3, 1863, OR vol. 13, 586; and Tomblin, *Bluejackets and Contrabands*, 319n51.

62. Tomb letter, OR vol. 13, 621–22, quoted in Tomb, *Engineer in Gray*, 60–61. The steamer *Memphis* then came and towed *Keystone State* back to Port Royal.

63. Browning, *Success Was All That Was Expected*, 140; Ingraham report, OR vol. 13, 618; Parker, *Recollections of a Naval Officer*, 296; Scharf, *History of the Confederate States Navy*, 675–78; and LeRoy correspondence, Letter of James Tomb, January 30, 1863, OR vol. 13, 622.

64. Among the other casualties was "Robert McKinsey, second-class boy (contraband), Robert Willinger, second-class boy, (contraband)

who both were scalded to death. Among wounded were Randy Goul, second-class boy (contraband) slightly scalded face and hands." Acting Assistant Surgeon C. H. Mason to Capt. H. S. Stellwagen, January 31, 1863, OR vol. 13, 581; Du Pont to Welles, February 1863, OR vol. 13, 577–78; W. E. LeRoy to DuPont, January 31, 1863, OR vol. 13, 582; and T. H. Eastman to Mrs. T. H. Eastman, February 3, 1863, OR vol. 13, 586. Lieutenant Commander Eastman later told his wife that they had mustered 196 men on board the morning of the attack and had buried 23 and would soon probably lose another 3 men.

65. Tomb, January 30, 1863, OR vol. 13, 622.

66. Tomb, 622; and Scharf, *History of The Confederate States Navy*, 679–82. Parker thought the proclamation "ill-advised." Parker, *Recollections of a Naval Officer*, 300.

67. *Savannah Republican*, February 2, 1863, extract enclosed to Gen. G. T. Beauregard to D. N. Ingraham, January 31, 1863, OR vol. 13, 601–7; and Tomb, January 30, 1863, OR vol. 13, 622.

68. Wise, *Lifeline of the Confederacy*, 205, 208, 209–10.

69. Cox, "Mobile in the War Between the States"; Friend, *West Wind, Flood Tide*, chap. 13, "So Daring a Plan"; Hearn, *Admiral David Glasgow Farragut*, chap. 20; Lewis, *David Glasgow Farragut*, vol. 2, *Our First Admiral*, chap. 20; and McPherson, *War on the Waters*, 206–7.

70. Browning, "'Go ahead, Go ahead'"; Johnston, "The Ram Tennessee at Mobile Bay," 402; Kinney, "Farragut Mobile Bay," 389–90; and Brooke, *John M. Brooke*, 242, 247. In a test of a 7-inch Brooke mounted on a temporary carriage on the CSS *Virginia* and loaded with a maximum 12-pound powder charge, the rifle fired a hundred-pound shell four and half miles.

71. Lewis, *David Glasgow Farragut*, 261; and Parker, "The Battle of Mobile Bay," 14–15.

72. Brigadier General Page to Gen. D. H. Maury, August 6, 1864, OR 21, 557–58; and Page, "The Defense of Fort Morgan," 408.

73. Parker, "The Battle of Mobile Bay," 14, 19.

74. Clark, *My Fifty Years in the Navy*, 96; and Hutchinson, "Bay Fight," 12. Parker ("The Battle of Mobile Bay," 15–16) quotes Farragut's general

order and a supplement on July 29. Lewis (*David Glasgow Farragut*, 260) has a copy of Farragut's sketch of the vessels' formation.

75. Johnston to Buchanan, OR 21, 579; and Brigadier General Page to Gen. D. H. Maury, August 6, 1864, OR 21, 557–8.

76. E. N. Kellogg to Father, August 7, 1864, LOC; see also Friend, *West Wind, Flood Tide*, 166. Charles Clark commanded one of the *Ossipee*'s gun divisions. "All our ships had their largest flags floating from peak, staff, and every masthead. From my position on the forecastle I counted nearly sixty. It was a beautiful and inspiring sight." Clark, *My Fifty Years in the Navy*, 95.

77. Johnston report, OR 21, 579. Seeing the ram steaming into combat, soldiers from both sides paused to watch the spectacle. The thick smoke obscured Farragut's view of the action, prompting him to climb up the *Hartford*'s port rigging until he reached the futtock bands where he held on to the futtock shrouds.

78. Parker, "The Battle of Mobile Bay," 26.

79. Wharton, *Battle of Mobile Bay*, quoted in Friend, *West Wind, Flood Tide*, 203. See also Webster, "An August Morning with Farragut"; and Hutchinson, "Bay Fight," 17.

80. Parker, "The Battle of Mobile Bay," 26; Lewis, *David Glasgow Farragut*, 268; and Page, "The Defense of Fort Morgan," 408. Page wrote, "Cheers from the garrison now rang out, which were checked at once, and the order was passed to sink the admiral's ship and then cheer."

81. Parker, "The Battle of Mobile Bay," 29.

82. Lewis, *David Glasgow Farragut*, 269; Friend, *West Wind, Flood Tide*, 182; and Hearn, *Admiral David Glasgow Farragut*, 262. Farragut also gave an order to *Metacomet*. Page, "The Defense of Fort Morgan."

83. Friend, *West Wind, Flood Tide*, 189.

84. Page, "The Defense of Fort Morgan," 408–10; see also Lewis, *David Glasgow Farragut*, 269.

85. Friend, *West Wind, Flood Tide*, 191–92.

86. Friend, 191–92.

87. Parker, "The Battle of Mobile Bay," 32.

88. Friend, *West Wind, Flood Tide*, 196–97, quoting Oliver A. Batcheller, "Battle of Mobile Bay, August 5, 1864," *Magazine of History* 14, no. 6 (December 1911): 227.

89. Clark, *My Fifty Years in the Navy*, 100–101. Her stern gun, "which could have raked us, was not fired, and Lieutenant Wharton, the officer who was training it, told me afterwards that the primers failed."

90. Kellogg to Father, August 7, 1864; see also Parker, "The Battle of Mobile Bay," 32; and Report of Commander Johnston, August 13, 1864, OR vol. 21, 580. Friend (*West Wind, Flood Tide*, 215) claims that Franklin Buchanan, determined to get the best of Farragut, ignored reports that the *Tennessee* had sprung leaks and was taking on water, and he told Johnston to stay the course and steer for the *Hartford*.

91. Kellogg to Father, August 7, 1864.

92. Kellogg to Father.

93. Friend, *West Wind, Flood Tide*, 198; and Lewis, *David Glasgow Farragut*, 271.

94. Kellogg to Father, August 7, 1864; see also Lewis, *David Glasgow Farragut*, 271; and Harrie Webster Papers, "An August with Farragut at Mobile Bay," LOC. Webster also wrote "The Battle of Mobile Bay in a Monitor," War Paper No. 14, Military Order of the Loyal Legion of the United States, Commandery of the State of California.

95. Friend, *West Wind, Flood Tide*, 219.

96. Clark, *My Fifty Years in the Navy*, 102.

97. Webster manuscript, LOC; see also Friend, *West Wind, Flood Tide*, 212; and Batcheller, "Battle of Mobile Bay," 229.

98. Friend, *West Wind, Flood Tide*, 212, 213; Parker, "The Battle of Mobile Bay," 32; and Conrad, "What the Fleet Surgeon Saw," 264.

99. Clark, *My Fifty Years in the Navy*, 102.

100. Batcheller, "Battle of Mobile Bay," 229; see also Clark, 103; Lewis, *David Glasgow Farragut*, 278; and Officers of the ram *Tennessee* who were in action, OR vol. 21, 579. "The guns of the *Hartford* went off at less than two-second intervals, a salute never to be forgotten." Clark, *My Fifty Years in the Navy*, 108.

101. Conrad, "What the Fleet Surgeon Saw of the Fight in Mobile Bay," 264.
102. Friend, *West Wind, Flood Tide*, 215; and Lewis, *David Glasgow Farragut*, 276–77.
103. Hutchinson, "Bay Fight," 20.
104. Friend, *West Wind, Flood Tide*, 214; and Marchand to Farragut, OR vol. 21, 466. "Our engines were kept in action, however, and the peculiar smashing sound which succeeded every discharge of our fifteen-inch gun told us below that the ram was not far way." Webster manuscript, LOC.
105. Clark, *My Fifty Years in the Navy*; see also Johnston, "The Ram Tennessee at Mobile Bay; Johnston report, OR vol. 21, 580; Lewis, *David Glasgow Farragut*, 273;
106. Johnston report, OR vol. 21, 58; and Lewis, *David Glasgow Farragut*, 277.
107. Lewis, *David Glasgow Farragut*, 277.
108. Lewis, 278–79; Clark, *My Fifty Years in the Navy*, 106–7; Buchanan to Mallory, OR vol. 21, 587; Log of the USS *Ossipee*, OR vol. 21, 841–42; and Hearn, *Admiral David Glasgow Farragut*, 283.
109. J. D. Johnston report to Buchanan, August 13, 1864, OR vol. 21, 580.
110. J. D. Johnston report to Buchanan, 580–81.
111. Lewis, *David Glasgow Farragut*, 278–79; Clark, *My Fifty Years in the Navy*, 106–7; Buchanan to Mallory, OR vol. 21, 587; and Log of the USS *Ossipee*, OR vol. 21, 841–42.
112. Lewis, *David Glasgow Farragut*, 278–79.
113. Clark, *My Fifty Years in the Navy*, 106.
114. J. D. Johnston report to Buchanan, OR vol. 21, 581.
115. Schoonmaker, Mobile Bay, Battle of, Ala., 1864, LOC.
116. Hearn, *Admiral David Glasgow Farragut*, 292–93.
117. Friend, *West Wind, Flood Tide*, 232, 237; Hearn, *Admiral David Glasgow Farragut*, 292–93; Mallory, OR vol. 21, 599–600; Lewis, *David Glasgow Farragut*, 281; Kellogg to Father, August 7, 1864, LOC; Johnston to Buchanan, enclosure, list of casualties on board the Confederate States ram *Tennessee*, OR vol. 21, 581; and Edward DeBois to Bennett, August 8, 1864, OR vol. 21, 596. The night after

the battle, the *Morgan* eluded the federal ships and reached Mobile's defenses. The *Gaines*'s men made it safely in small boats to Mobile.

118. Clark, *My Fifty Years in the Navy,* 111; and Friend, *West Wind, Flood Tide,* 226, 246.

119. Clark, *My Fifty Years in the Navy,* 111–12; Friend, *West Wind, Flood Tide,* 235–40, 246; and Lewis, *David Glasgow Farragut,* chap. 24.

120. Clark, *My Fifty Years in the Navy,* 111; see also Hearn, *Admiral David Glasgow Farragut,* 297. "The commander of Fort Morgan was General Randolph Page formerly an officer in our navy, where he had been known as 'Ramrod' Page," Clark explained.

121. Clark, *My Fifty Years in the Navy,* 111–12; see also Friend, *West Wind, Flood Tide,* 235–40; and Lewis, *David Glasgow Farragut,* chap. 24.

Chapter Seven. Naval Warfare on the High Seas

1. McPherson, *War on the Waters,* 112–13; and deKay, *The Rebel Raiders,* 4–7.
2. Browning, "The Confederate States Navy Department," 34–35.
3. Merli, "The Confederate Navy, 1861–1865," 128.
4. Delaney, "Strategy and Tactics," 196–97, 200; and Tucker, *Raphael Semmes and the Alabama,* 95.
5. Tucker, *Raphael Semmes and the Alabama,* 26; see also Kell, *Recollections of a Naval Life,* 146.
6. Kell, *Recollections of a Naval Life,* 147; see also Semmes, *Rebel Raider,* 13, 18–19. For Semmes' description of some of his officers, see Semmes, *Rebel Raider,* 34–35.
7. Chaffin, *The H. L. Hunley,* 37; and deKay, *The Rebel Raiders,* 17–18.
8. Shingleton, *High Seas Confederate,* 42; Boykin, *Sea Devil of the Confederacy,* chap. 9; and Campbell, *Sea Hawk,* 77–78.
9. Boykin, *Sea Devil of the Confederacy,* 102–3; Campbell, *Sea Hawk,* 79; and Shingleton, *High Seas Confederate,* 46–47.
10. Boykin, *Sea Devil of the Confederacy,* 102–3; Campbell, *Sea Hawk,* 79; and Shingleton, *High Seas Confederate* 44–45.
11. Shingleton, *High Seas Confederate,* 46–47.
12. Summersell, *The Cruise of the C.S.S. Sumter,* 72–74.

13. Kell, *Recollections of a Naval Life*, 187.
14. Semmes, quoted in Fullam, *The Journal of George Townley Fullam*, 14; see also deKay, *The Rebel Raiders*, 92–93.
15. Kell, *Recollections of a Naval Life*, 196.
16. Kell, 196.
17. Fullam, *The Journal of George Townley Fullam*, 48–49; see also Sinclair, *Two Years on the Alabama*, 197.
18. Summersell, *The Cruise of the C.S.S. Sumter*, 149.
19. Waddell was ambivalent about the ethics of targeting civilian ships. Schooler, *The Last Shot*, 42.
20. Waddell, *C.S.S. Shenandoah*, 104–5.
21. Waddell, 104–5.
22. Kell, *Recollections of a Naval Life*, 156; and Summersell, *Cruise of the C.S.S. Sumter*, 79–84.
23. Kell, *Recollections of a Naval Life*, 157–58; and Summersell, *Cruise of the C.S.S. Sumter*, 85–86.
24. Summersell, *Cruise of the C.S.S. Sumter*, 88–89.
25. Maffitt, *The Life and Services of John Newland Maffitt*, journal entry, January 21, 1863, p. 272. See also Boykin, *Sea Devil of the Confederacy*, 148–51.
26. Campbell, *Sea Hawk*, 88–89.
27. Campbell, 89–91.
28. Maffitt, *The Life and Services of John Newland Maffitt*, journal entry, February 12, 1863, p. 274.
29. Boykin, *Ghost Ship of the Confederacy*, 173.
30. Kell, *Recollections of a Naval Life*, 175; and Summersell, *Cruise of the C.S.S. Sumter*, 120.
31. A. L. Drayton Papers, diary, LOC; see also Campbell, *Sea Hawk*, 99–101; and Boykin, *Sea Devil*, 196–97.
32. A. L. Drayton Papers, diary. "C. W. Read, Capt., Pat J. Mattherson, Bob Matthews, A J. Stewart, J. Coffa, P. Murphy, Robertson, Dan Moore, McLeod, Billings, Lawson, Wilton, R. Murray and also Mr. Brown as 2nd and McDaniels." Campbell lists all eighteen crewmen and says Read promoted petty officers Billings, N. B. Pryde, and J. W. Matherson to master's mates. Campbell, *Sea Hawk*, 100, 102.
33. A. L. Drayton Papers, diary, LOC.

34. Campbell, *Sea Hawk*, 108–10.
35. Fullam, *The Journal of George Townley Fullam*, 47.
36. deKay, *The Rebel Raiders*, 186.
37. Ellicott, *The Life of John Ancrum Winslow*, 177–79; and Tucker, *Raphael Semmes and the Alabama*, 72–73.
38. Fullam, *The Journal of George Townley Fullam*, 190.
39. Semmes, *Memoirs of Service Afloat*, 370–87.
40. Kell, *Recollections of a Naval Life*; Ellicott, *The Life of John Ancrum Winslow*, 183; Tucker, *Raphael Semmes and the Alabama*, 76–77; and deKay, *The Rebel Raiders*, 194–95. Ellicott surmises that Semmes realized the war was nearing an end, and that he could not have the ship properly repaired nor reship his sailors if they were discharged. Ellicott, *The Life of John Ancrum Winslow*, 183.
41. McPherson, *War on the Waters*, 304; and Tucker, *Raphael Semmes and the Alabama*, 80.
42. Tucker, *Raphael Semmes and the Alabama*, 80; see also deKay, *The Rebel Raiders*, 195.
43. Kell, letter to H, June 20, 1864, in *Recollections of a Naval Life*, 221.
44. Ellicott, *The Life of John Ancrum Winslow*, 202–3; deKay, *The Rebel Raiders*, 198–99. Ellicott noted as well that one 32-pounder exploded in hammock netting, starting a fire, but the *Kearsarge*'s trained damage crew promptly extinguished it.
45. Ellicott, *The Life of John Ancrum Winslow*, 203; and deKay, *The Rebel Raiders*, 199–200.
46. Delaney, *John McIntosh Kell*, 173.
47. Summersell, *The Cruise of the C.S.S. Sumter*, 194–95; and Kell, *Recollections of a Naval Life*, 249–51. DeKay claims the *Deerhound* rescued forty-one officers and men, including eight wounded. deKay, *The Rebel Raiders*, 202.
48. Silverstone, *Warships of the Civil War Navies*, 211, 213, 215.
49. Waddell, *C.S.S. Shenandoah*, 85n20.
50. Waddell, 82–83n6, 95n26. Bulloch stated she was 1,600 tons, beams of iron, planked from keel to gunwale with East India teak, engines were direct acting with two 47-inch in diameter cylinders, nominal horsepower of 220, and she had a lifting screw.
51. Waddell, 102, 107; and Chaffin, *Sea of Gray*, 65.

52. Waddell, *C.S.S. Shenandoah*, 181, 184.

53. deKay, *The Rebel Raiders*, 98–99.

54. Kell, *Recollections of a Naval Life*, 190–91; see also Tucker, *Raphael Semmes and the Alabama*, 44.

55. Fullam, *The Journal of George Townley Fullam*, 41–42. The assertions came from Capt. George Hagar of the *Brilliant*.

56. Quoted in Bradford, "Raphael Semmes," 6.

57. Kell, *Recollections of a Naval Life*, 190–91; and Tucker, *Raphael Semmes and the Alabama*, 44.

58. Fullam, *The Journal of George Townley Fullam*, 37–38.

59. Kell, *Recollections of a Naval Life*, 201, 204.

60. Drayton Papers, diary, May 21, 1863, LOC.

61. Chaffin, *Sea of Gray*, 312.

62. Chaffin, 303.

63. Maffitt, *The Life and Services of John Newland Maffitt*, 380; Boykin, *Sea Devil of the Confederacy*, 102–3; Campbell, *Sea Hawk*, 79; and Shingleton, *High Seas Confederate*, 103.

Chapter Eight. Guns, Mines, and Experimental Craft

1. Morgan, *Recollections of a Rebel Reefer*, 80–81.

2. Trigg, "Daniel Trigg," 33–35.

3. Trigg, 33–35; and Coski, *Capitol Navy*, 37. The federal ships engaged a rebel battery at Fort Boykin and then steamed on past Fort Huger.

4. Trigg, "Daniel Trigg," 33–35.

5. Trigg, 33–35. A sketch of the Drewry's Bluff position shows Captain Tuckers' gun to the right just at the edge of the ninety-foot bluff and inside the fort six guns in emplacements at the fort's river edge facing north. A shell room and powder magazine were placed inside the fort well behind the guns.

6. Coski, *Capital Navy*, 42.

7. Morgan, *Recollections of a Rebel Reefer*, 80.

8. Sullivan, "The Marines," 157. See also Coski, *Capital Navy*, 42–43.

9. Morgan, *Recollections of a Rebel Reefer*, 81–82.

10. Morgan, 81–82.

11. Morgan, 82.
12. Morgan, 82.
13. Coski, *Capital Navy*, 44; see also Scharf, *History of the Confederate Navy*, 713.
14. Coski, *Capital Navy*, 52–54. According to twenty-four-year old Francis W. Smith, a Virginia Military Institute graduate who had been appointed a major of artillery in the Confederate army and given charge of the Drewry's Bluff battery, Sidney Smith Lee was "the poorest excuse of an officer I ever saw and worst of all, he gets all the credit for my work." Coski, 53. Although Admiral Buchanan and others believed that the navy had won the battle of Drewry's Bluff, that important post now became a joint army–navy command, which made life difficult for officers such as Smith. He acknowledged that the post had "a set of naval people who are first rate fellows, but commanded by an octogenarian imbecile." Coski, 53.
15. Coski, *Capital Navy*, 56.
16. Morgan, *Recollections of a Rebel Reefer*, 85.
17. Sullivan, "The Marines," 157; and Coski, *Capital Navy*, 54, 112.
18. Sullivan, "The Marines," 157.
19. Grady, "Hunter Davidson and the 'Squib.'" Following Virginia's secession, Davidson had resigned his commission in the U.S. Navy to join the Confederate States Navy and had been a gunnery officer on the CSS *Virginia*.
20. Crowley, "The Confederate Torpedo Service." A document signed by Navy Secretary Mallory referred to Crowley as an "electrician." Davidson himself referred to Crowley as his electrician in a letter dated May 1874 published in the *Southern Historical Society Papers*, vol. 2.
21. Crowley.
22. Crowley.
23. Crowley.
24. Crowley.
25. Calvin Gibbs Hutchinson, "Service on a Ferry-Boat," in Hutchinson Papers.
26. Quoted in Crowley, "The Confederate Torpedo Service."

27. Calvin Hutchinson to William Hill, May 19, 1864, Hutchinson Papers.
28. Coski, *Capital Navy*, 152; and J. C. Beaumont to Lee, May 11, 1864, OR vol. 10, 9–11.
29. Crowley, "The Confederate Torpedo Service."
30. Grattan, *Under the Blue Pennant*, 97–98. Grattan argued that Private Johnson thus probably saved other Union vessels from suffering a fate similar to *Commodore Jones*. Grattan, 98.
31. Rushmore to Welles, November 19, 1864, OR vol. 10, 29.
32. Anderson to Lee, May 18, 1864, OR vol. 10, 27.
33. Calvin Hutchinson to William Hill, May 19, 1864, Hutchinson Papers.
34. Crowley, "The Confederate Torpedo Service."
35. Curtis, "My Personal Remembrance of an Expedition," in A. O. Wright Collection of Confederate Navy Service Records, Library of Virginia.
36. Curtis, 1.
37. H. Davidson to Mallory, April 15, 1864, OR vol. 10, 604.
38. Curtis, "My Personal Remembrance of an Expedition," 1.
39. Curtis, 1.
40. Abstract log of the USS *Minnesota*, OR vol. 9, 603.
41. Enclosure, Birtwhistle to Lee, April 9, 1864, OR vol. 9, 594.
42. Lt. Cdr. J. H. Upshur to Lee, April 9, 1864, OR vol. 9, 593.
43. Curtis, "My Personal Remembrance of an Expedition," 2.
44. Curtis, 2.
45. Curtis, 2; and Lt. Cdr. J. H. Upshur to Lee, April 9, 1864, OR vol. 9, 593. Lee reasoned there was no excuse for the *Poppy*'s failure to respond to the call to run the torpedo boat down, and he recommended that acting ensign and pilot Isaac Miller, commanding the *Poppy*, have his appointment revoked and that he revert to his former grade of master's mate.
46. Curtis, "My Personal Remembrance of an Expedition"; see also Perry, *Infernal Machines*.
47. Grady, "Hunter Davidson and the 'Squib.'"
48. Browning, *Success Was All That Was Expected*, 290–91.

49. Chaffin, *The H. L. Hunley*, 169, 171–72.
50. Browning, *Success Was All That Was Expected*, 290–91.
51. Chaffin, *The H. L. Hunley*, 183–84; Ragan, *Union and Confederate Submarine Warfare* 10–12; and Delaney, "Strategy and Tactics," 207–8.
52. Chaffin, *The H. L. Hunley*, 183–84; Ragan, *Union and Confederate Submarine Warfare*, 10–12; and Delaney, "Strategy and Tactics," 206, 209.

Chapter Nine. Naval Warfare on the Rivers

1. Bennett, *Union Jacks*, 35; and Ringle, *Life in Mr. Lincoln's Navy*, 35.
2. African American pilots were not enlisted but were specially hired as pilots.
3. Campbell, *Confederate Naval Forces on Western Waters*, 16; Davis to Welles, OR vol. 23, 15; and Gregory's report, OR vol. 23, 15–16.
4. McPherson, *War on the Waters*, 25; and Patterson, *The Mississippi River Campaign*, 23.
5. Melton, "Shipbuilding," 91–92, 96–98.
6. Campbell, *Confederate Naval Forces on Western Waters*, 58–62, 78–82.
7. Campbell, *Confederate Naval Forces on Western Waters*, Chapter Two.
8. Campbell, 32.
9. Bennett, *Union Jacks*, 83.
10. Gosnell, *Guns on the Western Waters*, 108.
11. Warley, "The Ram Manassas," 89. See also Gosnell, *Guns on the Western Waters*, 108; Warley to Mitchell, June 8, 1862, OR 18:302–4; Campbell, *Sea Hawk of the Confederacy*, 39.
12. Tomblin, *Civil War on the Mississippi*, 199–202; McPherson, *War on the Waters*, 68–69; and Patterson, *The Mississippi River Campaign*, 163–65.
13. Brown, "The Confederate Gun-boat Arkansas," 572–73. See also Campbell, *Confederate Naval Forces on Western Waters*, 92–96; Tomblin, *Civil War on the Mississippi*, 113–16; Patterson, *The Mississippi River Campaign*, 158–59; and Davis report, June 6, 1862, OR vol. 23, 119–20.

14. Slagle, *Ironclad Captain*, 259–61; and Brown, "The Confederate Gun-boat Arkansas," 572–73.

15. Brown, "The Confederate Gun-Boat Arkansas," 572–73.

16. Tomblin, *The Civil War on the Mississippi*, 149.

17. Gosnell, *Guns on the Western Waters*, 128.

18. Read, "Reminiscences of the Confederate Navy," 353. See also Gosnell, *Guns on the Western Waters*, 104–6n17; and Smith, *CSS Arkansas*, loc. 216–19.

19. Gift, "The Story of the Arkansas," 163–67.

20. Walke, *Naval Scenes and Reminiscences*, 330.

21. Walke, *Naval Scenes and Reminiscences*, 330. See also Walke to Davis, July 15, 1862, OR vol. 19, 41–72; Soley, "Naval Operations in the Vicksburg Campaign," 555; Milligan, *Gunboats Down the Mississippi*, 82–85; and Joiner, *Mr. Lincoln's Brown Water Navy*, 84–87.

22. Campbell, *Confederate Naval Forces on Western Waters*, 114; Tomblin, 149.

23. Quoted in Smith, *CSS Arkansas*, loc. 27–29. Campbell says he gathered his crew together. Campbell, *Confederate Naval Forces on Western Waters*, 114.

24. In his description of the opening of the engagement, Brown wrote, "Directing our pilot to stand for the iron-clad, the center vessel of the three, I gave the order not to fire our bow guns lest by doing so we diminish our speed, relying for the moment on our broadside guns to keep the ram and the *Tyler* from gaining on our quarter which they seemed eager to do." Brown, "The Confederate Gun-boat Arkansas," 573.

25. Morrison, Civil War Diary of John G. Morrison, July 15, 1862, New York State Military Museum and Veterans Research Center.

26. Campbell, *Sea Hawk of the Confederacy*, 58; Campbell, *Confederate Naval Forces on Western Waters*, 116.

27. Campbell, *Confederate Naval Forces on Western Waters*, 117; and Gift, "The Story of the *Arkansas*," 53.

28. Morrison diary, July 15, 1862.

29. Read, *Reminiscences of the Confederate Navy*, 354. See also Campbell, *Sea Hawk of the Confederacy*, 60; and Smith, CSS *Arkansas*, loc.

28871–74, 2888–92. Pilots William Gilmore and James Brady took over, but neither was familiar with the Yazoo.

30. Brown, "The Confederate Gun-boat Arkansas," 580.

31. Morrison diary, July 15, 1862; see also Read, *Reminiscences of the Confederate Navy*, 354. "Our engines were stopped, and ranging up alongside with the muzzles of our guns touching him we poured in a broadside of solid shot, when his colors came down." Gift quoted in Campbell, *Sea Hawk of the Confederacy*, 62. As she was crossing, Morrison fired "a sixty-eight into her at less than two yards distance, with what effect I don't know. We then tried to bring our port broadside to bear on her but she was not in range." Morrison diary, July 15, 1862.

32. Morrison diary, July 15, 1862.

33. Lieutenant Gwin, July 15, 1862, and July 16, 1862, OR vol. 19, 36–37; and Brown, quoted in Gosnell, *Guns on the Western Waters*, 117.

34. Gwin, July 16, 1862, OR vol. 19, 36–37.

35. Brown, "The Confederate Gun-boat Arkansas," 575; see also Campbell, *Sea Hawk of the Confederacy*, 61–2; and Gosnell, *Guns on the Western Waters* 122.

36. Gosnell, *Guns on the Western Waters*, 115.

37. Campbell, *Sea Hawk of the Confederacy*, 65; and Brown, "The Confederate Gun-boat Arkansas," 576. Observing the Yankee rams poised to oppose him, Brown said, "Brady, shave that line of men-of-war as close as you can, so that the rams will not have room to gather head-way in coming out to strike us." Brown quoted in Gosnell, *Guns on the Western Waters*, 119.

38. Brown, quoted in Campbell, *Sea Hawk of the Confederacy*, 64–65.

39. Gift quoted in Gosnell, *Guns on the Western Waters*, 119.

40. "From Vicksburg," *Cincinnati Daily Gazette*, July 24, 1862.

41. Gosnell, *Guns on the Western Waters*, 121.

42. Gosnell, 121.

43. Anthony Francis O'Neil diary, July 15, 1862, LOC.

44. Trotter, *Ironclads and Columbiads*, 224–25; Campbell, *Storm over North Carolina*, 29; and Daniel B. Conrad, "Capture and Burning of the Federal Gunboat 'Underwriter,'" *Southern Historical Society Papers* 19 (1892): 93–99.

45. Richard H. Bacot to his sister, February 8, 1864, in Bacot Letters and Diaries.

46. Conrad, "Capture and Burning of the Federal Gunboat 'Underwriter.'"

47. Afterward, Wood praised Captain Wilson and his Marines for their "fine bearing and soldierly conduct." Conrad, *Rebel Reefers*, 67; Loyall, "Capture of the Underwriter"; Scharf, *History of the Confederate States Navy*, 396; and Campbell, *Storm over North Carolina*, 129–30. David M. Sullivan, "The Marines," 161, says 245 officers and men including 25 Marines, and Trotter, *Ironclads and Columbiads*, 225, says 285 officers and men including 25 Marines.

48. Richard H. Bacot to his sister, February 8, 1864, Bacot Letters.

49. Bacot to his sister. "We then went to Kinston NC and joined Cap J. T. Wood CSN who had 10 boats and 125 men and officers. While going on we rode in the boats which were lashed to flat cars. After hauling the boats down to the Neuse river with mule teams we embarked and pulled down the river 5 miles; to within a few miles of Newbern."

50. Conrad, *Capture and Burning of the Federal Gunboat Underwriter*.

51. Conrad, *Rebel Reefers*, 62; and Scharf, *History of the Confederate States Navy*, 396.

52. Wood to Mallory, February 11, 1864, OR vol. 9, 452.

53. Trotter, *Ironclads and Columbiads*, 226–27.

54. Loyall, "Capture of the Underwriter"; and G. Edgar Allen, February 2, 1864, OR vol. 9, 441.

55. Conrad, *Capture and Burning of the Federal Gunboat Underwriter*.

56. Conrad, 8.

57. Campbell, *Storm over North Carolina*, 136–37.

58. Loyall, "Capture of the Underwriter"; see also G. Edgar Allen, February 2, 1864, OR vol. 9, 441.

59. Loyall, "Capture of the Underwriter."

60. Conrad, *Capture and Burning of the Federal Gunboat Underwriter*.

61. G. Edgar Allen, OR vol. 9, 441.

62. Wood report, OR vol. 9, 452.

63. Bacot to sister, February 8, 1864, Bacot Letters and Diaries.

64. Parker *Recollections of a Naval Officer*, 326–27.

65. Driver, *Confederate Sailors*, 124, 294.

66. Gift to Cdr. Catesby Jones, February 13, 1864, OR vol. 9, 453.
67. Wood to Mallory, OR vol. 9, 452; and G. Edgar Allen to G. W. Graves, February 2, 1864, OR vol. 9, 441.
68. Trotter, *Ironclads and Columbiads*, 229–31; and Bacot to sister, February 8, 1864, Bacot Letters and Diaries.

Chapter Ten. Prisoners and Prison Camps

1. Union vessels also captured four wooden cruisers, the *Archer* (on June 28, 1863), *Florida* (on October 7, 1864), *Tallahassee* (seized by the British on April 9, 1865), and *Tuscaloosa* (on December 29, 1863), as well as smaller vessels such as the *Bombshell, Calhoun, De Soto, Ellis, Selma, Teaser,* and *Launch No. 3.* The *Morgan* surrendered and two, *Sea Bird* and *Sacanahm,* sank. CSS *Atlanta* was captured on June 17, 1863; *Baltic,* on May 10, 1865; *Columbia,* on April 26, 1865; *Eastport,* captured incomplete on February 8, 1862; *Missouri,* on June 3, 1865; *Nashville,* on May 10, 1865; *Tennessee,* on August 5, 1864; *Texas,* uncompleted on April 4, 1865.
2. Hain, *A Confederate Chronicle*, 93–95.
3. Hain, 97–98. The ship may have been intentionally run aground or sabotaged; the evidence is not conclusive.
4. Hain, 102–5. Two lists of prisoners from the *Atlanta* survive. The USS *Vermont* reported taking 114 Confederate crewmen on board. The *James Adger* took 116 men and an additional 12 men who may have been injured and were rejoining the crew. All but the cabin boy went to the POW camp at Fort Warren, where three more sailors joined them, George W. Quarles, B. R. Skelton, and Francis Beville, and Marine corporal Daniel Rioden. The *Savannah Republican* listed the twenty-two officers.
5. McPherson, *Battle Cry of Freedom*, 802.
6. Driver, *Confederate Sailors*, 322, 327, 118, 102, 100. Robert Driver has recorded the names of Confederate naval and Marine personnel from Virginia and Maryland held at Elmira, Point Lookout, Fort McHenry, Johnson's Island, Fort Warren, Fort Delaware, Camp Chase, Ship Island, and Camp Douglas.

7. Bush, *I Fear I Shall Never Leave This Island*, 44, 93, 120.

8. Driver, *Confederate Sailors*, 322, 327, 118, 102, 100.

9. Pickenbaugh, *Captives in Gray*, 21; Hain, *A Confederate Chronicle*, 107, 110; Tomb, *Engineer in Gray*, 44.

10. Tomb, *Engineer in Gray*, 43–44; see also Pickenbaugh, *Captives in Gray*, 200, 62–63.

11. *New York Times* quoted in Hesseltine, *Civil War Prisons*, 100.

12. *New York Times* quoted in Hesseltine, *Civil War Prisons*, 100; McPherson, *Battle Cry of Freedom*, 802; and Fetzer and Mowday, *Unlikely Allies*, xii–xv. McPherson cites the report of Brigadier General Ainsworth, June 29, 1903, in Rhodes, *History of the United States*, 507–8. The article includes a list of prisoners and cites the crew of the privateer schooner *Dixie*, blockade runner *Henry Middleton*, and the crew and passengers of the schooner *Colonel Lang*.

13. King, *Three Hundred Days in a Yankee Prison*, 84.

14. Joslyn, *Immortal Captives*, 48; see also Hesseltine, *Civil War Prisons*, 42–43; and Fetzer and Mowday, *Unlikely Allies*, 112–13.

15. Hesseltine, *Civil War Prisons*, 116.

16. Scribner and Scribner, *Ship Island Mississippi*, 61.

17. Quoted in Scribner and Scribner, *Ship Island Mississippi*, 61.

18. Scribner and Scribner, 61.

19. Bush, *I Fear I Shall Never Leave this Island*, 33–34, 51.

20. Handerson, *Yankee in Gray*; and Boyle, "A Prison Diary," in Walter Ralph Steiner Papers, LOC.

21. Josyln, *Immortal Captives*, 48; Fetzer and Mowday, *Unlikely Allies*, 114; Stokes, *The Immortal 600*, 21, 64–65; and Anderson, "A Confederate Prisoner at Camp Chase." Capt. Henry Dickinson, 2nd Virginia Cavalry, described two typical meals.

22. Bush, *I Fear I Shall Never Leave This Island*, 112.

23. Anderson, "A Confederate Prisoner at Camp Chase."

24. Anderson, "A Confederate Prisoner at Camp Chase."

25. King, *Three Hundred Days in a Yankee Prison*, 76–77. Camp Chase prisoner John H. King remembered that the prisoners' money was taken from them and tickets issued by the superintendent. "This

meant, of course, that we should only purchase from the sutler. . . . After a time, however, the sutler's store was closed and the victims left with the unredeemed tickets of the rascally superintendent."

26. Springer and Robins, *Transforming Civil War Prisons*, 38; Frohman, *Rebels on Lake Erie*, 15; Bush, *I Fear I Shall Never Leave This Island*, 119; and Hesseltine, *Civil War Prisons*, 42–43.

27. Bush, *I Fear I Shall Never Leave This Island*, 119.

28. Springer and Robins, *Transforming Civil War Prisons*, 38; and Frohman, *Rebels on Lake Erie*, 15. Kate Makely, in a letter to her husband, Wesley, who was imprisoned at Johnson's Island, listed the contents of a box she had sent to him: one coat, one pair pants, two pairs cotton socks, hat, neck ties, fifty paper collars, one pair shoes, one piece of soap, and an assortment of sundry foodstuffs. She wrote, "I hope the wine will be of benefit to you it is very good and good for desentery." Bush, *I Fear I Shall Never Leave This Island*, 119.

29. Makely spent much of his time reading that cold winter of 1865 and told her, "the weather has been so bad lately that I scarcely get out of my room at all, and I am very much put to pass the time." He asked her to send him several titles, including Washington Irving's *The Life of Mahomet*. Bush, *I Fear I Shall Never Leave This Island*, 39. See also Kate to Nessa, May 23, 1864, Kate to Nessa, January 7, 1864, in Bush, 87; and Makely to Kate, February 9, 1865, in Bush, 192.

30. Pickenbaugh, *Captives in Gray*, 9.

31. Boyle, "A Prison Diary," June 10, 1864; see also Boyle, May 29, 1864.

32. Boyle, July 1, 1864.

33. Boyle, June 28, 1864.

34. Hesseltine, *Civil War Prisons*, 182; and Handerson, *Yankee in Gray*.

35. Ivy, *Camp Chase*, iii, 92–95.

36. Ivy, iii, 92–95. The Camp Chase prison list does not reveal any Confederate States Navy or Marine Corps burials.

37. King, *Three Hundred Days*, 86; and Ivy, *Camp Chase*, 92–95.

38. John W. Rush, Letters from Camp Chase, January 6, 1865. See also King, *Three Hundred Days*, 94–96; Ivy, *Camp Chase*, iii, 92–95.

39. Pickenbaugh, *Captives in Gray*, 203.

40. King, 35–36.

41. Quoted in Hain, *A Confederate Chronicle*, 112–14.

42. Scribner and Scribner, *Ship Island, Mississippi*, 56–59.

43. Scribner and Scribner, 56–59.

44. Quoted in Scribner and Scribner, 59.

45. Quoted in Scribner and Scribner, 59.

46. Hollandsworth, "Union Soldiers on Ship Island."

47. Hollandsworth.

48. Charles E. Frohman, *Rebels on Lake Erie*, "Life in Prison," 16–17.

49. King, *Three Hundred Days*, 78–79; and Pickenbaugh, *Captives in Gray*, 98.

50. Quoted in Hain, *A Confederate Chronicle*, 115.

51. Virginia Dalton to Commander Goldsborough, December 17, 1861, CNSF, Prisoners, Release and Parole, A-W, 33–34. Lieutenant Dalton may have been Lt. Hamilton Henderson Dalton, who resigned from the U.S. Navy and was sent to Fort Warren 1861–62 and then exchanged. Driver, *Confederate Sailors*, 80–81.

52. King, *Three Hundred Days*, 91–93.

53. Anderson, "A Confederate Prisoner at Camp Chase."

54. Quoted in Hain, *Confederate Chronicle*, 115, 116, 117.

55. Butler to U.S. Grant, August 18, 1864, in War of the Rebellion Official Records of Union and Confederate Armies, OR ser. 2, vol. 7, 607.

56. Grant to Lee, October 2, 1864; Lee to Grant, October 1, 1864; Lee to Grant, October 3, 1864, in War of the Rebellion Official Records of Union and Confederate Armies, OR ser. 1, vol. 7, 906, 909, 914.

57. Watson, *Southern Service on Land and Sea*, 135. Some of the prisoners, Union sick and wounded men, may have come from Camp Lawton in Millen, Georgia, which held 10,000 POWs in November 1864.

58. Pickenbaugh, *Captives in Gray*, 51.

59. Inslee Deaderick to his father, David Deaderick, letter from Camp Chase prison camp.

60. Pickenbaugh, *Captives in Gray*, 199–201, quoting from the William S. Dillon diary, May 20, 1864; see also Bennett, *Union Jacks*, 80.

Chapter Eleven. Fighting to the Finish

1. Watson, *Southern Service on Land and Sea*, 140.
2. Melton, *Best Station of Them All*, 396–97; Watson, *Southern Service on Land and Sea*, 145; and Chapman to F. O. Pinkney, OR ser 1, vol. 11, 372–75.
3. Watson, *Southern Service on Land and Sea*, 145. See also Iverson Graves to Mrs. Sarah Graves, January 20, 1863, in Harwell, *A Confederate Marine*, 127–79; Trotter, *Ironclads and Columbiads*, 328; and Melton, *Best Station of Them All*, 396–97. Officers assigned to the battery included Lt. George Arledge of the *Atlanta* and Midn. Thomas Berrien.
4. Watson, *Southern Service on Land and Sea*, 145.
5. Watson, 146–47.
6. Watson, 147.
7. Watson, 147–48; see also Trotter, *Ironclads and Columbiads*, 389–94, 398–99.
8. Watson, *Southern Service on Land and Sea*, 148, 150. See also Melton, *Best Station of Them All*, 399–400; and Trotter, *Ironclads and Columbiads*, 328, 386–87.
9. Watson, *Southern Service on Land and Sea*, 150.
10. Watson, 157.
11. Watson, 158.
12. Jack, *Memoirs of E. A. Jack Steam Engineer*, 37–38.
13. Jack, 37–38.
14. Watson, *Southern Service on Land Sea*, 159–60.
15. Bacot to sister, March 27, 1865, Bacot Letters and Diaries, State Archives of North Carolina, Raleigh.
16. Bacot to sister, March 27, 1865, Bacot Letters and Diaries.
17. Semmes, *Memoirs of Service Afloat*, 803.
18. Coski, *Capital Navy*, 215–16; W. F. Shippey, C.S.N., "A Leaf from My Log-Book," *Master Society Papers* 12, no. 184: 416–21, quoted in Scharf, *History of the Confederate States Navy*, 742–43; and

Donnelly, "Confederate Navy Forlorn Hope," *Military Affairs*, vol. 28, no. 2 (Summer 1964): 73–78. https://www.jstor.org/stable/1983758.

19. Shippey, "A Leaf from my Log-Book," quoted in Scharf, *History of the Confederate States Navy*, 742–43.

20. Shippey.

21. Wilson, *Willie Wilson's War*, 36.

22. Shippey, "A Leaf from my Log-Book."

23. Wilson, *Willie Wilson's War*, 36–37.

24. Wilson, 36–37.

25. Wilson, 37.

26. Coski, *Capital Navy*, 219–20.

27. J. T. Chappell extract, A. O. Wright Collection, Library of Virginia.

28. J. T. Chappell extract.

29. Minor, *Confederate Naval Cadet*, 43–45, 48; and Coski, *Capital Navy*, 222.

30. Melton, *Best Station of Them All*, 412–13; and Werlich, *Admiral of the Amazon*.

31. Jack, *Memoirs of E. A. Jack Steam Engineer*, 38–39.

32. Werlich, *Admiral of the Amazon*; see also Melton, *Best Station of Them All*, 415–16.

33. Melton, *Best Station of Them All*, 415–16.

34. Coski, *Capital Navy*, 221; and "The 'Aye, Ayes' at Sayler's Creek." The article also cites Donnelly's *The Confederate States Marine Corps*, and Richard Wheeler's *Witness to Appomattox*.

35. Jack, *Memoirs of E. A. Jack Steam Engineer*, 38–39.

36. Jack, 38–39.

37. Watson, *Southern Service on Land & Sea*, 160–62.

38. Watson, 160–62.

39. Watson, 160–62.

40. Watson, 162.

41. Watson, 163–64; and Styple, *Writing and Fighting the Civil War*, 343.

42. Wilson, *Willie Wilson's War*, 37–38.

43. Wilson, 38.

Epilogue

1. Bennett, *Union Jacks*, 209.
2. Boykin, *Sea Devil of the Confederacy*, 281.
3. Campbell, *Confederate Naval Forces on Western Waters*, 221; see also McPherson, *War on the Waters*, 224; and Editor to Dawson in Dawson, *Reminiscences of Confederate Service*, 177.
4. Symonds, *The Civil War at Sea*, 169. Symonds argues the Civil War was a "total war."
5. Merli, "The Confederate Navy 1861–1865," 128, 140. He did, however, note that the Southern efforts in Europe lacked coordination and suffered from divided counsel. Foreign uncertainty about the outcome of the Civil War resulted in obstacles thrown in the way of the South's procurement program abroad.
6. Merli, 128.
7. Wegner, "The Union Navy," 112; and Symonds, *The Civil War at Sea*, 170.
8. Howarth, *To Shining Sea*, 202–3.
9. Symonds, *The Civil War at Sea*, 170.
10. Quoted in Campbell, *Storm over North Carolina*, 228.
11. Buhl, "Maintaining 'An American Navy,'" 157.
12. Campbell, *Sea Hawk of the Confederacy*, 192.
13. Shingleton, "The Officers," 239, 113.
14. Coski, *Capital Navy*, 247; and Eggleston, "Captain Eggleston's Narrative."
15. Tomb, *Engineer in Gray*, 134.
16. Stickney, *Promotion at the Bottom of the Sea*, 157–58; and Driver, *Confederate Sailors*, 44–45, 373–74, 99, 10, 295–96, 23, 25.
17. Driver, *Confederate Sailors*, 171, 142–43, 123, 139.
18. Beverly Wilson, foreword to Wilson, *Willie Wilson's War*.
19. Quoted in Campbell, *Confederate Naval Forces*, 221.

Bibliography

Manuscripts

Library of Congress, Washington, D.C. (LOC)

Billings, Assistant Paymaster Luther Guiteau. Articles and photographs, OCLC 71060539.

Boyle, Francis A. "A Prison Diary," in Walter Ralph Steiner Papers, 1780–1937, MSS5591.

Cuddy, Thomas C. Papers, 1858–1861, LCCN mm 79000967, MSS967.

Deaderick, Inslee. David Anderson Deaderick Collection, LCCN mm 79001020, MSS1020.

Drayton, A. L. Papers, 1863, LCCN mm 82062950, MMC-1861.

Harrison, James O. Papers, 1803–1913, LCCN mm 78025106, MSS25106.

Journal of the Congress of the Confederate States of America 1861–1865, U.S. Serial Set Numbers 4610–4616, https://memory.loc.gov/ammem/amlaw/lwcc.html.

Kellogg, Edward Nealy. Papers, and Edward Stanley Kellogg Papers, 1858–1937, LCCN mm 70052985, MSS52985.

O'Neil, Anthony Francis. Diary, in Charles O'Neil Papers, 1833–1927, LCCN mm 70052449, MSS52449.

Schoonmaker, Cornelius M. Papers, 1833–1931, Manuscript Division, LCCN mm 70052944, MSS52944.

Smith, Daniel Angell. Papers, 1863–1905, LCCN mm 70055996, MSS55996.

Webster, Harrie. Papers, 1889–1913, Manuscript Division, LCCN mm 70052464, MSS52464.

Nimitz Library, U.S. Naval Academy, Annapolis, Maryland

Hart, John E. Letter, U.S. Naval Academy Digital Collection.

A. O. Wright Collection of Confederate Navy Service Records,
1922–1925. Accession 20976. Personal papers collection, The Library
of Virginia, Richmond, Virginia. http://ead.lib.virginia.edu/vivaxtf/
view?docId=lva/vi01117.xml

Chappell, Samuel M. Letter, December 1, 1922, to A. O. Wright, containing
the reminiscences of his father, John T. Chappell, of Richmond,
who served aboard the *Patrick Henry* and the *Virginia* during his
service in the Confederate Navy.
Curtis, John. A. "My Personal Remembrance of an Expedition on Board
of the Spar Torpedo Boat 'Squib.'"

Confederate Navy Subject File (CNSF), National Archives and
Records Administration (NARA), RG 45. https://catalog.archives.gov
/id/1756242. Searchable database available at fold3, https://www
.fold3.com/title/779/confederate-navy-subject-file

Inglehart, Osborne, MD. CNSF, Medical, ML 109–11.

Other Collections

Bacot, R. H. Letters and Diaries. State Archives of North Carolina, Raleigh,
North Carolina.
Freeman, Robert J. *Journal of Medical and Surgical Practice aboard the C.S.*
Steamer Atlanta. Confederate States of America Medical Records,
M 217, Manuscript Collection. McCain Library, University of
Southern Mississippi.
Gibbes, Robert Reeve. Diary, 1861–1865. Port Columbus National Civil
War Naval History Center.
Hamilton Fish Papers. Southern Historical Collection, University of
North Carolina, Chapel Hill, North Carolina.
Hutchinson, Calvin Gibbs. Papers, 1862–1912. Henry E. Huntington
Library, San Marino, California.
Mallory, Stephen. Diary and Reminiscences, 1861–1872. Southern Histor-
ical Collection, University of North Carolina, Chapel Hill, North
Carolina.

Martin, Asa T. Letters (1861–1862). Civil War Letters Collection, Auburn University Digital Library, http://diglib.auburn.edu/collections /civilwardiaries/.

Minor, Lewis Willis. Papers. 1730–1965, Accession #3988, 3988-b, 3988-c, Albert and Shirley Small Special Collections Library, University of Virginia, Charlottesville, Virginia.

Morrison, John G. The Civil War Diary of John G. Morrison, 1861–1865. New York State Military Museum and Veterans Research Center, Saratoga Springs, New York.

Parrott, Enoch Greenleafe. Papers, 1780–1874. Beinecke Library, Yale University, New Haven, Connecticut.

Perry, Charles Smith. Letters. Dr. Charles V. Smith Collection, Joyner Library #470, East Carolina University, Charleston, South Carolina.

Pugh, John. Pugh family papers. A Guide to the Pugh Family Papers, 1807–1907. Briscoe Center for American History, University of Texas, Austin, 2009–11.

Rush, John W. Letters (1861–1863). Civil War Letters Collections, RG 2, Auburn University Libraries, Auburn, Alabama.

———. Letters from Camp Chase. Civil War Collection, Subseries 1.1: Civil War Era Documents, 1860–1865, Box 6, Emory University, Oxford, Georgia.

Weber, George. Letters, 1861–1862. Accession 27467, Personal Papers Collection, Library of Virginia, Archives Branch, Richmond, Virginia.

Publications

Allison, Elsie. "Confederate Matrons." Honors thesis, University of Richmond, 1998.

Anderson, James W. "A Confederate Prisoner at Camp Chase: Letters and A Diary of Private James W. Anderson." Edited by George C. Osborn. *Ohio State Archaeological and Historical Quarterly* 59, no. 1 (1950): 46.

"The 'Aye, Ayes' at Sayler's Creek." *Alabama Confederate* 17, no. 1 (January 1998).

Barratt, Peter. *Farragut's Captain: Percival Drayton 1861–1865*. Unpublished manuscript, 2016.

Batcheller, Oliver. "Battle of Mobile Bay, August 5, 1864." *Magazine of History* 14, no. 6 (December 1911).

Bell, Andrew M. *Mosquito Soldiers: Malaria, Yellow Fever, and the Course of the American Civil War*. Baton Rouge: Louisiana State University Press, 2010.

Bennett, John D. *The London Confederates: The Officials, Clergy, Businessmen and Journalists Who Backed the American South during the Civil War*. Jefferson, NC: McFarland, 2008.

Bennett, Michael J. *Union Jacks: Yankee Sailors in the Civil War*. Chapel Hill: University of North Carolina Press, 2004.

Block, W. T. "Requiem for a Confederate Gunboat: The CSS *Josiah H. Bell*." N.d. www.wtblock.com/wtblockjr/josiah_h_bell.htm.

Bollet, Alfred Jay. *Civil War Medicine: Challenges and Triumphs*. Tucson, AZ: Galen Press, 2002.

Bown, Stephen R. *Scurvy*. Toronto: Thomas Allen, 2003.

Boykin, Edward C. *Ghost Ship of the Confederacy: The Story of the Alabama and Her Captain Raphael Semmes*. New York: Funk and Wagnalls, 1957.

———. *Sea Devil of the Confederacy: The Story of the Florida and John Newland Maffit*. New York: Funk and Wagnalls, 1959.

Bradford, Gamaliel, Jr. "Raphael Semmes: A Last Confederate Portrait." *Atlantic Monthly* 112 (1913): 6.

Brewer, James H. *The Confederate Negro: Virginia's Craftsmen and Military Laborers, 1861–1865*. Tuscaloosa: University of Alabama Press, 2007.

Bright, Leslie S., William H. Rowland, and James C. Bardon. *C.S.S. Neuse A Question of Iron and Time*. Raleigh: Division of Archives and History, North Carolina Department of Cultural Resources, 1981.

Brooke, George M., Jr. *John M. Brooke Naval Scientist and Educator*. Charlottesville: University Press of Virginia, 1980.

Brown, Isaac N. "The Confederate Gun-boat 'Arkansas.'" *Battles & Leaders* 3: 572–80.

Browning, Robert M., Jr. "The Confederate States Navy Department." In *The Confederate Navy: The Ships, Men and Organization 1861–65*, edited by William N. Still Jr., 21–39. Annapolis, MD: Naval Institute Press, 1996.

———. "'Go ahead, Go ahead." *Naval History Magazine* 23, no. 6 (December 2009).

———. *Success Was All That Was Expected*. Washington, DC: Brassey's, 2002.

Buhl, Lance C. "Maintaining 'An American Navy." In *In Peace and War*, 2nd ed., edited by Kenneth Hagan, 145–73. Westport, CT: Greenwood, 1984.

Bulloch, James. *Secret Service of the Confederate States in Europe*, vol. 1. New York: G. P. Putnam, 1884.

Bush, Daniel R., ed. *I Fear I Shall Never Leave this Island: Life in a Civil War Prison*. Gainesville: University Press of Florida, 2011.

Butler, Benjamin. *Autobiography and Personal Reminiscences of Major General Benjamin F. Butler*. Boston: A. M. Thayer, 1892.

Calcutt, Rebecca Barbour. *Richmond's Wartime Hospitals*. Gretna, LA: Pelican, 2005.

Campbell, R. Thomas. *Confederate Naval Forces on Western Waters: The Defense of the Mississippi River and Its Tributaries*. Jefferson, NC: McFarland, 2005.

———. *Sea Hawk of the Confederacy: Lt. Charles W. Read of the Confederate Navy*. Shippensburg, PA: Burd Street Press, 2000.

———. *Southern Thunder: Exploits of the Confederate States Navy*. Shippensburg, PA: White Mane, 1997.

———. *Storm over North Carolina: The Confederate Navy's Struggle for Eastern North Carolina*. Nashville: Cumberland House, 2005.

Cary, Constance. *Refugitta of Richmond: The Wartime Recollections Grace and Gay of Constance Cary Harrison*. Edited by Nathaniel Cheairs Hughes Jr. and S. Kittrell Rushing. Knoxville: University of Tennessee Press, 2011.

Chaffin, Tom. *The H. L. Hunley: The Secret Hope of the Confederacy*. New York: Hale and Wang, 2008.

————. *Sea of Gray: The Around-the-World Odyssey of the Confederate Raider Shenandoah.* New York: Hill and Wang, 2007.

Chatelain, Neil P. *Fought Like Devils: The Confederate Gunboat McRae.* Bloomington, IN: AuthorHouse, 2014.

Clark, Charles E. *My Fifty Years in the Navy.* Boston: Little, Brown, 1917.

Clayton, W. F. *A Narrative of the Confederate Navy.* Weldon, NC: Harrell's Printing House, Pee Dee Historical Association, 1910.

Conrad, Daniel B. "Capture and Burning of the Federal Gunboat 'Underwriter.'" *Southern Historical Society Papers* 19 (1892): 93–99.

————. "What the Fleet Surgeon Saw of the Fight in Mobile Bay." *United Service: A Monthly Review of Military and Naval Affairs* 8 (1892).

Conrad, James Lee. *Rebel Reefers: The Organization and Midshipmen of the Confederate States Naval Academy.* Boulder, CO: Da Capo Press, 2003.

Coski, John M. *Capital Navy: The Men, Ships, and Operations of the James River Squadron.* Campbell, CA: Savas Publishing, 1996.

Cox, Benjamin. "Mobile in the War Between the States." *Confederate Veteran* 24, no. 5 (May 1916).

Crowley, R. O. "The Confederate Torpedo Service." *Century* 56, no. 2 (June 1898).

Culpepper, Marilyn Mayer. *Women of the Civil War South: Personal Accounts from Diaries, Letters and Postwar Reminiscences.* Jefferson, NC: McFarland, 2004.

Cunningham, Horace Herndon. *Doctors in Gray: The Confederate Medical Service.* Baton Rouge: Louisiana State University Press, 1993.

Curtis, Frederick. "The 'Congress' and the 'Merrimack.'" Retold by Frank Alden in *New England Magazine* 25, no. 6 (February 1899): 687–93.

Curtis, Richard. "History of the Famous Battle between the Iron-clad MERRIMACK C.S.N. and the Iron-clad MONITOR and the Cumberland and Congress, of the U.S. Navy." Hampton, VA: Houston Print and Publishing House, 1957.

Dalzell, George W. *The Flight from the Flag: The Continuing Effect of the Civil War on the American Carrying Trade.* Chapel Hill: University of North Carolina Press, 1940.

Davis, William C. *A Government of Our Own: The Making of the Confederacy.* New York: Free Press, 1994.

———. *Look Away: A History of the Confederate States Army.* New York: Free Press, 2003.

Dawson, Francis W. *Reminiscences of Confederate Service, 1861–1865.* Edited by Bell I. Wiley. Baton Rouge: Louisiana State University Press, 1980.

Dear, Ian, and Peter Kemp. *Oxford Companion to Ships and the Sea.* 2nd ed. Oxford: Oxford University Press, 2007.

deKay, James T. *The Rebel Raiders: The Astonishing History of the Confederacy's Secret Navy.* New York: Ballantine, 2002.

Delaney, Norman C. *John McIntosh Kell of the Raider Alabama.* Tuscaloosa: University of Alabama Press, 1973.

———. "Strategy and Tactics." In *The Confederate Navy: The Ships, Men and Organization 1861–65,* edited by William N. Still Jr., 193–213. Annapolis, MD: Naval Institute Press, 1996.

Denney, Robert E. *Civil War Medicine: Care & Comfort of the Wounded.* New York: Sterling, 1995.

Donnelly, Ralph W. "Confederate Navy Forlorn Hope." *Military Affairs,* vol. 28, no. 2 (Summer 1964): 73–78. https://www.jstor.org /stable/1983758.

———. *The Confederate States Marine Corps: The Rebel Leathernecks.* Shippensburg, PA: White Mane, 1989.

Driver, Robert J. *Confederate Sailors, Marines, and Signalmen from Virginia and Maryland.* Westminster, MD: Heritage, 2007.

Dudley, William. *Going South: US Navy Officer Resignations and Dismissals on the Eve of the Civil War.* Washington, DC: Naval Historical Foundation, 1981.

Durkin, Joseph T. *Stephen R. Mallory, Confederate Navy Chief.* Chapel Hill: University of North Carolina Press, 1954.

Eggleston, John R. "Captain Eggleston's Narrative of the Battle of the Merrimac." *Southern Historical Society Papers* 41 (1916): 166–78.

Ellicott, John M. *The Life of John Ancrum Winslow, Rear-Admiral, United States Navy, Who Commanded the U.S. Steamer Kearsarge in Her*

Action with the Confederate Cruiser Alabama. New York: G. P. Putnam's Sons, 1902.

Elliott, Robert G. *Ironclad of the Roanoke: Gilbert Elliott's Albemarle.* Shippensburg, PA: White Mane, 1999.

Escott, Paul. *Military Necessity: Civil-Military Relations in the Confederacy.* Westport, CT: Praeger Security International, 2000.

Evans, Clement, ed. *Confederate Military History, in Twelve Volumes.* Vol. 12: *Alabama and Mississippi.* Atlanta: Confederate Publishing, 1899.

Fetzer, Dale, and Bruce Mowday. *Unlikely Allies: Fort Delaware's Prison Community in the Civil War.* Mechanicsburg, PA: Stackpole, 2000.

Foote, Shelby. *The Civil War: A Narrative: Fort Sumter to Shelbyville.* New York: Vantage, 1986.

Fox, Stephen. *Wolf of the Deep: Raphael Semmes and the Notorious Confederate Raider CSS Alabama.* New York: Vintage Civil War Library, 2008.

Freemon, Frank R. *Gangrene and Glory. Medical Care during the American Civil War.* Chicago: University of Illinois Press, 2001.

Friend, Jack. *West Wind, Flood Tide: The Battle of Mobile Bay.* Annapolis, MD: Naval Institute Press, 2004.

Frohman, Charles E. *Rebels on Lake Erie.* Columbus: Ohio Historical Society, 1965.

Fullam, George Townley. *The Journal of George Townley Fullam, Boarding Officer of CSS Alabama.* Edited by Charles Summersell. Tuscaloosa: University of Alabama Press, 1973.

Furer, Julius Augustus. "Bureau of Medicine and Surgery." In *Administration of the Navy Department in World War II.* Washington, DC: U.S. Department of the Navy, 1959.

Gardner, Donald Ray. "The Confederate Corps of Marine." Master's thesis, Memphis State University, 1973.

Gift, George W. "The Story of the Arkansas." *Southern Historical Society Papers* 7 (1887): 163–67.

Gosnell, H. Allen. *Guns on the Western Waters: The Story of the River Gunboats in the Civil War.* Baton Rouge: Louisiana State University Press, 1949.

Grady, John. "Hunter Davidson and the 'Squib.'" *Civil War Monitor*, June 9, 2014. https://www.civilwarmonitor.com/blogs /hunter-davidson-and-the-squib.

Grattan, John W. *Under the Blue Pennant*. Edited by Robert J. Schneller Jr. New York: Wiley, 1999.

Hain, Pamela Chase. *A Confederate Chronicle: The Life of a Civil War Survivor*. Columbia: University of Missouri Press, 2005.

Handerson, Henry E. *Yankee in Gray: The Civil War Memoirs of Henry Handerson*. Literary Licensing, 2011. Originally published, Cleveland: Press of Western Reserve University, 1962.

Harwell, Richard. *A Confederate Marine: A Sketch off Henry Lee Graves and Excerpts from the Graves Family Correspondence, 1861–1865*. Tuscaloosa, AL: Confederate Publishing,1963.

———, ed. "Diary of Captain Edward Crenshaw of the Confederate States Army." *Alabama Historical Quarterly* 1 (1930), part 5.

Hasegawa, G. R., and F. Terry Hambrecht. "The Confederate Medical Laboratories." *Southern Medical Journal* 96, no. 2: 1221–30.

Hearn, Chester. *Admiral David Glasgow Farragut: The Civil War Years*. Annapolis, MD: Naval Institute Press, 1998.

———. *The Civil War: Virginia*. London: Salamander, 2005.

Hesseltine, William B. *Civil War Prisons: A Study in War Psychology*. Columbus: Ohio State University Press, 1930.

Holcombe, Robert. "Types of Ships." In *The Confederate Navy: The Ships, Men and Organization 1861–65*, edited by William N. Still Jr. Annapolis, MD: Naval Institute Press, 1996.

Hollandsworth, James G., Jr. "Union Soldiers on Ship Island during the Civil War." *Mississippi History Now*. N.d. http://www .mshistorynow.mdah.ms.gov/articles/211/union-soldiers-on -ship-island-during-the-civil-war.

Horigan, Michael. *Elmira: Death Camp of the North*. Mechanicsburg, PA: Stackpole, 2002.

Howarth, Stephen. *To Shining Sea: A History of the United States Navy, 1775–1998*. Norman: University of Oklahoma Press, 1999.

Humphreys, Margaret. *Marrow of Tragedy: The Health Crisis of the American Civil War*. Baltimore: Johns Hopkins University Press, 2013.

Hunter, Alvah F. *A Year on a Monitor and the Destruction of Fort Sumter*. Edited by Craig L. Symonds. Columbia: University of South Carolina Press, 1991.

Hutchinson, William Francis. "The Bay Fight: A Sketch of the Battle of Mobile Bay, August 5th, 1864." Personal Narratives of the Battles of the Rebellion series, no. 8. Providence, RI: S. S. Rider, 1879.

Jack, E. A. *Memoirs of E. A. Jack Steam Engineer, CSS Virginia*, edited by Alan B. Flanders and Captain Neale O. Westfall. White Stone, VA: Brandywine, 1998.

Jeter, Katherine B. *A Man and His Boat: The Civil War Career of Lieutenant Jonathan H. Carter, CSN*. Lafayette: Center for Louisiana Studies, 1996.

Johnson, Charles Beneulyn. *Muskets and Medicine: Or, Army Life in the Sixties*. Philadelphia: F. A. Davis, 1917.

Johnson, John. *The Defense of Charleston Harbor: Including Fort Sumter and the Adjacent Islands, 1863–1865*. Charleston, SC: Walter Evans & Cogswell Co., 1883.

Johnson, Robert Underwood, and Clarence Clough Buel. *Battles and Leaders of the Civil War: Being for the Most Part Contributions by Union and Confederate Officers*. 4 vols. New York: Thomas Yoseloff, 1936.

Johnston, James D. "The Ram Tennessee at Mobile Bay." In *Battles and Leaders of the Civil War: Being for the Most Part Contributions by Union and Confederate Officers*, edited by Robert Underwood Johnson and Clarence Clough Buel, 4:401–6. New York: Thomas Yoseloff, 1936.

Joiner, Gary D. *Mr. Lincoln's Brown Water Navy: The Mississippi Squadron*. Lanham, MD: Rowman and Littlefield, 2007.

Jones, John Beauchamp. *A Rebel War Clerk's Diary at the Confederate States Capital*. Vol. 1. Lawrence: University Press of Kansas, 2015.

Jones, Virgil C. *The Civil War at Sea*. Vol. 1, *The Blockaders*. New York: Holt, Rinehart and Winston, 1960.

Joslyn, Muriel Phillips. *Immortal Captives: The Story of 600 Confederate Officers and the United States Prisoner of War Policy*. Gretna, LA: Pelican, 1996.

Keeler, William Frederick. *Aboard the U.S.S. Monitor, 1862: The Letters of Acting Paymaster W. F. Keeler, U.S. Navy to His Wife Anna.* Annapolis, MD: Naval Institute Press, 1964.

Kell, John McIntosh. *Recollections of a Naval Life Including the Cruises of the Confederate States Steamers.* Washington, D.C.: Neale, 1900.

King, John Henry. *Three Hundred Days in a Yankee Prison: Reminiscences of War Life, Captivity, Imprisonment at Camp Chase, Ohio.* Atlanta: J. P. Daves, 1904.

King, John R. *My Experience in the Confederate Army and in Northern Prisons.* Conneaut, OH: Martha Stump Benson, 1994.

Kinney, John C. "Farragut at Mobile Bay." In *Battles and Leaders of the Civil War: Being for the Most Part Contributions by Union and Confederate Officers,* edited by Robert Underwood Johnson and Clarence Clough Buel, 4:379–99. New York: Thomas Yoseloff, 1936.

Knauss, William H. *The Story of Camp Chase: A History of the Prison and Its Cemetery, Together with Other Cemeteries Where Confederate Prisoners Are Buried, Etc.* Columbus, OH: General's Books, 1994. Reprint, CreateSpace Independent Publishing Platform, 2013.

Langley, Harold. *A History of Medicine in the Bureau of Medicine and Surgery Early U.S. Navy.* Baltimore: Johns Hopkins University Press, 2000.

———. "Shipboard Life." In *The Confederate Navy: The Ships, Men and Organization 1861–65,* edited by William N. Still Jr. Annapolis, MD: Naval Institute Press, 1996.

Lester, W. W., and William J. Bromwell, eds. *A Digest of the Military and Naval Laws of the Confederate States to the End of the First Congress under the Permanent Constitution.* Columbia, S.C.: Evans and Cogswell, 1864. Available at *Documenting the American South,* http://docsouth.unc.edu/imls/digest/menu.html.

Lewis, Charles Lee. *David Glasgow Farragut.* Vol. 2, *Our First Admiral.* Annapolis, MD: Naval Institute Press, 2014.

Littlepage, Hardin B. "A Midshipman Aboard the VIRGINIA," 3 parts. *Civil War Times Illustrated* 13 (1974).

Lonn, Ella. *Desertion during the Civil War.* Lincoln: University of Nebraska Press, 1998.

Loyall, Benjamin P. "Capture of the Underwriter New Bern 2 February 1864." In *History of Several Regiments and Battalions from North Carolina, in the Great War 1861–65*, edited by Walter Clark, 5:325–33. Raleigh, NC: E. M. Uzzell, 1901.

Luraghi, Raimondo. "Background." In *The Confederate Navy: The Ships, Men and Organization 1861–65*, edited by William N. Still Jr., 1–20. Annapolis, MD: Naval Institute Press, 1996.

———. *A History of the Confederate Navy*. Annapolis, MD: Naval Institute Press, 1996.

Lynch, John S. "Civil War Confederate Naval Office of Medicine and Surgery." *Military Medicine*, November 1999.

Maffitt, Emma. *The Life and Services of John Newland Maffitt*. New York: Neale, 1906.

Marvel, William. *The Alabama & the Kearsarge: A Sailor's Civil War*. Chapel Hill: University of North Carolina Press, 1996.

McAdams, Benton. *Rebels at Rock Island: The Story of a Civil War Prison*. De Kalb: Northern Illinois University Press, 2000.

McCallum, Jack. "Medicine, Naval." In *The Civil War Naval Encyclopedia*, edited by Spencer Tucker, Paul G. Pierpaoli Jr., and William E. White. Santa Barbara, CA: ABC-CLIO, 2011.

McFall, F. Lawrence. *Danville in the Civil War*. Lynchburg, VA: H. E. Howard, 2001.

McGuire, Judith. *Diary of a Southern Refugee during the War, by a Lady of Virginia*. Lexington: University Press of Kentucky, 2013.

McPherson, James M. *Battle Cry of Freedom*. New York: Oxford University Press, 1988.

———. *Embattled Rebel: Jefferson Davis as Commander-in-Chief*. New York: Penguin, 2014.

———. *The Negro's Civil War*. New York: Ballantine, 1965.

———. *Tried by War: Abraham Lincoln as Commander in Chief*. New York: Penguin, 2008.

———. *War on the Waters: The Union & Confederate Navies, 1861–1865*. Chapel Hill: University of North Carolina Press, 2012.

Melton, Maurice. *The Best Station of Them All: The Savannah Squadron, 1861–1865*. Tuscaloosa: University of Alabama Press, 2012.

———. "Shipbuilding." In *The Confederate Navy, The Ships, Men and Organization, 1861–65*, edited by William N. Still Jr., 91–111. Annapolis, MD: Naval Institute Press, 1997.

Merli, Frank J. "The Confederate Navy, 1861–1865." In *In Peace and War: Interpretations of American Naval History, 1775–1984*, 2nd ed., edited by Kenneth Hagan, 126–44. Westport, CT: Greenwood, 1984.

Milligan, John. *Gunboats Down the Mississippi*. Annapolis, MD: Naval Institute Press, 1965.

Minor, Hubbard T. *Confederate Naval Cadet: The Diary and Letters of Midshipman Hubbard T. Minor, with a History of the Confederate Naval Academy*. Edited by R. Thomas Campbell. Jefferson, NC: McFarland, 2007.

———. "Diary of a Confederate Naval Cadet," *Civil War Times Illustrated* 13, no. 8 (December 1974).

Morgan, James. "A Most Realistic War College." Naval Institute *Proceedings*, March–April, 1916.

Morgan, James Morris. *Midshipman in Gray: Selections from Recollections of a Rebel Reefer*. Edited by R. Thomas Campbell. Shippensburg, PA: Burd Street Press, 1997.

———. *Recollections of a Rebel Reefer*. New York: Houghton Mifflin, 1917.

Musicant, Ivan. *Divided Waters: The Naval History of the Civil War*. New York: Harper Collins, 1995.

Nevins, John. "Black Americans in the Confederate Navy and Marine Corps." *On Deck!* N.d. http://www.navyandmarine.org/ondeck /1862blackCSN.htm.

Osborn, George C. "Writings of a Confederate Prisoner of War," part 1. *Tennessee Quarterly* 10, no. 1 (March 1961): 74–90. https://www .jstor.org/stable/42621065.

———. "Writings of a Confederate Prisoner of War," part 2. *Tennessee Quarterly* 10, no. 2 (June 1961): 161–84. https://www.jstor.org /stable/42621074.

Page, Richard L. "The Defense of Fort Morgan." In *Battles and Leaders of the Civil War: Being for the Most Part Contributions by Union and Confederate Officers*, edited by Robert Underwood Johnson and Clarence Clough Buel, 4:408–10. New York: Thomas Yoseloff, 1936.

Parker, Foxhall. "The Battle of Mobile Bay, and the Capture of Forts Powell, Gaines, and Morgan by the Combined Sea and Land Forces of the United States under the Command of Rear-Admiral David Glasgow Farragut, and Major-General Gordon Granger, August 1864." Boston: A. Williams & Co., 1878.

Parker, William. *Recollections of a Naval Officer 1841–1865*. New York: Scribner, 1883.

Patterson, Benton Rain. *The Mississippi River Campaign, 1861–1863: The Struggle for Control of Western Waters*. Jefferson, NC: McFarland, 2010.

Perry, Milton. *Infernal Machines: The Story of Confederate Submarine and Mine Warfare*. Baton Rouge: Louisiana State University Press, 1985.

Phillips, Dinwiddie B. "Surgeon of the 'Merrimac,' Notes on the Monitor-Merrimac Fight." In *Battles and Leaders of the Civil War: Being for the Most Part Contributions by Union and Confederate Officers*, vol. 1, edited by Robert Underwood Johnson and Clarence Clough Buel. New York: Thomas Yoseloff, 1936.

Pickenbaugh, Roger. *Captives in Gray: The Civil War Prisons of the Union*. Tuscaloosa: University of Alabama Press, 2009.

Porter, John W. H. *A Record of Events in Norfolk County, Virginia, from April 19th, 1861 to May 10th, 1862, with a History of the Soldiers and Sailors of Norfolk County, Norfolk City and Portsmouth, Who Served in the Confederate States Army or Navy*. Portsmouth, VA: W. A. Fiske, Printer, 1892.

Quarstein, John V. *The CSS Virginia: Sink before Surrender*. Charleston, SC: History Press, 2012.

Ragan, Mark. *Union and Confederate Submarine Warfare in the Civil War*. New York: Da Capo, 1999.

Ramsey, Ashton H. "Most Famous of Sea Duels: The Merrimac and the Monitor." *Harpers Weekly* 31 (February 1912).

Read, Charles W. "Reminiscences of the Confederate Navy." *Southern Historical Society Papers* 1, no. 5 (May 1876): 331–62.

Reidenbaugh, Lowell. *27th Virginia Infantry.* Virginia Regimental Histories series. Lynchburg, VA: H. E. Howard Publishing, 1993.

Rhodes, James Ford. *History of the United States.* Vol. 5, *From the Compromise of 1850 to the McKinley-Bryan Campaign of 1896.* New York: Macmillan, 1920.

Richardson, James D., ed. *The Messages and Papers of Jefferson Davis and the Confederacy: Including Diplomatic Correspondence, 1861–1865.* Vol. 1. New York: Chelsea House, 1983.

Ringle, Dennis J. *Life in Mr. Lincoln's Navy.* Annapolis, MD: Naval Institute Press, 1998.

Robertson, James L., Jr. *Civil War Virginia: Battleground for a Nation.* Charlottesville: University of Virginia Press, 1991.

Robinson, William M., Jr. *The Confederate Privateers.* Columbia: University of South Carolina Press, 1994.

Rodgers, William Warren, Jr. *Confederate Homefront: Montgomery during the Civil War.* Tuscaloosa: University of Alabama, 2001.

Sanders, Charles W., Jr. *While in the Hands of the Enemy: Military Prisons of the Civil War.* Baton Rouge: Louisiana State University Press, 2005.

Scharf, J. Thomas. *History of the Confederate States Navy from Its Organization to the Surrender of Its Last Vessel.* New York: Rogers & Sherwood, 1887.

Schooler, Lynn. *The Last Shot: The Incredible story of the CSS Shenandoah and the True Conclusion of the American Civil War.* New York: HarperCollins, 2005.

Schroeder-Lein, Glenna R. *The Encyclopedia of Civil War Medicine.* Armonk, NY: Sharpe, 2008.

Schultz, Jane E. *Women at the Front: Hospital Women in Civil War America.* Chapel Hill: University of North Carolina Press, 2004.

Scribner, Theresa A., and Terry G. Scribner. *Ship Island Mississippi: Roster and History of a Civil War Prison*. Jefferson, NC: McFarland, 2012.

Semmes, Raphael R. *Memoirs of Service Afloat during the War between the States*. New York: Kennedy & Sons, 1869.

———. *Rebel Raider, Being an Account of Raphael Semmes' Cruise in the C.S.S. Sumter*. Selected and supplemented by Harpur Allen Gosnell. Chapel Hill: University of North Carolina Press, 1948.

Shingleton, Royce. *High Seas Confederate: The Life and Times of John Newland Maffitt*. Columbia: University of South Carolina Press, 1994.

———. "The Officers." In *The Confederate Navy: The Ships, Men and Organization 1861–65*, edited by William N. Still Jr., 112–32. Annapolis, MD: Naval Institute Press, 1996.

———. "Seamen, Landsmen, Firemen and Coal Heavers." In *The Confederate Navy: The Ships, Men and Organization 1861–65*, edited by William N. Still Jr., 133–46. Annapolis, MD: Naval Institute Press, 1996.

Silverstone, Paul H. *Warships of the Civil War Navies*. Annapolis, MD: Naval Institute Press, 1989.

Sinclair, Arthur. *Two Years on the Alabama: A Firsthand Account of the Daring Exploits of the Infamous Confederate Raider*. Boston: Lee and Shepard, 1895.

Slagle, Jay. *Ironclad Captain: Seth Ledyard Phelps and the U.S. Navy, 1841–1864*. Kent, OH: Kent State University Press, 1996.

Smith, Myron, Jr. *CSS Arkansas: A Confederate Ironclad on Western Waters*. Jefferson, NC: McFarland, 2011.

Soley, James R. "Naval Operations in the Vicksburg Campaign." *Battles and Leaders*, 3 (1956): 555–70.

———. "The Union and Confederate Navies." In *Battles and Leaders of the Civil War: Being for the Most Part Contributions by Union and Confederate Officers*, edited by Robert Underwood Johnson and Clarence Clough Buel, 1:611–31. New York: Thomas Yoseloff, 1936.

Spencer, Warren F. *The Confederate Navy in Europe*. Tuscaloosa: University of Alabama Press, 1983.

Springer, Paul J., and Glenn Robins. *Transforming Civil War Prisons: Lincoln, Lieber, and the Politics of Captivity*. New York: Routledge, 2015.

Stickney, John M. *Promotion at the Bottom of the Sea: The Blue and Gray Naval Careers of Alexander F. Warley, South Carolina.* Columbia: University of South Carolina Press, 2012.

Still, William. "The Common Sailor." *Civil War Times Illustrated*, February 23, 1985.

Still, William N., Jr., ed. *The Confederate Navy: The Ships, Men and Organization 1861–65.* Annapolis, MD: Naval Institute Press, 1996.

Still, William N., Jr. *Iron Afloat: The Story of the Confederate Ironclads.* Nashville: Vanderbilt University Press, 1971.

Stokes, Karen. *The Immortal 600: Surviving Civil War Charleston and Savannah.* Charleston, SC: History Press, 2013.

Styple, William B., ed. *Writing and Fighting the Civil War: Soldier Correspondence to the New York Sunday Mercury.* Kearney, NJ: Belle Grove, 2000.

Sullivan, David M. "The Marines." In *The Confederate Navy, The Ships, Men and Organization, 1861–65,* edited by William N. Still Jr. Annapolis, MD: Naval Institute Press, 1997.

Summersell, Charles Grayson. *The Cruise of the C.S.S. Sumter.* Tuscaloosa, AL: Confederate Publishing, 1965.

Symonds, Craig L. *The Civil War at Sea.* New York: Oxford University Press, 2013.

———. *Confederate Admiral: The Life and Wars of Franklin Buchanan.* Annapolis, MD: Naval Institute Press, 2008.

Thompson, Brooks, and Frank Lawrence Owsley Jr., eds. "The War Journal of Midshipman Cary." *Civil War History* 9, no. 2 (June 1963): 187–202. https://doi.org/10.1353/cwh.1963.0032.

Thompson, Samuel B. *Confederate Purchasing Operations Abroad.* Chapel Hill: University of North Carolina Press, 1936.

Time-Life Books. *The Blockade: Runners and Raiders.* The Civil War Series 3. Alexandria, VA: Time-Life Books, 1983.

Tomb, James H. *Engineer in Gray: Memoirs of Chief Engineer James H. Tomb, CSN.* Edited by R. Thomas Campbell. Jefferson, NC: McFarland, 2005.

Tomblin, Barbara Brooks. *Bluejackets and Contrabands: African Americans and the Union Navy.* Lexington: University Press of Kentucky, 2009.

————. *Civil War on the Mississippi: Union Sailors, Gunboat Captains, and the Campaign to Control the River*. Lexington: University Press of Kentucky, 2017.

Trigg, Angela. "A Romantic Adventurer: The Life of Daniel Trigg of Abington Virginia." Master's thesis, Georgia State University, Atlanta, 1997.

Trotter, William R. *Ironclads and Columbiads: The Civil War in North Carolina: The Coast*. Winston-Salem, NC: John F. Blair Publisher, 1989.

Tucker, Spencer. *Raphael Semmes and the Alabama*. Fort Worth, TX: Ryan Place, 1996.

Turner, Maxine. *Navy Gray. A Story of the Confederate Navy on the Chattahoochee and Apalachicola Rivers*. Tuscaloosa: University of Alabama Press, 1988.

"Uniform and Dress of the Navy of the Confederate States," Naval War Records, Office Memoranda No. 7, Washington, DC: Government Printing Office, 1898. Available at Naval History and Heritage Command, https://www.history.navy.mil/content/history/nhhc/research/library/online-reading-room/title-list-alphabetically/u/uniforms-usnavy/uniform-and-dress-of-the-navy-of-the-confederate-states.html.

U.S. Navy Department. *Official Records of the Union and Confederate Navies in the War of the Rebellion*. Washington, DC: Government Printing Office, 1894–1919. 30 vols. in 2 series + Index.

U.S. Surgeon General's Office. *The Medical and Surgical History of the War of the Rebellion*, 1861–1863, vol. 1, pt. 3. Washington, DC: Government Printing Office, 1888. Available at U.S. National Library of Medicine Digital Collections, https://collections.nlm.nih.gov/bookviewer?PID=nlm:nlmuid-14121350RX3-mvpart#page/772/mode/2up.

Waddell, James l. *C.S.S. Shenandoah: The Memoirs of Lieutenant Commanding James I. Waddell*. Edited by James D. Horan. New York: Crown, 1960.

Waitt, Robert W. *Confederate Military Hospitals in Richmond*. Richmond Civil War Centennial Committee, 1964.

Warley, Alexander. "The Ram Manassas at the Passage of the New Orleans Forts." In *Battles and Leaders of the Civil War: Being for the Most Part Contributions by Union and Confederate Officers*, edited by Robert Underwood Johnson and Clarence Clough Buel, 1:90–91. New York: Thomas Yoseloff, 1936.

Watson, Robert. *Southern Service on Land and Sea: The Wartime Journal of Robert Watson CSA/CSN*. Edited by R. Thomas Campbell. Knoxville: University of Tennessee Press, 2002.

Webster, Harrie. "An August Morning with Farragut at Mobile Bay." In *Civil War Chronology 1861–1865*. Washington, DC: Naval History Division, Navy Department, 1971.

Weeks, Dick. "The Civil War Sailor's Life." *Shotgun's Home of the American Civil War* website, http://www.civilwarhome.com/sailorlife.html.

Wegner, Dana. "The Union Navy." In *In Peace and War: Interpretations of American Naval History, 1775–1984*, 2nd ed., edited by Kenneth Hagan, 107–25. Westport, CT: Greenwood, 1984.

Wells, Tom H. *The Confederate Navy: A Study in Organization*. Tuscaloosa: University of Alabama Press, 1971.

Werlich, David P. *Admiral of the Amazon: John Randolph Tucker, His Confederate Colleagues, and Peru*. Charlottesville: University Press of Virginia, 1990.

Wheeler, Richard. *Witness to Appomattox*. New York: Harper & Row, 1989.

Wilson, William Francis. *Willie Wilson's War, 1861–1865: An Account of Some of the Civil War Experiences of Midshipman W. F. Wilson, C.S. Navy*. Edited by Beverly E. Wilson (n.p., 1969). Nimitz Library.

Wise, Stephen. *Lifeline of the Confederacy: Blockade Running during the Civil War*. Columbia: University of South Carolina Press, 1988.

Wood, John Taylor. "First Fight of the Ironclads." In *Battles and Leaders of the Civil War: Being for the Most Part Contributions by Union and Confederate Officers*, edited by Robert Underwood Johnson and Clarence Clough Buel, 1:692–711. New York: Thomas Yoseloff, 1936.

Young, Matthew. "Irony Clad: The Remarkable Odyssey of the *U.S.S. Water Witch*." Columbus State University. N.d.

INDEX